AN HISTORICAL SKETCH
OF
THE NATIVE STATES OF INDIA

AN HISTORICAL SKETCH OF THE NATIVE STATES OF INDIA

IN SUBSIDIARY ALLIANCE WITH THE BRITISH GOVERNMENT

WITH A NOTICE OF THE MEDIATIZED AND MINOR STATES

COLONEL G. B. MALLESON

'It is only by attracting attention to the prominent figures in Indian history, by casting light upon the salient features of their career and making them stand out boldly from the canvas, that it will ever be possible to interest the general reader in Indian affairs'

The Times, Feb, 20, 1872

Published by

Facsimile Publisher
12 Pragati Market
Ashok Vihar, Ph-2
Delhi-110052
facsimilepublisher.com

Distribution Network
gyanbooks.com
India, USA, Canada, UK, Australia, France

ISBN : 978-93-5324-545-0 (HB)
First Published, London, 1875

2nd Impression 2020

Printed at: Gyan Press, Delhi.

An Historical Sketch Of The Native States Of India
Author: Colonel G. B. Malleson

AN HISTORICAL SKETCH

OF

THE NATIVE STATES OF INDIA

IN SUBSIDIARY ALLIANCE WITH THE BRITISH GOVERNMENT

WITH A NOTICE OF THE MEDIATIZED AND MINOR STATES

BY

COLONEL G. B. MALLESON, C.S.I.

BENGAL STAFF CORPS

GUARDIAN OF HIS HIGHNESS THE MAHARÁJÁ OF MYSORE, AND AUTHOR OF 'HISTORY OF THE FRENCH IN INDIA' ETC.

'It is only by attracting attention to the prominent figures in Indian history, by casting light upon the salient features of their career and making them stand out boldly from the canvas, that it will ever be possible to interest the general reader in Indian affairs'

THE TIMES, *Feb.* 20, 1872

LONDON

LONGMANS, GREEN, AND CO.

1875

TO

THE MOST HONOURABLE

THE MARQUIS OF SALISBURY

This Work,

COMPILED IN THE KINGDOM OF WHICH
BY THE INITIATIVE TAKEN IN THE YEAR 1866 HE MAY BE
REGARDED AS THE SECOND FOUNDER,

Is by Permission

RESPECTFULLY INSCRIBED.

PREFACE.

THE WANT of a condensed historical sketch of the Native dynasties now reigning in India has been felt alike in that country and in England. Proposals to supply the want have from time to time been mooted. Had any of these been carried to their legitimate conclusion, the present publication would never have seen the light.

It happened, however, that information reached me in the course of last year that the labours in the same direction of a gentleman most competent to do justice to the subject had been indefinitely postponed. I had just then completed a literary work on which I had for some time been engaged, and the desire to supply a great public want induced me to take up the dropped thread.

Indian subjects had long been familiar to me, and the history of several important Native States had previously engaged my study and attention. I should, nevertheless, have felt myself unequal to the task of conducting to completion a work so extensive, had I not possessed in my library all the authorities necessary for the purpose. I made a diligent use of the materials thus at my disposal, and gave my undivided time and attention to the subject. The work is now completed. If it should fail to fulfil the expectations of those who have felt the want of such a book of reference, I can assure them that I have grudged no toil, and, dependent entirely as I was on my own exertions, have spared no pains to bring it as nearly as possible to the required standard.

Such a work must necessarily be of the nature of a compilation. This aspires to be nothing more. I have gone to the best authorities and have deliberately robbed them. In the widest sense of the term, I have been 'the burglar of others' intellects.' Of Colonel Tod's 'Annals and Antiquities of Rajasthan;' of Captain Grant Duff's 'History of the Mahrattas;' of Sir John Malcolm's 'Central India,' I have availed myself largely. Chiefly, however, certainly more generally, are my obligations due to Mr. Aitchison's invaluable collection of 'Treaties, Engagements, and Sunnuds,' a work which contains within it all the modern part of the information I have condensed, and which must always constitute a material basis for such a compilation as the present. I owe much likewise to Elphinstone's 'History of India;' to Ferishta's 'History of the Dekkan;' to a work published anonymously in 1833, entitled 'An Historical Sketch of the Princes of India;' to an admirable summary, evidently officially inspired, of the history of the several states of India attached to the 'Agra Gazetteer' for 1841 or 1842; to the Gazetteers of Hamilton and Thornton; and to a printed summary compiled in the Foreign Department in 1869, by Mr. Talboys Wheeler. I have made passing references to various articles in the 'Calcutta Review' and in 'Asiatic Researches;' to the works of Mill, Thorn, Stewart, and others; but those specially mentioned constituted my main sources of supply. Nor, when mentioning my obligations, can I omit the name of my valued friend Mr. Runga Charlú, Controller to the household of the Máhárájá of Mysore, a gentleman whose vast range of learning, great acquaintance with affairs, sound comprehensive views, and lofty character render him an invaluable ally to anyone engaged in literary work.

Of the Native States treated of in the first six parts of this volume, all, I think, may fairly be classed amongst those which are in subsidiary alliance with the British Government. The seventh part gives a brief account of the states and estates, classed as 'Mediatized and Minor,' which though under the suzerainty of, are not in direct alliance with, the British Government. There remain then the countries in Asia which have entered into treaties with the Government of British India. These are practically independent. They may be said broadly to comprise Persia, Belúchístán, Afghánistán and the frontier tribes, Nipál, Gúrkhá, Sikkim, Bhútan, Burma, and Siam; and their history may perhaps form a separate volume.

One word as to the mode of division I have adopted. I have thought it convenient, instead of grouping states according to their individual size, to follow the natural order of the divisions in which they lie. Thus beginning with Rájpútáná—the division containing the oldest monarchies in India, probably in the world—and taking after it its neighbours in Central India and Bundelkhand, I have followed in succession with Western, Southern, and North-Western India. I have indicated the history of the principal states in these six divisions with such detail as a mere sketch of them seemed to authorise, and with as much precision as the authorities to which I had access would permit. If I may not have succeeded in accomplishing all that has been desired, I shall at least have opened a pathway to others alike more competent and commanding more secret sources of information.

With respect to the spelling of the cities and provinces of India, I have followed the system laid down by Professor Blochmann in his 'Geography of India and Burma.'

CONTENTS.

PART I.

RÁJPÚTÁNÁ.

PART II.

CENTRAL INDIA AND MÁLWÁ.

PART III.

BUNDELKHAND.

PART IV.

WESTERN INDIA.

PART V.

SOUTHERN INDIA.

PART VI.

NORTHERN INDIA.

PART VII.

MEDIATIZED AND MINOR CHIEFS.

APPENDICES.

LIST OF MAPS.

HISTORICAL SKETCH

OF THE

NATIVE STATES OF INDIA.

INTRODUCTORY CHAPTER.

INTROD. CHAP.

THE affairs of India command at present an interest far greater than was bestowed upon them at any previous time. This is as true of that not inconsiderable portion of the country which still remains under native rulers as of the larger portion which has come under the direct sway of the British Government. The country has passed through various stages of its political history, and these afford useful subjects of study to the historian and to the statesman. The first stage comprised the long and comparatively peaceful period when, prior to the invasion of Mahmud of Ghizní, the nation owned the sway of sovereigns of its own race and faith. This would undoubtedly be the most interesting portion of its history for the study of the character and the institutions of the people in their native integrity. But though there are abundant traces of the country having then attained a high degree of prosperity and civilisation, so little is known in regard to the details of the principles of the government, or the condition of the people during this time, and so completely have all traditions connected with them been effaced by the long period of foreign rule which followed, that a study of the history of this epoch

INTROD. CHAP.

seems of value to the investigator of antiquarian researches rather than to the practical statesman. That the energies belonging to this purely native progress long ago exhausted themselves, was seen conspicuously in the manner in which all the once powerful Native States succumbed to the inroads of the Mahomedan invader.

The invasion of India by Mahmud of Ghizní, in the early part of the eleventh century, introduces us to the second, or Mahomedan, period of Indian history. The Mahomedan Empire properly commences from the establishment of the seat of government at Delhi, by Kutb-ud-dín, in the year 1206; and from that date to the decline of the empire in 1707 is one of the longest periods of foreign rule which any country has ever witnessed. This fact is in itself a most instructive subject for study, as bearing on the character of the conquered and conquering races and their institutions. The Mahomedan rule soon attained the status of a great empire; and during a considerable portion of the Mogul period, from Akbar to Aurangzíb, as well as in some of the preceding reigns, the Courts of Agra and Delhi, alike in their magnificence and in the largeness of their public measures, did not merely rival, but surpass, the best European Governments of the day. The institutions of Akbar in particular, the very advanced principles of toleration and justice to the conquered race which he introduced into his government—the influence of which was felt in several succeeding reigns—are worthy of imitation by the most enlightened Governments of any period. This great warrior, though belonging to an age which had but scarcely emerged from barbarism, recognised the sound principle that a Government must rest on the affections of the people. The measures which he adopted with this view for breaking down the barriers between the conquering and the conquered races are worthy of all praise. With the noble race of Rájpúts, in particular, he entered into intimate relations. He so far overcame their prejudices that their principal families gave their daughters in marriage to himself, and to his children; while their sons led his armies to the field, achieved his conquests, and filled the principal offices in his administration. The Hindú States of Rájpútáná were under his rule more powerful, more prosperous and more influential, that they are at the present day; and when we are further told that this enlightened ruler authorised Hindú widows to marry, mitigated the horrors of Satí, and forbade marriages before the age of puberty—measures the re-introduction of some of which have been laurels to the ablest administrators of our own day—it is impossible not to admire the wisdom and large-heartedness of his policy.

But the Mahomedan rule, like all other despotisms, contained within itself the seeds of decay. A Government which owes its success entirely to the personal character of the ruler affords no guarantee for continued progress. Akbar was a great ruler, but it was impossible even for Akbar to provide that he should be succeeded by another Akbar. To this defect, inherent in all personal governments, was added another of even greater magnitude in the unsettled rules of succession among children by several wives. The bloody contests and the unfeeling murders resulting from this cause distracted, and still continue to distract, the best of Mahomedan rules, as is painfully witnessed even at the present day, in the troubles which surround our ally of Afghánistán. The latter part of almost every reign of the successors of Akbar was clouded and unsettled by these contests, and when finally the bigoted Aurangzíb departed from the wise principles of toleration introduced by his great ancestor, and by cruelties, persecutions, and repeated acts of faithlessness alienated the affections of his allies and subjects, the Mogul empire began rapidly to decline. After a long and brilliant reign, during which he extended the limits of his empire farther than any of his prede-

INTROD. CHAP.

cessors, lived to see the death of Sivají, the founder of the power that was to supplant his own; even to wreak vengeance on his successor—this great potentate, amidst all his triumphs, felt and felt keenly, before he descended into his grave, that the sceptre was departing from the Mogul. 'His last letters,' says Elphinstone, 'showed the failure of his hopes in this world, his dread of that to come.'

Upon the ruin of the Mogul rose the power of the Márhátás, whose predatory career forms the third stage in Indian history. For more than a century these active, restless, lawless warriors undoubtedly exercised a predominant sway over Indian affairs, holding a considerable extent of territory under their own direct rule, and extorting contributions from most of the other Governments in the country. But their career, which was one of rapine and plunder, has scarcely any claim to the attributes of a settled government, much less to those of a great empire.

From the final breaking down of the Márhátá confederacy, in 1817, commences the absolute sovereignty of the great power which is yet destined to play an important part in the future history of this ancient nation. The territorial acquisitions and the influence of the English Government commenced from the middle of the eighteenth century, but its undisputed supremacy and claim to empire can properly reckon only from the complete crippling of the Márhátás in 1817. The time which has elapsed from that event to the present day is indeed but short, but the rapid changes which have taken place, even in this short interval, and the great strides in material and mental progress which have been made, cannot fail to convince the thoughtful native that his country has now entered upon a career which has no parallel in its previous history, whilst the stable character of the government, and the settled principles of its action, give the guarantee that the career thus commenced is destined to progress without material interruption. Comparisons have often been challenged and made between the Mogul and the British rule in India, but such comparisons between a power which was still enveloped to a certain degree in barbarism, and one which is wielding all the resources, the knowledge, and the enlightened principles of a civilisation entirely modern and very recent, can only be regarded as ostentatious. There are, however, as already noticed, favourable features in the Mahomedan rule which the English Government cannot lay claim to, and which it would be profitable for the English statesman to lay to heart. The Mahomedan Government was one which in every sense of the term lived in the country, acting upon the people and reacted upon by them in the most direct manner. The splendour of their Courts and the wealth of their aristocracy redounded to the benefit of the people, amongst whom all their acquisitions were spent in a manner calculated to stimulate and encourage native art, whilst the administration of public affairs was to a great extent, if not entirely, in the hands of the natives who held the principal offices in the civil administration, and enjoyed no small share in the command of the armies. These advantages, which touch the mainspring of national life and prosperity, are necessarily wanting in the British system, and it must be admitted that, in the opinion of the natives, this detracts somewhat from the benefits which that system otherwise confers. The superior science and resources of the British nation have annihilated whatever native arts or manufactures had been in existence, and have introduced nothing in their stead, whilst the exclusiveness of their national character and the still more exclusive nature of the administrative machinery adopted in India, have shut out the people from all share in the political administration of their affairs. The British Government, in fact, professes to administer the vast vital interests of an extensive nation by means of a foreign agency fluctuating and uncertain in its character, and without availing itself to any considerable extent of the aid and counsels of the people whose interests are mainly affected by its legislation.

In making these remarks I am simply asserting a fact to which it is necessary to allude in marking the striking differences between the system of the British rule and of that which preceded it: they are advanced for that purpose only. Sure I am that the distinguished statesmen by whom the government of British India has been, and continues to be administered, had and have no object more at heart than the improvement of the country and the advancement of its people. If there should be any doubt upon that subject, the noble despatch of the Duke of Argyll, transmitted to India in 1871, would be sufficient to dissipate it. That despatch contained within it the germs of a system by which the natives of India will be gradually brought more largely into the administrative machinery.

Meanwhile it is a satisfaction to reflect that, owing to the more recent policy of the British Government, there still survive many native States independent as to their internal action, which afford now, and for years to come will continue to afford, some opening for native talent and native ambition, some opportunities for solving the great question of native advancement. These States, containing nearly 600,000 square miles, and inhabited by forty-eight millions of people, are scattered over the different parts of India. They are peopled by almost all the nationalities into which the country is divided. They thus form so many centres where the Sikh, the Mahomedan, the Rájpút, the Márhátá, and the Dravidian can each bring out to the best advantage whatever may be peculiar and excellent in his national character and national institutions, under the generalising influence of English principles and English civilisation. Their opportunities for this lie essentially in the future. Deprived centuries ago of their independence, ground down by the Márhátás, restored to ease and safety by the British in 1817, they had not till within the last sixteen years shaken off the mistrust engendered partly by a retrospect of the past, but more even by the sight of the absorbing process occasionally put into action around them. But the Royal Proclamation transmitted to India by the present Earl of Derby in 1859, and the unmistakable manner in which the spirit of that proclamation has been carried out, have dissipated all alarms. Never were loyalty and good feeling more widely spread amongst the native princes of India than at the present moment. The moral influence thus gained gives the paramount power opportunities for urging the feudatory chiefs to adopt measures of progress and liberality. It is to be hoped that in the course of time there will be cemented between that power and its feudatories a confidence and affection such as can be born only of a complete comprehension of the native modes of thought on the one side, and an appreciation of the great moral ends aimed at by modern civilisation on the other. An understanding of that description would be the certain prelude to the grounding of a system compared to which that even of Akbar was 'the baseless fabric of a vision.' When not only the higher governing classes —who already appreciate the truth—but the great mass of Englishmen employed in India shall have schooled themselves to believe that real predominance consists alone, not in belonging to a mis-called dominant race, but in predominance in learning, in ability, in the higher mental qualities and moral powers of a man, irrespective of his colour, his nationality, and his creed; when, too, the native shall have completely learned, as he is fast learning, that to take part in the affairs of the present age it will be necessary to abandon prejudices which restrict his progress, then only may we feel confident that India is entering upon a path which will tend to her advancement in greatness, and open out careers for her sons.

INTROD. Judging from the increasing numbers of thoughtful minds who now-a-days devote themselves to the consideration of these important questions, the subject will, it is certain, sooner or later attract earnest attention, and be treated in a manner which its importance demands. Meanwhile it is possible that the task may be facilitated by a sketch giving an insight into the past career and history of the Native States. That career, it must be owned, displays little of the action of the people, but, like the history of all Governments of the past, consists simply in the wars, the exploits, and the successions of their rulers. But the story is by no means wanting in events of interest, or in indications of life and vitality calculated in many instances to excite the pride of the rulers and the ruled of these States in their past. And pride in the past, I need hardly say, affords the best guarantee for development and improvement in the future.

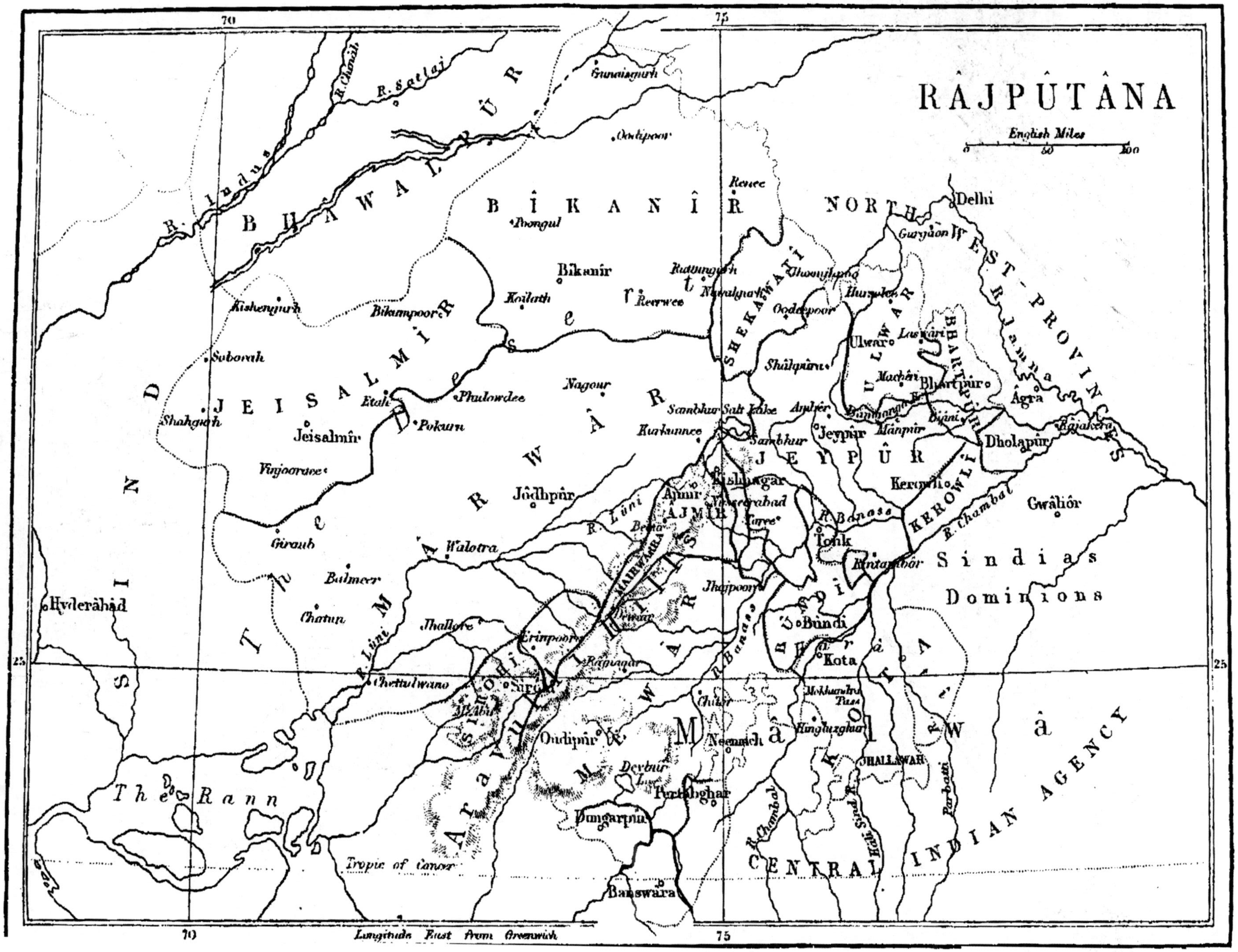

RÂJPÛTÂNA
English Miles
0
50
100
NORTH WEST PROVINCES
R. Jamna
Delhi
Gurgâon
Âgra
Dholapûr
Gwâliôr
Sindias Dominions
CENTRAL INDIAN AGENCY
BIKANÎR
Bikanir
Poongul
Koilath
Reerwee
Ruttungurh
Nawulgurh
Renee
Oodipoor
Gunaisgurh
BHAWALPÛR
R. Satlaj
R. Chenâb
R. Indus
JEISALMÎR
Jeisalmîr
Kishengurh
Bikampoor
Soborah
Shahgurh
Etah
Pokurn
Phulowdee
Vujooraee
MÂRWÂR
Nagour
Jôdhpûr
Kurkunnee
Sambhur Salt Lake
Sambhur
Walotra
Giraub
Balmeer
Chatun
Jhallore
Chettulwano
R. Lûni
SINDH
Hyderâbâd
The Rann
Tropic of Cancer
SHEKAWATI
Ghoonjhano
Oodeypoor
Shâlquru
ULWAR
Ulwar
Laswâri
Machâri
BHARTPÛR
Bhartpûr
Bijani
Mânpûr
Amber
JEYPÛR
Jeypûr
Kerowli
KEROWLI
R. Chambal
R. Banass
Tonk
Rintambôr
Kishngar
Ajmîr
AJMÎR
Nusseerabad
Taree
Beawr
MAIRWARA
Jhajpoor
Dewair
Erinpoora
Râjnagar
Sirohi
Abu
Oudipûr
Neemuch
Chitôr
Deybur
Pertabghar
Dungarpur
Banswara
Bûndi
Kota
Mokhundra Pass
Hinglazghar
JHALLAWAR
R. Kali Sind
Parbatti
Arâvulli
MEWÂR
MÂLWÂ
70
75
25
Longitude East from Greenwich

PART I.—RAJPÚTÁNA.

CHAPTER I.

ÚDAIPÚR OR MEWÁR.

AREA—11,614 sq. miles. POPULATION—1,161,400.
REVENUE—About 4,000,000 rupees.

CHAP. I.

'WITH the exception of Jaisalmír,' writes the learned author of the 'Annals and Antiquities of Rájásthán,' 'Mewár is the only dynasty of these races which has outlived eight centuries of foreign domination in the same lands where conquest placed them. The Ráná still possesses nearly the same extent of territory which his ancestors held when the conqueror from Ghizní first crossed the "blue waters" of the Indus to invade India; while the other families now ruling in the north-west of Rájásthán are the relics of ancient dynasties driven from their pristine seats of power, or other minor branches who have erected their own fortunes. This circumstance adds to the dignity of the Ránás, and is the cause of the general homage they receive, notwithstanding the diminution of their power. Though we cannot give the princes of Mewár an ancestor in the Persian Noshírvan, nor assert so confidently as Sir Thomas Roe his claims to descent from the celebrated Porus, the opponent of Alexander, we can carry him into regions of antiquity more remote than the Persian, and which would satisfy the most fastidious in respect to ancestry.'

The origin of the family of the present Ráná of

PART I.

Údaipúr is lost in antiquity. According to the best authenticated tradition, the sovereign of that part of the country had been treacherously murdered in the second century of the Christian era. His favourite wife, who was absent at the time, alone escaped the general slaughter. She was then pregnant, and in due course gave birth to a son. As soon after his birth as was practicable she made over the boy to a Brahman woman, with directions that he should be brought up as a Brahman. She then mounted the pile to rejoin her lost lord. The boy was Bappú Báwul, the ancestor of the Ránás of Údaipúr.

Brought up as a Bhíl, amongst the Bhíls, the child soon became known as the most daring son of the forest. He killed birds, chased wild beasts, and was the leader of his comrades in all their exploits. One day, after a deed of more than ordinary daring, the youths who accompanied him declared they would elect him as their King. One of them, to note their choice, cut his finger, and with the blood issuing from the wound made the royal mark on his forehead.[1] They then repaired to the chief of the tribe, who confirmed all that they had done.

On attaining manhood Bappú Báwul sought a wider field for his operations. He established a great reputation, connected himself by marriage with the royal house of Málwá, expelled the 'barbarians' who had usurped his family domains, and finally fixed the seat of his government at Chítor, where he ruled the whole of Rájpútáná. He died at the patriarchal age of a hundred years.[2]

[1] This remarkable ceremonial is still kept up, a Bhíl being still the principal actor in the investiture, and the material used for marking being his own blood. It is stated also, and there can be no doubt of the fact, that the custom was adhered to forty years ago, that whenever the Ráná of Údaipúr crossed the Mahí river, an individual, of a tribe descended from a Chohan Rájpút by a Bhíl mother, was sacrificed, his throat being cut, and his body thrown into the river. — *Vide An Historical Sketch of the Princes of India.* 1833.

[2] The legend adds that, 'advanced in years, he abandoned his children and his country, carried his arms west to Khorassan, and there

I have stated that the legend records the birth of Bappú Ráwul as having taken place in the second century of the Christian era; but later investigations have proved beyond a doubt that he reigned in the eighth century, his capture of Chítor having taken place about 728 A.D. Between him and Samársi, the twenty-third king of his race, occurs a break of nearly five hundred years. Of the events of these years the industry of Colonel Tod has obtained a trace, but it would be foreign to my present purpose to enter upon a subject so vast and so remote. Samársi, who flourished in the twelfth century, was a great warrior. The bard of the period describes him as being the 'Ulysses of the host; brave, cool, and skilful in the fight; prudent, wise, and eloquent in council; pious on all occasions; beloved by his own chiefs, and revered by the vassals of the Chohan.' In alliance with his brother-in-law Prithwi-Raj, the Hindú King of Delhi, Samársi went forth to meet the Tartar invaders of India. The battle which ensued lasted three days (1193) and terminated in the defeat of the Hindús, and the death of Samársi and all his chiefs.

Samársi was succeeded by his son Kárna, and he, a few years later, by his cousin Ráhap, son of Samársi's brother. This prince first changed the title of the Sovereign of Údaipúr from Ráwul to Ráná, by which it has ever since been known.

From Ráhap to Lákamsi, a space of half a century, nine princes of Chítor were crowned. Of these nine, six fell in battle. This period is described by contemporary annalists as a period of 'confusion and strife within and without.' I therefore pass it over.

Ráná Lákamsi succeeded to his father's throne in 1275. It was during his reign that Chítor had the first experience of Mahomedan invasion. Whilst he was yet a lad, his uncle, the Regent Bhímsi, beat off an attack

established himself and married new wives among the barbarians, by whom he had a numerous offspring.'—Tod.

of Alla-ú-dín, King of Delhi, upon Chítor. But in 1303 the attack was renewed. The Ráná, surrounded by all his sons but one—and that one he had sent away to preserve the duration of his race—after defending the place to the utmost, met the assailants in the breach and carried death into, or met it in, the ranks of the enemy. Yet the surviving son did not despair. He had, too, with him the son of his eldest brother, the renowned Hámir, destined to be the saviour of his country. Noticing the capacity of the latter, the Ráná resigned in a short time the kingdom in his favour. Left untrammelled, Ráná Hámir soon made the country so unpleasant to Alla-ú-dín that that prince was glad to make over Chítor to Mal-déo, the Rájpút chief of Jálor, whom he had enrolled amongst his vassals, and to return to Delhi. In a few years (1313) Hámir recovered the capital of his ancestors, and, it is asserted by the Hindú writers, defeated and took prisoner the successor of Alla-ú-dín, who was marching to recover Chítor; nor did he release his captive until he had surrendered four conquered districts and paid a lakh of rupees and a hundred elephants for his ransom. Under the rule of this great prince, the glories of Rájpútáná revived. He was the sole Hindú prince of power left in India. All the ancient dynasties had been crushed; and the ancestors of the present princes of Jodhpúr and Jaipúr, and many others, brought their levies, paid homage, and obeyed the summons of the great ruler who had asserted the valour of the Hindús, and established their rule in the part of India most congenial to them.

The administration of Hámir is stated to have been mild and paternal, and to have brought great prosperity to his subjects. He died, full of years, in 1365, 'leaving a name, still honoured in Mewár, as one of the wisest and most gallant of her princes, and bequeathing a well-established and extensive power to his son.' [1]

The son, Khaitsi Ráná, was a worthy successor of his

[1] Tod's *Rájásthán.*

great father. He added to his dominions by several conquests, and even obtained a victory over the Emperor Humayún at Bakról. Unhappily he was slain in a family broil with his vassal, the chief of Bunaoda, whose daughter he was about to espouse.[1]

He was succeeded (1383) by Lakha Ráná, an able man, a capable warrior, and a great patron of the arts. He, too, increased his dominions; but, more than that, he settled his frontier, and discovered and worked silver mines in Jaoara. He was, likewise, victorious against the Mahomedan King of Delhi, Mahomed Shah Lódi, but in driving that monarch's army from Gya was slain. His name still lives as of the ruler who was at once the patron of arts and the benefactor of his country.

The death of Lakha Ráná left the throne to a minor, Mókalji. His rights were zealously guarded in his early youth by his elder brother Chonda, self-excluded from the inheritance.[2] On his coming of age, he evinced all the high qualities of his race, and he achieved no inconsiderable renown in the field; but in the midst of his triumphs he was assassinated at Madaria by his uncles,

[1] Tod's *Rájásthán*.

[2] The history of the self-exclusion of Chonda is curious. It is thus told by Colonel Tod:—'Lakha Ráná was advanced in years, his sons and grandsons established in suitable domains, when "the cocoa nut came" from Rinmul, Prince of Márwár, to affiance his daughter with Chonda, heir of Méwar. When the embassy was announced, Chonda was absent, and the old chief was seated in his chair of state, surrounded by his court. The messenger of Hymen was courteously received by Lakha, who observed that Chonda would soon return and take the gage; "for," added he, drawing his fingers over his moustachios, "I don't suppose you send such play-things to an old greybeard like me." This sally was of course applauded and repeated: but Chonda, offended at delicacy being sacrificed to wit, declined accepting the symbol which his father had even in jest supposed might be intended for him; and as it could not be returned without insult to Rinmul, the old Ráná, incensed at his son's obstinacy, agreed to accept it himself, provided Chonda would swear to renounce his birth-right in the event of his having a son, and be to the child but the first of his "Rájpúts." He swore to fulfil his father's wishes.'

Right loyally he observed them. But it was an unfortunate policy that required the sacrifice. The right of primogeniture was compromised, and the making the elder branch of the family a powerful vassal clan with claims to the throne proved more disastrous in its consequences than the arms of the Moguls and the Márhátás.

PART I.

the natural brothers of his father, for an unintentional offence.[1]

The successor of Mókalji was Kúmbho Ráná (1419). He is reported to have been one of the ablest princes who ever sat upon a throne. He possessed, it is said, the energy of Hámir, the artistic tastes of Lakha, and a genius as comprehensive as either, and he was more fortunate. As a warrior he was unsurpassed amongst Hindú sovereigns. He inflicted, in 1440, a terrible defeat upon the allied Mahomedan sovereigns of Málwá and Gujrát, taking the former prisoner, and 'setting him at liberty not only without ransom, but with gifts.' Subsequently he defeated the forces of the King of Delhi, erected thirty-two fortresses for the defence of his dominions, and fortified the passes. He was a man of literary tastes, and a poet himself. Nor, considering that he married the most beautiful Hindú princess of the age, can he be regarded as insensible to female beauty.

Kúmbho Ráná had enjoyed a prosperous reign of fifty years when (1523) he was assassinated by his son! The cause of the parricidal act was simply lust to reign.

The parricide, by name Údá, but known in the annals as Hatiáro or the Murderer, did indeed succeed, but he ruled but a short time. In the four years of his administration he lowered the character of his race and diminished the glory of his country. He was driven from the country by his brother Raemal, and, fleeing to Delhi, was struck dead by lightning.

Raemal succeeded in 1474. His first act was to defeat the King of Delhi, who had espoused the cause of his nephews, in a pitched battle. He then pardoned the nephews, who became faithful and valiant subjects. He was very successful likewise in the wars he carried on with the Mahomedan King of Málwá. Unfortunately his domestic happiness was marred by the disunion amongst his sons. The episode recounting their feuds is one of

[1] Tod.

the most interesting and instructive in the annals of Rájpútáná, but it would be out of place in this volume.[1]

RaemalRáná died, after a prosperous reign, in 1509. He was succeeded by his son, Sánga Ráná. 'With this prince,' writes Colonel Tod, 'Mewár reached the summit of her prosperity. To use their own metaphor, "he was the urn on the pinnacle of her glory." From him we shall witness this glory on the wane; and, though many rays of splendour illuminated her declining career, they served but to gild the ruin.'[2]

Some idea of the glory of Sánga Ráná may be gathered from the enumeration of the retinue by which he was followed when he marched to the battle-field. 'Eighty thousand horses,' writes the authority already quoted, 'seven Rájás of the highest rank, nine Ráos, and one hundred and four chieftains bearing the title of Ráwul and Ráwut, with five hundred war elephants, followed him to the field. The Princes of Márwár and Ambar did him homage, and the Ráos of Gwáliár, Ajmír, Sikri, Raésen, Kalpí, Chandérí, Búndí, Gagraon, Rampúra, and Abú served him as tributaries or held of him as chief.'

Sánga Ráná was a great ruler. His first act was to allay the disorders occasioned by the intestine feuds of his family. He then organised his forces to repulse the invasion of the Mahomedans from Delhi and Málwá. These he defeated in eighteen pitched battles, in two of which —those of Bakról and Ghatolli—he was opposed by Ibrahim Lodi in person. But the invasion of the famous Báber came then to decide whether Hindostan was to be the spoil of the Mussulman or appanage of the Hindú. Victory seemed at first to smile on the latter. When the vanguards of the two armies met at Kanúa, near Sikri, on February 11, 1527, the Tartar invaders, though reinforced from their main body, were repulsed with heavy loss. 'If,' writes Elphinstone, 'the Ráná had pressed on during the first panic it is probable he would have ob-

[1] *Vide* Tod's *Rájásthán*. [2] *Ibid.*

PART I.

tained an easy victory; he chose to withdraw to his encampment after his success, and thus allowed Báber ample time to take up a position and to fortify his camp, so as to make it a difficult matter to assail him.'

On March 16 following, the decisive battle took place. Báber sallied from his entrenchments, at the head of all his army, and attacked the Hindús at Biána. For several hours the battle raged fiercely, but, when the result was most doubtful, the chief of Raysín, by name Sillaidi, who commanded the van of the Hindú host, deserted to the enemy, and Sánga Ráná was forced to retire from the field, himself wounded and the choicest of his chieftains slain. He retreated towards the hills of Mewár, having announced his fixed determination never to re-enter Chítor but with victory. Had his life been spared he might have redeemed the pledge, but the year of his defeat was the last of his existence. He died at Baswa, on the frontier of Mewár, not without suspicion of poison.

It is, perhaps, not unfitting to record in this place the account given of the personal form and qualities of one who was not only the most famous representative of the most ancient existing dynasty in the world, but also the most famous Hindú sovereign in India. 'Sánga Ráná'—writes the author of the 'Rájásthán'—'was of the middle stature, but of great muscular strength; fair in complexion, with unusually large eyes, which appear to be peculiar to his descendants. He exhibited at his death but the fragments of a warrior. One eye was lost in the broil with his brother, an arm in the action with the Lódi King of Delhi, and he was a cripple owing to a limb being broken by a cannon ball in another, while he counted eighty wounds from the sword or lance on various parts of his body. He was celebrated for energetic enterprise, of which his capture of Mózaffer, King of Málwá, is a celebrated instance; and his successful storm of the almost impregnable Rinthambór, though defended by the imperial General, Ali, gained him great renown. He erected a small palace at Kanúa, on the line which he determined should be the northern limit of Mewár, and, had he been succeeded by a prince possessed of his foresight and judgment, Báber's descendants might not have retained the sovereignty of India.'

SángaRáná was succeeded, in 1530, by his eldest surviving son, Ratna Ráná. He reigned only five years, but before he died had the satisfaction of seeing Báber depart, leaving the territories of his father undiminished. He was succeeded, in 1535, by his brother Bikramajít. This prince was daring and foolhardy, but without talent. Defeated in the field by Bahádúr, King of Gujrát, he was besieged by that monarch in Chítor. This famous capital, after a desperate and bloody defence, was taken and sacked. But Bahádúr, summoned to move against Humáyun, soon left his conquest, and Bikramajít Ráná recovered his capital. But he had learned nothing and forgotten nothing. His insolence to his nobles caused a rebellion. He was deposed and put to death, and Banbír, natural son of the brother of Sánga Ráná, appointed to reign in his stead. Banbír Ráná reigned, however, only until such time as the posthumous son of Sánga Ráná was able to assert his rights. The name of this prince was Údai Singh. He ascended the throne in 1541–2. He was a weak, yielding character, born to be ruled by others. Such characters are usually governed by the daring and the unscrupulous. Údai Singh Ráná was no exception to the rule. Attacked in 1568 by the great Akbar, his capital, after another desperate defence, again succumbed. Údai Singh fled to the forests of Rajpiplí, and died there four years later, after an unhappy and inglorious reign.

His son, Pertáp Ráná, 'succeeded to the titles and honours of an illustrious house, but without a capital, without resources—his kindred and clans dispirited by reverses.' He possessed, however, many of the noble qualities of his grandfather. Never despairing, nobly supported by his adherents, the princes and clansmen of the family, he established himself at Komulmír, and reorganised the country for a prolonged struggle with the invader. Alone of all the sovereign princes of Rájpútáná he refused to ally his house with the Mogul. He refused this 'degradation,' as he considered it, whilst yet struggling for existence; even when he saw the sovereign of Jodhpúr enriched by four provinces, bringing with them a revenue of nearly 16,00,000 rupees, for merely making the concession. But virtue did not remain always unrewarded. It is true that in the plain of Huldighát (1576) he met with a crushing defeat from the son of Akbar, afterwards his successor; and, after a series of encounters with adverse fortune, determined, with his family and trusting friends, to abandon Mewár, and found another kingdom on the Indus. He had already set out, when the unexampled devotion of his minister placed in his hands the means of continuing the contest. Turning upon his adversaries, he smote them in the hinder part, and in one short campaign (1586) recovered all Mewár—Chítor, Ajmír, and Mándelgarh alone excepted. Cut off from Chítor, he established a new capital at Údaipúr, a place which subsequently gave its name to the kingdom. He died in 1597, leaving behind him a reputation for 'undaunted heroism, inflexible fortitude, that which "keeps heroism bright," and perseverance.'

Amra Ráná, the eldest son, succeeded to the throne of Údaipúr. He was too fond of ease and dignity to be a great warrior, but he did, nevertherless, achieve some great things. In 1608 he defeated the Imperial army at Déweir. Jehángír, to revenge himself, made over Chítor to Súgra, uncle of Amra, but who had deserted his family. But the experiment failed. Súgra reigned in solitary grandeur for eight years, without conciliating a single Rájpút noble. Then his conscience smote him, and he restored Chítor to its rightful owner. With that fortress the Ráná acquired no less than eighty of the chief towns or fortresses of Mewár.

But a great trial was awaiting him. The Prince

Khúrm, afterwards the Emperor Shah Jehán, was about to invade his dominions. Again did the Ráná collect all his disposable forces, 'the might of their hills.' But all was in vain. He could not resist the overwhelming force of the Moguls, and after seeing his cities captured and his lands laid waste, sued for peace. What followed is thus recorded by the Emperor Jehángír himself: 'On Sunday, the 26th, the Ráná, with respect and due attention to etiquette, as other vassals of the empire, paid his respects to my son, and presented a celebrated ruby, well known in possession of this house, and various arms inlaid with gold; with seven elephants of great price, which alone remained after those formerly captured, and also nine horses as tribute. My son received him with princely generosity and courtesy, when the Ráná, taking my son by the knee, begged to be forgiven. He raised his head, and gave him every kind of assurance and protection, and presented him with suitable khiluts, an elephant, horses, and a sword.'

CHAP. I.

In other respects Shah Jehán treated the Ráná with great generosity. He restored to him all the country conquered since the time of Akbar, and raised his son, Karran, to a high rank amongst the military chiefs of the empire.

But the disgrace had crushed the heart of Amra Ráná. He abdicated shortly afterwards in favour of Karran, and shut himself up in a palace a mile outside the city of Údaipúr, nor did he once again cross its threshold.

Karran Ráná ascended the throne of his ancestors in 1621. In the rebellion of Khúrm (Shah Jehán) against his father, Jehángír, he took the part of Khúrm, and afforded him an asylum at Údaipúr. This act of gratitude to one who had been kind to his father did not affect the feelings of Jehángír towards him. He died after a peaceful reign in 1628.

His son, Juggut Singh, succeeded him. Regarding this prince, the Emperor Jehángír recorded in his memoirs, when the prince visited him at the age of twelve years, that 'his countenance carried the impression of his illustrious extraction.' He reigned twenty-six years—years of uninterrupted tranquillity. To him Údaipúr is indebted for those magnificent works which bear his name. A full description of these is given by Tod in his 'Annals of Rájásthán.' I, who have seen them, can bear witness to the accuracy of his description.

Ráj SinghRáná, his son, succeeded him in 1654. This prince showed his high blood by bearing off as his bride a Rájpút lady of the house of Márwár, who, solicited in alliance by the bigoted Mahomedan Aurangzíb, had appealed to the chivalry of the Ráná, sending him this message: 'Is the swan to be the mate of the stork?—a Rájpútní, pure in blood, to be wife to the monkey-faced barbarian?' Ráj Singh attacked and cut up the imperial guards sent for the lady, and carried her off as his bride to Údaipúr.

But he was to come to issue with Aurangzíb on grounds upon which he was even more absolutely in the right. About the year 1676 it pleased that fanatical prince to re-impose a tax called the jezia, *i.e.*, a poll-tax on unbelievers in Mahomedan orthodoxy. This act of bigotry roused a very bitter feeling amongst the Hindús generally, but especially so in the heart of their representative sovereign, the Ráná of Údaipúr. He wrote the noblest letter which a man under such circumstances could pen, and sent it to Aurangzíb.[1] But this letter lashed Aurangzíb to fury. He summoned his sons and his vassals from all parts of India, and dashed upon Údaipúr. But Ráj Singh was more than a match even for his hardened warriors. Retreating before his advanced troops, he drew them into the recesses of the country, and then overwhelmed them. Finally, after more than one great victory, he forced Aurangzíb to quit his country, and carried the war into regions ruled by

[1] *Vide* Appendix A.

the Mahomedans. He died in 1681, when a projected peace, signed by his successor, had afforded him the certainty that his labours had not been in vain. He is described as having possessed, in war, in chivalrous feeling, and in love of art, the qualities which most adorn a man.

Jai Singh Ráná succeeded his father, and signed the peace alluded to with Aurangzíb—a peace by which the right of imposing the jezia was renounced. Jai Singh had shown capacity in early youth, but he became indolent and uxorious. His reign is almost entirely a reign of domestic broils. He died in 1700, and was succeeded by his son Amra, who had been in revolt against him.

Amra II. reigned sixteen years. His rule is chiefly remarkable for the formation of a league amongst the Rájpút powers to defend themselves against the Mahomedans. But this league was unfortunately accompanied by conditions certain to breed, and which did breed,[1] internecine quarrels. These quarrels led in their turn to appeals to a stronger power, and it naturally happened that the stronger power took advantage of the quarrels and the appeals to help itself. It will be seen how Údaipúr suffered from this cause. Such sufferings, however, occurred subsequently to the demise of Ráná Amra II., which event took place in the year 1716.

Ráná Sangrám Singh succeeded his father and reigned till 1734. Under his rule Mewár was respected, and the greater part of her lost territory was regained. He was

[1] This triple alliance was formed between the Rájás of Jaipúr and Jodhpúr on the one side, and the Ráná of Údaipúr on the other. By it all connection with the Mogul empire, domestic or political, was renounced. Nuptial engagements between the contracting parties, renounced by Údaipúr since the time of Akbar, were to be renewed. It was stipulated that the sons of such marriages should be heirs, or if the issue were females, they should never be dishonoured by being married to a Mogul.

But the remedy was worse than the disease. It was a sacrifice of the rights of primogeniture, introducing domestic strife, and alternately giving ingress to the Márhátás as partisans and umpires in family disputes—a position of which these knew well how to take full advantage.

PART I.

a patriarchal ruler, wise, just, and inflexible, steady in his application to business, and an excellent financier. He had the good fortune to be served by an excellent minister, Behari Dás Panchóli.

Ráná Juggut Singh II., his son and successor, revived the defensive alliance with the Rájpút States, previously negotiated by Ráná Amra. He was too fond of pleasure to govern. He preferred, it is said, an elephant fight to warfare. Hence, under his rule, the kingdom passed through a rapid stage of decline. He was embarrassed in the first place by the want of cohesion amongst the Rájpúts engendered by the rivalry of their princes, then by the growing power and increasing audacity of the Márhátás. Then, instead of trusting, as his ancestors had done, to the valour of the Rájpúts, he must needs call in the aid of Múlhar Ráo Holkar to fight his battles. These causes contributed to give the Márhátás a firm hold on Rájásthán, and when Ráná Juggut Singh died, in 1752, the abasement of his country was sealed.

Ráná Pertá Singh II. lived three inglorious years. During the whole period Údaipúr was subject to invasions from the Márhátás, conducted in succession by Sutwaji, Jankoji, and Ragonáth Ráo. Ráná Ráj Singh II. succeeded his father in 1755. He reigned seven years, during which the country became so impoverished by invasions of, and war contributions imposed by, the Márhátás, that the Ráná was compelled to ask pecuniary aid from the Brahman collector of the tribute, to enable him to marry the Rahtór chieftain's daughter! To such a low ebb had the country fallen!

His uncle, Ráná Arsi, succeeded him in 1762. The ungovernable temper of this prince and his insolent behaviour to the highest nobles of his country caused the greatest misfortunes. Not only did the nobles rebel and support the claims of a pretender to the throne, but Sindhia, Holkar, and the Rájá of Jodhpúr, taking advantage of the distractions of the country, made the most of their opportunity. In the ten years of his reign Ráná Arsi lost in war six of his most important districts, besides having to pay large sums in contributions. Although, thanks to the fidelity and daring spirit evinced by a leading merchant, Amra Chand, he triumphed over the pretender, he did not escape the vengeance his cruelty and insolence had provoked from the spear of the assassin. He was murdered in 1772.

His son and successor, Ráná Hámir, was as unfortunate as his father. Throughout his reign 'the demoralisation of Mewár was complete: her fields were deluged with blood, and her soil was the prey of every paltry invader.'[1] Rebellion and invasion went hand in hand, and though these were repressed and subdued during the lifetime of the noble minister, Amra Chand—a man of whom it can be recorded that, though many years virtual ruler of Údaipúr, he did not leave behind him 'funds sufficient to cover the funeral expenses,' and whose splendid reputation still lives—yet, after his death, confusion became worse confounded, and six more districts were wrenched from the falling kingdom.

His brother, Ráná Bhím Singh, succeeded in 1778. He enjoyed a long reign of fifty years. It has been said of him that in the course of this period he witnessed greater changes and reverses of fortune than any prince of his illustrious house. And it is true. From his accession to the period of the Márhátá war with the English his country experienced a treatment not dissimilar to that which had been meted out to it under his immediate predecessors. It is true that reverses were tinged by occasional gleams of good fortune, but these were few and far between. It might have been hoped that the humiliation of the two leading Márhátá powers by Lake and Wellesley, in the beginning of the nineteenth century, would have procured some respite for Údaipúr. But the contrary happened. The introduction by Lord Corn-

PART I.

wallis of the non-intervention system left that and other Rájpút countries a prey to the raids of Sindhia, Holkar, Amír Khan, and subsequently of the Pindárís. To such a state of dependency and distress was the Ráná eventually reduced, that he—the head of all the Hindú dynasties —was forced to owe to Zálim Singh, regent of Kotá, the receipt of an allowance, for his support, of a thousand rupees a month. This state of degradation exposed him to the insults of his nobles and feudatories, the more powerful of whom retired to their forts, and directed all their efforts, not to save the kingdom, but to maintain their own domains.[1]

This state of things lasted till the end of the Pindárí war in 1817. The consequence was that when the British army, in the course of that campaign, entered Mewár, they found its fields laid waste and its cities ruined, the authority of the Ráná set at naught, all the elements of social order dissolved, or in the course of rapid dissolution.

A remedy was at once applied. The British Government took the country of Údaipúr under its protection, convened the nobles, and prevailed upon them to restore the territories they had usurped from the Ráná, whilst he, on his part, promised to protect their rights. With respect to the British, the Ráná engaged to acknowledge their supremacy, to abstain from political correspondence, to submit disputes to their arbitration, and to pay one-fourth of the revenue as tribute for five years, thereafter three-eighths in perpetuity. The treaty embodying these conditions was signed on January 13, 1817, and the following month the several bands of plunderers and Márhátá horse were expelled the Ráná's territories.

The disorganisation in the administration had, however, become so rooted that necessity forced upon the officer first nominated as British Agent—the Colonel Tod from

[1] For the fate of the Ráná's beautiful daughter, Kishna Komari, the struggle for whose hand ruined Rájpútáná, *vide* Appendix C.

whose exhaustive work I have so largely quoted—the whole conduct of affairs. The reforms he introduced were so beneficial, that in the course of three years, whilst greatly ameliorating the condition of the children of the soil, they almost doubled the revenue. Having thus practically demonstrated the mode in which it was possible to administer affairs, Colonel Tod, by direction of his Government, transferred the reins to the native authorities of Údaipúr. The experiment was not satisfactory. In the two succeeding years large debts were incurred, the revenues were anticipated, the tribute to the British Government left unpaid. Again were the officers of the State put into leading strings, and good management re-introduced. Again, too, in 1826, was the administration re-transferred to the native authorities. Once more, unfortunately, failure supervened. In the course of a few months disorder reigned rampant, and the revenue fell almost to the same low figure from which it had been raised by the decided measures taken in 1818. 'Within a few months the extravagance and oppression became as great as they had ever been before, and the roads became almost impassable to single travellers.' [1]

Bhím Singh died in 1828, and was succeeded by his son Jowan Singh. The new ruler was, unfortunately, a man of no character, addicted to vicious habits and low pursuits. It can be easily imagined that under such a rule State affairs did not prosper. Within a few years of his accession the tribute again fell heavily into arrear, the State became overwhelmed with debt, and there accrued an annual deficit of two lakhs of rupees. To such an extent was maladministration carried that the Ráná had to be warned that unless he could keep his engagements with the British Government a territorial or other sufficient security would be required.

The same year that Jowan Singh received this warning,

[1] Aitchison's *Treaties*.

PART I.

1838, he died without natural issue. His adopted son, Ráná Sirdar Singh, succeeded him. He was a harsh, overbearing man, very unpopular with his chiefs. He died in 1842, before the financial embarrassments bequeathed to him by his successors had been cleared off.

His younger brother, Ráná Surúp Singh, succeeded to the throne. To relieve his government, the British reduced the tribute to two lakhs of rupees annually (June 1846). His reign of nine years is chiefly noticeable for the continual contests in which he was engaged with his feudatory chiefs, most of whom, descendants of former Ránás, possessed exclusive privileges, on which the Ráná attempted to infringe. These disputes were finally settled in 1861.

In that year Surúp Singh died, and was succeeded by his nephew Sambhú Singh, who was a minor. The administration was first entrusted to a council of regency, aided by the advice of the Political Agent. But the members of the council soon exhibited signs of turbulent opposition and misconduct. Acts of cruelty were allowed to go unpunished, and every kind of opposition was thrown in the way of the Political Agent. At length it became necessary either to form a new council, or to appoint some one chief to act as regent. As no chief to whom this duty could be entrusted was available, it was determined to nominate a council of three, consisting of a president and two members. As the nobleman nominated as president insisted, however, on absolute and uncontrolled powers, the proposition fell to the ground, and the British Resident was directed to retain charge of the administration, assisted by two members; he was also ordered to associate the young Ráná with himself in the business of the State, so as to fit him as far as possible for the direct management of affairs. Under this arrangement the financial condition of the country improved greatly.

Máhárána Sambhú Singh attained his majority and assumed the direct government of the country on November 17, 1865. Though not without capacity, he was not a successful ruler.

CHAP. I.

Since the foregoing sketch was written, intelligence has been received of the death of the Máhárána Sambhú Singh. This event took place at Údaipúr, on October 7, 1874.

Sambhú Singh, who at the period of his demise had lived only twenty-seven years, was childless. His nearest of kin were his two uncles, brothers of his father, Sakat Singh and Sohan Singh; but the Máhárána had the right of excluding both of them by adoption. This right he exercised when his recovery was regarded as impossible, in favour of Surjun Singh, son of the elder uncle, a boy about sixteen years old. This prince has been installed as Máhárána.

The Máhárána has received the right of adoption. He is entitled to a salute of seventeen guns.

CHAPTER II.

JAIPÚR.

AREA—15,000 sq. miles. POPULATION—1,900,000.
REVENUE—36,00,000 rupees.[1]

CHAP. II.

THE kingdom of Jaipúr, better known amongst the Ráj-púts as the kingdom of Amber or Dhúdar, was founded by Dhola Raë in the year 957. Dhola Raë was thirty-fourth in descent from Rájá Nál, traditional founder of the kingdom and city of Nárwár. Rájá Nál is said to have been lineally descended from Kush, the second son of Ráma, King of Kóshula, whose capital was Ayódhia, the modern Oudh. Hence the reigning family in Jaipúr

[1] A large portion of the revenues of the State is alienated in jaghirs and religious grants. I record here the available receipts.—Aitchison's *Treaties.*

has been known from time immemorial as the Kutchwa family or rule.

The exploits of Dhola Raë can only be traced in the fabulous legends of the period. This much is clear—that he conquered the country inherited by his descendants. That part of Rájpútáná was then divided amongst petty Rájpúts and Mína chiefs, all owing allegiance to the Hindú Kings of Delhi. These he conquered in succession, and marrying the daughter of the Prince of Ajmír, he laid the foundations of a kingdom destined to be permanent.

Killed in battle, Dhola Raë was succeeded by his posthumous son by the daughter of the princess of Ajmír, named Kankal; he, again, by his son Maidul Ráo, a warrior and conquerer; and he, in his turn, by Húndéo. Kúntal followed him, and he it was who completed the subjugation of the other aboriginal race of the Mínas.

His successor, Pujún, was one of the most famous of the earlier monarchs of the dynasty. He married the sister of Pírthí Raj, King of Delhi, and commanded a division of that monarch's armies in many of his most important battles. He twice signalised himself in repelling invasions from the north, and, commanding at the time on the frontier, he defeated Sháb-ú-dín in the Khyber pass, and pursued him towards Ghizní. His valour mainly contributed to the conquest of Mahóba, the country of the Chundails, of which he was left governor; and he was one of the sixty-four chiefs who, with a chosen body of retainers, enabled the King of Delhi to carry off the Princess of Kanouj. But in this service Pujún lost his life.

From Pujún to Pírthí Raj there is nothing to record. The names of the intermediate sovereigns were Malèsi, Bijul, Rajdeo, Kítun, Kontul, Júnsi, Udaikurn, Nursing Bunbír, Udharun and Khundrasèn.

The ascent to the throne of Pírthí Raj marks an era in the dynasty. He had seventeen sons, of whom twelve reached man's estate. To these twelve and to their successors he assigned twelve chambers in the house of Kutchwa; and he limited the future right of his succession in his dominions to the descendants of those twelve chambers. Of Pírthí himself little is known but that he made a pilgrimage to the Indus, and that he was assassinated by his own son, Bhím, 'whose countenance,' says the chronicle, 'was like the mouth of a demon.'

From Pírthí Raj we come down to Bahárma, the first prince of the dynasty who paid homage to the Mahomedan power. He followed the fortunes of Báber, and received from Humáyun, prior to his expulsion by the Pathán dynasty, a high imperial title as ruler of Amber.

His son, Bhagwán Dass, became still more intimately allied with the Mogul dynasty. He was the friend of Akbar, and gave his daughter in marriage to Prince Selim, afterwards Jehángír—one of the first instances on record of a prince who 'sullied Rajpút purity by matrimonial alliance with the Islamite.' [1]

Bhagwán Dass had no children, but was succeeded by his nephew Maun Singh, son of his youngest brother. This prince was the most brilliant character at Akbar's court. As the emperor's lieutenant he was entrusted with the most arduous duties, and added conquests to the empire from Khóten to the ocean. Orísá was subjugated by him, Ásám humbled and made tributary, and Kábul maintained in her allegiance. He held in succession the governments of Bengal and Behár, of the Dekhan and of Kábul. He had the weakness, however, to interfere in the succession to the throne of Akbar in favour of Khúsrú, eldest son of Jehángír, and his own cousin. Though too powerful to be openly chastised, Maun Singh was never forgiven. He died governor of Bengal in 1615.

Ráo Bháo Singh succeeded him—a man of no mark. Nor was Máhá, who followed him, of more note. Upon

[1] Tod. Elphinstone relates (p. 439) that Bahármal 'had, at an early period, given his daughter in marriage to Akbar.'

PART I.

his death, Jehángír, on the advice, it is said, of Jóda Bai, his Rájpútni wife, gave the kingdom of Amber to Jai Singh, nephew to Maun Singh, a young man of great promise.

It was a fortunate selection. Jai Singh, known in history as the Mirza Rájá, restored by his conduct the glories of the family name. He performed great services during the reign of Aurangzíb, who bestowed on him one of the highest dignities of the empire. He made prisoner the celebrated Sivají, but afterwards, finding that his pledge of safety was likely to be broken, was accessory to his escape. But this instance of good faith was more than counterbalanced by his previous desertion of Prince Dára, in the war of succession, a desertion which crushed the hopes of that brave prince, and caused the death of his son Solimán. His conduct with respect to Sivají, combined with the haughtiness of demeanour which he assumed in later years, alienated Aurangzíb, who from that moment determined to destroy him. A foolish vaunt which the Rájá was in the habit of making in his durbar, and which reached the Emperor's ears, only intensified this resolve.[1] He found it difficult for some time to meet anyone who would or could execute his wishes. He had recourse, therefore, to the diabolical expedient of appealing to the ambition of the Rájá's son. He promised the throne of Jaipúr to Kírut Singh, younger son of Jai Singh, to the prejudice of his elder brother, Rám Singh, if he would assassinate his father. Kírut Singh consented, mixed poison with his father's opium, then returned to claim the investiture. Aurangzíb, however, only gave him a district. From this period, says the chronicle, Amber declined.

Rám Singh, who succeeded Jai Singh, and his son and

[1] It was the custom of the Rájá, sitting with his twenty-four chiefs in durbar, to hold up two glasses, one of which he called Satára (Sivají), the other Delhi (Aurangzíb). Then, dashing one to the ground, he would exclaim: 'There goes Satára; the fate of Delhi is in my right hand, and this, with like facility, I can cast away!'—Tod, whom I have followed almost textually.

successor, Bishen Singh, were men of little mark. The third in order, Jai Singh II. better known as Sowaè Jai Singh, deserves more notice. This prince came to the throne in 1699, eight years prior to the demise of Aurangzíb. He served with distinction in the Dekhan, but on the emperor's death he sided with Prince Bedar Bukt, son of Prince Azim, who had at once declared himself emperor. With these he fought the battle of Dholpúr (June 1707) which ended in their death and the elevation of Bahádúr Shah. For his opposition Jaipúr was sequestrated and an imperial governor sent to take possession; but Jai Singh entered his estates, sword in hand, drove out the imperial garrisons, and formed a league with the Ráná of Údaipúr and the Rájá of Jodhpúr for their mutual defence against Mahomedan aggression.[1]

Jai Singh II. was, perhaps, the most cultivated sovereign that ever reigned in India. He was fond of art, of mathematics, and of science. In astronomical knowledge he was not inferior to the best of his European contemporaries. He drew up a set of tables from which astronomical computations are yet made and almanacs constructed; he caused Euclid's Elements, the best treatises on plain and spherical trigonometry, and Napier's Logarithms, to be translated into Sanscrit.

He built a new city for his capital, the marble city of Jaipúr, the only one in India erected on a regular plan. He built observatories, with instruments of his own invention, at Delhi, Jaipúr, Banáras, and Mathurá, upon a scale of Asiatic grandeur, and their results were so correct as to astonish the most learned.

But besides the construction of a capital and objects of science—of which I have enumerated only a part—Jai

[1] By one of the clauses of this agreement, the Rájás of Jaipúr and Jodhpúr, with the view to recover the privilege of marrying with the Údaipúr family, forfeited by their matrimonial connection with the Moguls, agreed that, on the occasion of such alliances, the issue of the Údaipúr princess should succeed to the throne in preference to elder sons by other wives. It was an unfortunate arrangement, and brought great disasters both on Jaipúr and Údaipúr.

PART I.

Singh erected, at his own expense, *caravanserais* or public inns, for the free use of travellers in many of the provinces. He carried on these works in the midst of perpetual wars and court intrigues. And although he did not entirely escape the debasing influence of the latter, he not only steered his country through its dangers, but raised it above the principalities around it. He sustained the Mogul empire as long as the representative of the Mogul rights would exert himself to support them, but when he found himself unable to inspire the wretched Farokhsír even 'with the energy of despair,' he gave up the task and devoted himself with renewed energy to his favourite pursuits, astronomy and history. On the accession of Mahomed Shah in December 1720, Jai Singh was called from his philosophical studies and appointed the emperor's lieutenant for the provinces of Agra and Málwá in succession, and it was during this interval of comparative repose that he erected those monuments which irradiate this dark epoch of the history of India.[1] He procured at this time also the repeal of the jezia or polltax on infidels, imposed by the bigotry of Aurangzíb, and he repressed the incursions of the Jâts. Re-appointed in 1732 lieutenant for the Mogul in Málwá, he saw that it was vain, in the disorganised state of the empire, to attempt to repel the aggressions of the Márhátás. With the full consent, then, of Mahomed Shah, he formed an intimacy with the famous Báji Rao, and induced the emperor in 1734 to transfer to his keeping the province of Málwá. The influence he thus obtained was usefully employed in checking the excesses of the Márhátás, and in delaying their advance on the capital. During the invasion of Nádir Shah he wisely held aloof from participating in a contest in which there was no hope of success. Jai Singh II. died in 1743, after a prosperous reign of forty-

[1] From his observations of seven years at the various observatories he constructed a set of astronomical tables—these were completed in 1728.

four years. They had been years of prosperity for Jaipúr in the midst of the general declension of the other states and kingdoms of Hindostan. He had added to it the districts of Deóti and Rajúr, and he had governed it wisely and well. He is said to have been vain, and fond of strong drink. Yet he will ever be remembered as one of the most remarkable men of his age and nation. 'Science,' says Colonel Tod, 'expired with him.' His eldest son, Isuri Singh, succeeded him. Yet, according to the convention made with Údaipúr, the right of succession lay with his younger brother, Madhú Singh, son of a princess of Mewár. And Madhú Singh not only preferred his claims, but at a great cost[1] obtained the aid of Holkar to support them. He succeeded, and probably would have proved a successful ruler but for the troubles brought on him by the rising power of the Jâts. The long quarrels with that people were brought to an issue by a battle, which, though the Jâts were defeated in it, proved destructive to Jaipúr in the loss of all her chieftains of note. Madhú Singh himself died four days later. Had he lived, it is thought that he might have prevented the decline of the State of Jaipúr. He inherited no small share of his father's learning, and cultivated the society of men of science. He built several cities, of which that called after him, Madhúpúr, near the celebrated fortress of Rinthunbór, the most secure of the commercial cities of Rájwárra, is the most remarkable.

Pírthi Singh II., a minor, succeeded, under the guardianship of the mother of his younger brother Pertáp. She was an ambitious and unscrupulous woman, under the evil influence of her paramour, a low-born elephant-driver. After nine years of her dissolute sway, Pírthi Singh II. died from a fall from his horse, not however without suspicion of having been poisoned. Before he died he had married two wives, from one of whom was

[1] The districts of Rampúra Bhaupúra and Tonk Rampúra, with 840,000*l.*, were assigned to Holkar as payment for his support.

begotten a son, Maun Singh. The youth, however, was spirited away by his mother's relatives, and taken, first to his maternal roof, subsequently to Gwáliár, there to grow up under the protection of Sindhia. The half-brother, Pertáp Singh, son of the dissolute Ráni, succeeded Pírthi Singh II. He ruled the country twenty-five years. During his minority Jaipúr was a prey to constant feuds, in the course of which, while she had the good fortune to be rid by poison of the Ráni and her elephant-driver, she suffered greatly from Márhátá depredations and Márhátá insolence. On attaining his majority Rájá Pertáp was determined to rid himself of those locusts. He formed accordingly that league with Rájá Bíjé Singh, of Jodhpúr, which commenced so happily with the defeat of the Márhátás at Tonga (1787). But this triumph was short-lived. The defeats sustained at Patun and Mairta (1791), and the disruption of the alliance with Jodhpúr brought back the enemy. Holkar imposed a heavy annual tribute on the State, which he afterwards transferred to Amír Khan. From that period to the year 1803 the country was alternately desolated by Sindhia's armies and hordes of other robbers, who frequently contested with each other the possession of the spoils.

Pertáp Singh was a gallant prince and not deficient in judgment; but neither his gallantry nor his prudence could contend successfully against so many obstacles. He died in 1803.

His son and successor, Rájá Juggut Singh, ruled for nearly sixteen years with the disgraceful distinction of being the most dissolute prince of his race or of his age. His life did not disclose one redeeming virtue amidst a cluster of effeminate vices, including even cowardice. He was a debauchee, a spendthrift, and a libertine, without a spark of honour or virtue in his composition. It was the lust excited in him by the fame of Kishna Komári, the beautiful daughter of the Ráná of Údaipúr, which provoked that contest which, with the aid of the faithless marauder, Amír Khan, brought ruin to Rájpútáná.[1] To dwell upon the life of such a man would be to record actions from which an honourable mind recoils. He died unpitied, unlamented, even by his creatures, December 21, 1818.

CHAP. II.

Yet during his reign an event occurred which was to connect Jaipúr with the British. In 1803 a treaty was signed uniting that country in a subsidiary alliance with the alien nation. The Rájá, however, fulfilled his obligations very imperfectly, and Lord Cornwallis, who had resolved to abandon the system of subsidiary alliance, declared the connection with Jaipúr to be dissolved, and withdrew that State from the protection of the British Government. This policy was pursued by Sir George Barlow, notwithstanding the remonstrances of Lord Lake, made both on the grounds of general policy and good faith.[2]

The expediency of the dissolution of this alliance was considered to be very questionable by the Home Government, who in 1813 directed that Jaipúr should again be taken under protection whenever an opportunity might offer. But owing to the outbreak of the war with Nepâl it was considered better to postpone any such measure until it could be adopted as part of the general scheme for the suppression of the Pindárís. In 1817, when negotiations were opened, it was found that the cancelment of the previous treaty had rendered the Jaipúr State reluctant to enter into a fresh alliance. In time, however, the increasing necessities of the State, the example of its neighbours, and the apprehension of being excluded from British protection, the continued exactions of Amír Khan's troops, and the arrangements in progress for forming separate engagements with the small states dependent on Jaipúr, led at length to her accepting a treaty. By this (April 2, 1818) the protection of the British Government was extended to Jaipúr; the Máhá-

[1] *Vide* Appendix C.

[2] Aitchison's *Treaties*.

PART I. rájá agreed to furnish troops on the requisition of the British Government, and to pay an annual tribute of eight lakhs of rupees until the revenue should exceed forty lakhs, after which five-sixteenths were to be paid in addition to the eight lakhs. The fresh duty urged on the Máhárájá after the conclusion of the treaty was the resumption of the lands usurped by the nobles, and the reduction of the nobles to their proper relation of subordination to the Máhárájá. Through the mediation of Sir David Ochterlony agreements were entered into similar to those formed at Údaipúr. The usurped lands were restored to the Máhárájá, and the nobles were guaranteed in their legitimate rights and possessions.[1]

Rájá Juggut Singh left no issue, legitimate or illegitimate, and no provision had been made for a successor during his life. But as it was necessary to inaugurate a successor 'to light the funeral pile,' it became incumbent to nominate some one. The choice fell upon a distant relative, Móhun Singh, son of the ex-prince of Nárwár, the fourteenth in descent from Pirthi Raj I., Rájá of Jaipúr. But as the election was void, in consequence of its having been made without the due forms and in favour of one not nearest in order of succession, it is probable that a civil war would have ensued but for the timely discovery that one of the widowed queens of Juggut Singh was *enceinte*.

At three o'clock on April 1, a council of sixteen queens, widows of the late prince, and the wives of all the great vassals of the State, assembled to ascertain the fact of pregnancy, whilst all the great barons awaited in the ante-chambers of the *zenána* the important response of the council of matrons. When it was declared that the Bhattiáni queen was pregnant beyond a doubt, they consulted until seven, and then they sent in a declaration,

[1] Aitchison's *Treaties*, from which the account in the text is almost literally taken.

acknowledging their unanimous belief of the fact; adding that, 'should a son be born, they would acknowledge him as their lord, and to none else pledge allegiance.'[1]

On April 25, 1819, four months and four days after Juggut Singh's death, a son was ushered into the world with the usual demonstrations of joy, and received as autocrat of the Kutchwas; whilst the youthful interloper was removed from the throne, and thrust back into his native obscurity.[2]

The young child was named Jai Singh. The Government was assumed in his name by his mother. But during the minority of the young prince, Jaipúr was a scene of corruption and misgovernment, and the British Government found it necessary to appoint an officer to reside at the capital, and to authorise him to interfere in the internal administration of the State, with a view of guarding the interests of the British Government, and securing the payment of the tribute.[3]

In 1834–35 the British Government having found it necessary to march a force into Shaikháwatí for the purpose of settling that province, took possession of the Jaipúr share of the Sambhur salt lake as a security for the repayment of the expenses of the campaign. Whilst these, and arrangements connected with Shaikháwatí were being matured, Rájá Jai Singh died at Jaipúr under circumstances which could not fail to raise the strongest suspicions that his premature demise had been compassed by the minister, Sanghí Jotharám, and Rúpa Budárun, a female attendant in the palace. Jotharám had been the paramour of the late Rání, and under her influence had acquired great power in the State, supplanting in the office of minister the nominee of the British Government. The agent to the Governor-General proceeded therefore to Jaipúr to make inquiries, reform the administration, and assume the guardianship of the infant left by the Rájá. The strong measures he adopted led

[1] Tod. [2] *Ibid.* [3] Aitchison.

to the formation of a conspiracy by Jotharám. The life of the agent, Colonel Alves, was attempted, and his assistant, Mr. Blake, was murdered. The murderers were seized and executed by order of the minister, and Jotharám and his fellow conspirators were imprisoned for life in the fort of Chanár.[1] The young Rájá, Rám Singh, was placed under the guardianship of the British political agent. Under his superintendence, a council of regency, consisting of five of the principal nobles, was formed, and to their decision all measures of importance were submitted. The army was reduced, every branch of the administration was reformed, and satí, slavery, and infanticide were prohibited. The tribute was found to be far in excess of a due proportion of the revenue; a remission was therefore made in 1842 of forty-six lakhs of rupees, and the annual amount was reduced to four lakhs.[2]

Máhárájá Rám Singh did good service during the mutinies. For this he received a grant of the district of Kôte-kassim, under a promise to respect the revenue settlements made whilst the district had been under British management. He also received the privilege of adoption.[3]

Rám Singh is an intelligent prince, and devotes his best energies to the development of the resources of his country. With this object he has opened out roads, constructed railways, and given a great impulse to education. During the scarcity of 1868 he abolished transit duties on the importation of grain into his domains; and in the affairs of government generally he has shown an intelligent appreciation of the requirements of the age.

Máhárájá Rám Singh is extremely fond of the society of cultivated Englishmen and women. He has twice been a member of the Legislative Council of the Viceroy of India.

The Máhárájá is entitled to a salute of seventeen guns.

[1] Aitchison. [2] Aitchison's *Treaties*. [3] *Ibid.*

CHAPTER III.

JODHPÚR OR MÁRWÁR.

AREA—35,672 sq. miles. POPULATION—1,783,600.
REVENUE—about 17,50,000 rupees.

THE great kingdom of Kanouj, one of the four great Hindú sovereignties which existed in Hindostan for centuries previous to the invasions of Mahmud of Ghizní, came to an untimely end in the year 1193. Her last monarch, Jaichund, the representative of the race of the Rahtórs, proceeding, according to the Hindú legend, 'from the spine of Indra,' succumbed in that year to the invasion of Shab-ú-dín, King of Ghór, and was drowned in the Ganges whilst attempting to escape. With his death Kanouj ceased to be a Hindú city, and the name of Rahtór ceased to be heard on the banks of the 'sacred stream.'

Eighteen years subsequently to this event, two grandsons of Rájá Jaichund, by name Séoji and Saitram, abandoned the land of their birth, and, followed by two hundred retainers, and journeying westward towards the great desert, arrived at Kolúmund, twenty miles from the present site of Bíkánír, not then in existence.

The two brothers offered their services to the chief of the tribe of which Kolúmund was the place of abode, then at war with a neighbouring clan. The offer was accepted, and it was mainly due to the efforts of the two Rahtórs that victory inclined to Kolúmund. In the fight, however, Saitram was slain. The chief, to repay the debt he owed to the surviving brother, gave to Séoji his sister in marriage with an ample dower. Séoji then prosecuted his journey, and, after many adventures, alternately valiantly fighting and treacherously murdering, he planted his standard in 'the land of Khér' amidst the sand-hills of the river Lúni.

Séoji left three sons, the eldest of whom, Asot'háma, succeeded him. He established his second brother at Idar, on the frontiers of Gujrát, and the youngest at Okamundálá. He died, leaving eight sons, all of whom became heads of tribes, of which four still survive. He was succeeded at Khérdhur by his son Dúhur. Dúhur connected his reign with the past and the future. He endeavoured to recover Kanouj and to conquer Mundúr, destined to be the capital of his race. He failed in both attempts.

It will suffice to give the names of his successors, always the eldest sons in order of birth, till I come to the real conqueror of Mundúr. They were Raepal, Kanhul, Jalhun, Chado, Thído, Silko and Bírundéo, all men of renown in local warfare, under whom the family possessions were increased. Bírundéo was succeeded by his son Chonda, who conquered Mundúr, the ancient capital of Marú or Márwár, and made of it the chief city of the Rahtórs. He conquered likewise Nagore and the province of Godwar, and finally made firm his fortunes by marrying a daughter of the family he had expelled from Mundúr. He was blessed with fourteen sons, the descendants of four of whom still exist.

Chonda was killed at Nagore in the year 1402. He was succeeded by his son Ráo Rinmul.

Ráo Rinmul, during the lifetime of Ráná Lakha of Mewár, assisted that prince in his wars, and behaved as the first of his vassals. Upon the death of Ráná Lakha, however, he interfered in the affairs of Márwár in a manner which brought death to himself, and threatened his dominions with ruin.

In a note to the sketch of Údaipúr (page 13) I have given the reason why Chonda, the eldest son of Ráná Lakha, was content to resign his rights of succession to the throne of that kingdom in favour of Mókaljí, the youngest son of his father by Hansa,[1] daughter of Ráo Rinmul.

On the death of Răná Lakha, Chonda acted as guardian to his infant brother. But his administration was thwarted and interfered with by Ráo Rinmul, whose relatives fastened like locusts on the pleasant pasturages of Mewár. Indeed Rinmul seems to have cherished the idea of transferring the rule over the country to the Rahtór family.

As a prelude to the carrying out of this idea a brother of Chonda's was assassinated, and the life of the young Răná was threatened. But, at this crisis, Chonda suddenly swept down upon the Rahtórs, killed Ráo Rinmul, and scattered his followers. The eldest son of Ráo Rinmul, Joda, succeeded in escaping, but so utterly demoralised that he was forced to leave even Mundúr to its fate. All seemed lost to the Rahtórs. But Joda was a man of vigour and capacity. Carefully concealing his movements, he enlisted partisans, surprised two of the sons of Chonda at Mundúr, slew one there; the other, in his flight, on the boundary of the Godwar province. Then, wisely deeming the renunciation of a portion of his territory to be the most efficacious means of saving the remainder, he sued for peace, offering to restrict the boundary of his dominions to a line passing the spot on which the younger son of Chonda had fallen, 'as the price of blood and to quench the feud.' That is, he offered to cede the province of Godwar. The cession was accepted, and peace was made.

Joda, I have said, was a man of vigour and capacity. He had already displayed the first quality; it now devolved upon him to show what he possessed of the second. Instead of wasting his reign in fruitless wars, he devoted himself to the settlement of his country. He reinstated in their

[1] Hansa is variously stated to be daughter and sister of Ráo Rinmul. Even Colonel Tod writes of her under Mewár as the daughter, under Márwár as the sister.

PART I.

hereditary estates the ancient proprietors of the soil. Then, not satisfied with the ancient capital, he laid in 1459 the foundations of a new city, which he named after himself, Jodpúr or Jodhpúr, and which, in its turn, has given its name to the entire territory. He died in 1489 at the age of sixty-one. He had had fourteen sons, of whom the eldest surviving, second in order of birth, Súrajmul, succeeded him.

Of this prince the only record is that he reigned twenty-seven years, and had at least the merit of adding to the stock of Séoji. He had five sons, the eldest surviving of whom, Ganga, succeeded him. He died almost immediately, leaving a son of the same name, who established himself notwithstanding the armed opposition of his uncle Sága. In his reign, too, the Rahtórs had first to encounter in their own land Mahomedan invasion. Serving under the command of Sánga, Ráná of Mewár, they gained some successes, but had finally to succumb to the prowess of the Emperor Báber at the fatal field of Biána.[1]

Ganga died in 1532, and was succeeded by his son, Maldéo. This prince gained a great and lasting renown as a warrior and statesman. He regained Ajmír and Nagore, and made numerous conquests in the countries bordering on his dominions. Not content with this, he enclosed the city of Jodhpúr with a strong wall, built many forts and fortresses, and caused fortifications to be erected in the more salient parts of the country. Invaded by Shir Shah, he raised an army of 50,000 men, and reduced that monarch to great extremities. Shir Shah indeed was able to extricate himself solely by the device of instilling suspicion of some of his adherents into the mind of Maldéo. This caused the prince to countermand an assault which could scarcely have failed. The suspected leaders then vindicated their fidelity by an attack with their own followers on the camp of Shir Shah.

[1] *Vide* Údaipúr, p. 16.

Though they nearly penetrated to the quarters of the emperor, they were overwhelmed by numbers and almost annihilated. Maldéo had then no resource but to submit.

An incident, slight in itself, served subsequently to increase the misfortunes of Maldéo. He had refused an asylum to the Emperor Humáyún, when Humáyún was a fugitive. Yet he lived to see the son of Humáyún sitting on the throne of Delhi. Nay more, he lived to see that son, the great Akbar, enter, as an enemy, at the head of an army, the country from which he had repelled his father as a fugitive.

It was in 1561 that Akbar invaded Márwár. He captured Malakôt and Nagore, and transferred them to another Hindú family. Eight years later Maldéo saw himself compelled to sue for peace. He refused indeed to sue in person, but sent his son, the second in rank, Chundersén, to act for him. But Akbar was so incensed at this slight, as he conceived it, that he consigned Jodhpúr itself to the same Hindú prince, Raë Singh, upon whom he had conferred Malakôt and Nagore. Then ensued war to the knife. The old Rahtór chief had to stand a siege in his own capital, and finally on succumbing, to pay in the person of his recognised heir, Údai Singh, the homage he had refused before. The brother, Chundersén, held out for seventeen years, remaining all the time irreconcileable alike with his family and the Mahomedan invader. He was finally killed in battle.

The old Rájá, Maldéo, broken in spirit, died about 1573.[1] He left twelve sons,[2] of whom the third, Údai Singh, succeeded him.

Under this prince, the independence of Márwár ceased to exist. Údai Singh acknowledged the suzerainty of the

[1] Tod says in one place 1615 A.D. in two others, 1569 A.D. Both are manifestly incorrect. Akbar resented the non-appearance of Maldéo at his durbar in 1570, and assigned his dominions to Raë Singh in 1572. Maldéo was then alive, but he did not survive the last event more than one or two years.

[2] Of the two elder, the eldest had been banished, the second killed at Biána.

PART I.

Mogul. He was the first prince, moreover, of Rájpút race who gave his sanction to a matrimonial union between the race of the Rahtórs and the Mahomedan conqueror. He allowed his sister, Jod Bai, to marry the Emperor Akbar, not giving indeed, but receiving a dower, in the shape of all the districts wrested from Márwár by the bridegroom, Ajmír excepted, and likewise several rich districts in Málwá, whose revenues doubled the resources of his own domains. With the aid of his brother-in-law, Údai Singh diminished the power of his nobles, and curtailed the overgrown estates of the landowners for the benefit of the smaller peasantry. In the new settlement which he made he added fourteen hundred new villages to the fisc. In return for the aid thus given to him by Akbar, he supplied him plentifully with troops, of a quality inferior to none others in his army, for his expeditions.

Údai Singh survived his father, Maldéo, thirty-three years. He left thirty-four legitimate children; of these the eldest, Súr Singh, succeeded him.

Súr Singh was a great warrior. He was serving with the emperor's army at Lahore, where he had commanded since 1591–2, when intelligence reached him of his father's death. Much esteemed by Akbar for his military talents and brilliant services, he was commanded by that prince to attack, on his return to his dominions, Sirohí, a town in Rájpútáná, and capital of the hilly districts by which it was surrounded, the chief of which refused to acknowledge the emperor as his liege lord. Having completed this service he carried his arms against the King of Gujrát, completely defeated him at the battle of Dhúndoca, and brought about the submission of the country. On the death of Akbar, Súr Singh attended at the court of his successor, Jehángír, accompanied by his son and heir, Guj Singh, who was invested by the monarch on that occasion with a sword, to mark the distinguished valour he had displayed at the escalade of Jhalúr.

This Rájá added greatly to the beauty of his capital, and left several works, some of them of no small utility, which bear his name. He greatly lamented the necessity under which he found himself to accompany the Mogul emperor in all his expeditions, and shortly before his death caused a column to be erected on which were engraven words cursing any of his race who should ever in the future even once cross the Narbadá. Rájá Súr died in 1620, leaving six sons and seven daughters.

His eldest son, Guj Singh, succeeded him. He was in the imperial camp at Búrhanpúr, on the river Táptí, when he heard that he had been called to the throne. He, too, grew high in favour at the imperial court, received many favours from Jehángír, and was nominated his viceroy of the Dekhan. Like his father, too, he was a great warrior, and for his skill and daring obtained the title of 'Barrier of the Host.' He embroiled himself, however, with Prince Khúrm, afterwards Emperor Shah Jehán, for refusing to espouse his cause against his elder brother Khúsrú,[1] and when, in consequence, his confidential adviser was murdered by order of Prince Khúrm, he threw up his post in the army and returned to his native land. When, shortly afterwards, Prince Khúsrú died suddenly, and Khúrm seemed to threaten his father's throne, Jehángír appealed to the Rájpút chiefs to support him against filial ingratitude and domestic treason. The appeal was nobly responded to by Rájá Guj and by the Rájás of Jaipúr, Kotá, and Búndí; and by their efforts the rebellion was put down. When, prior to the decisive battle near Banáras, the Emperor met his Rájpút allies, he showed so much pleasure at the zeal displayed by Rájá Guj, that he not only took him by the hand, but, what was more unusual, kissed it.

Rájá Guj was killed in an engagement with some free-

[1] Tod says Prince Purvez; but Shah Jehán never feared Purvez. It was the murder of his eldest brother Khúsrú that cleared his way to the throne.

PART I.

booters in Gujrát in 1638. He had excluded his eldest son Amra from the succession in consequence of his violent disposition and turbulent conduct. The throne, therefore, descended to the second son, the renowned Jeswant Singh. The subsequent career of Prince Amra is one of the most striking and sensational stories in the history of Hindostan. It will be found at the end of this volume.[1]

The prince who now ascended the throne has left a name in the annals of Hindostan which will never die. More than once the destinies of India lay in his hands. The fate of Dára and the fortunes of Aurangzíb were alike at his disposal. He was not a great man in the true sense of that term, for he acted from interest, not from principle; was ready to change his side and to employ treachery. It is true that all his treacheries were directed against the Mahomedan enemies of his race and country, his one object being, by exciting divisions amongst them, to rid the country of the hated invaders. He was a scholar, a patron of the arts, a great general, utterly fearless, an active politician, and taken altogether, regard being had to the prevailing *morale* of the period, a man of whom the Rájpút race has reason to be proud. His reign embraces forty-three years of the history of Hindostan. I regret that the scope of this work will only allow me to give an outline of it. He ascended the throne in 1638, and from that time to 1658, a period of twenty years, was engaged mainly in the Dekhan under Prince Aurangzíb. In this and various other services he greatly distinguished himself. In 1638, the emperor became seriously ill. His eldest son, Dára Shekó, assumed the office of Regent. One of his first acts was to nominate Rájá Jeswant Singh his viceroy in Málwá. When, shortly afterwards, the ambitious designs of Aurangzíb began to develop themselves, Jeswant Singh was appointed generalissimo to oppose that prince. In the battle that followed, at a place fifteen miles south

[1] *Vide* Appendix B.

of Ujjén, since named Futtehabad, Jeswant Singh was defeated. He owed his defeat to his too great daring. He wished to crush the two brothers, Aurangzíb and Morad, at one blow, and delayed till their junction had been effected. This gave time to the wily Aurangzíb to corrupt the Mahomedans in his army, and their desertion on the field of battle brought about a defeat. Both armies remained, however, where they had fought, and Jeswant Singh was allowed to retreat unmolested the next morning.

The result of the battle, however, and of another equally successful, fought against Dára, was that Aurangzíb drove his brother from the regency, and assumed it himself. One of his first acts after his usurpation was to send a pardon to Jeswant Singh and a summons to his presence to join him in opposing his brother Shúja. Jeswant Singh obeyed the summons. But he did so only to be revenged. When the armies of the rival brothers were about to join battle at Kujwa, midway between Allahabad and Etawah, Jeswant Singh, in pursuance of an agreement made with Shúja, suddenly attacked the rear of Aurangzíb's army. Had Shúja then attacked, the fate of Aurangzíb had been sealed. But he delayed till the sun had risen. Jeswant Singh, then, finding himself unsupported, loaded his camels with the plunder of the camp and set off for Agra, leaving the two brothers to fight it out. In the battle which ensued between them Shúja was defeated. Meanwhile, Jeswant Singh lay in close vicinity to Agra, expecting Prince Dára Shekó, whose claims he was resolved to support. That prince had fled, after his defeat by Aurangzíb, to the banks of the Indus. But levying some troops, he entered Gujrát, raised an army there, and set out to effect a junction with Jeswant Singh at Agra. He delayed, however, unhappily, so long that the latter could no longer maintain his position, but was forced to retire upon Jodhpúr. He reached his capital in safety, deposited there his spoils, and then had an interview with Dára at Mairta. The moment for effective movement had, however, been lost. Aurangzíb, having crushed Shúja, was advancing in great force. Still this prince had seen so much of Rájpút valour in the Dekhan, that he did not feel very confident of the issue of a contest. He sent, with this view, a message to Jeswant Singh, not only assuring him of forgiveness, but offering him the viceroyalty of Gujrát, if he would withdraw from the contest and remain neutral. Jeswant Singh agreed, and accepted a commission to serve under Prince Moazzim against the rising power of Sivají.

Dára, thus deserted, was compelled to succumb to Aurangzíb, but Jeswant Singh had no idea of keeping faith with his Mogul lord. Hardly had he reached the Dekhan than he opened a correspondence with Sivají and planned the death of the imperial general, Shaista Khan, and the proclamation of the young prince as emperor. Information of the transaction reached Aurangzíb, but he concealed his knowledge of it till he had disposed of all his rivals; he then replaced Jeswant Singh by Jai Singh, Rájá of Jaipúr.

From that time, neither party trusting the other, it seemed as though he would succeed who showed himself the greater master in wile. Sent again with supreme powers to the Dekhan, Jeswant Singh again so incited the ambition of Prince Moazzim as to necessitate his removal from so dangerous a post. He received an order to proceed at once to take up the post of viceroy of Gujrát, but on arriving at Ahmedabád he found it had been a trick to draw him from the Dekhan. He proceeded then to his own dominions.

But even there, Aurangzíb did not consider himself as secure from the machinations of so powerful a vassal. He had tried secret means to rid himself of him, but these had all failed. He resolved, therefore, to send him to a distance. A rebellion had opportunely broken out in Kábul; he accordingly sent Jeswant Singh to quell it.

Jeswant set out, leaving his son, Pírthí Singh, in charge of his ancestral domains. CHAP. III.

But hardly had he reached Kábul than Aurangzíb commenced his measures for the destruction of his family. He invited Pírthí Singh to court, treated him with marked affability, and as a sign of his favour, gave him a robe of honour. But the robe was poisoned. Pírthí Singh put it on in the royal presence, and expired a few hours later in great agony.

When the news of his son's death reached Jeswant Singh he broke down utterly. He saw that his great enemy had gone beyond him in revenge, and felt his heart pierced by a poisoned sword. Two other sons, Juggut Singh and Dulthumun, fell victims about the same time to the climate of Kábul. Their deaths caused the overflowing of his cup; he died of a broken heart (1678).

At the time of his death his wife was in the seventh month of her pregnancy. In due time she was confined of a boy, who was called Ajít Singh. As soon as she was able to travel she set out on her return home. But the vengeance of Aurangzíb had not been satiated. As soon as the party reached Delhi, he demanded from the escort the person of the young prince. It was impossible to oppose force to such an order; but the address of the leader of the party, Dúrga Dás, supplied its place. Having obtained leave to send off the women of the party to their homes, he first retained one of the attendants to personate the Ráni, substituted a child for the young prince, and then sent off the mother and son with the women. But no long time elapsed before the suspicions of Aurangzíb were aroused, and he demanded that the Ráni and her child should be brought into the citadel. The Rájpúts played their parts to perfection by refusing to surrender the widow and son of their Rájá. This for some time blinded the suspicions of Aurangzíb, but at length they were renewed, and he again insisted, and the escort still refusing, sent troops to enforce his de-

PART I.

mands. The Rájpúts, after a desperate resistance, were cut to pieces and dispersed. Then, for the first time, did the emperor discover the trick that been played upon him. But it was too late. The Rání and her child had had time to reach Jodhpúr.[1] Aurangzíb, however, with his usual acuteness, feigned to disbelieve the story of the escape, and for many years treated the child he had captured as the undoubted heir of Jodhpúr.

The faithful Dúrga Dás reached Jodhpúr soon after these events, and took the lead in preparing the country for the impending invasion of Aurangzíb. Of the war which followed, it is not necessary to give a detailed account. It will suffice to say that for a long time the Mogul arms were irresistible. The country was laid waste, the villages burned, the women and children carried off. This was one result. There was another, even of greater importance. The tie which had till then bound the Rájpúts to the Moguls was severed, never to be renewed.

At length the craft of Aurangzíb was turned against himself. Dúrga Dás gained over his son Akbar, who proclaimed himself emperor. He was indeed foiled, but the contest continued with increasing advantage to the Rájpúts. They began, in their turn, a war of reprisals, and with greater or less mitigation, hostilities continued till the death of Aurangzíb in 1707.

Before this event occurred, Ajít Singh had obtained his majority, and had begun to rule, though not as yet in Jodhpúr. But after Aurangzíb's death he recovered his capital, and though he lost it once again, it was again re-

[1] Colonel Tod gives a different version of the escape of the boy. He states that, rather than surrender their prince, the Rájpúts caused the women to be blown up by gunpowder; that they then went to meet death at the hands of the Moslems in the streets of Delhi, whilst the boy was conveyed away in a basket of sweetmeats. Such is the Hindú legend, but it is neither so probable nor so well authenticated as the account given by Elphinstone, which I have mainly followed. He credits the Rání, however, with having two sons; but I think it clear there was but one.

covered, and the kingdom re-established in almost its former state of prosperity. It was this prince who entered into the triple alliance with Ráná Amra of Údaipúr and the Rájá of Jaipúr, to resist Mahomedan aggression and to undertake no matrimonial engagements with princes of that religion.

CHAP. III.

Ajít Singh was a prince of great vigour of mind and body. Born amid the snows of Kábul, exposed from his earliest youth to the frowns of fortune, he set himself to work to redeem his country from bondage to the invader. This was the one aim—the one object, of his life. He inherited an invincible hatred to the very name of Moslem, and was never scrupulous as to the means he employed against the members of that hated race. He succeeded. Never could the imperial forces overcome him. He gave deliverance to his country.

His death was most tragical. Unable to rid themselves in any other way of one so much dreaded, the court of Delhi bribed his son, Abhi Singh, then on the spot, by the offer of the viceroyalty of Gujrát, to have his father murdered. Abhi accepted the bribe, and carried out the project by means of his brother, Bukht Singh.

Abhi Singh succeeded to the throne of Jodhpúr in 1731, but his whole reign was passed in a contest with his fellow-assassin and brother, Bukht Singh. He was indolent, cruel, and fond of ease and opium. He repaid the gift of the viceroyalty of Gujrát by aiding in its partition, and annexing to Márwár the rich provinces of Bínmahl, Sambúr, and others. Colonel Tod truly adds: 'This additional reward of parricide has been the cause of all the civil wars of Márwár.' Abhi Singh died in 1750, and was succeeded by his son, Rám Singh, a youth of nineteen, of an impetuous and overbearing disposition. An insult offered to him at his installation by his uncle, Bukht Singh, the murderer of his grandfather, so enraged the young Rájá that he deprived his uncle of his fief of Jhalúr, and moved with an army to

PART I.

enforce his order. But he was defeated and driven from the throne, which his uncle at once occupied.

Rájá Bukht Singh was a man of noble presence, of herculean frame, generous, intrepid, well versed in the literature of his country, and but for his one great crime, would have ranked with the heroes of Márwár. He raised the *morale* of his country, and inspired his countrymen with a determination to resist foreign aggression. He reigned only three years, but in that time he completed the fortifications of Jodhpúr, and developed in many ways the resources of the country. He was poisoned by his relative, the aunt of the expelled Rám Singh. Bíjey Singh, his son, succeeded him; but hardly had he received the homage of his people than he was called upon to meet his cousin, Rám Singh, who was advancing with an army to assert his claims, assisted by the Márhátás. In the battle which ensued, Bíjey Singh was defeated, and sought refuge in flight. But the most unfortunate result of the battle for Márwár was that the Márhátás now took root in the land. The murder of their chief, Jyapa, gave them a pretext to change their *rôle* of auxiliaries to that of principals, and they speedily availed themselves of it, expelling Rám Singh.

This prince died in exile at Jaipúr, in 1773. He was succeeded as titular sovereign by his former rival, Bíjey Singh, but the Márhátás had for a time real possession of the land. The reign of Bíjey was full of vicissitudes and warfare, internal and external. He first planned the diminution of the power of the nobles, already encroaching upon his own. But he was forced, in the course of the contest which ensued, to yield more of his already diminished authority. Seemingly acquiescent, he planned revenge, and inviting the principal chiefs of Márwár to the funeral of his family chaplain, or gúrú, he had them assassinated. This great blow was decisive. Although the son of one chieftain rose in revolt, he was speedily subdued; and Bíjey Singh, to divert the attention of the others from the past, led them all against the robbers of the desert. They conquered Amerkôt, the key to the valley of the Indus from Sinde; curtailed the territories of Jaisalmír, on their north-west frontier; then sweeping back, recovered the rich province of Godwar from Méwar. Returning from these conquests, Bíjey Singh allied himself with Pertáp Singh, king of Jaipúr, for the expulsion of the Márhátás. The two armies met at Tonga, in 1787, and engaged in a battle in which the Márhátás, though aided by the infantry under the Chevalier de Boigne, were defeated. By this victory the Rájá recovered Ajmír. But De Boigne wiped out this defeat on June 20, 1791, at Patan, and on September 12 following at Mairta, in both of which actions the Rájpúts were completely vanquished. By them Ajmír was lost for ever to Márwár, and a contribution was imposed on the country of sixty lakhs of rupees.

Bíjey Singh did not long survive these losses. His last years saw him the slave of a beautiful concubine, whose insolence estranged the nobles, and procured her own assassination; not, however, before she had persuaded the Rájá to adopt one of his grandsons as her son and his successor.

Bíjey Singh died in 1793. He had had seven sons, six of whom survived him. Their names, in order of birth, were Zálim Singh, Sawant Singh, Shir Singh, Bhím Singh, Goman Singh, and Sirdar Singh. Of these, Zálim Singh was the rightful heir; but Bíjey Singh, to please his concubine, had adopted Maun Singh, his grandson, the son of Shir Singh. But on his death, the fourth son, Bhím Singh, seized the throne, defeated Zálim Singh, then by poison or the sword killed his four remaining brothers and their sons, the adopted son of the concubine, his own nephew, Maun Singh, alone excepted. This young prince had taken refuge in Jhalúr. Thither Bhím Singh pursued him, and despairing of taking the place by assault, subjected it to a rigorous blockade. But whilst

PART I.

the blockade continued, he managed to disgust his nobles to such an extent that they withdrew from him, and retired to their estates. Nevertheless the blockade was persisted in. It was made more and more rigorous; the besieged were reduced to something approaching starvation, when suddenly, November 1803, Bhím Singh died. The besieged prince naturally succeeded him.

Proclaimed at once Rájá, Maun Singh would appear to have retained the follies of heedless youth untempered by the adversities which should have strengthened his character. Just about the time of his accession, the English had triumphed over Sindhia, and were following Holkar in his headlong flight. With a view to effect a permanent settlement in Rájpútáná, they offered to Maun Singh the alliance which would have secured to him his territories. He concluded the treaty, but did not ratify it, proposing another. With a fatuity quite incomprehensible, he at the same time gave aid to the one enemy who could injure him, viz. Jeswant Ráo Holkar. The British Government therefore cancelled the treaty, and left Márwár to its own resources. It was this folly on the part of Maun Singh that caused his country to fall, a few years later, a prey to the depredations of Amír Khan.

Meanwhile the widow of Bhím Singh had given birth to a posthumous son, Dhókul Singh, to whose cause several of the nobles rallied. Under the charge of the chief of Pokurwa, he was presented to several chiefs as their lord, and then, to preserve him from any attempt on his life, he was sent to the desert, to be cared for by the chiefs of Shaikhawáti.

The reign of Maun Singh was one of continued warfare brought about by his own folly. He engaged in a disastrous war with Jaipúr for the hand of the daughter of the Ráná of Údaipúr. For the details of this tragical story I must refer the reader to the appendix to this volume.[1] In the war which followed he was alternately opposed and supported by the adventurer, Amír Khan, whose freebooters devastated the lands of Jaipúr, of Mewár, and Márwár, committing atrocities not to be counted. The appearance on the field, too, of the lad Dhókul Singh, as a pretender to the crown, supported by a large party of nobles, added to the troubles and perplexities of the Rájá. To escape these, he at last feigned madness, and abdicated in favour of his son, Chutter Singh.

It was whilst this young prince was holding the reins of sovereignty that the British Government offered, and Amír Khan accepted, the terms which freed Rájpútáná from the depredations of that marauder. This was followed by a treaty between the British Government and Jodhpúr (January 1818), by which the British protection was extended to that country, and certain conditions were made assuring the suzerainty to the British. But just at this crisis Chutter Singh died.

Within a short interval after his son's death, Rájá Maun Singh threw off his feigned insanity and re-assumed the Government. Secure now against external enemies, his native character disclosed itself, and he gave loose to all his smothered passions. He put to death or imprisoned almost all the chiefs who, during his feigned insanity, had shown any unfriendly feeling towards him. He confiscated property to the value of one million sterling. The name of justice became unknown—treachery and cold-blooded cruelty were the inspiring deities at Jodhpúr.

At length a crisis arrived. Many of the nobles, 'the flower of their country,' found asylums in the neighbouring states of Kotá, Mewár, Bíkánír, and Jaipúr. Thence they addressed remonstrances to the British authorities. The British authorities induced the Rájá to listen to terms of accommodation, and he promised to reinstate

[1] *Vide* Appendix C.

the self-exiled chiefs in their possessions (February 1824). But he did not alter his line of conduct. Consequently, in 1827, the recusant nobles levied their adherents, and calling on the posthumous son of the late Rájá, Dhókul Singh, to lead them, prepared to invade Jodhpúr from the Jaipúr territory. Upon this, Rájá Maun Singh urged upon the British Government that the time had arrived when he was entitled to the aid of British troops to support him on the throne; that the attack by which he was threatened was not an internal insurrection but a foreign invasion emanating from, and supported by, Jaipúr. The answer of the British Government was clear and decided. 'If,' they said, 'insurrection should be so general as to indicate the desire of chiefs and subjects for the downfall of the prince, there does not exist any reason for our forcing on the state of Jodhpúr a sovereign whose conduct has totally deprived him of the support and allegiance of his people against unjust usurpation, or against wanton but too powerful rebellion. The princes of protected states may fairly perhaps call upon us for assistance, but not against universal disaffection and insurrection, caused by their own injustice, incapacity, and misrule. Princes are expected to have the power of controlling their own subjects, and if they drive them into rebellion they must take the consequences.'

At the same time that the British Government laid down the sound and salutary principles enunciated in this despatch, it administered a sharp remonstrance to the Máhárájá of Jaipúr, and called upon Dhókul Singh to retire from the confederacy.

But the evil day was only adjourned. It is noticeable in the history of sovereigns, European and Asiatic, that those whose youth and middle age have been fiery, tempestuous, passionate, treacherous, and cruel, almost invariably succumb, in the third division of their existence, to the influence of priests. Maun Singh was no exception to this rule. But the priestly influence which swayed him made him neither less cruel nor less tyrannical than before. On the contrary, his evil passions became intensified to such an extent that the British Government was forced to interfere.

At the close of the rainy season of 1839, a force under Colonel Sutherland was marched to Jodhpúr, to restore tranquillity and, if possible, good government to the country. Jodhpúr was occupied five months. Maun Singh then executed an engagement by which he bound himself to respect the ancient usages of the country in determining the rights of the nobles. He agreed that a British political agent should reside at his court to assist the Rájá, the council of nobles, and the ministers in carrying on the government. Two of his evil advisers were dismissed, sequestrated lands were restored upon terms agreed to by the parties interested; an arrangement was concluded for the payment of arrears due on account of tribute and legion expenses, and for the punctual payment of such claims for the future; an amnesty for the past was granted by the Rájá to his nobles who had been in rebellion; and the British Government consented to extend a pardon to those who had been instrumental in subverting the true interests of Márwár.

Rájá Maun Singh died in less than four years after this event, leaving no son, natural or adopted. Dhókul Singh, the posthumous son of Rájá Bhím Singh, then preferred his claims; but they were rejected. The nearest representative families were those of Ídar and Ahmednagar, and it was left to the widows, nobles, and chief officials to select the future ruler. Their choice fell upon Tukht Singh, chief of Ahmednagar, whom, with his son, Jeswant Singh, they invited to Jodhpúr. Some negotiation ensued regarding the retention of Ahmednagar by the family of Tukht Singh, but it was decided that the right of succession lapsed by the acceptance of power in

PART I.

Jodhpúr, and that Ahmednagar should revert to Ídar, from which state it had been separated in 1784.

Máhárájá Tukht Singh ascended the throne of Jodhpúr in 1843. He traces a lineal descent back to Rájá Ajít Singh, of whom he is the great-grandson. But the hopes that had been entertained regarding his capacity for ruling were destined to be blighted. Soon after his accession the country fell into a state of disorder, little inferior to that which had prevailed under his predecessor. The Rájá showed himself avaricious, careless of affairs, and difficult of access. The management of the country fell then into the hands of subordinates, whose only desire it seemed to be to minister to the ruling passion of their master.

To such an extent did misgovernment proceed, that in 1867 the nobles would have organised an insurrection but for their fear of the paramount power. An act of cupidity perpetrated in that year intensified their feeling of dissatisfaction. The case was this. The thákur, or feudal lord, of Ghánerao died, leaving a brother, his rightful heir. Instead, however, of allowing the fief to devolve upon the brother in natural course, the Rájá despatched a force to seize it for one of his numerous sons. This emboldened the thákurs to represent their well-founded grievances to the British Government. They showed how they had been tyrannised over and oppressed, excluded from the royal council, and prohibited from leaving their property to adopted sons. Specific acts of gross misgovernment were dwelt upon, and especially the confiscation of Ghánerao.

In reply, the Máhárájá was 'called to order,' and it was hoped that the remonstrance of the British Government might not be without its effect; but the insolent behaviour of His Highness during the durbars in Rájpútáná in 1869–70 would seem to indicate that, like his immediate predecessor, Maun Singh, he is incorrigible.[1]

[1] When the late Viceroy, the Earl of Mayo, visited Rájputáná in 1871, he held a durbar at Ajmír, to which the Ráná of Udaipúr and the

The State of Jodhpúr did good service during the mutinies, and the right of adoption was duly bestowed upon the Máhárájá. CHAP. III.

CHAPTER IV.

BÚNDÍ.

AREA—2,291 sq. miles. POPULATION—220,000.
REVENUE—5,00,000 rupees.

THE city of Búndí, which, like all the cities in Rájpútáná, has given its name to the principality, was founded, in the year 1342, by Ráo Déva. Ráo Déva, in the Hindú legend, is said to have been lineally descended from Anhul or Agnipala, the first Chohan,[1] the date of whose birth loses itself in the mists of time. His later predecessors had felt the Moslem's sword, and had fled from Asèr to Mewár. Sallying thence, Ráo Déva, in 1342, occupied the Bandú valley, built the city of Búndí, exterminated, or almost exterminated, the indigenous CHAP. IV.

Rájá of Jodhpúr were invited. It had been officially decided some time previously, in strict accordance with custom, that on all state occasions when they might meet, the Ráná of Údaipúr should take precedence of the Rájá of Jodhpúr. But when this decision was communicated to Jodhpúr he refused to attend the durbar. It was explained to him that the question had long previously been settled and could not be reopened or discussed. But he remained obstinate. In vain did the political agent, in vain did his own son remonstrate with him. He refused to sit below Údaipúr. After waiting for him about an hour the Viceroy held the durbar with Jodhpúr's seat vacant.

After the durbar was over it was determined that so great a want of respect to the Viceroy of Her Majesty must be noticed. The Rájá then was directed to leave the camp at Ajmír at daybreak the following morning with the whole of his retinue. The friendly ceremony usual on such occasions was omitted, no salute was fired, and ultimately, after due consideration, it was decided that his salute should be diminished by two guns. Lord Mayo showed his sense of the loyal feeling of the Rájá's son by receiving him in private audience after the durbar.

[1] The Chohan was the last creation of the Brahmans to fight their battles against infidelity, and their only successful creation.

Mínás, and called the country Harawati (Harouti), or the country of the Haras.[1]

From Ráo Déva to Ráo Súrjun, a period of nearly two hundred years intervenes. Throughout this period the Haras had, whilst possessing independence, been quasi-vassals of the Ránás of Údaipúr, that is, their services had been indented upon in times of emergencies, and they had been given as much on account of the relationship engendered by marriages between the two houses as from any feeling of dependence. But with the accession of Ráo Súrjun in 1533 a new era began.

Ráo Súrjun had obtained, by means of Sawant Singh, a junior branch of his family, possession of the famous fortress of Rinthunbór. This fortress was greatly coveted by the Emperor Akbar. His arms had been victorious in Rájpútáná, Chítor had fallen, but he had ineffectually besieged Rinthunbór. According to the Hindú story he then effected by stratagem and courtesy that which he had failed to procure by force of arms. Rájá Maun, of Jaipúr, had a right of ingress to Rinthunbór. He proceeded there, accompanied by Akbar in the disguise of a mace bearer. The Emperor was recognised; due homage was paid to him, and he then made known his wishes. He offered, if Rinthunbór were yielded to him, to excuse the chiefs of Búndí from affiancing a princess to the Mogul sovereign; to exempt them from the poll-tax, from crossing the Indus, and from customs they considered degrading. He promised to grant them the privilege of entering the hall of audience completely armed; to respect their sacred edifices; never to place them under the command of another Hindú leader; not to brand their horses with the imperial mark (a flower on the forehead); to allow their bands to play in the

[1] So called from Ishtpal, ancestor of Ráo Déva, who lived in 1025. Ishtpal lay wounded to death, when the goddess of his race appeared, and sprinkling his dissevered limbs with the water of life, cured him. Hence the name Hara, from *Har*, signifying bones, thus collected.

streets of the capital, as far as the Red gate; and that Búndí should be to the Rájá what the capital of the Moguls was to Akbar. He promised also, a residence and right of sanctuary to the Ráo, in the sacred city of Banáras.

Above all these, the Emperor offered Súrjun Hara the government of fifty-two districts, whose revenues were to be appropriated without inquiry, on furnishing the customary contingent.

The offer was accepted; a treaty was drawn up on the spot; Ráo Súrjun renounced the suzerainty of Údaipúr, and was greeted as Ráo Rájá of Búndí. His kinsman, Sawant Singh, who was less pliant, sacrificed his life rather than allow the ownership of the fortress to pass to Akbar, and sacrificed it in vain.

Súrjun Singh did good service to his Mogul lord, and, as a reward, had two districts, Banáras and Chunar, added to his government. At the former of these he resided, and his administration greatly benefited not only that city, but the provinces over which he ruled. He established perfect security to life and property in these. He beautified and ornamented the city of Banáras, and constructed eighty-four edifices for various public purposes, and twenty baths. There he died, and was succeeded by his eldest son, Ráo Bhój. This Ráo and his second brother accompanied Akbar in his Gujrát campaign, and rendered splendid service, Ráo Bhój, on one occasion, killing with his own hand the leader of the enemy. He remained in the imperial camp till the death of Akbar in 1605, when he returned to his hereditary dominions. He died shortly afterwards at Búndí, leaving three sons, Ráo Ruttun, Hurda Nurayun, and Kesú Dás, the eldest of whom succeeded.

Faithful to the example of his father, Ráo Ruttun, with his two sons, Madhú Singh and Heri, joined the imperial army at Burhanpúr, at the time when Shah Jehán was threatening rebellion against his father. In the operations which followed, and which terminated in the discomfiture and flight of Shah Jehán, the two sons of Ráo Ruttun were severely wounded. To testify his sense of their and their father's services, and to show his acknowledgment of their fidelity, the emperor bestowed upon Ráo Ruttun the government of Burhanpúr. The reward bestowed upon the second son, Madhú Singh, though possibly equally well intended, dealt in reality a severe blow to the country of the race of Hara. For the emperor bestowed upon Madhú Singh, to be held by him and his heirs direct of the crown, the city of Kotá and its dependencies. Now Kotá was a city of Harawáti, and its dependencies were lands of Harawáti. The act of the emperor thus divided Harawáti into two parts, under separate rulers, who, though originally allied to each other by the bond of brotherhood, were to diverge more and more widely with the march of time.[1]

Ráo Ruttun was a man of a fine and noble character. He was universally respected. In his time no Moslem dared pollute the quarters where Hindús were stationed with the blood of the sacred kine; he established tranquillity throughout his government; founded the township of Ruttunpúr, and, by an act of vigour and neighbourly conduct, conciliated the esteem of the ancient suzerain of his house, the Ráná of Údaipúr. He was succeeded by his grandson, Chutter Sál.

This Ráo was nominated by the Emperor Shah Jehán governor of the imperial capital, a post which he held nearly throughout his reign. He served also under Aurangzíb in the Dekhan, and led the escalade in the storming of Kalberga. When at the time of the illness of Shah Jehán, his four sons each struck for empire, Chutter Sál, though serving in the camp of Aurangzíb, was faithful to the summons of his master, and baffling the

[1] Colonel Tod is of opinion that in this division the emperor acted designedly, 'as he dreaded the union of so much power in the hands of this brave race, and well knew that by dividing he could always rule both, the one by the other.'

preventive measures taken by Aurangzíb, succeeded in leaving his camp and reporting himself to the emperor. Subsequently, the Ráo of Búndí, with his Haras clad in their saffron robes, the ensigns of death or victory, formed the vanguard of the army of Dára Shekó at the battle of Dholpúr. Here, fighting valiantly, he was slain, struck in the forehead by a ball. His son, Bharut Singh, nobly continued the contest, but he and the choicest of his clan were slain. This battle, which gave the empire to Aurangzíb, was fought in June 1658. The sins of Chutter Sál were visited by the conqueror on his son and successor, Ráo Bháo. Aurangzíb gave a commission to Rájá Atmarám, Prince of Sheopúr, to reduce 'that turbulent and disaffected race, the Haras,' and to annex Búndí to the government of Rinthunbór. Atmarám attempted the task, and was successful in his first raids; but the Hara clans assembling, attacked, defeated, and drove him out, and not content with that, went on to blockade Sheopúr. The courage thus displayed by the Haras caused Aurangzíb to extend his forgiveness to the Ráo Bháo. He summoned him to court, and made him governor of Aurangábád. Here he erected many public edifices, and acquired much fame by his valour, his charity, and his piety. He died in 1682, and having no children, was succeeded by Anurád Ráo, grandson of his brother Bhím. The accession of Anurád was confirmed by the emperor, who, in order to testify the esteem in which he held his predecessor, sent his own elephant with the robe of investiture. Anurád accompanied Aurangzíb in his wars in the Dekhan, and on one occasion performed the important service of rescuing the ladies of the harem from the hands of the enemy. The emperor, in testimony of his gallantry, told him to name his reward. His reply was worthy of a Rájpút chief. He requested he might be allowed to command the van, instead of the rearguard, of the army. He distinguished himself at the siege and storm of Bijapúr, and subsequently in the Punjâb, when engaged in settling the northern countries of the empire. He died whilst engaged in that service.

Búdh Singh, his son, succeeded him. In the contest for empire which followed the death of Aurangzíb, this prince adhered to the cause of the legitimate heir, Bahádúr Shah; and it was in a great measure owing to his exertions that the terrible battle of Jajao (June 1707) gave victory to that monarch. For the signal services rendered on that day, Búdh Singh received the title of Ráo Rájá, was admitted to the intimate friendship of the emperor, and continued to enjoy it till his death. In the civil contentions which followed the death of Mahomed Shah, the prince of Hara, faithful to the traditions of his family, supported the royal house against the faction of the Seiads, often by demonstrations of force accompanied by loss of life. On the triumph of the Seiads, the Ráo Rájá returned to Búndí.

He returned, however, only to meet a new enemy in his brother-in-law, Jai Singh, Rájá of Jaipúr. This prince, in revenge for a private insult, and to gain for himself the suzerainty over the smaller states of Rájpútúná, conferred the title of Ráo Rájá of Búndí upon Dulíl Singh, Lord of Kurwar, and placed him in possession. His attempt to entrap Búdh Singh failed, owing to the courage of that prince and his Haras. Búdh Singh escaped to Beygú, whence he made many attempts, but all fruitless, to recover his patrimony. The Kotá Hara, Rájá Bhím, took advantage of his distress to seize upon and annex to Kotá the fiscal lands of Búndí east of the river Chambal.

Búdh Singh died in exile at Beygú. His sons were driven by Rájá Jai Singh even from that place of refuge. But on the death of that prince, in 1744, the eldest son, Omèda, then only thirteen years old, levied troops and attacked and carried some important posts in Búndí. He was aided by the new Rájá of Kotá, Dúrjun Sal, who, in his turn, had been threatened by the Rájá of Jaipúr, successor of Jai Singh. It would take too long to recount all the details of the struggle that followed. It must suffice to state that after fourteen years of exile Búndí was regained by Omèda, and he was recognised as its Ráo (1749).

Omèda lived a chequered life fifty-one years longer, for he survived till 1804. Still harassed by the tribute due to Jaipúr, his energies cramped and contracted by the exactions of the insatiable Márhátás, and his spirit haunted by the memory of a treacherous though well-deserved vengeance on a vassal who had betrayed him, he abdicated in 1771, and became a wandering pilgrim. In this guise, and under the name of Sri-ji, he visited every place of holy resort, of curiosity, or of learning, in Hindostan. He was greeted everywhere as a saint, regarded as an oracle, whilst the knowledge which his observation had accumulated caused his conversation to be courted and every word to be recorded.

Whilst on his travels, Omèda was recalled to Búndí by the death of his son, to superintend the education of his grandson. He was received with honour; and the suspicions with which interested sycophants had filled the mind of his grandson were dispelled. He carefully looked after the young Ráo's education for eight years, and died, as I have said, in 1804.

Before he died he had an opportunity to prove that the feeling of fidelity to the paramount power which had ever marked this branch of the Haras still burned brightly within his breast. On April 17, 1804, Lord Lake, commanding the British forces in India, had despatched a detachment under Colonel Monson to observe the movements of Jeswant Ráo Holkar. Monson advanced as far as Gúrí, whence, deeming further progress impossible, he retreated (July 8, 1804). The events of that retreat are historical. The course of the humiliating flight of our army led it through the territories of Búndí. Omèda cared not for the fact that it was a beaten force, followed

PART I.

by a revengeful enemy, which was passing through. In his mind it was the army of the paramount power, and he aided it to the utmost of his country's means, and with an absolute disregard of the almost certain consequences.

The young grandson, Bishen Singh, succeeded him. He was an honest man, possessed of an excellent heart, and an energetic soul. He cared not for unessential enjoyments, but loved the chase. He would bivouac for days in the lion's lair and would not quit the scene until he had slain the king of the forest, the only prey he deemed worthy of his skill. He had killed with his own hand upwards of a hundred lions, and tigers and boars innumerable.

He, too, was true to the paramount power. It happened that the territory of Búndí is so situated as to have been of great importance in 1817 in cutting off the flight of the Pindárís. In this work he co-operated heartily with the British Government, and rendered signal service. As a reward for these efforts, many districts, seized by Holkar half a century before, were restored without qualification, and others taken by Sindhia under conditions. Still, however, the districts seized unjustly by Kotá remained attached to that branch of the family.

By the treaty of 1818 Búndí was taken under the protection of the British Government. Bishen Singh died on May 14, 1821, and was succeeded by his eldest son, Rám Singh, then eleven years old.

He had scarcely reigned nine years before an event occurred, which, but for the supervising power of the British Government, would have caused hostilities between his country and Jodhpúr. The Ráo had married a daughter of the latter State. Report appears to have spoken censoriously of his treatment of his wife, for, in May 1830, a deputation, accompanied by three hundred men, arrived outside the city with the alleged object of securing some modification of the treatment experienced by the Princess of Jodhpúr. On the third day after its arrival, the minister of Búndí, Kishen Rám, a man of great talents and unblemished character,[1] was murdered by one of the Jodhpúr party. The young Ráo Rájá was determined not to permit such an offence to pass unpunished. Batteries were opened for three days against the place in which the Jodhpúr party had fortified themselves, and the water of the besieged was cut off. The two leaders of the party and the supposed instigators of the assassination were apprehended in an attempt to escape, and were publicly executed by the Ráo Rájá's orders. Persons of inferior note gradually surrendered themselves, and were sent beyond the Búndí frontier. On the sixth day, Batut Singh, a Jodhpúr nobleman, who had sworn to kill the Búndí minister, was himself killed. Taking his death, and the death of the two leaders before referred to, into consideration, the Búndí Government considered the assassination of the minister to be sufficiently avenged.

War with Jodhpúr would probably have followed, but the British Government, by its agent on the spot, put in its veto, and pacified matters.

During the mutiny of 1857, it would appear that the Máhá Ráo, Rám Singh, deviated from the traditions of his family, and showed himself indifferent to his allegiance to the paramount power. On this account, friendly intercourse was broken off with him and was not resumed till 1860. He received, however, a sunnud, conferring upon him the right of adoption. The Máhá Ráo is entitled to a salute of seventeen guns.

[1] During the administration of Kishen Rám, extending over six years and a half, the entire debt of Búndí had been paid off. He had maintained a regular system of finance; had caused the revenue, to the last rupee, to be paid into the treasury; had increased it from three to five lakhs; had accumulated a surplus of two lakhs; had placed all the establishments on an efficient footing, and paid the army with regularity. He was succeeded by his son.

CHAPTER V.

KOTÁ.

AREA—5,000 sq. miles. POPULATION—433,000.
REVENUE—2,500,000 rupees.

PART I.

WE have seen in the preceding chapter that Kotá was an offshoot from Búndí; that in the year 1625, Kotá and its dependencies were bestowed by the Emperor Jehángír upon Madhú Singh, second son of Ráo Ruttun, for his services in the campaign which forced Prince Shah Jehán to flee, almost unattended, from Burhanpúr. The dependencies alluded to consisted of three hundred and sixty townships, yielding an annual revenue of two lakhs of rupees.

Madhú Ráo, who assumed the rank and title of Rájá, ruled for several years. He added several outlying districts to his country, until it touched Málwá on the one side, and Búndí on the other. He was succeeded by his eldest son, Mókund Singh. Rájá Mókund Singh came to the throne in the year 1657. The illness of Shah Jehán that year brought about the struggle for empire amongst his sons to which I have alluded in the previous chapter. Mókund Singh, true to the traditions of his family, fought for the legitimate monarch and the son nominated to be his heir. At the battle of Ujjén, 1658, he and his four brothers led their vassals, clad in their saffron-coloured garments, with the bridal coronet, denoting death or victory, on their heads. The rashness of Jeswant Singh denied them the latter, but a glorious death it was almost impossible to prevent, and all five fell on the field. It happened, however, that the youngest, Kishór Singh, was afterwards dragged from amongst the slain, and though pierced with wounds, recovered. He lived to ascend the throne, and to be one of the most conspicuous commanders for the Mogul in the south of India.

Juggut Singh, son of Mókund Singh, succeeded to the dignity of Rájá. He reigned twelve years, passed principally with the imperial armies in the Dekhan.

His cousin, Paim Singh, followed. But he was so invincibly stupid, that the council of chiefs put him aside after a trial of six months, and sent him back to his family fief. He was replaced by Kishór Singh, the same who had so miraculously escaped at Ujjén. He displayed great military talents in the service of the Mogul. At the siege of Bíjapúr, he specially distinguished himself. He was slain at the escalade of Arcot.

His second son, Rám Singh, followed—the eldest son having been disinherited for refusing to accompany his father to the Dekhan. In the contest for empire which succeeded the death of Aurangzíb, Rám Singh sided with Prince Azím, and was slain at the battle of Jajao (June 1707).

Bhím Singh succeeded him. He espoused the cause of the Seiads in their struggles with their masters, the representatives of the Mogul, and was rewarded by these with high dignities. He seconded, also, the efforts of Jai Singh, of Jaipúr, to expel the elder branch of his family from the throne and country of Búndí. He annexed several districts, and expelling the Bhíls from their fastnesses, took possession of their lands. He was slain in an attempt to intercept and capture the famous Chin Kilich Khan, better known as Azof Jáh, Nizám-úl-Múlk, Subadar of the Dekhan. He did not die, however, before he had despoiled Búndí of the regal insignia of the Haras. Raja Bhím was the first prince of Kotá who had the dignity of 'Leader of Five Thousand' conferred upon him. He was likewise the first of his dynasty who bore the title of Máhá Ráo, or Great Prince—a title conferred by the head of all the Rájpút tribes, the Ráná of Údaipúr, and confirmed by the paramount power. He was succeeded by his eldest son, Arjún Singh. This prince died without issue after a reign of four years. Then ensued a civil war for the succession, in the course of which Kotá lost three important districts, Rampúra, Bhanpúra, and Kalapét. The civil war was terminated by the death of one of the claimants, Siam Singh, the brother next in succession to his predecessor.

The third brother, Dúrjun Sál, had then no rival, and occupied the royal seat (1724). His accession was acknowledged by the Emperor Mahomed Shah, at whose court Dúrjun Sál received the robe of investiture, and obtained the right to prevent the slaughter of kine in every part of the territories frequented by his nation. Dúrjun Sál was a successful ruler. He conciliated the leader of the Márhátás, the famous Bájí Ráo, and was presented by him, as an acknowledgment of services rendered, with the castle of Nahrgurh. And though his father had done something more than look on with complacency whilst the Rájá of Jaipúr was engaged in driving the elder branch of the family from their ancestral possessions, Dúrjun Sál not only aided the heir of that house, but finding Kotá threatened with the fate of Búndí, he defended his capital with so much vigour and skill that the aggressors were completely foiled. He could not, however, prevent his State from acknowledging the supremacy of the Márhátás, nor from paying tribute to Holkar.

Dúrjun Sál died without issue. He was succeeded by Ajít Singh, a lineal descendant of the Bishen Singh, who had been disinherited by his father, Rájá Rám Singh, for refusing to accompany him to the wars. He reigned only two years and a half, and was succeeded by his son, Chutter Sál. The prime minister of this prince was the talented Zálim Singh, then quite a young man. Chutter Sál was destined to have to witness, and fortunately to repel, another attack of Jaipúr on his principality. This took place in 1761. The legions of Jaipúr came on in overwhelming numbers, surprised the party left to guard the ford of the Chambal, and swept on triumphantly till they reached Butwarro. Here they found 5,000 Haras drawn up to receive them. Despising so small a number, they dashed upon them as upon an assured prey. But the Haras received them firmly. Not once, but twice, and thrice, the attack was repulsed. A fourth time came on the warriors of Jaipúr, and the battle was engaged in with redoubled fury. Whilst it was still doubtful, the cleverness of Zálim Singh decided in favour of Kotá. It happened that Mulhar Ráo Holkar, retreating from the disastrous field of Pánipat, was in close vicinity to the contending armies. He had refused to side with either, though pressed by both. But, at the crisis of the conflict, an idea struck Zálim Singh, which he instantly carried out. He rode to Mulhar Ráo, and said: 'The Jaipúreans have left their camp unguarded; you can plunder it!' No second hint was needed. The news conveyed to the Jaipúr host confounded it. They fled in dismay, and the claims of Jaipúr were never renewed.

Chutter Sál survived this elevation but a few years. He was succeeded by his brother, Goman Singh. This prince is described as having been at the time in the prime of manhood, full of vigour and intellect, and well calculated to contend with the storms gathering to burst on the devoted lands of Rájpútáná. But fortune smiled not on him. It happened that his minister, Zálim Singh, crossed him in love, and, it would seem, successfully. The Rájá did not possess sufficient generosity to forgive a success which was perhaps the highest testimony to his minister's merit, but dismissed Zálim from the office of minister. Zálim left Kóta at once, and proceeded straight to the court ofRáná Arsi of Údaipúr. He found that monarch under the tutelage of one of his vassals, the chieftain of Délwarra. His reputed talents gained him a warm reception, and the Ráná soon confided to

PART I.

him the misery of his condition. By a daring plan, which cost the Délwarra prince his life, the Ráná was released from his bondage. But a rebellion followed, and in the battle which ensued, Zálim Singh was taken prisoner. He fell into the hands of Trimbuck Ráo, father of the celebrated Ambají Inglia, and formed with him a friendship. Released from this bondage he returned to Kotá. The Rájá refused to receive him. Whereupon, choosing a favourable moment, he thrust himself into his presence, and was not only pardoned, but employed.

Probably the secret of his success lay in the fact that the Márhátás were swarming into Kotá, and the Rájá saw not how to expel them. Probably, too, he recollected Butwarro. Again, but in a different manner, did he succeed. The Márhátás were kept out, but only by the payment to them of six lakhs of rupees. Scarcely had they retired when the Rájá, Goman Singh, died. Before his death, however, he nominated Zálim Singh guardian to his infant son, Uméd Singh.

Uméd Singh was proclaimed as Máhá Ráo, but thenceforth Zálim Singh was the real chief of the state. He was a wonderful man—fond of power, unscrupulous as to the means he used, it must be admitted; but, on the other hand, he had a keen and vivid intellect, a distinct perception of the ends to strive for; a daring, a breadth of resources, a power of subduing difficulties, never surpassed. Under his administration, extending over forty-five years, the Kotá territory was respected by all parties—Mahomedan, Márhátá, and Rájpút. Whilst the other portions of that region were devastated and despoiled, Kotá reached the height of its prosperity, benefiting by the misfortunes of her neighbours. One of these was Búndí, from whom Zálim Singh snatched the rich districts of Indurgurh, Bulwan, and Anterdeh, retained ever since by the despoiler. The success of Zálim Singh was owing, in a great measure, to his personal character, to the justice and good faith for which he was celebrated. His word was regarded as good as the oath of other men, and, during the twelve years which elapsed between 1805 and 1817, few transactions occurred and few negotiations were contracted, without the intervention of Zálim Singh. This, too, it must be remembered, at a period when the British Government had withdrawn from all interference in the affairs of Rájpútáná.

When, in 1817, the British Government undertook to put down the Pindárís, Zálim Singh was the first of the Rájpút chiefs to co-operate with them. By his means a treaty was concluded between the Rájá of Kotá and the British Government in December 1817, by which Kotá was taken under the protection of the paramount power. The tribute formerly paid to the Márhátás was to be paid to the British Government; and the Máhá Ráo was to furnish troops according to his means when required. A supplementary article was added, vesting the administration in Zálim Singh and his descendants. Other clauses were inserted favourable to Zálim Singh, but it must be recorded, to his honour, that whilst the British Government was prepared to make a separate grant to himself personally of four districts ceded by Holkar, Zálim Singh insisted that they should be annexed to the Kotá State. The Máhá Ráo, Uméd Singh, who had been all his life a nonentity, died in 1820. His son, Kishór Singh, succeeded him. It became apparent, soon after his accession, that the anomalous system by which one person was recognised as the titular chief, and another was guaranteed as the actual ruler, would not be allowed to remain undisturbed. Nor was it. In December 1820, Máhá Ráo Kishór Singh left Kotá, called to his assistance his chiefs and vassals, and appealed to the neighbouring princes to assist him to expel Zálim Singh. Having assembled about 6,000 men, the Ráo advanced from Jaipúr into the Kotá territory, notwithstanding that he was aware that a body of British

PART I.

troops, called out for the purpose, barred his entrance thereto. A contest ensued (September 30, 1821) at Mangrúl, in which the Máhá Ráo's force was defeated, his brother was killed, and his adherents were put to flight.

The Máhá Ráo himself fled to Nathdwara, in Jodhpúr, but, after negotiating satisfactorily, returned on December 31 to occupy his pageant throne. He was guaranteed an annual allowance of 164,000 rupees for himself and his establishment; he was declared supreme within his own palaces, and had 300 men, of whom 100 were cavalry, placed at his disposal. On the other hand he recognised the perpetual administration of Zálim Singh and his heirs.

Zálim Singh, who had long previously attained the title of Ráj Ráná, died on June 15, 1824, and was succeeded by his son, Madhú Singh. The unfitness of this man for the office was notorious, but the terms of the treaty were imperative, and his succession was undisputed.

In 1828 Máhá Ráo Kishór Singh died, and was succeeded by his son, Rám Singh. Shortly after the Máhá Ráo's accession, Madhú Singh died, and his place and title devolved upon his son, Muddun Singh. The relations between this minister and the Máhá Ráo were never cordial, and in 1834 they reached such a pitch of hostility that it became necessary to make a rearrangement of the offices. It was finally resolved, in 1838, with the consent of the Máhá Ráo, to rescind the supplementary article of the treaty of 1818, which secured to the descendants of Zálim Singh the office of sole administrator of affairs, and to create a new and independent principality for them by dissevering certain districts from the main body of Kotá. This was accordingly done. Seventeen districts, yielding a revenue of twelve lakhs of rupees, and denominated the principality of Jháláwar, were made over to Muddun Singh.

This arrangement formed the basis of a new treaty

with Kotá. The Máhá Ráo's tribute was reduced by eighty thousand rupees, to be paid by Jhálâwar, and he agreed to maintain an auxiliary force at a cost of not more than three lakhs of rupees. It was with much reluctance that the Máhá Ráo agreed to the formation of this force; and in consequence of his repeated remonstrances the payment was reduced to two lakhs in 1844, and it was agreed that if this sum should prove insufficient, the difference would be paid from the Kotá tribute. At the same time the Máhá Ráo was warned that should he fail to make his payments punctually, a territorial security would be required both for the tribute and the payments for the auxiliary force.[1]

The arrangement made to sever Jhálâwar from Kotá worked well for both states, and caused all disagreements to cease.

In 1857, the auxiliary force previously referred to rose in revolt, and murdered the political agent and his two sons. Máhá Ráo Rám Singh made no attempt to put down the revolt or to aid the British officer. As a mark of the displeasure of Government his salute was reduced by four guns. He was subsequently, however, guaranteed the right of adoption.

The Máhá Ráo Rám Singh died on the evening of March 27, 1866, at the age of sixty-four. As soon as it became generally understood that the Ráo's days were numbered, a rumour spread abroad that one of his widows had expressed her determination to perish on the funeral pile. The political agent took measures at once to prevent the possibility of such an occurrence. He caused the apartments of the zenana to be locked and guarded, and directed that the news of the Máhá Ráo's demise should be withheld from the Ránís as long as possible. They were kept in ignorance of it for four hours. Then, however, one of the Ránís declared her intention of performing Satí, and indeed showed herself so violently

[1] Aitchison's *Treaties*.

PART I.

determined that she succeeded in bursting open the door. She was prevented, however, from leaving the zenana, and next morning the burning of the corpse took place without crime or disturbance.

Rám Singh was succeeded by his son, Máhá Ráo Chutter Singh. The Viceroy took the opportunity of his accession to restore to him the salute of seventeen guns enjoyed by his father prior to 1857.

CHAPTER VI.

JHÁLÁWAR.

AREA—2,500 sq. miles. POPULATION—220,000.
REVENUE—14,50,000 rupees.

CHAP. VI.

In the preceding chapter I have related how, in 1838, the bad feeling existing between the Máhá Ráo of Kotá and the descendants of the Ráj Ráná Zálim Singh was terminated by the creation of a new principality as a separate provision for those descendants. The principality thus created was called Jháláwar: it consisted of nineteen districts. It was subjected to the payment of a tribute of 80,000 rupees; and its chief was to receive the title of Máháráj Ráná.

The main exploits of the hero of the dynasty, Zálim Singh, have been related in the preceding chapter, but no account of his family was then given. His ancestors were petty chieftains of Hulwud, in the district of Jháláwar, in Káthíwár. Bhao Singh, a younger son of this family, left the paternal roof with a few adherents, to seek fortune amongst the numerous conflicting armies that ranged over India during the contests for supremacy amongst the sons of Aurangzíb. His son, Madhú Singh, came to Kotá when Rájá Bhím was in the zenith of his power. Although he had only twenty-five horse in his train, it is a proof of the respectability of his family, that the prince disdained not his alliance, but married his son, Úrjún, to the young adventurer's sister. Not long after, the estate of Nandta was entailed upon him, with the confidential post of *Foujdar*, which included not only the command of the troops, but that of the castle, the residence of the sovereign. This family connection gave an interest to his authority, and procured him the respectful title of Mámáh, or maternal uncle, from the younger members of the prince's family—a title which habit has continued to his successors. Muddun Singh succeeded his father in the office of *Foujdar*, and it then became hereditary in the family. Himmut Singh followed Muddun, and displayed great bravery and skill in many trying emergencies. He seconded the defence of Kotá, when it was assailed by the combined Márhátá and Jaipúr troops, and conducted the treaty which made her tributary to the former with such ability, that he gained influence sufficient to restore the ancient line of succession.[1] Zálim Singh was his nephew. How he gained his reputation has already been related.

Muddun Singh, first Máháráj Ráná of Jháláwar, was the grandson of Zálim Singh. He died in 1845, and was succeeded by his son, Pírthi Singh. This chief rendered good service during the mutinies by conveying to places of safety several Europeans who had taken refuge in his districts.[2]

He has been guaranteed the right of adoption, and receives a salute of fifteen guns.

[1] Tod's *Rajasthan*.

[2] Aitchison.

CHAPTER VII.

TONK.

AREA—1,800 sq. miles. POPULATION—182,000.
REVENUE—8,00,000 rupees.

PART I.

TONK is a town in Rájpútáná, on the right bank of the river Banás, 218 miles south-west of Delhi, and the capital of the principality of the same name founded by the famous freebooter, Amír Khan. Born in Rohilkhand, of Afghan parents, in the second half of the eighteenth century, Amír Khan, then twenty years old, and his younger brother, accompanied by ten followers, left their native province for Málwá, and took service there in the local militia. But other prospects soon opened to him. The troubles at Bhopál, caused by the death of Chutta Khan, led to the enlistment of men by different parties. Amír Khan, with six horsemen and sixty footmen, was engaged by the titular Nawáb, Hayat Mahomed. Here he remained about a year, then left Bhopál to take service with the Rájpút ex-chiefs of Ragúghur, who, expelled from their country by Sindhia, supported themselves and their followers by plunder.

In this service he greatly distinguished himself as a daring, fearless leader. A dispute with one of the chiefs caused him, however, to renounce it, to enlist under the Márhátá chief, Bálárám Inglia, then engaged, with the connivance of the minister of Bhopál, Múríd Mahomed, in pacifying that country. To Amír Khan was assigned the care of the fort of Futtehgurh, and the custody of the person of the Nawáb, Ghous Mahomed. But with the death of Múríd Mahomed, and the retreat of the Márhátás, his connection with Futtehgurh came to an end. He endeavoured indeed to transfer his services to the new minister, Vizír Khan, but before he had been employed for six months, that discerning statesman discovered his intriguing character, and dismissed him.

Just at that time, 1799, the reputation of Jeswant Ráo Holkar, as the rising star of the Márhátá chiefs, was at its zenith. To him, therefore, Amír Khan repaired, was received with open arms, and treated more as an equal than as a subordinate. Thenceforth, till the return of Jeswant Ráo from Hindostan, 1806, they followed the same path. Jeswant Ráo was the prince and leader, but Amír Khan, subordinate only to him, was sole commander of his own army, and entertained and dismissed whom he chose. Still his position was not enviable. For, often in want of money, he was constantly forced to commit outrages and depredations to appease the clamour of his troops for pay, and more than once, when unable to satisfy them, suffered considerable violence at their hands. In fact, his followers were rather depredators than soldiers, though undoubtedly able in the hour of need to strike a blow for the cause to which their master had pledged himself. The number of these followers gradually so increased that in the year 1806 they numbered 35,000 men, with 115 pieces of field artillery.

Prior to that period Holkar had assigned to Amír Khan estates (Jaghírs) in Málwá and Rájpútáná, forming the nucleus of the existing principality of Tonk. These Jaghírs, however, were insufficient to support the large number of troops I have noted. His bands, therefore, ranged over every part of Rájpútáná, Málwá, and Bandelkhand, indenting upon those countries for their support.

In 1806–7, leaving his brother-in-law, Guffúr Khan, to support his interests at Indúr, Amír Khan entered the service of Juggut Singh, Rájá of Jaipúr, then contending with the Rájá of Jodhpúr for the hand of the Princess of Údaipúr.[1] In the contest that followed, Jaipúr was,

[1] *Vide* Appendix C.

PART I.

at great cost to herself, successful. The Rájá of Jodhpúr saw himself reduced to his last resources, when, suddenly appealing to the avarice and ambition of Amír Khan, he induced that chief to change sides. Jaipúr was then cruelly ravaged. The indiscriminate pillage and slaughter brought both principalities to the very verge of ruin. The connection with them of Amír Khan was brought to a close by the sack of Nagore, and the treacherous murder of the real author of the war, Sevaí Singh, previously chief minister of Jodhpúr.

Rájpútáná thus devastated and brought to the verge of ruin, Amír Khan turned his arms against the Márhátá family which reigned in Nagpúr (1809). It is supposed that it was his intention to plant his own dynasty on the ruins of the Bhonsla. He was yet engaged in this expedition when he was recalled by the demonstrations of a British force against his own capital of Seronj. He was summoned almost immediately afterwards to the camp of Holkar, by the pressing messages of Guffúr Khan (1810). Having, as he thought, settled affairs in that quarter, he returned to fatten his followers once more on the spoils of Rájpútáná and Málwá. Nor were these countries relieved from his baneful presence until the success of the British in the Pindárí war enabled them to make a satisfactory and permanent settlement of those countries.

When the British army advanced, in 1817, towards Málwá, the offer was made to Amír Khan, then engaged in besieging the Jaipúr fort of Madhú Rájápúr, to accept the protection of the British Government under the condition that he should reduce his army to a certain specified number, and surrender his artillery at a valuation. On the other hand, he was informed that the Jaghirs originally assigned to him by Holkar would be guaranteed to him in sovereignty, but he was to relinquish the conquests made during his predatory career. The offer was a very liberal one. Amír Khan was more a Pindárí than the Pindárís. He had no hope that he could resist the strength put forth by the British, and doubtless he considered himself fortunate to be in a position to have such terms offered him. He accepted them; but, like a true waiter upon Providence, he delayed to ratify the treaty until he received intelligence of the result of the battle of Sítábaldí, when, considering the Márhátá game lost, he gave in, resolved to contribute to the maintenance of tranquillity and to begin a respectable life.

By the treaty Amír Khan was confirmed in possession of the districts of Seronj, Píráwá, Gogul, and Nímáhérá. To these the British Government added, as a free gift, the fort and district of Tonk-Rampúra; and a loan of three lakhs of rupees, afterwards converted into a gift, was made to him. The district of Palwal was also conferred on his son in Jaghír for life. In lieu of the revenue of this district, which it was found inconvenient to make over to the son, a monthly stipend of 12,500 rupees was assigned to him.

From that time Amír Khan renounced his predatory habits, and employed himself in settling his country, in building palaces and houses for travellers, and in improving his territory. Not content with this, he wrote an account of the events of his chequered life.

As he grew older, he made another advance in respectability. The man who had nearly ruined Rájpútáná, and sucked the life-blood of Jaipúr and Jodhpúr, became pious and devout; took to clothing himself in sackcloth, to reading the Korán, and associating himself with Múllas. It is due to him to add that he devoted great pains to the education of his twelve children. In 1832, when he went to Ajmír to pay his respects to the Governor-General, Lord William Bentinck, he was accompanied by six of his sons, five of them in chain armour. On that occasion he made a favourable impression. His manners are described as most frank and

PART I. agreeable; and his whole appearance was considered as forming an agreeable contrast to the ceremonious ostentation of the hereditary princes of Rájásthán.

Amír Khan died in 1834, and was succeeded by his son Vizír Mahomed Khan. This prince rendered good service during the mutinies, and received a sunnud from the Governor-General guaranteeing the succession to his family according to Mahomedan law in the event of the failure of natural heirs. He died on June 18, 1864, and was succeeded by his son, Mahomed Ali Khan.

Under the rule of this prince a grave complication arose which terminated fatally to the continuation of his own rule. It happened that in July 1865, the Thákur or lord of Láwa, a Rájpút vassal of the Nawáb, complained of the unusual demands which had been made upon him by the administration. Far from listening to the advice of the Governor-General's agent to give these demands a careful consideration, Mahomed Ali Khan assembled his forces and assaulted Láwa. He was, however, repulsed, with serious loss of life on both sides. For the moment, however, the affair was settled by the deputation to the spot of a British officer, and the future relations between the two parties were defined to the satisfaction of both.

But the Nawáb, Mahomed Ali Khan, was only dissimulating in order the better to effect his ends. It appears that the councils of the young Thákur of Láwa, Dhírut Singh by name, had been directed, since the affair of 1865, by his uncle, Réwut Singh, a stout soldier who had previously commanded a body of cavalry in the state of Alwar; on the advice of this uncle, the young Thákur, whilst steadily maintaining his own rights, had, between the years 1865 and 1867, made constant visits to Tonk to render there his feudal service. It was known, all this time, at Tonk that though he was weak and inexperienced himself, yet he was under the tutelage of his uncle, and that so long as the uncle lived, it would be

CHAP. VII.

difficult to gain an advantage over him. The uncle, therefore, was doomed.

To carry out this murderous project, the Nawáb, Mahomed Ali Khan, summoned in 1867 the Thákur to Tonk, to be presented with a dress of honour. Thither accordingly, the Thákur repaired, accompanied by his uncle and a few attendants. The reception of the uncle was most favourable. He was informed by the minister that the lands of Láwa which had been resumed by the Nawáb would be restored, and his satisfaction, as he returned from the interview, was unbounded. About nine o'clock the same evening, August 1, the uncle, Réwut Singh, was again summoned by the minister to consult with him regarding the dress of honour to be given the following morning. Réwut Singh at once proceeded to the minister's house, accompanied by his son, two kamdars or managers of affairs, and fourteen attendants. Réwut Singh, his son, and the two kamdars at once went upstairs, where they were massacred. The attendants below were also set upon by a party of Tonk sepoys, and all murdered but one, who escaped by being mistaken, by the colour of his turban, for a sepoy. The house in which the young Thákur had taken up his abode was at the same time surrounded by Tonk troops. For three days the young Thákur defended himself, resisting the demands of hunger and thirst, for he had neither food nor water for himself and his followers. On the fourth day, three persons came to him from the Nawáb, and persuaded him, under an assurance of safety, to permit himself to be conducted to the presence of that chieftain. Arriving in his presence the Thákur inveighed against the mode in which he had been treated, but the Nawáb simply informed him in reply that the past could not be recalled, and that if the Thákur had been present with his uncle he would have been treated in the same manner. On returning to his house, the Thákur found it still guarded by Tonk sepoys. There he remained till

August 8, when the arrival of a British officer procured permission for him to return to Láwa. Whilst these events had occurred at Tonk, a force of 1,000 infantry with 40 swivel guns had appeared before Láwa, and commenced firing upon the forts.

It was impossible that the suzerain power, the British Government, should allow so flagrant an outrage to pass unnoticed and unpunished. Nor did they. An inquiry was at once instituted. All the facts I have narrated were fully proved, and the Government decided that Nawáb, Mahomed Ali Khan, should be deposed and forced to reside outside the Tonk territories; that the minister, his instrument in the outrage, should be constituted a political prisoner, and all the sepoys attached to his office should be discharged; that the salute of the ruler of Tonk should be reduced from seventeen guns to eleven; and that Láwa should be for ever separated from Tonk and converted into a separate chiefship under the protection of the British Government. It was further decided to bestow the government of Tonk upon the son of the deposed Nawáb, his great uncle, Ibadúlla Khan, conducting the administration during his minority.

This decision was made known to the Nawáb by the Viceroy by means of a letter addressed to him; and to the nobles, chiefs, and people of the principality of Tonk by a proclamation of the Government of India.

In accordance with it, Ibrahím Ali Khan, the eldest son of the late Nawáb, was placed upon the throne in January 1868. He was then twenty years of age; very illiterate and extravagant. The state was thirteen lakhs of rupees in debt; there was not a rupee in the treasury, and the soldiers were from four to six months in arrears. On the representation of the great uncle, Ibadúlla Khan, of his own inability to cope with the circumstances that presented themselves, a council of regency was formed, composed of four influential noblemen, presided over by a British officer. The young Nawáb was likewise encouraged to attend the meetings of the council, to be initiated in state affairs. CHAP. VII.

The ex-Nawáb was allowed to reside at Banáras, on the understanding that he should not be permitted to leave the neighbourhood, except with the knowledge of the Governor-General's agent, and for purposes of sport or temporary recreation. He receives sixty thousand rupees a year. His minister and tool, Hákim Surwar Shah, is restricted to a residence in the fortress of Chanár, but he is allowed moderate freedom and exercise, and personal servants.

CHAPTER VIII.

KARAULÍ.

AREA—1,878 sq. miles. POPULATION—188,000.
REVENUE—3,00,000 rupees.

THIS small state lies to the south of Bharatpúr. To the east of it is Dholpúr; to the south-east runs the river Chambal, separating it from Gwáliár; to the south-west the river Banás, dividing it from Jaipúr; and to the north-west, also, is Jaipúr. CHAP. VIII.

The early records of this state are very obscure. It would appear to have had no separate history prior to the decline of the Mogul empire. In the history of the Márhátás, the Rájá of Karaulí is mentioned as a dependant of the Peshwa, to whom the Rájá paid a tribute of 25,000 rupees per annum. He was the first to accept the protection offered by the British Government in 1817. He agreed then to acknowledge the supremacy of the British Government, and in return for this he was guaranteed in his possessions, and the tribute paid to the Márhátás was remitted.

By the fourteenth article of the treaty of Púna (June 13, 1817) the Peshwa had resigned his rights to all

PART I.

his territories north of the Narbadá, those in Gujrát excepted, and the Rájá of Karaulí had in reality no option but to accept the protection of the British Government or to be absorbed. He chose the former course. Yet though his territories were thus preserved to him, his mind still hankered after some possessions south of the Chambal formerly belonging to him, and he resented the refusal of the British Government to grant him a guarantee for these. He took an early opportunity to show his ill-feeling. When, in 1825, the British were engaged in hostilities in Burmah, and Dúrjun Sál, cousin to the Rájá of Bharatpúr, rose in rebellion against his liege lord, the Rájá of Karaulí assisted the rebel with all the troops he could raise. After the capture of Bharatpúr, however, his zeal oozed out rapidly; he made humble professions of submission, and his misconduct was overlooked.

Beyond the adjustment of some border differences between Karaulí and Jaipúr, there seems to have been but little communication between the British Government and the Rájá of the principality, Hurbuksh Pál, till he died in 1858. He died childless. A son of his cousin, Pertáp Pál, was then nominated to succeed him, in the event of no posthumous child being born. One of the Ránís, however, shortly declared herself pregnant, and subsequently a mother. Her assertions, were, however, disputed by Pertáp Pál. A commission of inquiry was instituted; but no valid proof of the birth of the child having been submitted, the Governor-General's agent declared the statement to be untrue, and in the name of the British Government pronounced Pertáp Pál to be Rájá. This final recognition took place at the end of 1839, and early in 1840 the Rájá entered his capital in triumph. The Ránís, after vainly attempting to excite a civil war, quickly retired to Bharatpúr, where they were allowed to remain.

Pertáp Pál died in 1848. His reign had been a series of

mismanagements on the part of himself and his ministers. Want of money had led to oppression, and oppression to insubordination and outbreaks. Four times had a British officer been deputed to Karaulí to mediate and to settle affairs, but on every occasion he had failed. Pertáp Pál died childless. The family adopted Nursing Pál, a minor relative, as his successor. The British Government, however, withheld its recognition of the adoption until the first instalment of the debt of upwards of a lakh and a half of rupees, due to it by Karaulí, should have been paid. After some delay the young chief offered payment of the first instalment. But as the offer was not made unconditionally, and the money was to be advanced by a speculator for employment in Karaulí, it was not accepted. Meanwhile various parties were struggling for the guardianship of the young Rájá, and as the absence of the recognition of the latter gave these vitality and encouragement, the British Government deemed it expedient to withdraw the condition it had imposed. But in thus recognising the Rájá, a distinct warning was conveyed to him that payment of the debt would be exacted. At the same time, to control the factions and to baffle intrigue, an agent of the British Government was sent to Karaulí with instructions to assume the direct management of affairs.

The Rájá, Nursing Pál, died in 1852. The day before his death he had adopted as heir a distant kinsman, Bharat Pál. The Government of India proposed to treat the state as a lapse, and its annexation 'was only prevented by the interference of the Home Government on a threatened motion in the House of Commons.[1] Bharat Pál was, upon this, recognised by the British Government as Rájá of Karaulí, and arrangements were made for the due administration of his state during his minority. But meanwhile the various factions, for a long time previous busy at Karaulí, had made a discovery. It was

[1] *Quarterly Review*, 1858, p. 269.

ascertained that the adoption of Bharat Pál had been informal, by reason of the minority of the previous Rájá and the omission of certain necessary ceremonies; and it was urged that the claims of Madan Pál, as a nearer relative, were superior to those of Bharat Pál. This view was adopted by the chiefs of Bharatpúr, Dholpúr, Alwar, and Jaipúr. The facts above stated having been proved on inquiry, and Madan Pál having been accepted by the Ránís, by nine of the most influential Thákurs, by three-fourths of the lesser feudal chiefs of the state, and by the general feeling of the country, the recognition of Bharat Pál was annulled, and the claims of Madan Pál were admitted (1854). The direct interference of the political agent in the internal administration was then withdrawn, and the agency abolished the following year. But Madan Pál was warned that, in the event of his failing in the regular payment of the annual instalment of the debt (then reduced to 94,312 rupees), one or more districts would be occupied by the British till the whole of the debt should be liquidated.[1]

In 1857, Rájá Madan Pál rendered good service, aiding the British authorities by every means in his power. In consideration of this, the debt, which had then risen to 1,17,000 rupees, was remitted; a dress of honour was conferred upon him, and his salute was raised from fifteen to seventeen guns. In 1859, in consequence of the pecuniary embarrassments of the state, a political agent was deputed to assist the Máhárájá in the adjustment of his debts. The agent was instructed to put himself in the position of a friend and adviser to the Máhárájá, and not in that of an authoritative controller of affairs. He was withdrawn in 1861.[2]

I am not aware that anything has subsequently occurred calling for special notice.

[1] Aitchison's *Treaties*. [2] *Ibid.*

CHAPTER IX.

KISHNGARH.

AREA—720 sq. miles. POPULATION—70,000.
REVENUE—600,000 rupees.

THE principality of Kishngarh was founded in the year 1613 by Kishn, the ninth son of Údai Singh, Rájá of Jodhpúr. The permission to found this independent state was the price of blood. When Rájá Guj of Jodhpúr had refused to second the ambitious views of Prince Khúrm (Shah Jehán) against his father and sovereign, the Emperor Jehángír, Khúrm tried to gain his point by means of Govindas, a Rájpút of the Bhátí tribe, one of the foreign nobles of Márwár, and confidential adviser of the prince. But Govindas 'knew no one but his master and the king.' He refused. For this act of fidelity Khúrm had him assassinated. The instrument he employed to effect his purpose was Kishn, uncle to Rájá Guj; and the reward to the murderer was permission to found an independent principality. Kishn selected a spot beyond the limits of Márwár, and built there a town which, called after himself, perpetuates the memory of his crime. To follow the history of this small state in minute detail seems unnecessary. In fact, up to 1790, there is nothing to record. The inhabitants are mainly Jâts, the government was, and is, patriarchal; but the territory was too small to allow its ruler to take a prominent part in the many struggles by which the eighteenth century was characterised. Perhaps the smallness of its extent, combined with the barrenness of its soil, was advantageous to it; for there can be no reasonable doubt that to this circumstance it owed for a long time its immunity from the payment of tribute alike to the Moguls and the Márhátás.

PART I.

In the years 1790–91, however, a circumstance occurred which did bring the ruler of Kishngarh somewhat prominently forward,. and in a manner not very favourable to his character as a patriot. It will be recollected[1] that in 1787 the Rahtórs of Jodhpúr had united with the Kutchwas of Jaipúr to resist the Márhátás, and that they beat them at the battle of Tonga. The defeat was wiped out in 1790 and 1791 at Patun and Mairta. But on these occasions it was Bahádúr Singh, chief of Kishngarh, who betrayed his country by leading the Márhátás against his native land. It was no calculating spirit born of a desire to be on the winning side, that prompted him to this act. It was to revenge himself on his feudal lord, the Rájá of Jodhpúr, because he had foiled his attempt to despoil his brother of the share of the possessions which had devolved to him by right. The fatal battle of Mairta rivetted the chains of the Márhátás on Rájpútáná, the traitor chief alone being exempted from the general subjection.

Kalian Singh succeeded Bahádúr Singh. It was during his rule that Kishngarh was brought under British protection (1818). By the treaty then made it was stipulated that the Rájá should acknowledge the supremacy of the British Government and act in subordinate co-operation with it; that he should abstain from entering into negotiations with other states without its sanction, should refrain from aggression, should refer disputes to the arbitration and award of the British Government, and furnish troops when required according to his means. On the other hand, the British Government agreed to protect him; they guaranteed that he and his successors should be absolute rulers of the country; and they promised not to introduce British jurisdiction within it. Shortly after the signature of this treaty, Kalian Singh began to behave in a manner which argued either insanity or a total absence of principle. The personal service due to him by his Thákurs, or lords

[1] *Vide* Chapters II. and III.

of domains, appeared to him to be fairly subject to commutation for a money payment. But there being no guarantee that after the payment had been made the services would not be insisted upon, the Thákurs naturally refused to comply. One of the Thákurs, indeed, set up claims to independence. These men the Rájá wished to subdue and crush; but suddenly, in a freak of eccentricity, he started off to Delhi to lay his complaints before the titular sovereign who represented the house of Timour. At Delhi he employed himself in buying honorary privileges from the king, such as the right to wear stockings in the royal presence. Meanwhile his partisans had not been inactive at Kishngarh. They had enlisted troops, and even procured aid from Búndí, whilst the Thákurs had been by no means idle in responding. Hostilities actually commenced between the rival parties, the effects of which were injuriously felt in the British districts adjoining. Upon this it was represented to the Rájá that the British Government held him responsible for the conduct of his chiefs and their troops as well as for his own. This intimation would appear to have alarmed him, for on receiving it he quitted Delhi with some raw levies, reached Kishngarh, summoned his vassals, and marched against his rebellious barons. But his vassals soon showed that they had no intention to aid him in subjugating and oppressing men of their own order. One by one they deserted him, then suddenly uniting, menaced the capital, declaring their intention to depose Kalian Singh, and to proclaim his infant son. The Rájá, upon this, fled to Ajmír, and appealed to the British Government for aid, offering to farm to it the government of his province. The revolted barons likewise invoked British arbitration. The British Government, refusing the Rájá's offer, stated that no objection would be offered to his retirement to Delhi, and the formation of a regency to manage the country in his absence. Upon this, negotiations were entered into

PART I.

between the chiefs and his barons. These, however, produced no result. As a last resource, the barons offered to leave the dispute to the Máhárájá of Jodhpúr, provided the decision should receive the guarantee of the British Government; but this guarantee was refused. The chiefs then proclaimed the heir apparent as Rájá, laid siege to Kishngarh, and were on the point of capturing it, when the Rájá accepted the mediation of the British political agent. By his intervention terms were agreed upon, and Kalian Singh returned to Kishngarh. A very short period, however, proved that the pacification would not last; that the Rájá had no intention of keeping the terms to which he had agreed. The nobles again banded together, and shortly afterwards Kalian Singh retired from Kishngarh, and abdicated in favour of his son. He died in 1839, and was succeeded by his son, Pirthí Singh.

Since that time nothing has occurred worthy of special notice.

The Rájá of Kishngarh has been allowed the privilege of adoption. He is entitled to a salute of fifteen guns. His territories are situated between Ajmír and Jaipúr.

CHAPTER X.

DHOLPÚR.

AREA—1,626 sq. miles. POPULATION—500,000.
REVENUE—6,00,000 rupees.

CHAP. X.

DHOLPÚR is a small principality bounded on the north and north-east by the district of Agra; on the south-east by the river Chambal separating it from Gwáliár; and on the west by Karaulí. Although it has only existed as a separate principality for about seventy years, the family which rules it figured prominently in the history of India for the preceding eighty years. It will be necessary, then, to go back to the beginning of that period.

The ancestors of the present Ráná of Dholpúr were, about a hundred and fifty years ago, zamindárs or landholders of Góhad, then a small village, twenty-eight miles north-east of the fortress of Gwáliár. They belonged to the Jât caste,[1] were industrious, and of a very warlike disposition.

By the exercise of these qualities, the family brought themselves between the years 1725 and 1740 to the prominent notice of the Peshwa, Bájí Ráo, and amid the lawlessness and disruptions of the times, managed to assume a quasi-independence as lords of Góhad under suzerainty of the Márhátás. The chief who accomplished this feat died about the middle of the eighteenth century, and was succeeded by his nephew. He, being likewise a clear-headed man, contrived to enlarge his borders. With a wise prescience he held aloof from the great struggle for empire between the Márhátás and the warriors from the north, and when the fatal day of Pánipat (1761) had completely overwhelmed the former, he showed his sense of the importance of the defeat by proclaiming himself Ráná of Góhad, and seizing the fortress of Gwáliár. That independence remained unquestioned for six years. But, in 1767, the Márhátá power, carefully nursed in the interval, was beginning to feel all the symptoms of revival, and its general, Ragonáth Ráo, afterwards Peshwa, being then in Hindostan, thought that the opportunity should not be lost of reading the Ráná of Góhad a lesson which he would not forget. Accordingly he marched with his army to attack the town of Góhad. But the Ráná had in the meanwhile strengthened its defences; he had drilled his troops; and being a hardy, daring man himself, with an especial

[1] According to Colonel Tod, no mean authority, the Jâts are a mixture of the Rájpút and Jit or Gete race.

dislike to be ridden over roughshod, he gave the assailants some very hard and unpleasant work. He defended himself, in fact, so valiantly, that Ragonáth Ráo proposed at last to treat. An accommodation was agreed upon, by which, for a consideration of three lakhs of rupees, the Márhátás agreed to retire, and to recognise the independence, under their suzerainty, of the Ráná, Lakindár Singh.

I have been unable to trace the exact date when the Ráná of Góhad lost Gwáliár, but it was probably about this period. It fell into the hands of Mádhají Sindhia.

It was in his possession when, in 1779, the British Government entered into an alliance with that 'turbulent tributary'[1] of the Márhátás, the Ráná of Góhad. By this treaty the Government agreed to furnish the Ráná with a force for the defence of his dominions or for their enlargement from the Márhátás, to share with him their joint conquests, except the territories constituting his jaghír and then in possession of the Márhátás, and to embrace the Ráná in any treaty concluded with the Márhátás.

In pursuance of the terms of this treaty, a British force of 2,400 men, under the command of Captain William Popham, was sent into the Góhad country to expel thence the Márhátá marauders, and to concert measures with the Ráná (February 1780). Popham drove out the Márhátás, carried the fort of Lahar by storm, and on August 4 surprised and carried the fortress of Gwáliár, till then reputed impregnable. The fortress was transferred to the Ráná of Góhad. By the treaty made by the British with Mádhají Sindhia, dated October 13, 1781, Gwáliár and his other territories were guaranteed to the Ráná, 'so long as he observes his treaty with the English.' But the Ráná did not observe his treaty with the English. On the contrary, several acts showing that he was quite prepared to aid in the confederacy forming

[1] Grant Duff.

against them in 1781–2 were brought home to him, and as a consequence the treaty of mutual assistance was regarded as abrogated. Consequently, when Mádhají Sindhia, left free by the treaty of Salbye, attacked Gwáliár and Góhad, the English left the Ráná to his fate. It was too strong for him, for Gwáliár had to surrender after a protracted siege, Góhad was taken, and the Ráná was forced to constitute himself a prisoner.

But there was to be a turn again in the wheel. In 1802 the British declared war against the successor of Mádhají, Daolat Ráo. Ambají Inglia, his governor of the province of Góhad, seeing the rapid progress of the British arms, revolted, or pretended to revolt, against his master, and joined the British. With these he made a treaty by which he agreed to surrender to them the fortress of Gwáliár and certain districts which they intended to transfer to the Ráná of Góhad, on being himself guaranteed the remainder of the territory free of tribute. The ceded districts were made over to Ráná Kírat Singh, son and successor of Lakindár Singh, by a treaty dated January 17, 1804, with the exception of the fortress and city of Gwáliár, which the British retained.

Subsequently, in consequence of a dispute with Sindhia as to the meaning of the clause in the treaty of Surjí Anjengaom, by which he had agreed to renounce all claims on his feudatories with whom the British Government had made treaties, 'provided that none of the territories belonging to the Máhárájá situated to the southward of those of the Rájás of Jaipúr and Jodhpúr, and the Ráná of Góhad, of which the revenues have been collected by him and his Amildars, or have been applicable as Serinjámí (materials) to the payment of the troops, are granted away by such treaties'—Sindhia contending that the Ráná of Góhad could not be included, inasmuch as the pretensions of that family had been extinct, and their territories in Sindhia's possession for thirty years—the British Government determined to abandon Gwáliár and Góhad

PART I.

to Sindhia. But to compensate the Ráná, and in consideration of the fact that the failure in the stipulations of the former treaty had arisen from no fault of the Ráná, they agreed to grant him the pergunnahs of Dholpúr, Bárah, and Rajkérah. Thus it was that the *ci-devant* Ráná of Góhad became Ráná of Dholpúr.

Ráná Kírat Singh accepted the exchange, although, naturally perhaps, he would have preferred that the previous arrangement should remain unaltered. But he never forgave the Sindhia. When, in 1831, the Baiza Bai and her brother were ejected from Gwáliár, he showed his dislike to the government of Gwáliár by giving them a splendid reception. He died in 1836 at a good old age.

His son, Ráná Bhagwant Singh, succeeded him, and in 1837 was invested with a robe of honour by the British Government. In 1841 he showed in an unworthy manner that the hatred of Sindhia was in his blood. He desecrated a Jain temple, by dethroning the god Párasnáth, and substituting Máhádéo, the god of his own partisans, simply because the Jain votaries were connected with Gwáliár. Sindhia took up the matter as a personal affront, and appealed to the British Government. But it was explained to him that, however blameworthy the action might have been, it was not one that warranted the interposition of the paramount power.

In 1857, Ráná Bhagwant Singh did good service by rendering assistance to the British fugitives from Gwáliár. His minister, Déo Hans, however, incurred the displeasure of Government by plundering villages in the Agra district, and, in 1862, in consequence of the intrigues of that individual, and his endeavours to supplant his prince, it became necessary to remove him to Banáras, and place him under surveillance.

Ráná Bhagwant Singh has received the right of adoption, and is entitled to a salute of fifteen guns.

CHAPTER XI.

BHARATPÚR.

REA—1,974 sq. miles. POPULATION—650,000.
REVENUE—21,00,000 rupees.

THE state of Bharatpúr is bounded on the north by the British district of Gúrgaon; on the north-east by Mathurá; on the east by Agra; on the south and south-west by Karaulí and Jaipúr; and on the west by Alwar. It enjoys the distinction of being the only Jât principality of any magnitude in India, and has, perhaps, the only government of a truly national character where a great proportion of the people belong to the same tribe as the nobles and princes of the state. The tribe of Jâts—recognised by Colonel Tod[1] as the Getæ and Massagetæ of the ancient writers, the Jutes of Jutland, and consequently as the people who founded the first Teutonic kingdom in England,[2]—is said to have emigrated from the province of Múltán, during the seventeenth century, and to have settled in the Duáb as cultivators. But they are mentioned before this in history. They were Jâts who, in 1026, harassed Mahmud of Ghizní in his march from Somnâth to Múltán, and who, in the following year were nearly destroyed by him. They were Jâts who, in 1398, were encountered and massacred by Tamerlane on his march by Múltán towards Delhi; and, finally, they were Jâts who disquieted Báber during his advance through the Punjâb in 1525. Migrating, as I have said, to India, in the seventeeth century, they settled down in the Duáb. There, the native turbulence of their character brought upon them more than once the imperial wrath, and with it condign punishment. But the disruption which followed the death of the Emperor

CHAP. XI.

[1] *Journal Asiatique*, May 1827. [2] Freeman's *Old English History*.

PART I.

Aurangzíb offered a full scope for the play of their hardy and daring character. Taking advantage of the civil wars which then ensued, they, under their chief, Chúránam, erected petty castles in the villages, the lands of which they cultivated, and soon obtained the distinction of being denominated *Kuzzâks* or robbers, a title which they were not slow to merit, by their inroads as far as the royal abode of the Emperor Farókhsír. The Seiads, then in power, commanded Jai Singh, Rájá of Jaipúr to attack them in their strongholds. But the Jâts, even in the very infancy of their power, evinced the same obstinate skill in defending mud walls as that which, in more recent times, gained them such celebrity. They beat off their assailants. Not long after this, Badan Singh, brother of Chúránam, and who had been imprisoned by him, made his escape, and, invoking the aid of Rájá Jai Singh, induced him to renew the war. This time it was Jât against Jât, and the assailants triumphed. Chúránam and his son fled, and Badan Singh was proclaimed chief of the Jâts, and installed as Rájá, by Jai Singh, at Díg, destined also in after times to have its share of fame.

Badan Singh had a numerous progeny, and four of his sons, Súrajmal, Súbharam, Pertáp Singh, and Bírnarain obtained notoriety. He subjected several of the royal districts to his authority. He abdicated in favour of his eldest son, Súrajmal, having first made a provision for the youngest, Pertáp Singh. Súrajmal inherited all the turbulence and energy requisite to carry on the plans of his predecessors. His first act was to dispossess a relative named Kaima of the fortress of Bharatpúr, and to make it his capital. In 1754 he baffled the allied forces of the Vizír Ghazi-ú-din, the Márhátás, and the Rájá of Jaipúr, though in the end he preferred to compound with them by the payment of 7,00,000 rupees. Six years later he joined, at the head of 30,000 men, the great Márhátá confederacy which, under Seódaséo Bai, marched to Delhi to strike its great blow for the empire of India.

But the incompetency of the Márhátá leader made itself so patent, and his insolence was so galling to Súrajmal, that he withdrew from the confederacy, and thus escaped the blow at Pánipat, which crushed, and for the moment annihilated, the Márhátá power. He even did more. Profiting by the confusion consequent upon that terrible defeat, he seized and garrisoned Agra. Three years later he carried his audacity so far as to make an attempt on the imperial city. But when encamped close to the enemy, he went out hunting, was set upon by a party of Belúchí horse, and was slain.

His son, Jowahir Singh, succeeded him. He was defeated in an attempt to invade Jaipúr, and was subsequently assassinated. His brother, Ratan Singh, followed. He was assassinated by a Brahman from Mathurá, who had undertaken to teach the Jât prince the transmutation of metals, and had obtained considerable sums under the pretence of preparing the process. The day having arrived on which the transmutation was to take place, the Brahman saw no way of escape from the punishment due to his imposture but by driving his knife into his dupe. His son, Kesrí Singh, an infant, succeeded, under the guardianship of his uncle, Néwal Singh. Néwal Singh was a man of great ability, but events were too strong for him. He was unable to make head against his enemies in the field, and was forced to shut himself up in Díg. Here he died of dropsy in 1773.

Námal Singh, third son of Súrajmal, succeeded his brother by right as regent. But his younger brother, Ranjít Singh, ambitious to rule, threw himself into the arms of Mirza Najaf Khan, then wielding the supreme power of the Mogul, and invited him to espouse his cause. The Mirza did so, and took possession of Agra. But called away immediately afterwards into Rohilkhand, Námal Singh, taking heart, determined to carry the war into the enemy's country. He therefore marched on Delhi and occupied Sikunderábád. Attacked, and re-

PART I.

pulsed thence, he retired, only however to make a second onward movement, reinforced by the trained mercenaries of Samrú. They had reached Hódal, a town sixty miles south of Delhi, when they were attacked and dislodged by Mirza Najaf Khan, who had returned for the purpose, accompanied by Ranjít Singh. Námal Singh and Samrú then retired, first on Kótban and ultimately on the fortress of Díg, followed by the Mirza. The latter, finding Díg extremely strong, enticed the Jâts to Barsána, where he attacked and completely defeated them. Díg resisted for a twelvemonth before it was captured.

By this defeat, Ranjít Singh was enabled to get possession of Bharatpúr, though that alone remained of all the possessions of his family. By the intercession of his mother, however, with Najaf Khan, the latter restored to the family lands yielding nine lakhs of rupees. Subsequently, when the death of the Mirza in 1782 reopened the seams of disorder, the whole of the territories of the Jâts, including Bharatpúr, fell into the hands of Sindhia, but, again, on the intercession of the widow of Súrajmal, he restored to Ranjít Singh eleven districts, yielding ten lakhs. To these, three districts yielding four lakhs were subsequently added as a reward for services rendered to General Perron.

Meanwhile, by the death of his relations nearer to the succession than himself, Ranjít Singh had become Rájá of Bharatpúr. His previous career had not been fortunate for his country, but his reign was destined to connect his name and that of his capital with a deed of great daring, and, in Indian annals, of unsurpassed success.

Ranjít Singh had been one of the first of the petty chieftains of Hindostan who evinced a desire to connect their interests with the British Government. A treaty was therefore concluded with him at the beginning of the Márhátá war, by which he was guaranteed in the independent possession of his territories, and was permanently relieved from the payment of tribute to the Márhátás, and from the apprehension of exactions or encroachments of any foreign state. In the campaign against Daolat Ráo Sindhia which followed, Lord Lake was joined by a Bharatpúr contingent of horse, which did good service at the battle of Láswárí, and continued to serve with the British army until the end of the campaign. For his services in this campaign, the British Government transferred to Bharatpúr five districts, yielding seven lakhs of rupees.

It was on his return from Láswárí, in December 1803, that the Commander-in-Chief, Lord Lake, had an interview with Rájá Ranjít Singh, at Kanoár. It must have been in every respect satisfactory, for by his alliance with the British the Rájá had been compensated for the losses of the earlier period of his career, and no cause of dissatisfaction had been given to him. Yet it is certain that very shortly after this time he was in active correspondence with Holkar, then about to measure swords with the British.

When war did break out with Holkar, the Rájá of Bharatpúr was called upon to send his contingent to the army. This requisition he first evaded, afterwards refused. His contingent, in fact, joined Holkar, and fought with his troops against the British at Díg. It happened that when the routed troops of Holkar were pursued to the glacis of that fortress, November 1804, the Rájá's troops opened a destructive fire upon the pursuers.

This overt act of hostility showed the Rájá of Bharatpúr as a declared enemy. Thenceforth he was so dealt with, and the British army proceeded to attack his forts. Díg was carried by assault on December 23, and Bharatpúr invested on January 7. But Ranjít Singh, seeing that the fall of the fortress would be a certain prelude to his own overthrow, resolved to defend it with all the resources at his disposal. In this he was well seconded by his army and his people. He repulsed a first assault on January 9, a second on the 21st, a third on February 20, and a fourth on February 21, inflicting on the British army in all these a loss in killed and wounded of 3,203 men. But though Ranjít Singh had repulsed the British he was by no means confident of ultimate success. Between February and April Holkar had become once again a fugitive. Weary, then, of his allies, disliking the enormous expenses imposed upon him, and, above all, having a just dread of the pertinacity of the English general, he took advantage of receiving the intimation of the elevation of General Lake to the peerage to offer him his congratulations, accompanying them by a profession of his desire for peace, and of his readiness to proceed in person to the British camp. This offer met a corresponding return. Negotiations were opened, and on April 10 the terms of a treaty were agreed upon. By these, Rájá Ranjít Singh agreed to pay an indemnity of twenty lakhs of rupees (seven of which were subsequently remitted), and was guaranteed in the territories he had held prior to the suzerainty of the British Government. The districts which had been granted him in 1803 were resumed.

But though the Rájá of Bharatpúr lost by the line he had taken both money and territory, he gained in prestige and credit. His capital was the only fortress in India from whose walls British troops had been repulsed, and this fact alone exalted him in the opinion of the princes and people of India. For more than twenty years subsequently Bharatpúr was a 'household word' in their habitations; and it required a reversal of the result of the first siege to deprive the taunt of its efficacy and sting.

Rájá Ranjít Singh died in less than two years after his moral triumph, and was succeeded by his eldest son, Randbhír Singh. As a general rule this chief conducted his policy towards the paramount power by a system of irritating to the utmost limit of forbearance. Peace was however maintained, and in the Pindárí war (1817) the Rájá duly furnished his contingent of troops to the British army. He died, childless, on October 7, 1823, and was succeeded by his brother, Baldéo Singh. CHAP. XI.

Rájá Baldéo Singh reigned only about eighteen months, as he died on February 26, 1825. He left a son six years old, named Balwant Singh, whose succession was recognised by the British Government. His cousin, however, Dúrjun Sál, supported by the Rájá of Karaulí and others, attacked, dethroned, and imprisoned him. Upon this the British Resident at Delhi, Sir David Ochterlony, who was also the agent for Bharatpúr, promptly assembled a force to reinstate the rightful heir, and there can be little doubt that if he had been allowed to proceed, no serious hostilities would have followed. But the Governor-General, Lord Amherst, trusting that the family differences would be peaceably adjusted, and not considering that the recognition of an heir-apparent during the life-time of the father imposed upon it any obligation to maintain him under the circumstances which had occurred, disapproved of Sir David Ochterlony's policy, and summarily removed him from his post. But in the end, the Government of India was forced to take up and carry out the policy thus rejected, and under circumstances far less favourable. For Dúrjan Sál, in the interval, whilst negotiating and professing to leave the decision of his claims to the British Government, had been engaged in strengthening the fortifications, in levying troops, and in soliciting aid, which was secretly promised from the Rájpút and Márhátá states. The attitude of Dúrjan Sál, combined with the prestige attaching to his capital, produced at last so great an excitement and commotion throughout the country, that to prevent a general conflagration, the Government resolved in the end to adopt the policy of Sir David Ochterlony, viz., to replace Balwant Singh and expel the usurper. An army of 25,000 men, well provided with artillery, was collected, and sent, under the personal command of the Commander-in-Chief, Lord Combermere, against the fortress. The siege was begun in December 1825, but as the mud walls were of great height and sixty feet thick, fronted by a deep wet ditch, mining operations were resorted to. These commenced on December 23, and the mines were sprung on January 17 following, when a sufficient breach was effected, and the fortress carried by assault on the 18th. Dúrjun Sál was made prisoner, and sent to Allahabad; whilst the young Rájá was installed (February 5, 1826) under the regency of the principal widow of the late Rájá, and the superintendence of a political agent. The regent, however, Ráni Mirut Kour, having shown a great disposition to intrigue, and have gone so far on one occasion as to lock herself up with the young Rájá for several days in the palace, threatening to destroy herself if any opposition were offered to her, or any attempt made to remove him, was displaced, and the ministers were formed into a council of regency, with the entire administration of the government in all departments.

In 1830 the government of Bharatpúr sustained a great loss by the death of its chief minister, Jawáhir Lál. He had been the principal revenue minister for the twenty-five years preceding; and it is recorded of him that it was his thorough knowledge of revenue matters, combined with a degree of temper, patience, and forbearance, which have seldom, perhaps never, been surpassed, that enabled him to discharge the duties of his office in a manner most beneficial to the interests of his country. After his death a change for the worse was quickly perceptible, and the deterioration became so rapid, that, in June 1831, the British agent suggested the appointment, as finance minister, of Bhólanáth, a man of some reputation in the town. Matters then improved.

In 1835 Rájá Balwant Singh assumed charge of his government, and the political agency was withdrawn. The detachment of troops which had till then been stationed in the capital was also recalled, and the Rájá was left to the independent management of the country.

This freedom from restraint was not abused. From the accession of Rájá Balwant Singh to 1840 the affairs of the state continued to be managed by the minister Bhólanáth, and it would have been difficult to point to a state better governed during that period than was Bharatpúr. To such an extent was this appreciated by the British Government that in 1839 it excused the Bharatpúr state from the payment of the accumulated arrears of interest with which the unliquidated war charges incurred in 1825–6, and which amounted to 25,49,000 rupees, were burdened according to agreement. CHAP. XI.

Rájá Balwant Singh died in 1853, and was succeeded by his son, Jeswant Singh, a minor. The administration during his minority was conducted by five of the nobles under the superintendence of a political agent.

Subsequently nothing of prominent importance has occurred, unless the birth of an heir to the Máhárájá on January 26, 1868, be considered such.

The Máhárájá of Bharatpúr has been granted the right of adoption. He is entitled to a salute of seventeen guns.

CHAPTER XII.

ALWAR.

AREA—3,300 sq. miles. POPULATION—1,000,000.
REVENUE—16,00,000 rupees.

THE state of Alwar is bounded on the north by Gúrgaon and the native district of Kôt Kásin; on the east by Mathurá and Bharatpúr; on the south by Jaipúr, and on the west by Jaipúr. The principality itself forms a portion of Mewát, or the country of the Mewátís. CHAP. XII.

The Mewátís, who have long had the character of being a fierce, savage, and predatory race, played rather a prominent part, by the display of the qualities attributed to them, in the time of the early Mahomedan kings of Delhi. Their predatory expeditions, sometimes even to the very gates of the capital, at last roused indignation and desire for revenge. In 1266 Gheias-ú-dín Bulbun organised an expedition against them, and by a system of extermination, backed by the formation of local garrisons and other precautions, succeeded in ridding the country of upwards of a hundred thousand of them. A century and a half later the Mewátís endeavoured to take advantage of the disorder which followed the extinction of the house of Toghlak, but Seiad Mobárik inflicted upon them a crushing defeat (1429). From that time, for 300 years, they appear to have been content to plunder on a smaller scale. Indeed, their strength was insufficient to allow them to enter into competition with the plunderers on a princely plan. They wanted, too, organisation and a chief. But their time was fast coming. The disruption of law and order which followed the death of the Emperor Aurangzíb incited the Rájá of Jaipúr, in 1720, to wrest from the empire several territories, and amongst the number the country of the Mewátís. This remained with Jaipúr for about fifty years. But in 1764–74 disorder had reached the state of Jaipúr. The nobleman, Pertáp Singh, of the clan of the Masúkha Rájpúts, upon whom the jaghír of Macherí in Mewát had been conferred, took advantage of the confusion consequent upon a long majority, to strike for independence. In the war carried on by Mirza Najaf Khan with the Jâts, he united his forces at an opportune moment with those of the former, aided him to beat the enemy at Barsána and at Díg; and as a reward for this service obtained the title of Ráo Rájá, and a sunnud for Macherí, to hold it direct from the crown. In this way was Macherí severed for ever from Jaipúr. Not content, however, with that, Pertáp Singh took advantage of the weakness of Bharatpúr at this period to wrest from it the strong hill fort and fortified town of Alwar and other places in its vicinity.

Pertáp Singh, having thus gained a principality, next attempted to keep it in his family. The plan he is said to have adopted was at least ingenious. He wished so to arrange that the country might offer no temptations to an invader, no smiling fields inviting the encampment of large bodies of troops. His policy, therefore, was to discourage cultivation. On the other hand he fortified all the commanding positions, and held them by strong garrisons.

Pertáp Singh lived for about twenty years after the acquisition of Alwar. He died without male issue, but he had adopted a relative, Buktáor Singh, who succeeded him. In the reign of this chief the country, notwithstanding the precautions of his predecessor, was overrun by the Márhátás, a portion of it, indeed, was conveyed to their partisans. This is sufficient to explain why, when the Márhátá wars of 1803–6 broke out, Buktáor professed himself willing to accept the protection of the British Government, and concluded with it a treaty of offensive and defensive alliance. He co-operated in those wars, and although his Mewátís, in their normal love of plunder, did not spare, occasionally, the baggage of the British, yet he was rewarded for his services by the transfer to himself of the districts originally bestowed upon Bharatpúr, and subsequently forfeited by the Rájá of that place. To suit the convenience of both parties a partial exchange of territories was effected about this time between the Rájá of Alwar and the British.

Buktáor Singh evinced no gratitude to the paramount power, nor did he always show that he was guided by common sense. In 1808, for instance, he made an embankment across the Malmas Nai, the river flowing into the Bharatpúr territory, and supplying its people with the means of irrigation, and thus cut off a supply absolutely necessary for their fields. The British Government interfered, but a long time elapsed before the matter could be adjusted. Then, in 1811, the Rájá was seized by a religious frenzy, which could only be gratified by the persecution of his Mahomedan subjects. He destroyed their mosques, and seizing some of their devotees, he mutilated them, and sent their noses and ears to a neighbouring Mahomedan prince. His savage zeal did not stop there; and among other exploits, he caused the bodies of Mahomedans to be disinterred, and sent their bones out of the country.

Just about this time, also (1811), the British Government discovered that the Rájá had interfered in the affairs of Jaipúr in a manner which it was impossible for the paramount power to sanction. As no article in the treaty of 1803 expressly forbade this, a new agreement was drawn up (July 1811), by which the Rájá expressly agreed never to enter into any engagement or negotiation whatever with any other state or chief without the knowledge and consent of the British Government. Yet, the very next year (1812) he took possession of the forts of Dhobí and Sikráwa and the territory adjoining, and, though the British Resident at Delhi remonstrated, refused to restore them. It became necessary, then, to compel him. A force was organised and sent against him, but when the troops were within one march of his capital, Buktáer Singh yielded, restored the usurped territory, and paid three lakhs of rupees for the expenses of the expedition.

The Ráo Rájá Buktáor Singh died in 1815, leaving a nephew and adopted son, Benéi Singh, and an illegitimate son, Balwant Singh, both minors. A dispute then arose as to the succession. The cause of the nephew was supported by the Rájpút nobles, that of the illegitimate son by the Mahomedan faction, headed by Nawáb Ahmed Baksh Khan. A compromise was effected, and it was agreed that the nephew should enjoy the title, while the illegitimate son should exercise the power of the state. The British Government sanctioned this arrangement. It lasted till both boys had grown up. Then, however, the nephew, Benéi Singh, chafing at the restraints imposed upon him, caused Balwant Singh to be imprisoned, and the life of the Nawáb, Ahmed Baksh Khan, then on a visit to the British Resident at Delhi, to be attempted. The assassin was apprehended, and on investigation, the crime was traced to the instigation of certain persons at the court of Alwar. The surrender of these persons was demanded by the British Government, in order that they might be tried at Delhi. Rájá Benéi Singh refused to surrender them, and he persisted in his refusal until, after the fall of Bharatpúr in 1826, he learned that Lord Combermere was on his march to Alwar. He then gave them up. At the same time he made a provision for the dispossessed Balwant Singh.

But the conduct of Rájá Benéi Singh continued to show a defiant spirit. The persons accused of attempting to murder the Nawáb were, indeed, acquitted; but so strong was the suspicion against them that the Rájá was requested not to employ them in any offices of trust. Far from complying with this request, he bestowed upon those persons the highest offices in the state! For this reason the British Resident declined to visit the Rájá of Alwar as he had visited the other chiefs of Rájpútáná, and the following year (1827) the Governor-General refused to receive a deputation from his principality.

Again, in 1831, a correspondence was discovered between the courts of Alwar and Jaipúr, originating in the desire of Rájá Benéi Singh to do fealty to Jaipúr, and to receive a dress of investiture, for which he was prepared to pay a considerable sum of money. It was pointed out to the Rájá that such correspondence constituted a breach of his engagements.

In one or two other ways the Rájá continued to

PART I. display his defiance, and a threat of the march of British troops to enforce the law was almost always necessary to bring him to reason.

Ráo Rájá Benéi Singh died in 1857, just after the outbreak of the Mutiny. After his death the Mahomedan ministers acquired an ascendancy over his son, Séodán Singh, then thirteen years of age, which was obnoxious to the Rájpút nobles, who rose and expelled them (1858). The ministers were compelled to reside at Banáras under surveillance, and a political agent was appointed to Alwar to advise and assist the council of regency which was formed to conduct the administration during the young chief's minority. Ráo Rájá Séodán Singh attained his majority in September 1863.[1] A political agent continued, however, to remain at Alwar.

In 1864 the young Máhá Ráo paid a visit to Calcutta, and much impressed the Viceroy by his intelligence and force of character, though, in other respects, the impression was not favourable. The Viceroy warned him that in the event of commotions occurring at Alwar he must not expect British assistance to put them down. The warning was needed, for the same year the Máhá Ráo was accused of murdering his master of the horse, a Mahomedan; and though the charge of homicide could not be brought home to the Máhá Ráo, the circumstances were extremely suspicious. Shortly after he caused great scandal by his disputes with his Thákurs and his overbearing conduct towards Jaipúr. By this time the British agent had been recalled, and precautions taken to prevent bloodshed. But the Máhá Ráo was distinctly informed that he would have to bear the consequences of his own acts.

To mark his sense of the Máhá Ráo's misconduct, the Viceroy felt constrained at this period (1866) to refuse him the dress of investiture in recognition of his assumption of power. Subsequently, the conduct of the Máhá

[1] Aitchison's *Treaties.*

Ráo gave promise of amendment, and the Governor-General's agent having reported more favourably of his administration, a dress of investiture was bestowed upon him in 1867. CHAP. XII.

The Máhá Ráo of Alwar has received the right of adoption. He is entitled to a salute of fifteen guns.

Subsequently to the writing of the foregoing sketch, Máhá Ráo Séodán Singh died (October 1874). He left no children, and has been succeeded by Mangal Singh, son of Hurdéo Singh, the representative of the Thána family.

CHAPTER XIII.

BÍKÁNÍR.

AREA—17,676 sq. miles. POPULATION—539,000.
REVENUE—about 6,00,000 rupees.

THE state of Bíkánír was founded by Bíka Singh, sixth son of Rájá Joda of Jodhpúr. Followed by three hundred of his clansmen, Bíka quitted the paternal roof to found a new city in the wilderness. He of course went sword in hand, with a determination to slay or to be slain. The Sanklas of Jánglú fell before him. This brought him in contact with the Bhátís of Púgal, the daughter of whose chief he married. Settling down at Koramdésír, he built there a castle; then, gradually, by establishing his influence over the race of the Jàts or Getes, settled in the land, and of others who immigrated from more remote regions, he came at last to be elected lord of a community of nine cantons, containing 2,670 villages. The people led a pastoral life, their wealth consisting in their cattle, the produce and wool of which they exchanged with their neighbours. The conditions on which they offered CHAP. XIII.

PART I.

to bestow the supremacy over their community upon Bíka Singh were these:—

1. That he should make common cause with them against the cantons with which they were at variance.

2. That he would guard the western frontier against the irruption of the Bhátís.

3. That the rights and privileges of the community should be held inviolable.

On the fulfilment of these conditions, they relinquished to Bíka and his descendants supreme power, assigning to him, in perpetuity, the power to levy *dhúa*, or a hearth tax, of one rupee on each house in the canton, and a land tax of two rupees on each hundred bíghas[1] of cultivated land within their limits. As a security for the performance of their part of the contract by Bíka and his successors, Bíka bound himself and them to receive the mark of inauguration from the hands of the descendants of the elders, and that the throne should be deemed vacant until such rite had been administered.

Bíka then made war with the rival tribe of his new nation, the Johyas, and conquered them; then advancing against the Bhátís, won Bhágór from them. In this district he founded his capital, Bíkánír (1489), just thirty years after his departure from Mundúr.

Bíka died in 1495, leaving two sons by his first wife, Núnkarn, who succeeded him, and Garsi, who founded Garsisin and Arsisar.

Núnkarn conquered several districts from the Bhátís. He left four sons, the eldest of whom renounced his birthright to have a separate establishment in his father's lifetime. The second brother, Jáetsí, then succeeded Núnkarn. He, too, enlarged his borders. Kálian Singh, his eldest son, followed him, and then succeeded his eldest born, Rai Singh.

Rai Singh came to the throne in 1573. In his reign

[1] A bígha is five-eighths of an acre. The charge, therefore, was equivalent to six shillings and five pence per hundred acres.

Bíkánír rose to importance amongst the principalities of the Mogul empire, and Rai Singh became a satrap of his brother-in-law, the Emperor Akbar.[1] High honours were bestowed upon him by the emperor. He was made a leader of four thousand horse, received the title of Rájá, and the government of Hissar. Moreover, when Maldéo Singh, King of Jodhpúr, incurred the displeasure of Akbar, that sovereign transferred to Rai Singh the district of Nagore and afterwards his entire kingdom. Such transfers, however, were in effect nominal. But, armed with the emperor's favour, Rai Singh returned to Bíkánír, conquered Bhutnair, and rooted out the Johyas. Previous to his reign the Rájpúts had gradually been ousting the Jâts as proprietors of the soil, and the Jâts had been sinking to the position of labourers or serfs. This silent revolution was completed under Rai Singh. It was made absolute by the conquest of the territories of the Púnias, the last race of Jâts who had preserved their liberty. CHAP. XIII.

Rájá Rai Singh led a band of his warriors in all the wars of Akbar. He distinguished himself in the assault of Ahmedábád, slaying the Governor in single combat. He married his daughter to Prince Selim, afterwards Emperor, as Jehángír. Her son Purvez was one of those who unsuccessfully strove for the empire with Shah Jehán.

Rai Singh died in 1632, and was succeeded by his only son Karan. Karan supported the claims of Dára Shekó against Aurangzíb, and escaped the plot laid by the general of his antagonist to destroy him. He died in 1674, and was followed by his son, Anóp Singh. This prince held the governments of Bíjapúr and Aurangabád, was nominated a leader of 5,000 horse, accompanied Rájá Jeswant Singh to Kábul with the imperial forces, returned, and died at Bíkánír in 1709. His son, Sarúp Singh, succeeded. Sarúp Singh was killed in endeavouring to recover the castle and lands of Adóní, bestowed by

[1] They had married two sisters, princesses of Jaisalmír.

Aurangzíb on his father, and taken back on his quitting the imperial army. The two next Rájás, Sujaim Singh and Zoráwar Singh, were men of little note.

Rájá Guj Singh followed them. Throughout a long reign of forty-one years, this prince was engaged in border contests with the Bhátís and Bháwalpúr. He succeeded in rounding his borders by acquisitions from both. But he is chiefly famous for the number of his offspring. He had sixty-one children; 'though,' remarks the annalist, 'all but six were "sons of love."' He was succeeded in 1787 by his son, Ráj Singh.

Ráj Singh enjoyed his dignity only thirteen days, being removed by a dose of poison, administered by the mother of Súrat Singh, fifth son of the late Rájá. He left, however, two sons, Pertáp Singh and Jai Singh. But Ráj Singh had not been poisoned without an object. Súrat Singh at once assumed the office of regent, his two elder brothers, Súrtán Singh and Ajít Singh, fleeing the paternal roof to escape the fate of their brother. During the following eighteen months Súrat Singh conducted himself with great circumspection, and by condescension and gifts impressed the chiefs in his favour. Then he disclosed to some of them his determination to rule. His plans were, however, discovered, and the majority of the nobles determined to resist him, unfortunately only passively. Súrat Singh, an active and determined man, levied troops, attacked, and subdued them; then returned to Bíkánír, resolved to remove every obstacle between himself and the throne. One of his nephews had died; the other remained under the care of the sister of Súrat Singh, a virtuous woman. Unable to deceive her vigilance, Súrat Singh forced her into a marriage which she abhorred, and then, having rid himself of her, strangled, it is said with his own hands, his nephew and sovereign. He then proclaimed himself Rájá, a position in which his defeat of his elder brothers, who had levied a force to dispossess him, confirmed him.

It was in the year 1801 that Súrat Singh became undisturbed ruler of Bíkánír. He was a warrior, and made many acquisitions to his country, especially from the Bhátís; but in the Jodhpúr civil war he unfortunately took the wrong side, supporting the cause of the pretender, Dhókal Singh, and expending nearly five years' revenue in fruitless efforts on his behalf. This failure caused him to become oppressive to his people, and bigotry in his old age, the natural child of riotous and unscrupulous youth, making him more and more superstitious, he withdrew gradually from affairs, leaving his government in the hands of those who had been his associates, and who were not haunted by the same terrors. Before his death in 1828, his country was embraced in the general scheme of subsidiary alliances, formed by the British Government at the time of the Pindárí war. The Rájá was bound to subordinate co-operation, and the British Government engaged to protect his territories and to reduce his rebellious subjects to obedience. No tribute was exacted, none having been paid to the Márhátás. Súrat Singh left his country in a terrible state of anarchy and disorder: the chiefs were in open rebellion, the country swept by robbers, the very cultivators of the fields forced to arm in their own defence. He was succeeded by his son, Ratan Singh.

One of the first acts of the new Rájá was to proceed to invade the territory of Jaisalmír in revenge for former injuries, or supposed injuries, sustained by his subjects through subjects or servants of the former. The Rájá carried his operations, in direct breach of his treaty with the British Government, to the very gates of his enemy's capital. The ruler of Jaisalmír prepared an army to resent the injury, and the armies of Jodhpúr and Jaipúr assembled on their respective frontiers. The peace of Rájpútáná was in imminent danger, when the British Government interfered, and through the arbitration of the Ráná of Údaipúr the dispute was settled, both parties making reparation for the injuries done.

But there was but little improvement in the internal condition of the state. The Rájá continued on bad terms with many of his nobles, and he did not feel himself strong enough to coerce them. Under these circumstances, he applied for aid to the British Resident at Delhi (1830). The aid was promised under a misapprehension. But the British Government interfered, and informed the Resident that military aid should never be given to native states for the suppression of internal disturbances, except under the specific authority of Government. The Government also expressed an opinion that the case was not one in which they were called upon to interfere.

Meanwhile the squabbles between the Rájás of Bíkánír and Jaisalmír continued. They had reached such a point in 1835 that a British officer was deputed to effect a reconciliation. His mission was happily attended with success. Both Rájás renounced their previous ill-will to each other, and entered into a pact of friendship. A disposition to border encroachments was, however, manifested by the Rájá in other quarters, especially in the direction of Hissar; and it was not until strong means had been used that he desisted from his attempts.

Rájá Ratan Singh died in 1852. He was succeeded by Sirdár Singh, the present chief. Sirdár Singh did good service in the mutinies, both by sheltering European fugitives and by co-operating against the rebels in the districts of Hansi and Hissar. As a reward for these services he received a grant of forty-one villages, which, some years before, had been declared to belong to the Sirsa district. He received, likewise, the right of adoption.

Still the frontier outrages continued, and they proceeded to such a length in the Jodhpúr territory, that in 1861 the British Government was constrained to remind the Rájá of his treaty obligations. In the same year, too, his misgovernment of the forty-one Sirsa villages ceded to him for his services in the Mutiny, called for the intervention of the British Government. An inquiry before the Commissioner of Hissar showed that, whereas the total revenue demand against the villages between 1861 and 1867 had been 90,000 rupees, the Rájá's officials had exacted 2,00,000 rupees in excess of that sum. The Viceroy, upon this, addressed a letter to the Rájá, calling upon his Highness to maintain all concerned in the rights and privileges conferred upon them by the British Government, and to place an official of upright character in charge of the villages.

CHAP. XIII.

I am not aware of anything that has occurred subsequently in Bíkánír calling for notice.

The Rájá of Bíkánír is entitled to a salute of seventeen guns. His territory lies in the Rájpútáná Desert, east of Bháwalpúr.

CHAPTER XIV.

JAISALMÍR.

AREA—12,252 sq. miles. POPULATION—73,700.
REVENUE—5,00,000 rupees.

CHAP. XIV.

JAISALMÍR was founded in the year 1156 by Jaisal, Ráwul or Prince of the Bhátís, a branch of the Yádú race, whose power was paramount in India 3,000 years ago. Abandoning India, this tribe, led by the ancestors of Jaisal, is said to have settled in Mervo. Migrating thence, they conquered Afghánistán, making Ghizní their capital. Expelled thence by the King of Khorassan (supposed to have been Antiochus IV., the Great), they settled in and colonised the Punjâb, and founded the city of Salabhána.[1]

[1] Colonel Tod thinks, and it appears to me with some reason, that Salabhána and Lahore may have been one and the same place; at all

Driven from the Punjâb by the King of Ghizní,[1] they fled to the great Indian desert. There they intermarried with the ruling family of Amírkót, and subsequently with that of Jhalór. They then built a fortress in the desert, which they called Tanót, and made it their capital (A.D. 731).

Tanót remained the capital of the Bhátí tribe until, about the year 840, it was taken and sacked by the neighbouring clans, and all the people found in it put to the sword. The remnant that escaped under their Ráwul, Déoraj, managed, by a cunning device, to build another fortress, which, after himself, he named Déoráwal. This prince restored the fortunes of the family, conquering Lodorva, capital of the Lodra Rájpúts, and making it his own. His sixth descendant, Jaisal, considering that city open to invasion, built another ten miles from it, which on completion he called Jaisalmír, and transferred to it the royal residence (1156). This city still retains its pre-eminence, and has given its own name to the country.

Jaisal survived this event twelve years. I propose to give little more than the names of those of his successors in their order whose exploits do not seem to require special notice; but every important event will be recorded.

Jaisal was succeeded by Salbahan, a successful warrior, but who was ousted during his absence by his son, Bíjil. Salbahan was killed fighting against the Belúchís. Bíjil did not long survive him. His uncle, Kailán, followed and avenged his brother's death by defeating the Belúchís and slaying their leader. He governed prosperously for nineteen years.

Cháchick Déo, his son, succeeded in 1219, and ruled the country thirty-two years. His grandson, Karan,

events that the intervening distance could not have been great between the two cities. There is, he adds, a Sangala, south of Lahore, near the altars of Alexander, and a Sealkote. Salabhána, Salbahanpore, or simply Salpura, may have been erected on the ruins of Kampilanágri.

[1] The Bhátís had retaken Ghizní, and made it over to the grandson of their prince, who became a convert to Mahomedanism.

followed, ruling twenty-eight years. Both these princes were valiant and successful sovereigns. CHAP. XIV.

Of Lakhúr Sén, who next mounted the throne, it is recorded that 'he was so great a simpleton that when the jackals howled at night, being told that it was from being cold, he ordered quilted dresses to be prepared for them. As the howling still continued, though he was assured his orders had been obeyed, he commanded houses to be built for the animals in the royal preserves.' He ruled only four years, and was replaced by his son, Pompâl. But the temper of this prince was so violent that his nobles combined to dethrone him, replacing him by Jaetsi, the elder brother of Káwul Karan, and whose claims had been set aside in deference to the death-bed wishes of Káwul Cháchick.

Jaetsi reigned eighteen years. In the course of these his capital Jaisalmír was subjected to a siege from the troops of the Emperor Alla-ú-dín Khilji,[1] in revenge for some marauding carried on by his grandson. The siege, it is stated, had lasted eight years when Káwul Jaetsi died. On the accession of his son, Múlráj, the attacks of the besiegers increased in fury, and, though they were repulsed, the blockade became more strict than before. So great was the distress of the inhabitants, that the Káwul meditated sacrificing all the females of the place, and dying with honour on the field of battle. This plan was, in effect, ultimately carried out. Twenty-four thousand females were sacrificed by fire or the sword, then the men arming themselves, rushed on the foe, and, inflicting great slaughter, were destroyed to a man. The only survivors were the two nephews of Káwul Múlráj and a small force in the field commanded by Déóráj, son of Múlraj, who was soon afterwards carried off by fever (1295).

The Moslem garrison occupied Jaisalmír for two years, when they abandoned it. Some years later the

[1] Not as stated by the annalist, Alla-ú-dín Ghori, who lived about a century earlier.

PART I.

Rahtórs of Méhwo came and settled in the ruins, but they were driven out by the remnant of the Bhátís, led on by Dúdú, son of Jésur, who was elected Ráwul. Dúdú had the imprudence, however, to carry off the horses of the King of Delhi whilst they were being watered at a lake. In consequence, Jaisalmír was again attacked, and submitted to a sacrifice as horrible in all its details as that which preceded it (1306). Meanwhile the two nephews of Ráwul Múlráj had been taken to Delhi. By good service rendered there, the elder, Garsi, obtained a grant of his hereditary dominions, with permission to re-establish Jaisalmír. With his own kindred, and the aid of the vassals of his friend, Jagmál of Méhwo, he repaired thither, soon restored order, and established a sufficient force. He was, however, assassinated by the partisans of the relatives of Dúdú, son of Jésur. His brother Kêhur succeeded him, and by his consent the widow of Garsi settled the descent to the throne in the family of Hámir, their cousin, grandson of Ráwul Múlráj.

The next eight generations may be briefly passed over. They were represented by the Ráwuls Kailem, Cháchick Déo, Bersi, Jait, Núnkarn, Bhím, and Munóhurdas, under whom the country became not only resettled, but increased in extent. Munóhurdás, the last-named, who had murdered his nephew, the son of his predecessor, Bhím, was succeeded by Sabal Singh, the fourth in descent from Ráwul Núnkarn. When he ascended the throne the dependencies of Jaisalmír extended on the north to the Gárah River, on the west to the Indus; on the east and south they were bounded by Bíkánír and Márwár. Sabal Singh first diminished them by presenting a feudatory[1] of Márwár with the city and domain of Pókurn, which have since remained severed from Jaisalmír.

Amra Singh, son of Sabal, succeeded. He cleared

[1] The feudatory in question had been sent by the Rájá of Márwár to place Sabal Singh on the throne.

his country from robbers, and, anticipating an attack planned upon him by the Rájá of Bíkánír, completely frustrated his designs. He died in 1702, and was followed by Jeswant Singh. The reign of this Ráwul was unfortunate. Three districts, Púgul, Barmair, and Filódí, and other towns and territories were wrested from him by the Rahtórs, and the territory bordering the Gárah on the north by Dáod Khan, an Afghan chief from Shikarpúr. After his death ensued a contest for the throne between the brother and sons of the deceased prince. Ultimately this was decided in favour of the eldest son, Akhi Singh, who reigned forty years. He, too, lost another portion of his dominions, Déóráwal and all the tract of Khádál, to the son of Dáod Khan, the founder of Bháwalpúr.

Múlráj succeeded him (1762). The unhappy choice of a minister by this Ráwul completed the demoralisation of the Bhátí principality. This man, named Sarúp Singh, in the gratification of his animal desires, had deeply offended the nobles and the Crown Prince, Rai Singh. He was cut down by the latter in his father's presence. Then ensued a state of anarchy, the nobles wishing to depose Múlráj and to substitute Rai Singh, the latter steadily refusing. It ended by Rai Singh and his partisans going into exile. But the Ráwul Múlráj waited until Sálim Singh, son of his slaughtered favourite, Sarúp Singh, should be old enough to manage affairs. He then made him minister. Sálim Singh would appear to have been the very incarnation of evil, to have united the subtlety of the serpent to the ferocity of the tiger. He is described as having been in person effeminate, in speech bland; pliant and courteous in his demeanour; promising without hesitation, and with all the semblance of sincerity, what he never had the most remote intention to fulfil. He was a signal instance of the fact of the inadequacy of religious professions, though of a severe character, as a

PART I.

restraint upon moral conduct, for he was most devout amongst the devout.

It happened that the nobles exiled with Rai Singh had waylaid this man on his return from a mission to Jodhpúr, but their hearts softening to his entreaties, had allowed him to depart uninjured. As a return for this kindness, he had the nobleman who had been mainly instrumental in saving him, poisoned; he then dealt to his own brother and his wife, 'who knew too much,' the same fate; he had the castle in which the heir apparent, Rai Singh, and his wife were dwelling, fired at a time when it was impossible for them to escape, and they were burnt to death; their children he confined at Rámgurh, a remote corner of the desert, and there had them poisoned. He then declared Guj Singh, the third son of the third son of Múlráj, to be heir apparent. The other sons and grandsons of the Ráwul saved themselves by flight. But the measure of Sálim's atrocities was not completed by these acts. He put to death all those whose talent he had any reason to fear. The town of Jaisalmír was depopulated by his cruelty, and the trade of the country greatly interfered with by his harsh and unscrupulous measures.

It was during the reign of Ráwul Múlráj that Jaisalmír first came under the protection of the British. The Ráwul would gladly have accepted the British protection in 1808, but the policy which limited the British ascendency to the territories east of the Jumna prevented the formation of an alliance with him. In 1818, however, a treaty was concluded by which the state was guaranteed to the posterity of Ráwul Múlráj; he was to be protected from serious invasions and dangers to his state, provided the cause of the quarrel was not attributable to him; and he was to act in subordination to the British Government. No tribute was demanded.[1]

Two years later Ráwul Múlráj died, and was succeeded by his grandson, Guj Singh. This prince was

[1] Aitchison's *Treaties*.

fitted, from his years, his past seclusion, and the examples which had occurred before his eyes, to be the submissive pageant Sálim Singh required. He was isolated by his minister from the rest of mankind, except from the creatures in Sálim's pay, whose duty it was to watch and report every word and every gesture.[1]

Guj Singh was a minor when he ascended the throne. For the four years that Sálim Singh yet survived, that minister continued his career of cruelty, extortion, and misgovernment. It was this that led to those raids on the Bíkánír frontier, which caused the embroilments I have related in my account of that state. In the same spirit he constantly urged, in the name of his master, claims to territories possessed by other chiefs, and even threatened a visit to Calcutta to urge them. The Ráwul was then, however, distinctly informed that it was impossible, consistently with the engagements subsisting with other states, to attend to claims to territories possessed by those states. In 1824 an attempt was made to assassinate the minister. Sálim Singh was so persuaded that the assassin had been instigated by the Ráwul, that he sent off his family to his own jaghír. The same year he died, in the conviction, however, that he had fixed for ever the office of minister in his own family!

So firmly was the interest of this man established in the capital, that on his death his eldest son was appointed to the office, in conjunction with a younger son by a different mother, the favourite wife of the father. The eldest son, however, discovering, or pretending to discover, a criminal connection between that lady and her confidential servant, put both to death. For this act Ráwul Guj Singh, who had attained his majority, imprisoned him. His partisans rallied in his favour, but as the Ráwul was firm, and the British Government declined to

[1] Tod's *Rajasthan*.

interfere with the just authority of the chief of the state, the tumult subsided.

Subsequently the Ráwul took the administration into his own hands, and by measures of a just and conciliatory nature gained great popularity with his people. It was by his tact and judgment that the way to a pacification and good understanding with Bíkánír was made easy.

Nor was he ever other than a good friend to the British. His exertions, indeed, to supply the British army of the Indus (1838–9) with camels were such as to elicit the special thanks of the Government of India.

In 1844, after the conquest of Sindh, the forts of Shágar, Garsía, and Gatúra, which in bygone days had been wrested from Jaisalmír, were restored to that state. These forts were given over by Mír Ali Murád by order of the British Government, but no sunnud appears to have been given to the Ráwul on that occasion.[1]

Guj Singh died in 1846 without male issue. His widow adopted Ranjít Singh, who received, in 1862, a formal sunnud guaranteeing the right of adoption. He died in 1864 without leaving an heir.

The widow of Ranjít Singh adopted his brother, Bairí Sál. The young prince, however, who was only fifteen years old, refused to take his seat on the throne, giving as a reason that he thought he should never be happy as ruler of Jaisalmír. In consideration of his youth, the British Government allowed the question to remain in abeyance, and the installation to be deferred, affairs being, meanwhile, administered by his father, Thákur Kaisri Singh.

But in October of the following year (1865) the young prince had outgrown his scruples. He was then installed as Máhá Ráwul by the Governor-General's agent, his father, whose administration had given satisfaction to the people, continuing as minister.

The Máhá Ráwul of Jaisalmír is entitled to a salute of fifteen guns. His territories lie south-west of Bíkánír.

[1] Aitchison's *Treaties*.

CHAPTER XV.

SIROHÍ.

AREA—3,000 sq. miles. POPULATION—55,000.
REVENUE—80,900 rupees.

THIS territory is bounded on the north by Jodhpúr; on the north-east by Godwar; on the east by Mewár; and on the south by the state of which Barodah is the capital. It is separated by the Aráwalí range from the table lands of Mewár. CHAP. XV.

Sirohí is the one domain in Rájpútáná which maintained its independence, acknowledging the suzerainty of neither Mogul, Rahtór, nor Márhátá. Ruled over by men boasting descent from the Chohan Rájpúts, Thákurs as well as Ráo, the Bhíls, Mínas, and Grásias, who inhabited the country, lived a life of lawlessness and licence amongst their native hills. That life they called liberty, and as such they clung to it. Attacked repeatedly by the Rájás of Jodhpúr, they never acknowledged themselves conquered. Wild, and savage, and free, as they were at the beginning, so did they continue to the end.

But a time arrived at last when dissension came to weaken them. In the beginning of this century, their Ráo, from master and sovereign, became tyrant and oppressor. His name was Údibánjí. Such a transformation was not to be borne by the free Thákurs of the hills. Several broke out in revolt, and transferred their allegiance to more genial lords. Those that remained acted as became a people who loved liberty. Their prince had betrayed his trust and oppressed them. In return they deposed and imprisoned him. To act as regent during his lifetime they nominated another. This other was no alien; he was the brother to the deposed Ráo, Shéo Singh by name. Údibánjí, upon this, sent messengers to Jodhpúr, to implore the intervention of Rájá Maun Singh. Nothing could be more agreeable to Maun Singh. He and his predecessors had long claimed suzerainty over Sirohí, though they had been forced to content themselves with its verbal assertion. They had never been able to enforce it. But now, with a Déóra prince, the rightful claimant to the chieftainship, to welcome them, success seemed certain. An expedition was ordered. It marched; it entered the Sirohí territory, and it retired baffled, beaten, and humiliated. The sons of the hills had been too strong for the invader. Údibánjí remained a prisoner, and died in confinement.

But the invasion had been a formidable one, and the danger had been great. The princes of Údaipúr, Jodhpúr, and Barodah, the nearest neighbours of the Sirohí chief, lived under the protection of the new paramount power, the British. The value of the protection thus afforded to small states had been felt even in Rájpútáná. Amír Khan had ceased to desolate, the Pindárís to ravage. Every chief who had accepted it had been a gainer; he had had his possessions secured to him; and, in more than one instance—notably in that of Amír Khan—a successful and faithless marauder had developed into a pattern sovereign, given to piety and devoted to priests!

The advantages were so patent that the Regent, Shéo Singh, hastened to ask them for his small principality. They were granted. A treaty was concluded with the British Government, September 11, 1823, by which the regent acknowledged British supremacy, agreed to abstain from political intercourse with other chiefs, to govern in accordance with the advice of the British agent, to introduce an efficient administration, and to pay a tribute not exceeding three-eighths of the revenues. On its side the British Government extended its protection to the state, guaranteed the succession to the heirs of Údibánjí, should any of them survive Shéo Singh, and reserved to itself the right of regulating the transit duties.

Údibánjí having died without issue in 1847, Shéo Singh was acknowledged as Ráo, and his son as heir apparent. CHAP. XV.

Various circumstances, however, had combined to render the administration of the country at this period a matter of some difficulty. The invasion of Maun Singh, though repulsed, had disquieted the minds of the Thákurs or barons, and some of them felt inclined to strike for independence. Others had fallen off in the reign of Údibánjí. To quell their rebellion, the Ráo was compelled to raise a force, and to raise a force he had to borrow from the protecting power. A loan of a lakh and a half of rupees was accordingly made him, and a body of troops was sent by the British against the wild Mínas, who supported his most powerful vassal. Subsequently, by the mediation of the British Government, order was restored, and it was arranged that the Thákurs who had rebelled subsequently to the deposition of Údibánjí should return to their allegiance.

In 1845 the Ráo made over to the British some lands on Mount Abú, for the establishment of a sanitarium. The grant was fettered by several conditions, one of which was that no kine should be killed. The Ráo has always refused to cancel this condition.

In 1854, the state, at the earnest request of the Ráo, was taken under direct British management. The debt was then about two lakhs of rupees. It was soon found that the tribute, 30,000 rupees, was very much out of proportion to the total revenues of the state, 80,000 rupees, and it was reduced by one-half. The state was under British management in 1857, when the Mutiny broke out. The Ráo evinced on this occasion a most friendly disposition towards the paramount power, and as an acknowledgment of this his tribute was again halved, and reduced to 7,500 rupees.

In 1861, the Ráo, Shéo Singh, being stricken in years, made over the government to his son, Úméd Singh, he retaining, however, the honours and dignities of office.

PART I.

He died the same year. Ráo Uméd Singh still continued to be assisted by the British political agent, but in 1865, the debt having been entirely liquidated, the agent was withdrawn.

The early years of the rule of this chief were disturbed by the rebellion of his three brothers, who were dissatisfied with the provision made for them by their father; but they were subsequently pacified.

Since that period nothing of importance has occurred. Some correspondence did indeed take place on the subject of the extradition of criminals claimed by other states, and it was ruled by the British Government that the Ráo was bound to comply with all such demands.

The Ráo of Sirohí has been allowed the right of adoption. He is entitled to a salute of fifteen guns.

CHAPTER XVI.

DONGARPÚR.

AREA—1,000 sq. miles. POPULATION—100,000.
REVENUE—75,000 rupees.

CHAP. XVI.

THIS little state is bounded on the north and east by Údaipúr; on the south-east by Bánswárá; on the south and south-west by the Máhi Kanta districts.

The chief or Ráwul of Dongarpúr claims to represent a senior branch of the house of Údaipúr. His ancestors, from the time of Akbar, were dependents of the Moguls; and on the break-up of their empire after the death of Aurangzíb they fell into the hands of the Márhátás, by whom they were ground down and oppressed. The state was rescued from this bondage in 1818, by accepting the protection of the British power, in return for which it transferred from Dhár the tribute of 35,000 rupees it had annually paid to that power.

By a separate arrangement a sum of 35,000 rupees was paid in lieu of all arrears, and the annual amount of the tribute was proportionally diminished, until, after the expiration of three years, it should arrive at its maximum of Company's rupees, 27,387.

From some old records of this state it was ascertained in 1819 that the revenues had greatly decreased in more recent times, and it was hoped they might be restored to their pristine elasticity; but these hopes have not been realised.

In 1824, in consequence of internal commotions, some of the Thákurs having called in the aid of the Bhíls to assist them in their claims against the Ráwul, it became necessary to invoke the aid of the British Government. Troops were promised; but the requisition was sufficient. The Thákurs returned to their allegiance, and the troops to their quarters.

The commotions alluded to were due in a great measure to the character of the Ráwul, Jeswant Singh, a man incompetent as a ruler, and addicted to the lowest and most degrading vices. For his incompetency and maladministration he was deposed in 1825, and his adopted son, Kour Dalpat Singh, grandson of Sawant Singh, chief of Partábgarh, was made regent.

But under the rule of this chief the resources of the state deteriorated, and he found himself unable to manage his Thákurs. Under these circumstances he applied in 1831 for some assistance from the British Government to enable him to curb the undue pretensions of the refractory chiefs, and to reduce them to their normal condition of lords rendering loyal service to the Ráwul. In reply, the British Government informed him that they looked to the ruler of each independent state to adopt such measures as might be necessary to maintain his own power, and to preserve general tranquillity.

British troops were, however, occasionally employed

to assist the regent in repressing the Bhíls and other plunderers.

In 1844, the death of his grandfather, chief of Partábgarh, left Dalpat Singh heir to that state. The question then arose whether it might not be possible to unite the two states under one ruler. The Thákurs of Dongarpúr, however, showed themselves greatly averse to such a union, and it was not insisted upon. Finally, it was agreed that Dalpat Singh should be allowed to adopt a successor for Dongarpúr, and take up his own fief of Partábgarh. The boy he adopted, the son of the Thákur of Sablí, being a minor, it was decided that, while ruler at Partábgarh, he should continue at the same time to be regent of Dongarpúr.

This arrangement was apparently not agreeable to the late Ráwul, Jeswant Singh, for he made an attempt to recover his authority and to adopt as heir the child of another family. He was, however, unsuccessful, and, as a penalty, was removed to Mathurá, with an allowance of 1,200 rupees per annum.

The double government, as it may be called, though the term is scarcely accurate, was not a success. Dongarpúr had been badly administered whilst her ruler resided in the capital. She fared worse when he lived at Partábgarh. Maladministration was, however, endured for eight years, but then becoming quite unbearable, the affairs of Dongarpúr were removed from the hands of Dalpat Singh, and placed in those of a native agent appointed by the British Government. The Ráwul, Údai Singh, has subsequently attained his majority and has assumed the administration of affairs. The chief of Dongarpúr has been guaranteed the right of adoption. He is entitled to a salute of fifteen guns.

BÁNSWÁRÁ.

AREA—1,500 sq. miles. POPULATION—150,000.
REVENUE—300,000 rupees.[1]

CHAP. XVI.

THIS territory is bounded on the north by Dongarpúr and Údaipúr; on the north-east and east by Partábgarh; on the south by the dominions of Holkar, and on the west by a portion of Gujrát.

The Ráwuls of Bánswárá are of the same stock as the Ránás of Údaipúr, of whose country Bánswárá at one time formed a part. They are, in fact, descended from a younger brother of the founder of Dongarpúr, and their adherents and subjects are composed of the same classes —Rajpút Thákurs, and a large proportion of Bhíls—as are those of that state. Like Dongarpúr, too, Bánswárá suffered from the successive tyrannies of the Moguls and Márhátás, the latter of whom exercised an enormous amount of oppression in the country. The rise of the British power seemed to offer to the rulers and ruled a good opportunity of ridding themselves of these marauders. Accordingly in 1812, the Ráwul of Bánswárá proposed to become a tributary to the British Government on the sole condition that the Márhátás should be expelled. He engaged in fact to pay the British Government three-eighths of the revenue of his country in return for aid to expel the armies of Sindhia, Holkar, and Dhár. The Resident at Barodah, to whom this offer was made, referred the envoy to the Resident at Delhi. To him, therefore, the envoy was accredited, and though no steps were taken at the moment, yet five years later, the envoy, acting on the same credentials, concluded a treaty on the terms before offered, viz., the payment of three-eighths of the revenues in return for British protection (September, 1818).

[1] Of this sum the feudatories, thirty-three in number, receive 1,10,000 rupees.

PART I.

The Ráwul, however, whose name was Uméd Singh, either thinking that the time of danger had passed away, or that the terms, though of his own offering, were too exorbitant, refused to ratify the treaty. The British Government insisted that it was binding, but as in the meanwhile they had concluded with Dhár a treaty which transferred to them the tribute theretofore paid to that state by Dongarpúr and Bánswárá, they were not unwilling to revise the agreement. Accordingly negotiations were reopened, and a new treaty signed (November 25, 1818). By this the Ráwul engaged, in return for British protection and a promise to assist himself, his heirs, and successors against any relatives or connections who might prove refractory, to pay to the British Government all arrears of tribute due to Dhár or any other state, and, annually, whatever tribute the British Government might deem adequate to cover the expenses of protection, provided it did not exceed three-eighths of the revenues. Subsequently all arrears for tribute were limited to 35,000 rupees, and the annual payment settled at a sliding scale for three years, to be eventually fixed at 35,000 rupees, which is rather more than one-sixth of the present net revenue.

Up to the year 1824 Bánswárá continued to be subject to raids of Bhíls and other plunderers who made inroads from the neighbouring jungles. In that year, however, a great effort was made to put an end to this organised system of robbery. The effort was successful, and since that time Bánswárá has enjoyed much internal tranquillity. The effect of the suppression of these raids was shown in the rapid rise of the revenue subsequently to 1824. It was reported by the political agent that the rise would have been even more rapid but for the vices and misconduct of the Ráwul and his favourite minister.

The excesses of these men gradually led to their natural consequences. By 1835 the tribute due to the British Government had fallen considerably into arrear, the money intended to pay it having been spent in debauchery by the Ráwul, Bhowání Singh, son of the Uméd Singh who signed the treaty of 1818, and by his minister. It needed the strongest arguments on the part of the British agent to remedy this state of things. Remonstrances were useless, and it was only when the inevitable result of persistence in conduct so discreditable was pointed out to the Ráwul, that he agreed to dismiss his minister. Arrangements were then made to liquidate the arrears.

Bhowání Singh did not long survive the dismissal of his favourite. He left no male heir, but the chiefs, with the concurrence of the political agent, adopted the noble whose claims were best founded, Bahadúr Singh. On his death, without issue, the present ruler, Latchman Singh, was elected Ráwul. The election was opposed by Maun Singh, Thákur of Khandú, who conceived that his own son had preferable claims, but he eventually withdrew his opposition on receiving a remission of 1,300 rupees a year from the tribute due by him to Bánswárá. The Ráwul of Bánswárá has been granted the right of adoption. He is entitled to a salute of fifteen guns.

PARTÁBGARH.

AREA—1,460 sq. miles. POPULATION—150,000.
REVENUE—2,62,400 rupees.[1]

THE state of Partábgarh is bounded on the north and north-west by Údaipúr; on the east by Mundisúr, Jáorá, and Ratlam; and on the south-east by Bánswárá.

The Rájá of Partábgarh is descended from a junior branch of the family of Údaipúr. The ancestors of the reigning prince were officers of the Delhi emperors; and one of them, Sálim Singh, was so great a favourite with

[1] From this has been deducted 200,000 rupees enjoyed by the feudatories of the state.

Mahomed Shah, that he granted him permission to coin money in his own name. He accordingly founded a mint in Partábgarh, from which rupees called Sálim Sháhi rupees still continue to be struck off. These rupees are of less value than those of the British currency, the proportion being nearly five to four.

On the break-up of the Mogul empire the Rájá, Sáwant Singh, son of Sálim Singh, became tributary to Holkar. He attempted to release himself from those shackles in 1804, and actually made for the purpose a treaty, by which he accepted British protection, and transferred to the British Government the tribute theretofore due to Holkar. This treaty, however, having been dissolved by the policy of Lord Cornwallis, Partábgarh was doomed to suffer, fourteen years longer, the exactions of the Márhátás. But, in 1818, that policy was revoked, and in common with the other states of Rájpútáná, Partábgarh was then taken under British protection, the tribute, amounting now to 56,887 rupees per annum, being paid to the British, but accounted for by them to Holkar.

Between the years 1823 and 1826 much confusion and ill-feeling was excited in Partábgarh by the differences between the Rájá Sáwant Singh and his son and heir, Kour Díp Singh. Some years before the Rájá had entrusted to his son the administration of the affairs of the territory. But the Kour, having wantonly put to death certain persons who were obnoxious to him, the British Government insisted upon his removal from office and banishment. He was accordingly removed, and ordered to reside at a place called Déólah.

Kour Díp Singh went to his place of exile unwillingly, but finding it even more disagreeable than he had anticipated, he stayed there only a few months and then returned to the capital. There his conduct became so outrageous and threatening that it became necessary to call in British troops to escort the Kour to the fort of Kernora,

There he died on May 21, 1826. Meanwhile the old Rájá, Sáwant Singh, who had virtually abdicated in favour of the Kour about twenty years before, resumed office; but before his son's death he pardoned him and petitioned the British Government for his release. His prayer would have been complied with but he had paid the debt of nature before the sanction of the British Government could be acted upon.

The infirm state of the Rájá prevented his paying to the affairs of state the attention which they required. Consequently they fell into disorder. The confusion was increased by the carelessness of the Bhíls, Thugs, and other marauding and murdering classes. By British intervention, however, a successful blow was struck at their depredations.

The only grandson of Rájá Sáwant Singh, Dalpat Singh, had been adopted, in 1825, into the Dongarpúr family. When, therefore, Sáwant Singh died, in 1844, he left, according to the strict Hindú law, no real heir. It was arranged, however, as I have stated in the account of Dongarpúr, after some discussion, that Dalpat Singh should succeed his natural grandfather at Partábgarh, and act also as regent for Dongarpúr during the minority of a newly-adopted ruler to that state. At the end of eight years this arrangement was found so inconvenient that Dalpat Singh thenceforth confined himself to Partábgarh.

The Rájá of Partábgarh has been granted the right of adoption. He is entitled to a salute of fifteen guns.

PART II.—CENTRAL INDIA AND MÁLWÁ.

CHAPTER I.

GWÁLIÁR, OR THE DOMINIONS OF SINDHIA.

AREA—33,000 sq. miles. POPULATION—2,500,000.
REVENUE—93,10,000 rupees.

PART II.

THE founder of the family which now rules the state of which Gwáliár is the capital was Ránojí Sindhia. Of the origin of the family there are two accounts. Sir John Malcolm states that they were Sudras of the tribe of Kúmbí, or cultivators, and he thus describes the rise of the man who first made it famous :—'Ránojí Sindhia,' he writes,[1] 'the first who became eminent as a soldier, had succeeded to his hereditary office of Headman, or Patél, of Kumerkerrah, in the district of Wye, before he was taken into the service of the Peshwa Ballají Bishwanath, after whose death he continued in that of his son Bájírao Bullal. The humble employment of Ránojí was to carry the Peshwa's slippers ; but being near the person of the chief minister of an empire in any capacity is deemed an honour in India. The frequent instances of rapid rise from the lowest to the highest rank led men of respectability to seek such stations ; and it is probable that ambition, not indigence, influenced the principal officer of a village to become, in the first instance, the menial servant of Ballají Bishwanath. Ránojí's advancement, however,

[1] *Central India*, vol. i. p. 116.

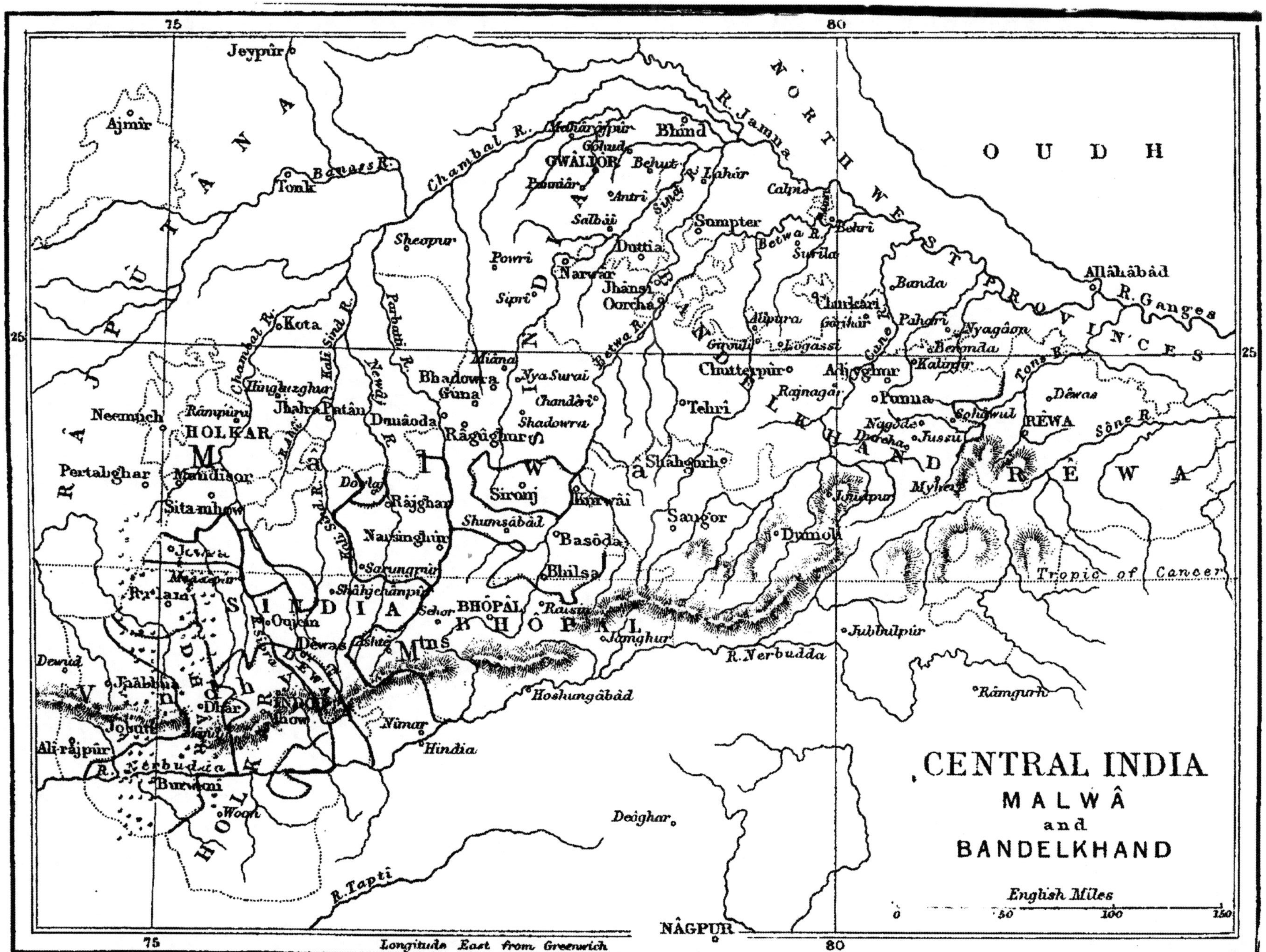

Edwd. Weller

London: Longmans & Co.

is imputed to accident. It is stated that Bájírao, on coming out from a long audience with the Sahú Rájá, found Ránojí asleep on his back, with the slippers of his master clasped with fixed hands to his breast. The extreme care of so trifling a charge struck Bájírao forcibly; he expressed his satisfaction, and, actuated by motives common to men in the enjoyment of such power, he immediately appointed Ránojí to a station in the pagah or bodyguard.'[1]

This somewhat sensational story, though generally believed, has not been altogether unquestioned. A writer, who, though anonymous, had evidently access to the best sources of information, and whose work[2] was read over and emended prior to publication by such high authorities as Mountstuart Elphinstone and Grant Duff, ventures to doubt it. His account of the origin of the Sindhia family is as follows:—'The Sindhia family,' he writes, 'were Patéls of Kumerkheir, near Sattara, and, in the absence of other information, we may judge of their respectability from the circumstance of the Emperor Aurangzíb selecting a lady from the family to give in marriage to the Rájá Sahú, about 1706, before deputing him to claim his inheritance as sovereign of the Márhátás. The lady died in 1710, when residing at Delhi with Sahú's mother. It was said of Ránojí that in early life he was a domestic of very inferior degree in the service of the Peshwa, viz., the carrier of his slippers: a story repeated by almost all writers of his history. But as the family had always been Silladars (cavaliers) nothing can be more improbable than that any member of it should serve in a menial office, more especially at a period when the army afforded an ample field for the display of

[1] Malcolm adds in a note: 'This anecdote receives confirmation from a letter of Captain Stewart, acting resident at Sindhia's Court, dated 3rd September, 1819. Ránojí (he observes) is stated, after he was promoted, to have carried with him, carefully packed in a box, a pair of the Peshwa's old slippers, which he never ceased to regard with almost religious veneration as the source of his rise.'

[2] *An Historical Sketch of the Princes of India.* Edinburgh, 1833.

PART II.

courage, talent, and birth. Ránojí, moreover, must have been a near relation of one of the Rájá Sahú's wives or princesses, and would, therefore, hardly be allowed to stand in the capacity of a domestic to the Peshwa, who was himself only the minister, or servant of Sahú.'

However this may be, it is certain that Ránojí was a man to make the most of his opportunities. He first attracted attention in 1725, when he was regarded as one of the most daring leaders of the Márhátá host. In 1736, at Delhi, he contributed greatly to the defeat of a body of 8,000 Mahomedan horse, who had sallied out to attack the Márhátá army. Two years later, in the campaign against Nizám-úl-Múlk, he was one of the three principal officers who led the Márhátás into action, and to whose efforts the successful result of the campaign, viz. the first foundation of the three states of Sindhia, Holkar, and Puar, was mainly due. In 1743, his character caused him to be selected as one of the securities for the observance of the treaty between the Peshwa and the Emperor Mahomed Shah. On this occasion he publicly declared that should the Peshwa not observe his contract he would quit his service.

Nearly half the conquests achieved by the Márhátás in Hindostan had been made over to Ránojí for the support of his troops. On his death, about 1750, he was in possession of half Málwá, and enjoyed a personal income of about sixty-five and a half lakhs of rupees.

Ranojí left three legitimate sons, Jyapa, Duttájí, and Juttabah. Of these the first was murdered at Nagpúr, in 1759, by emissaries of the Rájá of Jodhpúr; Duttájí was killed in action on the plain of Rudber, near Delhi, and Juttabah died at Kamber, near Dig.

But he had besides two illegitimate sons, Túkají and Mádhají. Of these Túkají [1] did not survive his father; but Mádhají lived to establish one of the most powerful and lasting native monarchies of Hindostan. But Mád-

[1] Grant Duff states he was slain at Pánipat.

haji did not immediately succeed to the chiefship of the clan. His nephew, Jankají, who was the son of Jyapa, became after his father's death in 1759, its recognised representative. But at the fatal battle of Pánipat, January 6, 1761, Jankají was taken prisoner and put to death. From that terrible overthrow Mádhají escaped, though at the cost of a wound which rendered him lame for life. Arriving at Púna, alone and unattended, he at once made an application to the Peshwa to be recognised as the chief of his father's house, and the inheritor of his jaghír. After much opposition offered by the Peshwa's uncle, Ragonáth Rao, the claims of Mádhají were admitted.

From this moment his rise was rapid though not easy. He had to meet and overcome all those obstacles, rather harassing than really formidable, which jealous mediocrity invariably seeks to cast in the way of a man whose ability and ambition are clearly recognised. But Mádhají was equal to every occasion. Appointed general of one of the divisions of the army sent by the Peshwa into Málwá in 1764, to recover the prestige lost at Pánipat, Mádhají took advantage of the many opportunities which presented themselves to establish himself firmly in the country north of the Narbadá. He is described by Sir John Malcolm as being, a little subsequent to this period, 'the nominal slave but rigid master of the unfortunate Shah Alum, Emperor of Delhi; the pretended friend, but the designing rival of the house of Holkar, the professed inferior in all matters of form, but the real superior and oppressor of the Rájpút princes of Central India; and the proclaimed soldier, but the actual plunderer of the family of the Peshwa.'

In 1766 Mádhají returned to Púna. Here his nominal employment was that of commandant of the household troops of the Peshwa, but the real influence of his strong practical character was almost irresistible. He used it on this occasion to support the claims of Ahalya Bai, widow of the deceased representative of the house

PART II.

of Holkar, to inherit the family possessions. When we come, in the history of that house, to notice the immense benefits conferred upon it by the administration of that illustrious lady, we shall perhaps be inclined to dissent somewhat from the opinion already quoted, that Mádhají was the designing 'rival' of the house of Holkar.

In 1769, Mádhají commanded one of the divisions of the army sent by the Peshwa under Visají Krishna against Northern India. Of this expedition Mádhají was the soul. It was due to the plan of operations advised by him, that the Mogul Emperor, Shah Alum, was induced to throw himself into the arms of the Márhátás. It was under his escort that the emperor re-entered his capital in December 1771. That accomplished, the Márhátás conquered nearly the whole of Rohilkhand, and established in that part of India a footing so firm that it was never seriously contested till they were driven from it thirty years later by Lord Lake.

The death of the Peshwa Madho Ráo in the following year, recalled Mádhají to Púna. The new Peshwa, Narain Ráo, did not long enjoy his honours, and then the mantle fell on the restless Ragonáth Ráo, the enemy of Mádhají. This latter, however, seeing that Ragonáth Ráo had enough upon his hands to occupy all his thoughts, employed the following two years in consolidating his power. This accomplished, he in concert with Túkají Holkar, suddenly declared against Ragonáth, whose imprudence was already imperilling the Márháta empire.

In the contest which followed, Mádhají first came in contact with the English, who had espoused the cause of Ragonáth Ráo. His first operations were eminently successful. He compelled the troops, commanded by Colonel Cockburn, with Mr. Carnac as his *adlatus*,[1] to retreat with great loss, to destroy their heavy guns and

[1] These officers and Colonel Egerton, who had led the army into the snare, were dismissed the service.—GRANT DUFF.

burn their stores, and finally, he forced upon them at Wargaum the most disgraceful treaty ever signed in India by a British commander.

The effect on Mádhaji's career was marvellous. In no country is prestige more powerful than in India, and Wargaum had given Mádhají prestige. Thenceforth with the Márhátás, as with his own countrymen, his influence was unbounded.

The arrival of General Goddard somewhat changed the aspect of affairs. But even in his contest with this general, Mádhají proved his right to be considered a commander of no ordinary ability. More acute than all his countrymen, he had thus early discerned in the English the capital enemy with whom the Márhátás would have to contest the empire of India, and he was unwilling to embark in such a contest, until he should have united all the native powers against their common foe. He felt that the contest was, for him, premature. He therefore used all his efforts to negotiate a peace. But Goddard was as far-sighted as Mádhají. It was necessary, he felt, to disarm so powerful an enemy with as little delay as possible. With this view, he attempted, April 3, 1780, to surprise him at Barodah. But though actually taken by surprise, Mádhají drew off his forces with consummate skill and little loss.[1] A second attempt, made on the 19th of the same month, was even less successful, Mádhají skilfully avoiding an action. By this line of conduct he effectually gained his end—the prolongation of hostilities until after the commencement of the rainy season. He lost, however, almost immediately afterwards, the fortress of Gwáliár, then reputed impregnable, but which succumbed to the skill and daring of Captain Popham in August of that year. Unable to pursue his operations against Sindhia in the interior, Goddard transferred his operations to the coast, and laid siege to Bassein. On December 10 he

[1] These details have already appeared in a memoir on Mádhají Sindhia in *Recreations of an Indian Official*, p. 373.

PART II.

defeated the Márhátá force sent to relieve it, and the place surrendered on the following day. Other operations, with varying fortunes, ensued, no great success, however, being obtained by the English, and their army on one occasion, April 23, 1781, suffering a decisive defeat. These operations gave Mádhají the opportunity he coveted, of planting his own power firmly in Central India. General Goddard at last perceived that, by confining his attack upon the Márhátá possessions to those districts farthest from the possessions of Sindhia, he was in reality playing the game of that ruler, who, whilst he was the mainstay of the Márhátá power in the field, cared nothing regarding the nation at whose expense his own possessions were extended. A resolution was accordingly arrived at to attack Sindhia in his own territory.

The attempt was first made by a British force under Lieutenant-Colonel Camac. The operations of Mádhají, on hearing of this movement, stamp him as a military genius of no common order. Learning that Colonel Camac's force was small, he resolved to overwhelm it before it could be reinforced. He hastened at once, with a large body of troops, in the direction of Sípri, but, too late to save that place, he came up with Camac at Seronj, and surrounded him. The English force was reduced to great straits by famine. Added to this a cannonade of seven days' duration made considerable havoc in its ranks. Feeling that a further continuance in his position would inevitably lead to his destruction, Camac resolved to retreat, having previously sent to the nearest division of British troops earnest requests for reinforcements. For seventeen days the retreat continued, our troops being followed up and harassed by Mádhají. But on the eighteenth day the Márhátá chieftain, for the first time in his life, allowed himself to be completely outwitted. As the only means of escape, Colonel Camac, at the dead of night, on March 28, attempted to surprise his enemy. His movements were entirely successful. Mádhají was completely defeated, and forced to give up the pursuit. A few days later, Colonel Camac was joined by a force under Colonel Muir. Mádhají, however, with the energy and spirit of a true Márhátá, soon recovered from his mishap; and, by his superiority in cavalry, he speedily reduced the English force to a state of inactivity. A few months later, Mádhají, perceiving that he had everything to lose from a contest carried on within his own territory, concluded a treaty with Colonel Muir, by which he bound himself to neutrality, agreed to exercise his good offices to bring about a general peace, recovered all his territory except the fortress of Gwáliár, and obtained from the English a promise to recross the Jumna.

This treaty was concluded just at the right time for the interests of Mádhají. The Government of India was, for many reasons, anxious to conclude the war with the Márhátás, to prevent it from attaining the proportions of a deadly struggle for existence. The defection of Mádhají from the confederacy was hailed, therefore, by them with the liveliest satisfaction, and prepared them to show towards that chieftain a consideration such as, under other circumstances, would undoubtedly have been denied him. Nothing could have more advanced the views of Mádhají at this conjuncture than his recognition by the English as an independent prince. Besides the great moral advantages flowing from that recognition, it would give him that of which he then stood greatly in need; it would give him time: time to consolidate his conquests, to give them a compact form, to gain for himself an independent footing amongst the several rulers of Hindostan; time, moreover, to watch the opportunity for recovering, free from any interruption on the part of the English, the stolen fortress of Gwáliár. That fortress the English had made over, after its capture, to the Ráná of Góhad, to be by him held solely on the condition of good behaviour. It required but a little arrangement on the part of Mádhají to bring about

PART II.

the apparent infraction of a condition so easy to set aside.

But, before he attempted this, he had been a consenting party to the treaty of Salbye, between the Peshwa and the English, which restored peace to every part of India but the Carnatic. Mr. Hastings was urged to the conclusion of this treaty by the doubtful fortunes of the struggle between Haider Ali and the coast army, and by the fear lest a man so ambitious as Mádhají might influence the Márhátá nation to cast in its lot with the great adventurer of Mysore. Náná Furnawís was anxious for peace, not less on account of the presence of English troops in the Márhátá territories, than of jealousy of the increasing power of Mádhají; whilst Mádhají himself, after long hesitation, after coquetting with Haider Ali and even obtaining the sanction of the Náná to a plan for the invasion of Bengal, came to the conclusion, for reasons already stated, that peace with the English would, for the moment, best advance his interests.

The treaty of Salbye, whereby, in addition to the former territories secured by him, he obtained the cession of Bharoch, promised him after the capitulation of Wargaum, had scarcely been signed, when Mádhají had proof of the wisdom of the course he had followed. The signature took place on May 17, 1782; the treaty was ratified on June 6 following, and was exchanged with the Peshwa on February 24, 1783. In the interval between the first signature and the final exchange, events had occurred at Delhi which opened out to Mádhají Sindhia a prospect, the realisation of which had ever been one of his fondest hopes, and had, nearly twenty years earlier, led to the campaign which ended on the fatal field of Pánipat.

Ever since the retreat of the Márhátás to their own country in 1773, the imperial government had been carried on under the auspices of Mirza Najaf Khan, the leader of the anti-Rohilla party in the state. His rule had, on the whole, been vigorous and successful. He had made the voice of the descendant of Timour once more respected at home and abroad, and under his energetic sway the empire seemed likely to attain a position such as it had not occupied since the death of Aurangzíb. But on April 22, 1782, Najaf Khan died. His death was the signal for anarchy and intrigue, for divided factions and contending rivals. This was the opportunity for which Mádhají had been longing. It seemed to him that the occupation of imperial Delhi, with the connivance of the English, opened out to him better prospects than an alliance with Haider Ali for the destruction of that nation. And when, towards the close of 1782, he received from Warren Hastings an assurance that the English would not interfere with his plans on Delhi, he made up his mind, and at once put in action the means he had so plentifully at his command.

Whilst these intrigues were pending, he made himself, in the first instance, secure in his own acknowledged dominions. To protect them the more effectually, he contrived a quarrel with the Rána of Góhad, and forced him to surrender Gwáliár,—the English, occupied, after the death of Haider, with his son Tippú, not caring to interfere. Everything having been placed upon a footing of order in his own territory, he caused himself, by means of his intrigues with one of the contending factions at Delhi, to be invited to that city in the name of the emperor. The timely assassination of one of the leaders of the contending factions made Mádhají arbiter of the situation. Meeting the imperial court near Agra, he accompanied it to Delhi, where, refusing for himself and for the Peshwa the office highest in name and in repute—that of Amir-úl-Amrah, or prime minister—he accepted for the Peshwa that of vicegerent of the empire, and for himself that of deputy to the Peshwa; thus, at the same time, acknowledging his fealty to the chief of the Márhátás, whilst retaining in his own hands alike the

PART II.

power and the right to exercise it. From this period till the defeat of the armies of Daolat Ráo Sindhia, by Lord Lake, in 1802, the imperial districts of Northern India were—some brief intervals alone excepted—administered and governed by the Márhátás, acting in the name of the imprisoned emperor.

For the five years following Mádhají's assumption of power at Delhi, he was engaged in a continuous struggle to maintain it. It was scarcely to be supposed that the Mahomedan factions would acquiesce tamely in his elevation. The country, moreover, was exhausted, and the necessity for raising a certain amount from its inhabitants did not increase his popularity. The Rájpúts, the Játs, the Síkhs, and some of his own followers, too, disputed his supremacy. Yet Mádhají was resolved not lightly to resign the imperial power. He enlisted two battalions of regular infantry under a foreign adventurer, named De Boigne, and as opportunity offered he largely increased this force and added greatly to its efficiency. He improved likewise the irregular troops, enlisting amongst them not only Rájpúts, but Mahomedans, and organising them on the basis of a disciplined army. His own energy and force of character not only inspired his men, but supplied even the losses occasioned by the treachery and misconduct of some of his adherents. Thus, after the battle of Jaipúr, lost by the desertion of his regular infantry, Mádhají delayed not a moment in securing his strong places; then, effecting a junction with a considerable force of Jâts, he sent a fresh army into the field underRáná Khan and De Boigne. Though this army was defeated near Agra on April 24, 1788, Sindhia so far rallied it as to meet the enemy, and completely beat them on June 18 following. The Moguls, under the ferocious Ghulám Kadir, committed after this event those terrible atrocities upon the unhappy descendant of Timour and his family, as well as upon the inhabitants of Delhi, which have made his name for ever infamous in history. His triumph was short-lived. On

CHAP. I.

October 11 Delhi was occupied by Ráná Khan and De Boigne, and a few days later Mádhají himself seated the blinded Shah Alum on his recovered throne. His power and authority were subsequently confirmed and consolidated by a great victory obtained by his army on June 20, 1790, over Ismael Beg, the last remaining Mahomedan noble possessing sufficient power and influence to interfere with his ambitious views. A second victory over Ismael Beg's allies, the Rájpúts, was gained on September 12 the following year; and Mádhají, sensible of the expediency of conciliating rather than driving to extremity that warlike people, granted them peace on easy terms.

In the first war with Tippú, 1790–92, Mádhají took no part. He was strongly of opinion that complete victory in such a contest would only be advantageous to the English, from whom a violent and persistent enemy would thus be removed, whilst the maintenance of Tippú at Mysore was by no means inconsistent with Márhátá interests. He condemned, therefore, strongly the conduct of Náná Furnawís, in aiding the British on such an occasion. He continued, then and subsequently, to consolidate his own authority in Hindostan, to meet the open efforts of Túkají Holkar and the secret efforts of Náná Furnawís to overthrow him, and to prepare against any attack from the north-west, constantly threatened as it was by the grandson of the Abdallí. He found, however, in the course of time, that, having placed his dominions in Hindostan on a footing of tolerable security, the best, and indeed the only efficacious mode of thwarting his Márhátá rivals was to proceed direct to Púna. Could he become the minister of the Peshwa, as well as the holder of the power of the Mogul, what a vista would open to him! He would then wield a power such as neither Aurangzíb nor Sivají, with all their efforts, had ever attained. To unseat Náná Furnawís, always plotting against him, and to occupy his place, became then the fixed and settled purpose of his mind. For no lighter purpose would he have left his territories in Hindostan and Central India, the seat of his real power. But the end he proposed to himself was so vast, so full of promise, so magnificent, that it seemed to him worth while to encounter even a dangerous risk. He set out for Púna, and marching slowly, ready at any moment to retrace his steps, he reached that city on June 11, 1793.

There was naturally an ostensible reason for his journey. He was to invest the Peshwa with the insignia of the office of vicegerent of the Mogul empire, conferred upon him by the emperor. This he did, despite the secret opposition of Náná Furnawís, with great pomp and ceremony. His secret object, however, was to gain the young Peshwa, Madhú Ráo Narain. This too, despite of the opposition, open as well as secret, he would, had he lived, undoubtedly have accomplished. Everything seemed to favour his purpose. Whilst at Púna he received intelligence of the complete defeat of the fast adherent and supporter of Náná Furnawís, Túkají Holkar—a defeat by which the army of that rival chieftain was almost entirely destroyed; he learned, too, of the capture of Ismael Beg, his sole Mahomedan adversary. He found, in fact, that he wielded unchecked the whole power of Northern and Western, and a great part of Central Hindostan. The spirit of the young Peshwa, too, chafing under the austere guardianship of the Náná, inclined more and more every day to the genial warrior, who encouraged him in his aspirations after the sports of the field and the pleasures of the chase. But it was not to be. At the very threshold of his fortunes, when success seemed within his grasp, Mádhají was attacked by fever and died. His death took place on February 12, 1794, in the vicinity of Púna. He had no children, nor had he made any adoption. He had, however, expressed a wish that his grand-nephew, Daolat Ráo, grandson of his co-illegitimate brother, Túkají, might succeed to his possessions; and this wish, after some opposition on the part of his widow, was carried into effect.

By the death of Mádhají Sindhia the Márhátás lost their ablest warrior and their most far-seeing statesman. In his life he had had two main objects: the one to found a kingdom, the other to prepare for the contest for empire with the English. In both, it may be said, he succeeded. The kingdom he founded still lives; and if the army which he formed on the European model was annihilated eight years after his demise by Lake and Wellesley, it had in the interval felt the loss of his guiding hand, as on the field it missed his inspiring presence. Had he lived, Sindhia would not have had to meet Lake and Wellesley alone; Mádhají would have brought under one standard—though in different parts of India—the horsemen and French contingent of Tippú, the powerful artillery of the Nizám, the whole force of the Rájpúts, and every spear which Márhátá influence could have collected from Púna, from Indúr, from Barodah, and from Nagpúr. The final result might not have been altered, but it would still have hung longer in the balance, and at least the great problem, in the terms in which it had presented itself to the mind of the greatest of Márhátá leaders—the problem of a contest between an united India and the English—would have been fairly fought out. As it was his death settled it. Thenceforth a sinister result became a question only of time.

Daolat Ráo Sindhia.

Daolat Ráo Sindhia was fifteen years old when he succeeded to the extensive dominions of his grand-uncle.

Young as he was, with a character still unformed, this prince had, at the very outset of his reign, to deal with problems which called for the wisdom of a practical statesman. The first of these was that raised by the death of the Peshwa.

On October 25, 1795, the Peshwa Madhú Ráo, in a fit of profound melancholy, deliberately threw himself from a terrace of his palace, and injured himself so much that he died two days later. An event more fraught with importance to India could scarcely have occurred. Madhú Ráo was young, well-disposed, and entirely dependent upon his minister, the famous Náná Furnawís. His nearest relative was his cousin, Bájí Ráo, son of Raghunát Ráo, a young man of great talent, utter unscrupulousness, and greater ambition, but detested by Náná Furnawís, who even then kept him in restraint in the hill fort of Sewnerí.

Daolat Ráo had already been to Púna. He had taken part in the almost bloodless campaign of 1795 against the Nizám, had renewed at Púna with Náná Furnawís the friendship which had existed, on the surface, between that minister and his father, and had already reached Jamgaon on his return to Hindostan, when he was recalled by an express from the Náná to deliberate as to the succession to the vacant Peshwaship.

The plan adopted by the Náná, in consultation with Holkar, Sindhia, and other chiefs, was to put aside Bájí Ráo, and to authorise one of the widows of Madhú Ráo to adopt an heir. But Bájí Ráo, apprised of this, began to manœuvre on his side. He first gained over Daolat Ráo's chief minister, Balloba Tattai, and then Daolat Ráo himself—the latter by the offer of territory bringing in a revenue of four lakhs of rupees, and the payment of the whole charge of his army during his stay at Púna.

Into the intrigues which followed it is not necessary here to enter. They mostly concern the youthful Daolat Ráo in that they were the cause of his concluding a marriage which cannot but be termed unfortunate. In their course Bájí Ráo, then under surveillance in the camp of Sindhia, had been started off by the minister of the latter, Balloba Tattai, towards Hindostan. Now this escort was commanded by Sukharám Ghatgay, a man of the most unscrupulous character. Bájí Ráo gained him over by promising to pay two millions sterling to Daolat Ráo on his becoming Peshwa; to have, then, Ghatgay appointed as Sindhia's prime minister: he arranged, too, that Ghatgay's daughter should marry Daolat Ráo; and that Ghatgay should obtain the village of Kagul, in inam.[1] Most of these conditions were subsequently carried out.

But before this happened Daolat Ráo had asserted the preponderance of his power in a very remarkable manner. A quarrel occurring in the house of Holkar consequent upon the death of Túkají Holkar, Daolat Ráo interfered to support the party of the imbecile son, Khásí Ráo, against his more able brother. The contest resulted in the death of the brother and the capture of his infant son. With a *crétin*, then, as the representative of Holkar, Daolat Ráo had apparently nothing to fear in Central India.

He fortified his influence likewise on the western coast by the capture of the fort of Kolábah, imprisoning the ruler, and transferring that principality to his near relative, Bábú Ráo Angria.

But all this time Bájí Ráo was anxious to get rid of him. He had already rid himself of his able minister, Náná Furnawís, and now he thought Daolat Ráo's turn had come. He executed his plans with an ingenuity of malice not to be surpassed. First, in March 1798, he married Ghatgay's daughter to Sindhia. This caused the latter to expend enormous sums of money. To meet his necessary payments, he asked Bájí Ráo to pay him the two millions he had promised. Bájí Ráo regretted his inability, but told Daolat Ráo that if he would appoint Ghatgay his minister, he would know how to raise the necessary sums. Ghatgay was consequently appointed, and he did succeed, by a system of extortion, torture, and oppression, unparalleled in the history of Western India, in screwing enormous sums out of the people. But by this proceeding, the very name of Sindhia became hateful to the masses.

[1] *Inam*, a gift from a superior, free from all rent to Government.

This was what Bájí Ráo had plotted. He thought now that the pear was ripe. He determined to rid himself for ever of Daolat Ráo. The scene that followed is thus told by the facile pen of Captain Grant Duff:—'In this state of things'—which I have described—'Sindhia's unpopularity having become extreme, Amrat Ráo (the adopted brother and prime minister of the Peshwa), with Bájí Ráo's cognisance, prepared Abba Kálí, the commander of one of the Peshwa's regular battalions, to be ready to rush in, upon an appointed signal, and seize Sindhia. Daolat Ráo was invited, on business, to the Peshwa's palace; but the invitation being declined, a positive order was sent by Bájí Ráo desiring his attendance. He obeyed the summons, and soon after he sat down, Bájí Ráo told him he had sent for him to desire an explanation of his conduct; and, suddenly assuming a tone of authority and decision for which the other was quite unprepared, he required of him to declare whether he was master or servant? Sindhia having answered with respect and humility, that he was the Peshwa's servant, and ready to show his dependence by his obedience, Báji Ráo reminded him of the insolence, violence, and cruelty which he and his servants had used, in numberless instances, towards the servants and subjects of his government, in the city, and even in his own palace; he declared that "the contempt and disrespect thus shown towards his person and authority he could bear no longer, and therefore ordered Sindhia to remove to Jamgaon." Daolat Ráo's reply was couched in the mildest terms; but whilst he expressed his willingness to obey, he declared his inability to move, from want of funds to pay his troops; "that he had incurred large debts by placing his Highness on the musnud, which it was incumbent on his Highness to discharge; when that was effected he would immediately quit Púna." At this moment Amrat Ráo asked his brother if he should give the signal; but Bájí Ráo's heart failed him; he had not courage to proceed in the design, and thus gave his friends the first decided proof of that imbecility which swayed most of the actions of his life. Sindhia withdrew from the presence in a manner the most respectful, but with a mind filled with suspicion and distrust; and Báji Ráo had afterwards the baseness, as well as the weakness, to tell him what Amrat Ráo had intended, and to advise him to be upon his guard.'[1]

Then followed a series of intrigues and counter intrigues, which often seemed to threaten open hostilities between Daolat Ráo and his liege lord. These were complicated by the complaints, ending in revolt, made by the widows of Mádhají that not only did they not receive the attention due to their rank, but that their ordinary comforts were circumscribed. After, as I have said, intrigue and counter intrigue, after shots had been exchanged, the mediation of the British resident solicited, and embassies for aid sent to independent powers, matters were compromised by the dismissal from office of the miscreant Ghatgay and his agent Garway, their confinement, and the release of Náná Furnawís.

But affairs still continued for some time in a very disordered condition. Daolat Ráo's treatment of the widows of his predecessor, still in revolt, had induced a large and influential body of chiefs to join their cause. The reappointment by Daolat Ráo of Balloba Tattai as minister did at least put an end to this scandal, as he used his great influence and judgment with effect in his master's cause, but still affairs did not prosper. There was a laxity of principle about Daolat Ráo which manifested itself in all the important transactions of his life. The death of the Peshwa's able minister, Náná Furnawís, in the year 1800, showed him again in the light of a man who would scruple at nothing to seize the property of others. He scrambled with the Peshwa for the dead man's possessions. This was always the case when money was

[1] *History of the Márhátás*, vol. iii.

PART II.

in question; but when it was a matter of personal revenge the two chiefs were ready to play into each other's hands. It would be waste of time to pursue further the infamous courses adopted by each, from the displacement of Balloba Tattai in favour of the infamous Ghatgay by Sindhia, to the ruin of the friends and adherents of the deceased Náná by the Peshwa.

At length Daolat Ráo felt it was absolutely necessary for him to return to Hindostan. The progress of Jeswant Ráo Holkar in Málwá was the immediate object which rendered that return imperative. He accordingly set out northwards towards the end of November at the head of the main body of his troops, and having secured bills from the Peshwa to the amount of forty-seven lakhs of rupees.

But his return was not allowed to accomplish itself without opposition from the ambitious Jeswant Ráo. In June 1801, this daring chieftain inflicted two successive defeats on strong detachments sent by Sindhia for the protection of Ujjén. The following month he made a bold attack upon Sindhia's great park of artillery, defended only by four battalions of infantry and a few cavalry; and though the gallantry of Sindhia's general, an Englishman named Brownrigg, caused his repulse, yet the attack showed to what lengths so determined an enemy might proceed.

At the same time the repulse saved Sindhia. Up to this time Daolat Ráo had displayed only an impetuosity, a recklessness, and a want of judgment, combined with an entire absence of scruple, which augured ill for the future. But, warned by the danger from which he had just escaped, he now hastened to concentrate his forces. Having accomplished this, he waited till he had been rejoined by his father-in-law, Ghatgay, and then marched on Indúr. Jeswant Ráo moved to its succour, and a battle took place on October 14, which terminated in the complete defeat of Holkar and the sack of his capital,

Had Daolat Ráo followed up this victory, Jeswant Rao's career was ended for ever. But he never, throughout his life, showed any of the great qualities of a general. He preferred to negotiate, and Jeswant Ráo, amusing him for a while, went off suddenly to renew hostilities in Khándesh. A force which Sindhia had despatched to oppose him, under Seodaséo Ráo, was completely defeated near Púna on October 25, 1802, by the intrepid Jeswant Ráo. But this defeat was more disastrous to the Peshwa than to Sindhia, as it forced the former to accede to the treaty of Bassein, a treaty by which 'he sacrificed his independence as the price of his protection.' To such a result had the divergence from the policy of Mádhají led the Márhátá power. He had invited union with a view to combination against the English. The disunion of those who followed him had placed one of the three great Márhátá chiefs, the highest in point of rank, very much in the power of the English.

Daolat Ráo was not insensible to the great mistakes which had been committed. In the treaty of Bassein he saw not only the subversion of the vast plans of his great uncle, but a threat against himself. Though invited to become a party to the defensive portion of the treaty, he expressly refused. And from this time he turned all his efforts to the welding together of the union, which had been the dream of Mádhají, and for the same purpose, viz., the expulsion of the English from Northern, Central, and Western India.

But he was too late. Holkar refused to join him. His preparations, though denied, were too patent. The Governor-General, therefore, Marquess Wellesley, with a wise prescience, determined to anticipate him, and to bring the question at once to a crisis.

It is no part of my plan to detail the military operations which followed. It will suffice to say that at Aligarh on August 29, at Delhi on September 11, at Assaye on the 23rd, at Agra on October 10 and 18, at

PART II.

Láswárí on November 1, at Argaum on November 29, 1803, Daolat Ráo had to admit the ruin of his ambitious hopes. His troops, especially those trained by De Boigne, and who greatly distinguished themselves at Láswárí, fought remarkably well; many died in their ranks; but they were not a match either for British soldiers, or for their own countrymen well led by a sufficient number of British officers. The battalions trained by De Boigne, and officered on a system analogous to that now known as the irregular system, could not stand against their countrymen and kinsmen, led by European officers four times as numerous as their own.

The result was that Daolat Ráo, roughly awakened from his dream, was forced to accept on December 30, 1803, very unfavourable conditions from his conqueror. By the treaty signed on that day, and known as the Treaty of Surjí Anjengaom, Daolat Ráo ceded to the British Government and its allies his territory between the Jumna and Ganges, and all situated to the northward of Jaipúr, Jodhpúr, and Góhad; the forts of Ahmadnagar and Bharoch and their districts; his possessions between the Ajunta Ghât and the Godavery. He renounced all his claims on the Mogul emperor, on the Peshwa, the Nizam, and the Gáikwár, as well as on the Rájás who had assisted the British, and whom he declared independent of his authority. There were other minor conditions which it is scarcely necessary to enumerate.

One article, however, must be stated. It was left optional to Daolat Ráo to become a party to the defensive alliance, receiving a subsidiary force, to be paid from the revenues of the territories already ceded. Daolat Ráo eventually agreed to this, and on February 27, 1804, a new treaty was drawn up at Burhanpúr, by which Daolat Ráo agreed to subscribe to the defensive alliance, and to permit the cantoning, near his boundary, but within British territory, of a subsidiary force of six thousand infantry. But the conditions of this second treaty were not acted upon.

It was, indeed, not the intention of Daolat Ráo that the conditions of the treaty of Surjí Anjengaom should be considered as binding on him for ever. And a circumstance occurred early in the following year which gave him great hopes of being able to shake it off altogether. On April 16, 1804, the Marquess Wellesley, unable to obtain any satisfactory assurance from Holkar, declared war against that chief. Notwithstanding Colonel Monson's mishap, Holkar was reduced, in the course of the campaign that followed, almost to extremities, when Daolat Ráo, instigated by his minister Ghatgay, expressed his determination to aid him. He preceded any overt demonstrations in his favour, however, by seizing the person of Mr. Jenkins, the acting British resident in his camp, and plundering his property. And although the Governor-General accepted the excuses made by Daolat Ráo for this outrage, the latter did not relax his preparations, but actually received in his camp Jeswant Ráo and other chiefs then fighting against the English. This act was looked upon by the British general as an act of hostility, and he advanced against Sindhia. But the two chiefs retreated to Ajmír. Here their hereditary rivalry broke out again, and Daolat Ráo found means to reconcile himself with the Governor-General. One good effect of the temporary union was the dismissal of the minister Ghatgay. He was succeeded by Ambají Inglia, a man more inclined to cautious and prudent counsels.

The replacement of the illustrious Marquess Wellesley by Lord Cornwallis at this conjuncture gave Daolat Ráo the opportunity of altering the treaty of Surjí Anjengaom to his own advantage. He had violated it in many particulars. Amongst other infractions he had retained Góhad and Gwáliár, he had allied himself with a chief in arms against the English, he had not respected the sacred character of an envoy. But Lord Cornwallis was pre-

PART II.

pared to overlook these errors committed by a prince smarting under defeat. He accordingly agreed to negotiate a new treaty on more liberal terms. By virtue of this, signed at Allahábád on November 23, 1805, Gwáliár and Góhad were ceded to Sindhia, the Chambal was constituted the northern boundary of his territory; the British Government bound itself not to make treaties with Údaipúr, Jodhpúr, Kotá, or any chiefs tributary to Sindhia or Málwá, Méwár, or Márwár, or to interfere in any arrangements he might make regarding them; it likewise granted to Daolat Ráo, his wife and daughter, a pension and jaghírs. He, on his part, relinquished the pension of fifteen lakhs of rupees granted to certain officers in his service, and resigned the main districts of Dholpúr, Barí, and Rájkerrah, reserved to him by the first treaty. He promised never to re-admit into his service the ex-minister Ghatgay. Such were the main provisions of the treaty; in other essential points the stipulations of the treaty of Surjí Anjengaom were adhered to. Though peace was thus restored to the dominions of Daolat Ráo, it by no means followed that it should be accompanied by internal tranquillity. And, in fact, the contrary was almost always the case. Daolat Ráo spent upon his army far greater sums than the revenues of the country could afford. To meet these constantly increasing expenses he had recourse to a system than which a worse could scarcely be devised. He sent his troops out into the districts to feed themselves on what they might wring from the ryots. The system of Napoleon, that of making war support war, has been often and justly blamed. But he at least made the inhabitants of the enemy's country pay for his victorious soldiers. Daolat Ráo made military rapine one of the principles of the administration of his own country. The result is thus recorded by Captain Grant Duff: 'Armies accustomed to rapine and violence in extensive regions were now,' he writes, 'confined to tracts comparatively small; the burden of their exactions became in many places intolerable, and districts, before cultivated and populous, were fast running to waste and violence.'

It can readily be imagined that the revenues of the country suffered in proportion. With every year they diminished. As for Daolat Ráo himself, the only reliable source of private income he possessed arose from the pension and jaghírs granted to him and to his family by the British Government. But even with that, so frequently was he embarrassed, that he was forced to take advances—at a ruinous rate of interest—from the bankers of the country.

The same cause, impecuniosity, probably prevented Daolat Ráo from taking advantage of the humiliation of Holkar by the British power, and of the consequent weakness of his dominions; nor can it be doubted that for many years that followed it was mainly instrumental in keeping him on terms of peace with his former conquerors.

When, however, it became necessary for the Government of India, in 1817, to deal with the Pindárís, a great temptation seemed to offer itself to the restless spirit of Daolat Ráo. The Pindárís had been the hangers-on of the Márhátá camps during all the wars in the latter half of the eighteenth century. It is true they had plundered as well as fought; probably indeed plundered more than fought. But to Sindhia they looked up as to their natural protector and liege lord. Strong in their own numbers, with his support they thought they must be irresistible. These, and other reasons at least as potent, were urged upon Daolat Ráo. He was very much inclined to give way. He would, indeed, have given way but for the prescience of the Marquis of Hastings, who, informed of his hesitation, promptly placed the British troops in such a commanding position as to force him to an immediate decision. He had grown too wise by experience to doubt, then. On November 5, 1817, he signed a treaty

PART II.

by which he agreed to locate his troops in positions from which they were not to emerge without the orders of the British Government; to give up the fortresses of Assírgarh and Hindia as security for the lines of communication and a guarantee for the performance of his engagements, and to surrender for three years the tribute of the Rájpút states.

But Daolat Ráo had been hesitating regarding other matters likewise. About this time the Peshwa had been endeavouring to resuscitate the old Márhátá confederacy, That Daolat Ráo, though he dared make no open demonstration in his favour, favoured secretly his plans, was proved by the fact that on the capture of his fortress of Assírgarh by the British on April 9, 1819, a letter was found in the possession of the Killadar directing him to obey all the orders of the Peshwa, at the time at war with the British. The penalty inflicted for this breach of faith was the permanent cession of the fortress to the English. The year prior to this discovery, Daolat Ráo had, by treaty (dated June 25, 1818) readjusted the boundaries of his dominions with the English, he resigning Ajmír and other districts, in exchange for lands of equal value.

Daolat Ráo survived the fall of the Peshwa (June 1818) nearly nine years—years of peace, but for him scarcely of prosperity. He died on March 21, 1827, at the comparatively early age of forty-eight. He had had a stormy and chequered career. The great projects of his predecessor had been scattered to the winds. Still he had fared better than his master, the Peshwa, better even than Holkar. He had, in fact, been preserved by the British power, in spite, as it were, of himself. Twice had he been thus saved. In 1805, the replacement of Marquess Wellesley by Lord Cornwallis secured to him peaceful possession of Gwáliár and Góhad, which he had seized, and with which he would not have parted without a severe struggle; in 1817, the occupa-

CHAP. I.

tion of his country by the orders of the Marquis of Hastings, preserved him from casting in his lot with the Pindárís. It was to these acts of his enemies, far more than to any statesmanlike policy and political foresight of his own, that he left behind him territories capable of realising a revenue, under proper management, of nearly a million and a half sterling. His dominions, in fact, remained at his death almost in the same state in which they had been left by the treaty of 1805. The acquisitions made from him by the British Government comprised the principal part of the Delta of the Ganges and Jamna, from the source of the latter river to near its confluence with the former. They included the city of Delhi, which, however, with a tract of country round it, was continued under the nominal authority of the titular emperor, the real authority being vested in the British Resident.[1]

Daolat Ráo left no son. Seeing that he had no prospect of offspring, he sent to the Dekhan, shortly before his death, for the children of some distant relations, that he might select one from amongst them. The candidates, five in number, not arriving at Gwáliár till after his death, the right of selection devolved upon his widow, Baiza Bai, daughter of the infamous Ghatgay, and who then filled the office of regent. She selected Múgat Ráo, a distant relative, eleven years old. The ceremony of adoption took place on June 17, 1827, and the boy was married the same day to the granddaughter of Daolat Ráo, by his daughter married to Dhubárí Ráo, Sénápatí.[1] The following day he was placed on the throne, under the auspices of the British Government, with the title of Ali Jah Jankojí Ráo, Sindhia.

Jankoji Ráo Sindhia.

The reign of this prince, which lasted over a period of sixteen years, was characterised by peace with his neighbours and turbulence within his own borders. In his early youth, and for ten years after his accession, the

[1] *Historical Sketch of the Princes of India.*

PART II.

ambition of his predecessor's widow, the Baiza Bai, caused him and his country endless trouble and annoyance. This lady began very soon to show that she intended to be the real ruler. Her late husband, she asserted, had nominated her to be regent during her entire lifetime. With a spirit worthy of the daughter of Ghatgay she began at once to put her plans into operation.

It must be admitted that the conduct of the British Government with respect to her claims was such as to encourage them. It declined to interfere beyond insisting that the Máhárájá's seal should be always used in official communications. It made no effort to provide for the future good government of the country by instilling right principles into the mind of the young prince, nor did it even insist that he should receive any education at all. As a consequence he remained uneducated.

Thus left to their own devices it is easy to understand how the stronger mind of the experienced woman triumphed over the youth and inexperience of the never strong-minded boy. For the moment the Baiza Bai gained the day. And, had she been endowed with good judgment and sense, she might have kept her position till her death. But she was the worthy daughter of Ghatgay, as unscrupulous, as ambitious, as headstrong, and as impulsive as he had been. Instead of consolidating her position by governing the country in such a manner as to gain the confidence of the people—instead of endeavouring to win the confidence of her ward—she oppressed the former, and she kept the latter in a seclusion which resembled confinement. Vain were his remonstrances. The Baiza Bai was jealous of his possible influence, and made him feel that she was so.

To such a mode of procedure there could be only one result. Scarcely had the young prince attained the age of sixteen than (October 1832) he fled from the palace, and took refuge with the British Resident.

CHAP. I.

In December of the same year, the Governor-General, Lord William Bentinck, paid a visit to Gwáliár. Before he arrived the Baiza Bai had become reconciled to the young Máhárájá, but the terms on which they lived had not improved. For her, then, the advent of the Governor-General was an event of great importance. He might side with her, or he might side with her ward. The efforts made by both parties to influence the Governor-General were incredible. But they found him impassive. He was apparently willing to recognise the Baiza Bai, so long as she did not attempt to interfere with the future rights of the Máhárájá. To all the solicitations of the latter he replied, therefore, that it was impossible for him to interfere, but that if the Máhárájá would abstain from all attempts to subvert the Baiza Bai's power, the British Government would prevent the regent adopting any other person, to the prejudice of his claim to the throne.

This negative policy satisfied nobody. Within seven months, then, of the departure of the Governor-General, the Máhárájá again left the palace, and took refuge at the residency; and although, by the Resident's persuasion, he was induced to return to the palace, the news of the step he had taken encouraged those who were discontented with the rule of the Baiza Bai to attempt a *pronunciamento* in his favour.

In point of fact, the Baiza Bai's rule had become so unpopular in the country, that the nobles and the people only wanted an excuse to rise against her. This excuse the conduct of the Máhárájá afforded. The day following his flight from and return to the palace, almost all the troops at Gwáliár rose in revolt against the Baiza Bai, and shouted for Jankojí Ráo. The Rání, alarmed, attempted to escape, but her flight having been intercepted, she in her turn took refuge at the residency. Here, however, she was allowed to remain only on the condition that she would resign the sovereignty and quit the country. She was forced to agree, and quitted Gwáliár for Dhol-

PART II. púr on July 13. The Máhárájá had been proclaimed sovereign at Gwáliár three days previously.

The proceedings of the Resident did not altogether meet the approval of Lord William Bentinck. He was censured for having called out the contingent to support the Máhárájá's authority, and the Government of India declared its indifference as to whether the Máhárájá or the Bai exercised the administrative power, its only object being to preserve general tranquillity and its own reputation, recognising the ruler supported by the popular voice. In accordance with this view, whilst the Government of India forbade the Baiza Bai to use her asylum in the British territory for the purpose of organising an invasion of Gwáliár, it placed no obstacle whatever in the way of the return of that lady to Gwáliár with the view of throwing herself upon the support of her own people.

Thenceforth, however, the Baiza Baí had no connection with the administration of Gwáliár, although she troubled the actual rulers in the vexatious manner of which an intriguing woman, in command of a large amount of money, is so well capable. But in the end, seeing every hope vanish, she renounced her ambitious views, and was allowed to return to Gwáliár, where she died in 1862.

Jankojí Sindhia was a weak ruler. During the greater part of his reign the administration was in the hands of his maternal uncle, Mámáh Sahib. But, to quote the words of Mr. Aitchison[1]: 'The court was one constant scene of feuds and struggles for power amongst the nobles; the army was in a chronic state of mutiny. The weakness of the internal government prepared the way for the hostilities with the British Government, which broke out shortly after the Máhárájá's death, and resulted in an entire change of policy towards the Gwáliár State.'

[1] Aitchison's *Treaties*, vol. iv. p. 208.

I have already stated that the reign of Jankojí was undisturbed by war. In fact the only two matters which connect his reign with foreign governments were the organisation of the contingent and the rounding of the borders of his territory by exchanges.

The reform of the contingent took place in the year 1837. Consisting originally, according to the treaty of 1817, of 5,000 horse, and reduced after the termination of the war to 2,000, it was resolved in 1837 to establish it on the footing of a regiment of cavalry, one of infantry, and a company of artillery, commanded by European officers. To induce Jankojí to agree to this arrangement, it was resolved to restore to him the districts in Khándesh which had been made over temporarily to the British Government, Sindhia paying in lieu a sum equivalent to their net revenues. The expenses of the contingent were defrayed in part from those revenues, in part from the revenues of the retained Ságar districts, and the tributes from the Rájpút states, formerly due to Sindhia.

Jankojí had no male children. In 1837, however, an attempt was made to substitute a male child for a female, to which his wife had just given birth. But the attempt coming to the knowledge of the Rájá, it naturally miscarried. On the death of his wife the year following, he married her sister, Tara Bai, then little more than a child, the daughter of Jeswant Ráo Gúrpóra.

In general matters the government of Jankojí showed itself eminently desirous to keep on good terms with the British Government. He gave every encouragement to the endeavours made by that Government to suppress Thagí and highway robbery—till then extremely prevalent; and he arranged for the trial and punishment within his own dominions of the prisoners charged and convicted. In 1838, when a mission from Nipál, supposed to entertain intentions hostile to the British Government, came to Gwáliár, its members were arrested and sent back. Similarly in 1839, he arrested and placed at the

PART II.

disposal of the British Resident an envoy from Dóst Mahomed, ruler of Afghanistán.

In January 1840, Jankojí received a visit from the then Governor-General, the Earl of Auckland. It was merely a complimentary visit, but at an Asiatic court such modes of showing honour are highly esteemed.

Just three years later—February 7, 1843—Jankojí Sindhia died. It will be seen from the sketch I have given of his life, that, at the best, his was a negative character. He did not possess one tittle of the genius of Mádhají, nor was he endowed even with the boldness and daring of his immediate predecessor. He took but little part in the government of the country. He was in that respect little more than a lay figure. His death, at the early age of twenty-seven, was certainly due neither to excess of work, to excess of horse exercise, nor to intellectual study.

The death of Jankojí without an heir, and without having adopted an heir, left the throne once more open to the intrigues of interested parties. But on this occasion the sound principle was adhered to of adopting the nearest relation. This nearest, though distant relation, was Bagírat Ráo, son of Hanwant Ráo, usually called Bábájí Sindhia, and he was only eight years old. The adoption made by the widow, Tara Bai, with the assent of the great nobles, was approved of by the British Government. But it then became necessary to appoint a regent. Now the prime minister at the time of the death of Jankojí, and indeed for several years previously, had been the Rájá's maternal uncle, Mámáh Sahib. Of him the British Resident had reported only two years previously, that he was 'the most capable of the ministers of state,' and 'certainly the person of most influence at present.' It is true the Resident had somewhat qualified this testimony to the merits of the Mámáh Sahib by an insinuation that he owed the retention of his position to the absolute confidence reposed in him by his master, 'for,' he adds, alluding to the influence, 'I am of opinion that it is likely to terminate with his nephew's, the Máhárájá's, existence.' But when, on the demise of the Máhárájá, this second part of the Resident's report appeared to be falsified by the selection of this very Mámáh Sahib by the chiefs present at Gwáliár to be sole regent, and the Resident reported that this selection had given universal satisfaction, the British Government could not but signify their approval.

But a few months showed that, in his report of two years before, the Resident had rightly divined that the influence of the Mámáh Sahib was bound up with the existence of the late sovereign. For three months, indeed, if we may except the revolt of one battalion, speedily suppressed, all was quiet. But intrigue had not the less been at work. It was impossible, with a young widow bent on power, it should have been otherwise. Either women in such a position will find men weak enough to bend to their vices, or there will be men ambitious and unscrupulous enough to make tools of the women. The intrigue in this case formed no exception to the rule.

There happened to be a woman in the palace, possessed, or believed to be possessed, of great influence with Tara Bai, named Morengi. This woman had struck up an intimate friendship with Dádá Khásjí-wála, a man who had been appointed controller of the palace under the Mámáh Sahib. The 'friendship' was soon suspected to cover a dangerous intrigue, and the woman was removed. But Dádá Khásjí-wála's movements still continued to excite suspicion. Mámáh Sahib reported his conduct to the Resident, and, going further, taxed the Dádá in person with want of loyalty. The latter assumed an air of virtuous indignation, denied the charge, and courted inquiry. Nothing could then be proved against him. But soon the object of his machinations became apparent. He assumed a haughtier tone. He openly bearded the regent. Suddenly, when the pear was ripe,

PART II. the widowed Ráni, Tara Bai, expressed to the British Resident her determination to dismiss the Mámáh Sahib from office.

From subsequent events it appeared that she had been made to believe that the Mámáh Sahib, whose daughter had been married to the Máhárájá, intended entirely to supersede her authority.

The British Resident remonstrated, but to no purpose. Mámáh Sahib, whose friends fell from him, as though he were infectious, on the news of his disgrace, was dismissed, and fled from Gwáliár. The Dádá Khásjí-wála became minister in his place.

The remarks made by the Governor-General at this crisis deserve to be quoted for the good sense they display. The Mámáh Sahib, he recorded, was clearly an incapable, who 'had proved himself quite unfit to manage men or women, and a minister of Gwáliár must manage both.' Lord Ellenborough saw no great offence to the British Government in the removal from office of a minister so incapable, nor did he wish to force upon the state an unpopular regent. 'Any form of administering the affairs of the Gwáliár State which may effect the object of frontier tranquillity will be satisfactory,' he wrote, 'to the British Government.'

It will thus be clear that the expulsion of the Mámáh Sahib and the installation in his place of the Dádá constituted no offence to the British Government. Such offence could only be created by divergence on the part of the Dádá from the peaceful foreign policy pursued by the government of Sindhia subsequent to the year 1819.

Unfortunately for himself, the Dádá did make that divergence. Probably having been installed by the favour of the army, he deemed it absolutely essential to keep the troops in a good humour and in a state of devotion to himself. The specific so successfully practised at Satory in 1850-51—the specific of 'sausages and champagne'—had not then been invented, nor probably would it have been quite suited to an eastern hemisphere. He was forced then upon a dangerous course. The army had forgotten Assaye and scarcely remembered Láswárí. A new race had grown up, a race into whose ears the triumphs of Mádhají, and the commanding position of Daolat Ráo had been sung from their earliest childhood. These men thirsted for action, and the Dádá soon found that to retain their confidence it would be necessary to fan their hopes.

With this object he in a short time dismissed from the army, even with ignominy, all those officers who were favourable to the British, replacing them by the scum of Márhátá society—men who were ready for plunder and pillage at any price. Large presents of money were made to the soldiery, and they were gradually brought to a state of indiscipline bordering on revolt.

But to escape one danger the Dádá had provoked another. The British Government could not at any time have tolerated a mutinous and hostile power—for its hostility was undisguised—within fifty miles of Agra. Still less was it possible for it to tolerate the existence of such an army, when another mutinous body of soldiers, the soldiers of the Punjâb, threatened its northern boundary. Lord Ellenborough, however, was averse from severe measures. The mischief seemed to have been caused by one man, the Dádá Khásjí-wála, and he not unreasonably hoped that with the removal of the Dádá it would disappear. The better to bring about this result, an officer in whom Lord Ellenborough had entire confidence, Colonel Sleeman, was appointed Resident at Gwáliár.

The report of Colonel Sleeman confirmed the pre-existing opinion that the Dádá was at the root of the mischief. He described him as turbulent, restless, and intriguing; an enemy of public order, and a fomenter of troubles with his neighbours; at the same time so deficient in personal courage, that it was his habit, in moments of difficulty, 'to conceal himself in the most sacred of the female apartments.'

PART II.

This report decided the Government. It determined to remove Dádá Khásjí-wála from Gwáliár to a place of security within its own territories. To give force to its orders, it directed the assembly at Agra of an army of exercise.

But before the British Government could take any action in the matter, affairs had come to a crisis in Gwáliár. The conservative party in the army, representing the views of those favourable to an alliance with the British, suddenly reasserted their position, and called for the dismissal of the obnoxious Dádá, as the cause of all the evil. The Dádá, to suppress this revolt, as he termed it, sent against the insurgents the troops who remained faithful to himself. But these were beaten, and the Dádá himself was seized. After some discussion he was sent off, under an escort, to the British camp at Agra. But either the escort was merciful, or the Dádá was profuse in his promises; he was allowed to return.

After his return the Gwáliár Durbar made one effort to procure permission for the confinement of the Dádá within the Gwáliár territories. But Colonel Sleeman was inexorable. Either, he said, the Dádá must be surrendered, or British troops would march on Gwáliár.

Still the Durbar hesitated, and the British troops accordingly broke ground. But it was not until the close approach of the Governor-General at the head of an army showed the impossibility of retaining the Dádá, that he was surrendered.

But by that time, the British army had advanced too far to recede without obtaining a guarantee against the recurrence of such a danger. It continued then to move forward, the Governor-General intimating to the Durbar his wish to settle matters at a personal interview between Tara Bai and the Máhárájá on the one side and himself on the other.

This interview was fixed for December 26. But the intelligence was extremely distasteful to the Gwáliár army. They determined then to fight for it. Massing the great body of their troops near the village of Máhárájpúr, they took the Commander-in-Chief, Sir Hugh Gough, by surprise, on the 28th, whilst a smaller detachment made a similar demonstration against the disjointed wing of the British army, under General Gray.

But it would not do. The Gwáliár troops fought well; they had everything in their favour; they inflicted on us considerable loss, but they were beaten; and Gwáliár lay at the feet of Lord Ellenborough.

The way in which this nobleman dealt with the prostrate State will always be quoted as a masterpiece of policy. He made a friend of it—a friend who stood the English in good stead during their troubles fourteen years later. By a treaty concluded on January 13, 1844, the sovereignty of the country was retained for Sindhia; the government during the minority of the Rájá was to be conducted according to the advice of the British Resident; the British Government pledged itself to maintain the just territorial rights of Gwáliár; a territory yielding eighteen lakhs a year was to be ceded to the British Government for the maintenance of a contingent force, and other lands for the payment of debts due, and the expenses of the war; and the army was to be reduced to 6,000 cavalry, 3,000 infantry, and 200 gunners with 32 guns.

This arrangement ensured peace, an improved administrative system, and gratitude. From 1844 to 1857 the history of Gwáliár was a history of peace and prosperity. In 1854 the young Máhárájá Alijáh Jaiají Ráo Sindhia became of age, and assumed the administration. Nor throughout the entire period were there the smallest symptoms of any disturbance of the political horizon.

Jaiají Ráo Sindhia.

But in 1857 the Bengal army mutinied. The prime minister of Jaiají Ráo, for four years previous to the outbreak, had been a Brahman, named Dinkar Ráo, one of the most honest, most far-seeing, and most capable men that Central India has ever produced. In his brief tenure of office he had introduced large and beneficial reforms in the internal administration of the country, had swept away numberless abuses, and had made life comparatively easy for the cultivator of the soil. In effecting these reforms it would have been impossible for him not to have given some offence to a few of the ambitious families whose folly had fourteen years before pushed Dádá Khásjí-wála to defy the British. But in a time of peace and prosperity the machinations of such men were powerless.

But the rumbling of the coming mutiny had not been unfelt in Gwáliár. It had given hope to the disaffected, and filled the minds of the aristocracy with ambitious ideas. But there were at least two men in that state free from the prevailing madness. These men were the Máhárájá, Jaiají Ráo, and his able minister.

From the very first, with the full concurrence and support of that minister, Jaiají Ráo determined to cast in his lot with the British. Not in vain had Lord Ellenborough, in 1844, displayed the prescient policy of a real statesman. Not in vain had he forborne from the lust of conquest, and restored to the minor sovereign intact his dominions, with a provision to secure their good administration during his minority. With an opportunity which Mádhají would have made decisive, which Daolat Ráo even would have clutched at, Jaiají Ráo took upon himself the task, which, under the circumstances of the feeling of the country, must have been pre-eminently difficult—the task of being loyal to his engagements to the British, even when British supremacy seemed lowered, and British authority had been shaken off in districts within fifty miles of his capital.

Full of these loyal ideas, Jaiají Rao's first movement was to send his own bodyguard to Agra to aid the Lieutenant-Governor of the North-West Provinces in the suppression of the revolt.[1] They rendered excellent ser-

[1] *Red Pamphlet*, Part II. pp. 192-3.

vice. His next was to place his entire contingent at the disposal of the same high officer. The offer was accepted. But it soon became evident that the causes which had induced the mutiny in the Bengal army had infected the sepoys of the Gwáliár contingent with the virus of revolt. At Hatrás, at Nímach, at Augar, at Lalatpúr, and finally on June 14, at Gwáliár itself, the sepoys of the contingent rose and massacred many of their British officers.

No sooner had these men revolted than they placed their services at the disposal of Jaiají Ráo, and begged him to lead them against the British in Agra. To give due credit to the loyalty of Jaiají Ráo Sindhia at this crisis it should be remembered that not only were the insurgents in possession of the capital of the Moguls, but the entire country to the north-west of Agra was in revolt. British garrisons were beleaguered at Káhnpúr and at Lakhnau, and it seemed as though one decisive blow would finish with the English dominion north of Bengal proper. Had the Máhárájá, then, acceded to the request of the sepoys, it was quite possible that with the 20,000 trained soldiers, men who afterwards gave evidence of the excellence of their discipline against General Wyndham at Káhnpúr, and against Lord Strathnairn after Jhánsí, he might have struck that fatal blow.

To say that he must have felt his power, is only to credit him with ordinary capacity, and his capacity is at least beyond the average. But he was loyal and true. Had the ablest member of the Council of India been at his ear he could not have inspired him with counsels more calculated to prove beneficial to the British cause than those which he and his minister, with the instinct of loyal natures, followed of their own free will.

Not only did the Máhárájá not accept the offer of his troops, but by dint of skilful management, by cajoling and by gifts of money, by pretended difficulties in the way of procuring carriage, he detained them. More than that,

PART II. when mutinous troops from Mau and the territories of Holkar passed through his dominions, he restrained his own troops from joining them. He succeeded, in fact, in retaining them in inaction till after Delhi had fallen, and Káhnpúr had been relieved. And when finally he did let them go, it was only that they might fall into the clutches of Sir Hugh Rose and Sir Colin Campbell.

It can easily be imagined that the loyalty of Jaiají Ráo to the British alliance had not made him popular with that large and augmenting class of self-seekers which the mutiny had called into existence. It was not long before the hostile feelings of these men were manifested. When in June 1858, the rebel troops under Tantia Tópí entered Gwálíár, not only had the power of the Máhárájá to restrain his own men vanished entirely, but these made common cause against him, and forced him and his minister to flee for British protection to Agra. He was restored in the course of the same month by Sir Hugh Rose.

The loyalty of Jaiají Ráo to the British Government did not pass unnoticed. His conduct, indeed, had been so pre-eminently faithful that nothing could have excused its being passed over. By a treaty dated December 12, 1860, lands were restored to Sindhia yielding three lakhs of rupees a year; and the exchange of lands he wished for for others of nearly equal value was arranged with the British Government. He received a sunnud conferring upon him the right of adoption, and permission to raise his infantry from 3,000 to 5,000 men, and his guns from 32 to 36. In place of the revolted contingent the British Government agreed to maintain a subsidiary force.

Subsequently the name of Jaiají Sindhia appeared in the first list of the Knights of the Star of India.

Since 1859 Jaiají Ráo has been his own prime minister. He has administered the country himself. His former minister, now Sir Dinkar Ráo, lives mainly at Agra, in which city his son is receiving the education of an English gentleman. CHAP. I.

It is strange that, like all his predecessors, without one exception, Jaiají Ráo Sindhia has no legitimate male descendant. He has had three sons, but they died. He possesses the power of adoption, and this power he exercised in November 1865, by the selection of a youth named Ganpat Ráo to be his successor. It has, however, been stipulated that in the event of his being blessed with offspring, his own son shall succeed him, Ganpat Ráo being provided with an estate returning an annual income of a lakh of rupees.

Of the revenues of the country 78,38,900 rupees are derived from the land; 14,70,202 from customs; the remainder from the tributes of feudatories. The customs' revenue is realised from transit duties on iron, tobacco, sugar, and salt, all other articles being free, and from jaghír and local taxes. No transit duties are taken on the portion of the Agra and Bombay road and its branches passing through Sindhia's territories, or on the roads connecting Gwáliar with Itáwah, Farrukhabád, Datiá, Jhansí, and Kalpí.[1]

The Máhárájá of Gwáliár receives a salute of nineteen guns. His territories may be described generally as being bounded on the north and north-west by the river Chambal; on the east by Bundelkhand and the central provinces; on the north by Bhopál and Dhár; and on the west by Dholpúr, Karaulí, Údaipúr, and Kotá.

[1] Aitchison's *Treaties*.

CHAPTER II.

INDÚR, OR THE DOMINIONS OF HOLKAR.

AREA—8,318 sq miles. POPULATION—576,000.
REVENUE—30,00,000 rupees.

PART II.

THE father of Mulhar Ráo, the founder of the dynasty of the Holkars, was a shepherd. To this occupation he added the more profitable trade of a weaver of blankets. He lived in the village of Hol, on the river Níra, whence he derived the surname Holkar—the adjunct kae or kur signifying inhabitant.

Mulhar Ráo first saw light about the year 1693. His father died when he was five years old, and his mother went shortly afterwards to live with her brother, a landholder in Khándesh. Mulhar Ráo was brought up as a shepherd, but soon disdaining the slothful life, he determined to devote himself to arms, and enlisted in a troop of horse, then on their way to Gujrát. He soon distinguished himself, and, it is said, in one of his first engagements, had the good fortune to slay with his own hand an officer of rank in the enemy's service. For this he obtained the command of twenty-five horsemen. Whilst on duty with this body of men on the family estate of his leader, Kantají Kadam, a party of the Peshwa's horse, on their way to Málwá, attempted to pass over the lands belonging to it. Mulhar Ráo disputed their passage, and displayed so much courage as to attract the notice of the Peshwa, who persuaded him to enter his service as commander of 500 men. This transfer was made with the consent of Kantají Kadam, and Mulhar Ráo showed his obligations to that family by adopting their colours as his own.

Mulhar Ráo appears to have joined the army of the Peshwa about the year 1724. Starting as the leader of

500 horse, he, in four years, raised himself to a far higher position. In 1728 he received from the Peshwa, as a reward for his services, a grant of twelve districts north of the Narbadá; in 1731 twenty districts were added to these, and at the same time the Peshwa, in a letter written with his own hand, confided the Márhátá interests in Málwá to his charge. The following year he filled the post of principal general under the Peshwa when the army of Dia Bahadúr, Subadar of the province of Málwá, was defeated by the Márhátás. Indúr, with the greater portion of the conquered country, was assigned to Mulhar Ráo for the support of his troops, and in 1735 he was left as general-in-chief of the Márhátá forces north of the Narbadá. In 1738 we find him the most daring assailant of the Mogul army under Nizám-úl-Múlk, and conducting to a favourable conclusion a warfare which confirmed to the Márhátás the sovereignty of the country between the Narbadá and the Chambal.

In 1739 he assisted at the expulsion of the Portuguese from Bassein—an enterprise which cost the besiegers, it is said, 500 men. He then rejoined the Peshwa to defend his territories against the threatened onslaught of Nadir Shah. But this never took place.

In the eleven years that followed, Mulhar Ráo continued to increase his fame and his possessions. In this interval he never met with a single check, and this continued success no doubt served to encourage the ambitious designs which gradually forced themselves upon him, and which, it seemed to him, could be crowned only by the replacement at Delhi of the Moguls by the Márhátás.

With this object in view, we find him in 1751 assisting the Vizír Safdar Jang in preserving Oudh from the Rohillas. In this war he greatly added to his reputation as a leader. The mode in which on one occasion he succeeded with a small body of troops in a night attack on the masses of the enemy is thus recorded by Sir John Malcolm: 'He directed torches and lights to be tied to the horns of several thousand cattle, which were driven in one direction, while in another he placed lights upon every bush and tree, and, when this was done, marched silently in the dark by a different route to attack. The enemy, pressed in one quarter by an actual assault, and seeing lights in several others, thought themselves surrounded and in danger of destruction; they dispersed and fled in dismay, leaving their camp to be plundered by the conquerors, whose leader acquired just increase of fame from the victory.'

For his conduct in this campaign, Holkar received a grant of twelve and a half per cent. on the revenues of Chandúr, and honours in addition.

At Pánipat Mulhar Ráo divided with Sindhia the command of the right wing of the Márhátá army. Prior to that battle he had been treated with the greatest indignity and insult by the commander-in-chief, Sudaséo Ráo. Again and again had Sudaséo spurned the advice offered him by the practised warrior. 'Who wants the advice of a goatherd?' was the reception given to these wise counsels. In one of the skirmishes, or rather battles of a secondary rank, on his way to join the headquarter camp, Mulhar Ráo had been surprised and defeated, but this had not prevented his junction with the main body, nor had it held him back from inflicting in subsequent skirmishes great losses on the enemy. He had advised Sudaséo to adhere to Márhátá tactics, to retreat, to draw the heavy-armed enemy after him, then suddenly to overwhelm him. The advice, as I have said, was scornfully rejected. The result was that on January 6, 1761, the Márhátá power, was dealt an almost fatal blow on the field of Pánipat.

It has been asserted that in that fatal battle Mulhar Ráo did not fight with his old spirit, and that he left the field early in the day. He did not, it is certain, exhaust all the powers of his men. He kept something in hand in case of an overthrow. But his partisans assert that he did this because he believed defeat to be certain, and that he kept a portion of his troops in reserve to cover the retreat of the remainder. It is certain that he alone, of all the Márhátá leaders, retired with some amount of order.

CHAP. II.

After Pánipat Mulhar Ráo retired to his possessions in Central India, and employed himself in reducing his vast acquisitions to coherence and order. In this he succeeded well, for he was a man of generous instincts, considerate, yet firm, and these qualities ensured his popularity amongst his people. He died in 1765, at the ripe age of seventy-six, leaving a name amongst the Márhátás which, even now, stands second only to that of Mádhají Ráo Sindhia, and second to him only in the science of politics. He left behind him a principality bringing in an annual gross revenue of 75,00,000 rupees.

Mulhar Ráo Holkar had had but one son, Khandí Ráo, who was killed at the siege of Khumbír, near Díg, some years before Pánipat. But Khandí left behind him by his wife, Ahalya Bai, a son named Málí Ráo. This boy, however, who showed symptoms akin to madness, did not survive his grandfather more than nine months. The administration was then assumed by Ahalya Bai.

Ahalya Bai.

The rule of this estimable lady, which lasted thirty years, was not, however, established without some opposition. The scheming Ragonáth Ráo, uncle to the then Peshwa, and afterwards Peshwa himself, used all the means in his power to procure the adoption of a child whose movements, by means of his agents, he might always control. But in this attempt he was defeated not less by the firmness and prudence of Ahalya Bai, than by the stedfast attitude assumed by Mádhají Sindhia, who, aided by other Márhátá chiefs and the Peshwa himself, declared himself determined to support the legitimate rights of the widow of Mulhar Ráo's son.

Thus firmly established, the first act of Ahalya Bai was to select a commander-in-chief of her forces. It need not be said that in those days, when the principle was

PART II.

universally recognised that power was to him who wielded the sword, this was a task which called for the nicest discrimination of character. Ahalya Bai proved that she was endowed with that discrimination. Her choice fell upon Túkají Holkar, a man of the same tribe, but not related to her husband's family. He was a man of mature years, unobtrusive and unambitious, whose character was formed, and who had won the respect of all parties. A better choice could not have been made. Bound together by feelings of mutual respect and mutual esteem, Ahalya Bai and Túkají conducted the affairs of the state for thirty years—thirty years of happiness and prosperity for the people, such as they had never known before and have but rarely known since.

The mode in which this 'coalition government' was conducted has been thus described by Sir John Malcolm: 'When Túkají was in the Dekhan,' he writes, 'all the territories of the family south of the Satpúra range were managed by him, and the countries north of that limit were under Ahalya Bai, to whom the different tributaries also made their annual payments. While he was in Hindostan he collected the revenues of the territories that had been acquired there and in Bundelkhand, and also the tributes of Rájpútáná. The districts in Málwá and Nimár continued as usual under the direction of Ahalya Bai; and her authority was on such occasions extended over the possessions in the Dekhan. The treasures of the family, which were very considerable, remained with Ahalya Bai; and she had besides personal estates yielding annually four lakhs of rupees, which, with the hoard above mentioned, were entirely expended at her discretion, while all the rest of the receipts were brought into a general account, and applied to the expenditure of the government. The accounts of receipts and disbursements were kept with scrupulous exactness; and Ahalya Bai, after paying the civil and militia charges, sent the balance that remained in the public treasury to supply the exigencies of the army employed abroad.'

It would appear, moreover, from the same writer, that wherever he might be, Túkají always referred, on every occasion in which the general interests of the country were implicated, to Ahalya Bai, and that the ministers at the several foreign courts were deputed directly from her.

During thirty years of rule perhaps no prince or princess ever conciliated more respect from foreign sovereigns than did this illustrious Hindú lady. She was extremely pious, much given to devotion, yet she fouud time to attend to the important affairs of state which pressed themselves daily on her attention. It was her habit to transact business every day in open durbar. 'Her first principle of government,' says Sir John Malcolm, 'appears to have been moderate assessment, and an almost sacred respect for the native rights of village officers and the proprietors of lands. She heard every complaint in person; and although she continually referred causes to courts of equity and arbitration, and to her ministers for settlement, she was always accessible; and so strong was her sense of duty on all points connected with the distribution of justice, that she is represented as not only patient, but unwearied in the investigation of the most insignificant causes where appeals were made to her decision.'

Her hours for transacting business were from 2 P.M. to 6 P.M., and again from 9 P.M. to 11 P.M. By her unremitting attention to business she was able during her long reign to maintain such excellent relátions with her neighbours that her dominions were but once invaded, and then unsuccessfully. Nor was her internal administration less successful. In no part of India were the people so happy and contented as were those in the dominions of Holkar.

Amongst other of the acts by which her reign will be remembered, was the founding of Indúr, the present

PART II.

capital of the country. A village when she came to the administration, it was soon transformed, under her auspices, into a wealthy city. She built likewise several forts, and caused to be constructed, at considerable cost, a road over the Vindhya range, where it is almost perpendicular. She spent likewise large sums of money on religious edifices.

She died at the age of sixty, worn out with care and fatigue. According to Sir John Malcolm, to whose history of Central India the reader is referred for a more detailed account of this famous lady, 'she was of the middle stature, and very thin; her complexion, which was of a dark olive, was clear; and her countenance is described as having been to the last hour of her life agreeable. . . . She was very cheerful, seldom in anger, possessed a cultivated mind, was quick and clear in the transaction of public business, and even flattery appears to have been lost upon her.'

Her death, which occurred in 1795, was lamented far and wide.

It is not necessary to give more than a cursory glance at the military achievements of Túkají during the reign of Ahalya Bai. We find him in 1780 employed in Gujrát in conjunction with Mádhají Sindhia against the English, under Colonel Goddard; and in 1786 aiding the Nawáb of Savanór against his master, Tippú Sultan, whose troops he defeated. In 1792 he introduced European tactics and discipline among his troops, four battalions being thus disciplined and placed under a Frenchman, the Chevalier Dudrenec. At the battle of Lukhairí, near Ajmír, these four battalions formed part of Holkar's army, 30,000 strong, which fought against Sindhia's forces, commanded by Gopál Ráo Bhao, consisting of 20,000 horse, and 9,000 regular infantry, disciplined in the European fashion, and commanded by De Boigne, who planned the attack. Dudrenec's battalions fought till they were nearly annihilated, and Holkar lost all his guns. The stand made by Dudrenec, however, encouraged Túkají to persevere in the system.

Túkají Holkar survived Ahalya Bai only two years. He died in 1797, leaving four sons, Khásí Ráo and Mulhar Ráo by his wife, and Wittóji and Jeswant Ráo by a concubine. Of the legitimate sons Khásí Ráo was half-witted, but Mulhar Ráo gave promise of great things. The four young men were invited to the Peshwa's court at Púna on their father's death, and it was hoped that the succession would devolve upon the high-spirited Mulhar Ráo. But just at that moment Daolat Ráo Sindhia was supreme at the court of the Peshwa, and it suited the ambitious views of that unscrupulous ruler to see Holkar's dominions governed by a fool. He therefore gave the whole might of his support to Khásí Ráo, attacked Mulhar Ráo in the night, slew him, and took his son, Khandí Ráo, prisoner. Wittóji and Jeswant Ráo escaped, but the former turned freebooter, was captured whilst marauding in the Dekhan, and was put to a cruel death.

All the hopes of the subjects of Holkar now turned to Jeswant Ráo. This prince, fleeing from Púna, had sought refuge with the Rájá of Nagpúr, but had been treacherously imprisoned. After a short confinement, however, he escaped, and for a year or so led the life of a proscribed fugitive. But in the course of that life he had many opportunities of displaying the innate strength and daring of his nature, his lofty views and his generous ideas. The breezes wafted exaggerations of these qualities to Indúr, and the whole army longed for him to appear. At length he arrived. Then, as if instinctively, the entire army, including the trained infantry and artillery of the Chevalier Dudrenec, the Patans of Amír Khan, and the Pindárí auxiliaries, went over to him in a mass.

Jeswant Ráo Holkar.

Jeswant Ráo, ignoring the claims of the imbecile Khásí Ráo, at once assumed the regency in the name of

PART II.

his nephew Khandí Ráo, but, as he subsequently caused the latter to be poisoned, his reign may be said to begin from this date (1798). He found in Indúr a great part of the treasure accumulated by Ahalya Bai, and he commenced his reign by a declaration that he intended to make regular payments to his troops. But his necessities, exaggerated by an ambitious nature, soon made him burst the bonds he had proposed to himself. He found he was compelled to feed his army by the plunder of others. He did not scruple then to lay waste alike the territories of Sindhia, and the territories of his liege lord the Peshwa. It was the story of these devastations that caused Daolat Ráo Sindhia to leave Púna for his own territories.

But as a general, Daolat Ráo was no match for the daring Jeswant Ráo. The latter, counting the initiative as three-fifths of a victory, attacked, in June 1801, the disciplined forces of Sindhia, under Hessing at Ujjén, and completely defeated them. He then, in July, made a daring attack upon Sindhia's great park of artillery on the north bank of the Narbadá, and though he was repulsed, still succeeded in alarming Sindhia, who advanced upon Indúr. The battle that ensued at that place was most desperately contested. Well had it been for the Márhátá power had Holkar triumphed, for the victory of Daolat Ráo paved the way to the ruin of the Peshwa and the treaty of Bassein.

Jeswant Ráo was indeed badly beaten; and had Sindhia displayed any of the qualities of a politician, his ruin had been assured. But dallying away the time in a fruitless attempt to treat, he left the game in the hands of his vanquished rival. Jeswant Ráo had lost his army, but rallying round him the daring spirits who traded in adventure, he first plundered Rájpútáná, then devastated Khándesh, and marched on Púna. Near this place he defeated, on October 25, the general of Sindhia, and possessed himself of the capital of the Peshwa.

Had the Peshwa, Bájí Ráo, taken counsel of anything but his fears, he would have endeavoured to negotiate with Holkar, whilst waiting the arrival of Daolat Ráo Sindhia, with an overwhelming force. But Bájí Ráo Peshwa possessed one of those natures that could not wait. To obtain a temporary triumph, he signed a treaty (Bassein) which made him virtually a vassal of the British, and escorted by a British force, thenceforth virtually his jailors, recovered his capital.

Jeswant Ráo then returned to his own dominions, thence to watch, though not to partake in, the war which ensued between Sindhia and the British. Had he lent the weight of his support to his brother Márhátá chieftain, the result might have been different. Why he did not still remains a mystery. Probably he thought, as Napoleon III. thought in 1866, that the struggle would be long and doubtful, and that he might then step in with the overpowering prestige of an arbitrator. But the struggle, though sharp, was short and decisive. Yet no sooner had Sindhia been beaten than Jeswant Ráo showed the British Government that he, too, was prepared to meet their conquering forces.

He entered into the struggle with a decision and energy characteristic of the man. And at first fortune smiled on him. He compelled Colonel Monson to retreat with great loss. He at once invaded the British territories. But he had to experience then the fate of every native power which has yet contested supremacy with the British. At Futtehgarh, at Díg, and on other minor occasions, he was completely beaten. He fled then for refuge to Bharatpúr, and aided in the repulse of the British from that place. A peace having been concluded with the Rájá of Bharatpúr, he fled to the Punjâb. Pursued by Lord Lake with the energy which marked all that general's movements, Jeswant Ráo, hopeless of all but his life, threw himself on the mercy of the conqueror, admitting that 'his whole kingdom lay upon his saddle's

PART II.

bow.' To his surprise the British Government restored to him all his territories, and the few that they alienated at the time they gave back to him the following year.[1]

Hardly had Jeswant Ráo returned to Indúr than he set himself to work to remodel his army. He carried out this reform on a very intelligent plan. His army had become overgrown, and want of discipline had made it a rabble. He at once reduced its numbers to a figure proportionate to the revenues of his dominions, and amongst the reduced numbers he established a system of order and discipline. The predatory horse, which he had found more prompt to plunder than efficient in the field, he summarily discharged.

The result of these innovations was that the disbanded troopers not only turned against him, but actually proclaimed his nephew, Khandí Ráo, a boy of eleven years of age, Rájá in his stead. To rid himself for ever of the prospect of such a rival, Jeswant Ráo first pacified the mutineers, and then had his nephew poisoned. By similar means he rid himself very shortly afterwards of his legitimate brother, Khásí Ráo, and of his wife, who was then in a state promising to present her husband with an heir.

Having thus removed all competitors from his path, he set himself to work with redoubled energy to complete his military reforms. He began to cast cannon, labouring at the forges with his own hands. The effects of this hard labour, aggravated by excessive drinking, soon showed themselves. His temper, always violent, became unbearable. Unless his orders were carried out on the spot, he became excited beyond measure. Gradually his mind began to wander; the tension on his brain had become too great. His madness became too evident, and in 1808 he was placed under restraint. Many attempts

[1] More detailed accounts of Jeswant Ráo's military exploits are to be found in Malcolm, Grant Duff, Thorn, and the Author's *Essays and Lectures on Indian Historical Subjects*—Essay 'Lord Lake.'

were made to bring about his recovery, but they all failed. After remaining one year in a state of madness, he sank into one of complete fatuity. In this he lingered two years longer, dying at last on October 20, 1811, in the city of Bambúra.

Jeswant Ráo was of middling stature, and of strong and active build. His complexion was dark, and he had suffered much from the loss of an eye, but its expression was agreeable from the animation given to it by his constitutionally high spirits. His character is thus, and, I think, very fairly, summed up by Grant Duff: 'The chief feature,' he writes, 'of Jeswant Ráo Holkar's character was that hardy spirit of energy and enterprise which, though like that of his countrymen, boundless in success, was also not to be discouraged by trying reverses. He was likewise better educated than Márhátás in general, and could write both the Persian language and his own. His manner was frank, and could be courteous, and he was distinguished by a species of coarse wit very attractive to the Indian soldiery. He had few other commendable qualities; for, although sometimes capriciously lavish, he was rapacious, unfeeling, and cruel, and his disposition was overbearing, jealous, and violent.'

On Jeswant Ráo becoming insane, the regency had been assumed by his favourite mistress, Túlsa Bai, a woman of great beauty, most fascinating manners, and considerable talents. She adopted a young boy, then not four years old, the son of another mistress,[1] and during his minority, which would be long, she flattered herself she would be allowed to administer the affairs of the country. As prime minister she retained Balarám Sét, who had filled the same office under Jeswant Ráo, and whom she believed to be devoted to her interests.[2]

[1] A woman of low caste, a Kumár or pot-maker.

[2] Sir John Malcolm relates that Túlsa Bai was married prior to her acquaintance with Jeswant Ráo; that he saw her, fell in love with her, and in a few days she was in his house and her husband in prison.

PART II.

But to keep in proper restraint the newly-formed army, proud of its strength and conscious of its power, something more was necessary than the control of a woman whose chief claim to her position was her surpassing loveliness. The troops almost at once assumed a licence bordering on revolt. Many of the neighbours seized without scruple outlying districts of which they themselves had been robbed. The cohesion which had existed in the dominions of Mulhar Ráo and Ahalya Bai was now dissolved, and decay and dismemberment seemed to threaten the entire edifice. The demands of the troops became at last so insolent and so rapacious, that Túlsa Bai was forced to take refuge in the fortified town of Gungrao. There, in pursuance of a dark intrigue, and instigated by her paramour, Ganpat Ráo, a man of no talent, she caused her minister, Balarám Sét, to be executed. But this deed of violence, far from stopping the clamours of the troops, increased them to such an extent that the regent and the infant Rájá, worsted in the field, fled for refuge to Alót.[1] Just about this time (1817) the Pindárí war broke out. An English force was assembling near Újjén. The opportunity appeared to Túlsa Bai too advantageous to be lost. She sent to the English commander an earnest request that she and the youthful Rájá might be received under British protection. But whilst negotiations were proceeding to effect this object, war broke out between the British and the Peshwa, and a large and predominating party in the durbar of Holkar announced their intention to adhere to the fortunes of the titular chief of all the Márhátás. In this conjuncture the regent, Túlsa Bai, found herself powerless. The command of the army was seized by Patán leaders, hostile to any accommodation with the English. As a first preliminary to hostilities with that

Eventually, the husband received as compensation for the loss of his handsome wife, a horse, a dress, and a small sum of money.

[1] A town sixteen miles south-west of Gungrao.

nation, these leaders caused the person of the Rájá to be seized, the regent Túlsa Bai to be executed, and her paramour and minister, Ganpat Ráo, to be secured.

Túlsa Bai was beheaded on December 20, 1817. Her accomplishments and character are thus described by Sir John Malcolm: 'Túlsa Bai,' he writes, 'was not thirty years old when she was murdered. She was handsome, and alike remarkable for the fascination of her manners and quickness of intellect. Few surpassed her in fluent eloquence, which persuaded those who approached her to promote her wishes. She rode with grace, and was always, when on horseback, attended by a large party of the females of the first families of the state. But there was never a more remarkable instance than in the history of this princess, how the most prodigal gifts of nature may be perverted by an indulgence of vicious habits. Though not the wife of Jeswant Ráo, yet being in charge of his family, and having possession of the child who was declared his heir, she was obeyed as his widow. As the favourite of the deceased, and the guardian of their actual chief, she had among the adherents of the Holkar family the strongest impressions in her favour; but casting all away, she lived unrespected, and died unpitied.' The day after the murder of Túlsa Bai, the army of Holkar, under its Pathán leaders, was completely defeated at Mehidpúr. The little Rájá, Mulhar Ráo, then about sixteen, was present at the action, seated on an elephant. He is stated to have behaved with spirit, but to have burst into tears when he saw his men fleeing in confusion. The treaty of Mundisúr, concluded a fortnight later (January 6, 1818), deprived him of nearly two-thirds of his dominions, and he was reduced to the position of a dependent sovereign. The terms of the treaty may thus briefly be stated. To the British Government were abandoned all Holkar's possessions within and to the south of the Satpúra range; he relinquished all claims or conquests from the Rájpút

PART II.

states; he ceded to the Rájá of Kotá four districts formerly rented by him; and to Amír Khan and Gafúr Khan the jaghirs held by them of the Holkar family, the latter, however, binding himself to maintain a contingent of 600 horse. In return, the British Government took the remaining territories under its protection. These remaining territories yielded then an actual annual revenue of upwards of twelve lakhs of rupees, but they were capable of much development; they now produce thirty lakhs.

The minister with whom the treaty of Mundisúr had been negotiated, Tantia Jógh, bent all his attention, after the signature of the treaty, to discharge superfluous troops and establishments, and to restore the finances of the country. In this praiseworthy endeavour he received encouragement and assistance from the British authorities—an encouragement and assistance without which all his efforts would have been futile. For the treasury was empty, and the country disorganised. But by small loans from time to time advanced by the British Government, Tantia Jógh was enabled to tide over the difficulty.

Mulhar Ráo Holkar.

Two insurrections broke out in 1819, which added greatly to the difficulties of the minister's situation, and thus retarded the settlement of the country. One of these was occasioned by an impostor personating Mulhar Ráo Holkar, and the other by the pretensions of Harí Ráo Holkar, cousin of the Máhárájá. The impostor, whose real name was Krishna Koer, assembled a considerable force to the west of the Chambal, and kept the field for some time, supported by a body of mercenaries; but he was at length encountered by the contingent under British officers formed by the minister at Mehidpúr, and his party was broken and dispersed. He then fled to Kotá, was recognised and imprisoned, but finally pardoned and released as having been an instrument in the hands of others. The insurrection of Harí Ráo Holkar was less

CHAP. II.

formidable, for soon becoming sensible of the folly of his enterprise, he threw himself on the generosity of his cousin, who, it is said, was disposed to pardon him, but was dissuaded from this purpose by Tantia Jógh, who deemed it imprudent he should be left at liberty to disturb the peace of the country. He was, therefore, thrown into prison at Mahaisir.

In the years 1821 and 1822 further disturbances arose, which were only finally suppressed by the intervention of the British troops.

In April 1826, the able minister who had striven so zealously to retrieve the fortunes of his country died. He was succeeded by Raojí Trimbak. But a year later Raojí was displaced by a relative of the late minister, Daejí Bakshí. But this individual proving himself incompetent, Appah Ráo Krishna, a clever, active Pundit, was nominated to the high office.

Second only to the tranquillisation of the country, the most important event which characterised the reign of Mulhar Ráo was an agreement made with the British Government, securing to it the exclusive right to purchase opium in Málwá. Serious difficulties, however, having resulted from these arrangements, the monopoly was abandoned in 1829, and a transit duty was levied on the opium in its passage through the British territory to the sea-coast.

Mulhar Ráo Holkar took little part in public affairs himself. He was dissolute and extravagant, and was cursed with the fatal facility of yielding to the influence of worthless favourites. None of the three ministers who had succeeded Raojí Trimbak were men of mark. As a natural consequence, the revenue had fallen, and the country gradually verged to the state in which it had been before the battle of Mehidpúr—an empty treasury and a mutinous soldiery. In 1829 the eyes of the Rájá were opened to the impending catastrophe. Giving promises of reform and amendment, he persuaded his

PART II. mother, who had made large accumulations, to relieve his pecuniary embarrassments, and at her desire the minister Appah Ráo Krishna was dismissed, and the executive charge of the government entrusted to Madho Ráo Furnawís.

Mulhar Ráo Holkar died four years later (October 1833), at the early age of twenty-eight, a victim to debauchery and dissipation. He left no issue; but, at the moment of his death, his widow, Gótuma Bai, with the concurrence of her mother-in-law, adopted the infant son of Bápú Holkar, said to be of the same tribe and lineage as Mulhar Ráo, and not many degrees removed from Túkají Holkar. This child, not four years old, was publicly installed on January 17, 1834, by the style and title of Máhárájá Martand Ráo Holkar, the executive government still continuing in the hands of Madho Ráo Furnawís. The British Government recognised the succession, though declining to bind itself to support it if it should appear subversive of the authority of any other party, or contrary to the wishes of the majority of the chiefs and followers of the Holkar family.

But it soon appeared that the pretensions of Martand Ráo were not to pass unquestioned. The cousin of the late Rájá, Harí Ráo Holkar, was still alive, though in confinement at Mahaisir. From this he was forcibly released by his partisans on the night of February 2, 1834, and proclaimed without delay at Maindlaisar. Thousands flocked to his ranks; the infant child was abandoned, and on April 17 Harí Ráo Holkar was installed as Máhárájá in the presence of the British Resident. Martand Ráo was banished from the country, and granted an allowance of 500 rupees a month on condition of his resigning all claims to the succession.

Harí Ráo Holkar.

The new sovereign was quite unfit to rule. He was weak, timid, and superstitious. An imprisonment of nearly fifteen years had sapped up all his energies. All his acts betrayed incapacity. After, in the manner of his race, wreaking vengeance upon those who had supported the pretensions of his rival, he unearthed from a distant part of India an individual named Rívají Phansia, a man who for the preceding fifteen years had lived obscure and in poverty, and made him prime minister. The character of Rívají soon showed itself. He knew nothing of the country, he was naturally devoid of ability, and long poverty had made him avaricious and self-seeking. He was, besides, a drunkard. His first act was to marry his eldest son, Rájá Bhao, also a drunkard, to a natural daughter of the Máhárájá, and to bestow upon them a valuable pergunnah; thus, by his first act, alienating from the impoverished State at least a twelfth part of its revenues.

Under the management of this man the revenues began to decrease and the expenditure to augment, until in 1834 the extraordinary result was reached that whilst the former had dwindled down to 9,25,000 rupees, the latter had become swollen to 23,69,000. But this would appear to have been a part of the minister's system. He thought to trade on the timorous nature of Harí Rao by representing the army as being on the verge of mutiny, which he alone could suppress. Hence he augmented and decreased the number of troops at his pleasure, according to the fancied exigencies of the moment. To meet the extra expenditure he had recourse to loans from soucars or bankers at a ruinous rate of interest.

This state of things could not long continue. In 1835 a conspiracy was formed, mainly, it was said, by Madho Ráo Furnawís, the last minister of the Rájá Mulhar Ráo. On September 8 of that year a body of 300 armed men, led by two officers of the late Rájá, entered Indúr. Far from meeting any opposition in the city they were allowed to reach the palace unmolested, were admitted into it, and were even joined by some of the Rájá's troops. Had they pushed on, the enterprise would have succeeded. But the two leaders went in the first instance to ask instruc-

PART II.

tions from the widow of Mulhar Ráo, then occupying rooms in the palace. She received them with reproaches, and refused to lend her support. Meanwhile the troops faithful to Harí Ráo attacked the invaders. The two leaders, seeing that all was lost, threw themselves on their own swords. A general massacre then ensued, not a man of the invaders or of those who had joined them escaping.

This conspiracy only increased the timidity of Harí Ráo; and his minister, nursing his fear, so fortified the palace that he made of it a prison guarded by a lawless rabble. The proper business of the government fell into stagnation, and the disorder in the finances increased As for Harí Ráo, his alarm was so great that for fifteen months after the conspiracy he never once left his apartments.

At length the crisis came. Rívají Phansia could raise no more money. He had ruined the credit of the State. He had then no course to pursue but to retire. This he did in November 1836. He was succeeded by Salikrám Mantrí, the agent of the firm of bankers of which Tantia Jógh had been the head.

But the country had become so disorganised that it became necessary (1837–8) for the British Government to interfere. Harí Ráo Holkar was accordingly informed that the British Government would consider it its duty to assume the management of the country under its own officers should the Resident of Indúr be unable at a certain fixed period to report a material amelioration in the state of affairs within his dominions.

This notification had a wonderful effect. A capable and well-qualified officer, Abbají Buláb, was appointed minister, and a very few months later, several important reforms had been effected. Expenses were cut down, the corrupt officers of revenue were removed, remissions were granted in the districts which had suffered most from over-exaction, and an improved revenue system was introduced. By these means it became possible before long to pay off the arrears of the civil and military establishments.

In an autograph letter to Harí Ráo, the Governor-General, Lord Auckland, expressed himself pleased with the measures thus taken by that prince.

Harí Ráo died on October 24, 1843, at the age of forty-eight. He left no male offspring, his only son by his wife, Híra Bai, a person of an obscure family, having died when quite young. Two years before his death he had adopted as his heir and successor Khandí Ráo, a boy thirteen years of age, son of an obscure zamindar, and very distantly related to the reigning family. Khandí Ráo was at once recognised by the British Government. But he lived litttle more than three months.[1] 'He was never married. There was no lineal heir to the State, and there was no one possessing a legitimate right to adopt. The nomination of a successor was therefore declared to rest exclusively with the British Government, and the Resident, Sir Robert Hamilton, was instructed to make a selection in such a way as to show that it was manifestly the sole act of the British Government. The mother of Harí Ráo Holkar, who was greatly respected by the people, and had been associated with the Resident in the administration before Khandí Ráo's death, pleaded the claims of Martand Ráo, but Government refused to select him, and proposed to nominate the younger son of Bhao Holkar if he should be found, on inquiry, to be the most eligible. The Resident thereupon declared in full durbar the desire of the British Government to perpetuate the state of Holkar by the selection of a successor from amongst those eligible to such a distinction, that the Mah Sáhiba had pointed out the younger son of Bhao Holkar as a fit successor, and that the Governor-General, having a great respect for the Mah Sáhiba, had determined to bestow the chieftainship on him. Three days thereafter, without waiting for instructions, the Resident installed the

[1] Aitchison's *Treaties.*

PART II.

boy with all the formality of an hereditary chieftain. For this serious departure from his instructions the Resident was severely censured, and informed that by his proceeding an opportunity had been lost to Government of marking an important line of policy. In a letter to the young chief the Governor-General laid down the conditions on which the state was conferred on him. This letter was declared to have the force of a sunnud, and the Máhárájá was required to present a nuzzer of 101 gold mohurs on its delivery.'[1]

Túkaji Ráo Holkar.

The new sovereign, then about ten years old, assumed the name of Túkají Ráo Holkar. He attained his majority in 1852, and from that date has managed the affairs of his state.

Little occurred to mark the administration of Túkají Ráo prior to the outbreak of the mutiny in 1857. He had then a military establishment consisting of about 2,000 regular and 4,000 irregular infantry; of 2,000 regular and 1,200 irregular cavalry; of 500 artillerymen and 24 field guns. The irregular portion of these broke from his control under the influence of the excited passions of the hour, and suddenly besieged the Resident, the late Sir Henry Durand, in the Residency. With some difficulty, and solely to ensure the safety of the women and children under his charge, Colonel Durand retired to Bhopál. Thence he hastened towards Aurangábád to direct the movements of the column advancing from Bombay to restore order in Central India. He met this force at Assírgarh, and so impressed his strong character on the direction of its movements, that not only was the rebellious fort of Dhár taken, but Nímach was very seasonably relieved after two actions fought at Mundisúr. These victories not only broke the spirit of Holkar's mutinous soldiers, but also cowed them so completely that at Indúr they ignominiously laid down their arms before the man whose life, only a few weeks earlier, they had

[1] Aitchison.

treacherously attempted. Order was then restored in Central India.

CHAP. II.

The Government of India did not connect Túkají Holkar with the rebellion and outrages of his troops. He received in 1862 a sunnud guaranteeing to him the right of adoption, and he was subsequently nominated a Knight of the Star of India.

From that time to the present day nothing has occurred in the territories of Holkar meriting special notice.[1] The matters which have been raised between him and the British Government have been more or less questions of detail, and in respect to these the action of the British Government has been more than liberal. In 1864 arrangements were concluded with the Máhárájá for the cession of land for a line of railway to connect Indúr with the great Indian Peninsula line at Nimar.

The present prime minister of Holkar is Sir Madhava Ráo, K.C.S.I., a Brahman from the south of India, one of the most acute and accomplished men of his race.

The Máhárájá is entitled to a salute of nineteen guns.

CHAPTER III.

BHOPÁL.

AREA—6,764 sq. miles. POPULATION—663,656.
REVENUE—13,76,252 rupees.

CHAP. III.

THE principality of Bhopál was founded at the close of the seventeenth century by an Afghán nobleman, Dóst Mahomed Khan, who served under the emperor Aurangzíb. Dóst Mahomed had been nominated by the emperor, about the year 1690, superintendent of the district of

[1] It has been stated, and I believe truly, that throughout Holkar's dominions no private individual possesses permanent, heritable, or alienable rights in land. Every cultivator is a tenant at will of the Máhárájá.

PART II.

Bhairsía, and he took advantage of the convulsions which followed the death of the emperor to declare himself Náwab of the territory which, partly as a reward for services rendered, partly by stratagem, and partly, it is said, by treachery, he had acquired in the emperor's lifetime. This territory he called Bhopál, after the principal town within its limits.

Dóst Mahomed Khan survived the emperor sixteen years. He died in 1723, at the age of sixty-six, leaving behind him a great reputation as a man of capacity and courage. His death was the signal for a struggle for power. There were two claimants to the succession. One, Yar Mahomed, the elder but illegitimate son, the other, Sultán Mahomed, younger but legitimate. The cause of Yar Mahomed was espoused by the Nizám, and Sultán Mahomed resigned in his favour, receiving as compensation the fort of Ráthgurh and its dependencies.

Yar Mahomed possessed little of the ability of his father, nor did his son and successor, Feyz Mahomed, compensate for his sire's deficiencies. Yet they had both one great merit. Though they possessed little ability themselves, they were eager to encourage it in others. During their reigns the affairs of the state were managed by Hindú ministers, men of honesty and singular talents.

Feyz Mahomed was a fanatic or religious recluse. But he was harmless. He was not a persecutor, but was content to practise his austerities upon himself. His death, after a reign of thirty-eight years, was little felt. His brother and successor, Mahomed Yassein, survived him only a few days. The third brother, Hyat Mahomed, who followed, possessed a proportionate share of the fraternal intellect, and no more.

Many stirring events, however, happened during his long reign of twenty-nine years. First may be mentioned the contest of the English with the Márhátás, ending for the moment in the shameful convention of Wargaum. In consequence of that convention the very safety of

British interests on the western coast seemed to depend upon the opportune arrival of a force of 4,000 or 5,000 men, which Warren Hastings, with the wonderful prevision for which he was distinguished, had despatched, in anticipation of disturbances, from Bengal. This force, making its way through Central India, met with numberless obstacles and impediments to its progress. The Rájpút and other powers whose territories were touched, were all more or less dependent on the Márhátás. They all refused their aid. All, I should have said, but one—and that one was Bhopál. When the difficulties in the way of the advance of the English general, Goddard, appeared insurmountable, Bhopál offered him a friendly hand. Not only did she open out a path for him through her territories, but she furnished him plentifully with supplies. This was the beginning of a friendship which has never been broken, and which, genuine on both sides, has operated to the advantage of both.

The next stirring events—for two came simultaneously—in the reign of Hyat Mahomed, were the invasions of the Pindárís and the Márhátás. The former swept like locusts over the land, and the latter, called in to expel them, began to vie with them in plundering. In this crisis, with an imbecile sovereign on the throne, and intriguers tearing the state to pieces by their selfish manœuvres, Bhopál was saved by the appearance on the stage of a young cousin of the Nawáb, Vizír Mahomed by name, who, having been driven into banishment for rebelling against a minister subsequently deceased, returned to offer his sword to his country in her danger. The talents, the daring, the engaging qualities of this young soldier of fortune worked wonders. He expelled the Pindárís, drove out the Márhátás, and in less than eight months restored to Hyat Mahomed the security of his throne.

But he had deserved too much for the small minds of the members of the ruling family. The heir apparent,

PART II.

Ghous Mahomed, especially looked upon him with suspicion. He was too popular, and must be got rid of. The office of dewan or prime minister happened to be vacant, and the claims of Vizír Mahomed were in every one's mouth. To get rid of Vizír Mahomed it was necessary to appoint some one else to the office, who, looking upon him as a rival, would endeavour to crush him.

This policy was carried out. Muríd Mahomed Khan, a lineal descendant of the legitimate son of the founder of the family, was made minister. His first act was to send Vizír Mahomed to act against the Márhátás in the field; his next to 'feather his own nest.' He did this so unblushingly that he drove the people to revolt, and then sent for the Márhátás to support him.

This was Vizír Mahomed's opportunity. He flew at once to Bhopál to defend it against the foreign foe. With his inadequate means he might not have succeeded, but, fortunately, a disturbance in the territories of Sindhia caused the Márhátás to be recalled. They left, taking with them the cause of their invasion, Muríd Mahomed Khan, who died from terror in their hands.

The way was now open for Vizír Mahomed. He became minister. He found, it is true, an empty treasury, an impoverished state, and a dwindled army. In return he gave himself to the State. It resulted from this gift that in a short time order was restored to the finances, and victory to the standards of Bhopál. A little longer period and the State would have been pronounced cured of her misfortunes. But again jealousy struck him down. To support him, first the Pindárís, then the Márhátá hosts, were called in by the son of the sovereign, the imbecile Ghous Mahomed.

Just at this period the father, Nawáb Hyat Mahomed, died, and Ghous became ruler. Far from resting his support on his countrymen, however, he recognised the Márhátás only as his protectors. Vizír Mahomed had withdrawn for the moment, but, watching his opportunity, he returned, and expelled the Márhátás. From that moment Ghous Mahomed was but the nominal Nawáb; Vizír Mahomed became real ruler.

For the nine years that followed, Vizír Mahomed was engaged in warring for the defence of his country. Compelled in 1809 to ally himself with the Pindárís, then pursued by the British, he laid before the British commander a clear statement of the necessities of his position, and expressed his earnest desire to enter into friendly negotiations with the rising power. Nothing was agreed upon at the time, but the design never left the mind of the minister of Bhopál. Four years later he was attacked and besieged in the capital by the combined armies of Sindhia and the Rájá of Berar. For nine months he, with a gallantry and fortitude never surpassed, with a garrison very small in proportion to the number of the assailants, withstood their attacks, and had the proud satisfaction of repulsing them. Next year Sindhia threatened to renew the siege, but was withheld by the interference of the British Government, which began now to discern, though still dimly, the importance of Bhopál.

Eighteen months later (1816) Vizír Mahomed died at the age of fifty-one, leaving behind him the reputation of being the greatest warrior, the most skilful and dashing leader, and the wisest politician of that part of India. He was succeeded as minister by a son worthy of himself, Nuzzer Mahomed, whose granddaughter now reigns in Bhopál.

Though this minister held office for less than four years, his administration was of lasting consequences to his country. He succeeded, the year after his accession (1817), in concluding an arrangement with the British, whereby Bhopál was guaranteed to himself on condition of his aiding the British army with a contingent, and co-operating with it against the Pindárís—a condition which was faithfully observed. The following year these terms were made the basis of a formal treaty of perpetual friend-

PART II.

ship and alliance. In return for furnishing a contingent of 600 horse and 400 infantry, he received five districts in Málwá, subject to an annual assignment on them of 6,000 rupees to their former manager.

Under the sway of this able man the finances of the country recovered their elasticity, and districts which had been lost in former wars were recovered. In fact, a new era of prosperity was dawning on the principality, when the accidental discharge of a pistol by his brother-in-law, Foujdar Khan, a child eight years old, deprived Bhopál of her ablest ruler and worthiest citizen.

Nuzzer Mahomed had had but one wife, the daughter of Nawáb Ghous Mahomed, known as the Kúdsia Begum. She had given birth to but one child, a daughter, Sekunder Begum, who will live in history as the famous Begum of Bhopál.

Upon the death of Nuzzer Mahomed it was arranged, with the consent of the Bhopál nobles and the sanction of the British Government, that his nephew, son of his elder brother, Múnír Mahomed Khan, should marry Sekunder Begum, and should succeed as Nawáb, and that, meanwhile, until this marriage should have taken place, the regency should be placed in the hands of the widow, Kúdsia Begum.

This arrangement took effect. The Kúdsia Begum, then only seventeen years old, commenced her regency by continuing in office the ministers of her late husband, and by following their advice. But with the march of time the love of power grew strong within her. Her daughter had been betrothed to her cousin Múnír Mahomed Khan. But when, after six years of rule (1827), this man claimed the hand of his promised bride, and demanded to be invested with the sovereign authority, the Kúdsia Begum fired up, gave him a point-blank refusal, and cancelled the matrimonial engagement. Though Múnír objected to this treatment, the Begum carried the day. Acting in concert with the nobles of the state it was decided that

Kúdsia Begum should continue to rule for a time unfettered; that the engagement with Múnír Mahomed should be cancelled, he receiving, instead, a jaghír of 40,000 rupees, and resigning all his claims in favour of his brother Jehángír Mahomed Khan.

This Jehángír was yet young, and the Kúdsia Begum, anxious to maintain her power, deferred the celebration of the marriage on various pretences. At last it could no longer be postponed, and it took place in April 1835. But the dissensions were thereby only increased. There were then three parties struggling for power—the Kúdsia Begum, her daughter, Sekunder Begum, and the daughter's husband, Jehángír Mahomed Khan. Had Jehángír been content to wait, he would probably have gained the mastery for a time. But in his impatience to be *facile princeps*, he planned a *coup d'état*, his design being to seize the person of the Kúdsia Begum and confine her. His arrangements were well made, and up to a certain point well carried out; but at the decisive moment his heart failed him. He let the Begum go when she was in his power.

The failure rebounded upon himself. A civil war ensued. In the course of this Jehángír was defeated, and then besieged in the Fort of Ashta. The siege lasted two months, at the end of which time both parties agreed to accept the mediation of the British Government. It was then arranged that, in consideration of the Begum receiving a life jaghír of 60,000 rupees, the administration of the state should be entrusted to Jehángír. In accordance with this, Jehángír received his investiture on November 29, 1837, with the full consent of the Kúdsia Begum.

Thenceforth that lady appears no more on the scene. But her absence did not restore peace. In the Sekunder Begum the Nawáb had a wife with abilities far greater than his own, an ambition as lofty, and a mind more even and more resolute. Their quarrels were incessant. At last

PART II.

Sekunder Begum, knowing Jehángír's character, and feeling that with time and patience the day was her own, left him to go and live with her mother.

The result was what she had foreseen. After six years of weak and dissolute rule, Jehángír died. On the occurrence of this event various means were attempted to place her, either alone or conjointly with the Kúdsia Begum, at the head of the administration, but they all failed, as the Begum intended they should fail. Eventually, in February 1847, Sekunder Begum was appointed sole regent for her only child, a daughter.

In this office the Begum had a large field for the exercise of her talents, and she fully justified all the expectations that had been formed of her. In six years she paid off the entire public debt of the state; she abolished the system of farming the revenue, and made her own arrangements directly with the heads of villages; she put a stop to monopolies of trades and handicrafts; she brought the mint under her own management; re-organised the police, and made many other improvements. In fact she displayed in all departments of the State an energy, an assiduity, and an administrative ability such as would have done credit to a trained statesman.

She had originally been appointed regent till her daughter should attain the age of eighteen, but on the marriage of the latter with the commander of the forces, Bukshí Báker Mahomed Khan, the period was extended three years. This, however, did not satisfy the Begum. She desired to be regarded as ruler in her own right, and although, in consequence of the British Government having previously recognised her daughter, Shah Jehán Begum, the request could not be complied with at the time, events soon after occurred which gave her a claim that was irresistible. Meanwhile she remained actual ruler, her daughter having resigned her right to govern during her mother's lifetime.

She was guiding the State vessel when in 1857 the

storm of the mutiny burst upon her. She was equal to the occasion, true to the traditions of her country, to her plighted word, to the sentiments of truth and honour. As early as April of that year she communicated to the British agent the contents of a lithographed proclamation which had reached her, urging the overthrow and destruction of the English. In the month of June she expelled from Bhopál a native whom she found engaged in raising troops for a purpose he did not care to avow. In July she afforded shelter to the British officers who had been driven from Indúr by the mutinous troops of Holkar. She did all this under great difficulties: when the contingent raised in Bhopál and commanded by British officers had mutinied, when her mother, who had become a bigot, and her uncles, who were weak-minded and priest-ridden, were urging her to declare a religious war against the infidel. But the Begum never faltered. She was true to the last. She caused the British officers to be conducted in safety to Hoshungábád; then with infinite tact allayed the excitement in her capital; put down the mutinous contingent with a strong hand, and finally restored order in every part of the Bhopál territory. Then, when the tide turned, and British supremacy began to vindicate itself, she was as prompt in another way with her aid. Supplies, soldiers, all that she had that could be useful, she gave with a liberal hand.

For these services Sekunder Begum received for Bhopál a grant of the district of Bairsía, confiscated from Dhár; she was recognised (December 1859) as ruler in her own right of Bhopál, with succession to her daughter, and succession to her descendants according to the Mahomedan law; four guns were presented to her; and on September 1, 1863, her Highness was invested by the Viceroy with the dignity of the highest grade of the most exalted order of the Star of India.

She, too, was liberal and generous. Those of her

PART II. own subjects who rendered good service in 1857 were largely and handsomely rewarded.

Two months later her Highness left Bhopál with a suite on a pilgrimage to Mecca, leaving her daughter under the protection of the British Government. It had been at one time her intention to extend her journey to Medina, and thence possibly to England, but the annoyance she met with from marauders induced her to return after an absence of nearly eight months. She arrived at Bombay in June, 1864, remained there four or five months, and then returned to Bhopál.

Her Highness lived four years longer, still governing Bhopál with wisdom and prudence. She died on October 30, 1868. The intelligence was received by the Government of India 'with profound regret.' An extract from the order issued on that occasion will be found in the appendix.[1]

The daughter, Begum Shah Jehán, at once succeeded. She, too, has one child, a daughter, Sultán Jehán, who was married on February 1, 1875, to Mír Ahmed Ali Khan Bahadúr, a nobleman of Afghán descent. She has learned English.

The Begum of Bhopál receives a salute of nineteen guns.

CHAPTER IV.

DHÁR.

AREA—2,691 sq. miles. POPULATION—125,000.
REVENUE—4,37,000 rupees.

CHAP. IV. THE family of the Puars of Dhár descends from a Rájpút tribe settled in Málwá in a remote era, whence the branch now reigning in Dhár emigrated at an early age to the

[1] *Vide* Appendix D.

vicinity of Púna. Sivají Puar, the first of this branch who brought himself at all prominently forward, was a Patél[1] of the village of Múltán, thirty miles north-east of Púna, where the descendants of that branch of the family retained thirty years ago, and probably retain still, the hereditary office of Patél. Sivají Puar had one son, Krishnají, who, as well as his three sons, Bábájí, Ryají, and Kerújí, were cultivators of the soil, and at the same time silladars. Bábájí had two sons, Sámbájí and Kálojí, who became military commanders in the service of the famous Sivají. Three sons of Sámbají; viz. Údají, Anand Ráo, and Jugdéo, fought likewise under the successor of Sivají, Sahú Rájá, in the Márhátá army, and from the circumstance of that direct service under the chief of all the Márhátás, their descendants claim precedence over Sindhia and Holkar, who had served only under the Peshwa. Of the three members of the family last mentioned, Údají Puar attained considerable rank. He was not only entrusted with a high command, but treated with great consideration by Sahú Rájá and his minister, Bájí Ráo.

Údají Puar, however, incurred the displeasure of the all-powerful Peshwa, and was imprisoned. His name does not again occur in history, though his descendants are still Patéls of Múltán. The leadership of the family devolved, after the imprisonment of Údájí, upon his brother, Anand Ráo, at the time Patél of Kaorá. This leader was vested with authority to collect the Márhátá share of the revenue of Málwá and Gujrát in 1734. Subsequently he settled in Dhár, and this province, with the adjoining districts and the tributes of some neighbouring Rájpút chiefs, was then assigned for the support of himself and his adherents. He is thus considered as the founder of the principality of Dhár.

Anand Ráo Puar died in 1749, and was succeeded by his son, Jeswant Ráo. This prince was the first of the

[1] Head man or chief.

PART II.

family who received the title of Rájá of Dhár. He was remarkable alike for his valour and generosity, and his name is still held in remembrance by the inhabitants of Málwá. Like many other of the Márhátá leaders, he fell at the fatal battle of Pánipat in 1761.

His son, Khandí Ráo Puar, a boy only two and a half years old, succeeded him. His long minority was most disadvantageous to the family interests. Holkar and Sindhia scrupled not, whilst recognising the young Rájá as their superior in rank, to despoil him of slices of his dominions. But the climax of misfortune seemed to be reached when Ragonáth Ráo, the Peshwa, harassed by his enemies, sent, in 1774, his chief wife and family to take refuge in Dhár. The wife, Anundí Bai, was delivered there of a son, Bájí Ráo, afterwards last of the Peshwas. This event caused all the enemies of Ragonáth Ráo to crowd at once into the principality to seize the person of his heir. Khandí Ráo, who, though still under major age, had assumed the direction of affairs, had taken part with Ragonáth Ráo, and therefore his dominions were considered a fair prey by the invaders. These were at once occupied, and were only restored on the surrender of Anundí Bai and her child, who were carried prisoners to Púna.

Khandí Ráo Puar did not long survive this event. He died in 1780, at the early age of twenty-one. He left his wife, the daughter of Govind Ráo, Gáikwár, pregnant. Six months later she gave birth at Barodah to a son, who was called Anund Ráo.

Anund Ráo Puar remained at Barodah, under the care of his mother and grandfather, till the year 1797. He was then seventeen. His assumption of authority was opposed by the minister, Rung Ráo Úrekur, who had conducted the administration in his absence. Rung Ráo, however, was unable to maintain his usurped authority, and fled to the court of Holkar. Holkar, whilst pretending to open negotiations with Anund Ráo Puar for the return of his minister, plundered and laid waste the country. The minister, seeing he was not in earnest, fled to Daolat Ráo Sindhia, and instigated that prince to attack Dhár. Daolat Ráo, nothing loath, not only threatened to resume the country, basing his threats upon pretended orders from the Peshwa, but, in the course of the seven years that followed, annexed the districts of Augur and Soneil, besides all the Dhár possessions in Haraotí, and extorted large sums from the Rájá. Two years later, one of Sindhia's leaders, Sambají Jugga, again attacked the weakened principality, and took, after an action fought at Budnáoar, the whole of that district, to satisfy the demand made by order of Sindhia for 75,000 rupees. A desire to regain his territory induced Anund Ráo to raise and pay over that sum. But before the territory had been restored, he died. This event, and the confusion that ensued, led to the retention by Sindhia of both money and territory. It is believed that Anund Ráo Puar was poisoned by his sister, who was a very dissolute woman. Her supposed object was to obtain the reins of government which she hoped to guide by means of a child she would have then adopted. But these hopes, if entertained, were completely frustrated. She was seized and put to death, with several real or presumed accomplices, a few days after her brother's death.[1]

On the death of Anund Ráo Puar, his widow, Mína Bai, assumed the government. She was pregnant at the time. To assure herself, therefore, at such a time, against the intrigues of her enemies, and especially those of Morári Ráo, an illegitimate relation of her late husband, she formed a party to support her interests at Dhár, and went to Mandú for her confinement. In due course she gave birth there to a son, whom she called Ramchunder Ráo. As soon as she was convalescent she returned to

[1] Malcolm.

PART II.

Dhár, completely thwarted, by her firmness and prudence, the efforts of Morári Ráo; and then, summoning to her aid from Barodah a body of troops upon whom she could depend, applied all her energies to restore the fortunes of the country. It must not be imagined that the country was properly administered at this period. Nothing could be further from the fact. There was indeed no administration at all. The principality had been so devastated that no attempt was made to collect a regular revenue. It would have been fruitless to attempt it. Morári Ráo, too, still occupied one corner of it, always threatening the remainder. Under these circumstances, the only way to provide supplies for the ordinary wants of the State was to make predatory incursions on the Rájpút countries in the neighbourhood.

Whilst the administration was thus worked on a hand-to-mouth principle, the boy Rájá, Ramchunder Rao Puar, died. The mother, still resolved to rule, at once adopted, with the concurrence of Holkar and Sindhia, her sister's son, a boy of about the same age, under the name of Ramchunder Puar. During the eight years that followed Dhár continued a prey to her overgrown neighbours. Morári Ráo died, but other enemies rose up. She could not even keep out the Pindárís. To such a length did spoliation reach, that when the British entered Málwá in 1817 to annihilate the power of those freebooters, the only portion of the ancient principality remaining in possession of the Rání was the town of Dhár itself, and this had been maintained solely by the firmness and courage of Mína Bai! The revenue did not exceed from 20,000 to 30,000 rupees!

Then began a new era for the family of Puar. Dhár was taken (January 10, 1819) under the protection of the British Government, several districts which it had lost were recovered and restored to it, and such arrangements were made with the paramount power as would ensure to the recovered districts sufficient time to rally from the state of impoverishment to which they had been reduced.

By these arrangements, and by an addition to them made two years later, the principality of Dhár was made to consist of the districts of Dhár. Budnáoar, and Nalcha. It received, likewise, an annual payment of 1,10,000 rupees from the British Government for the district of Bairsía and the tribute of Allí-Mohun, ceded in 1821 to the British Government. Its tributary rights over the Rájpút states of Bánswárá and Dongarpúr had been ceded to the British Government in 1819.

From the moment of the interference of the British the condition of Dhár began rapidly to improve. The State had an able minister in the person of Bapú Ragonáth. Under his administration during the minority of the Rájá, the disorderly rabble of foreign mercenaries was dismissed, and their place supplied by an efficient body of 300 horse and 800 foot, which, with the ordinary police of the country, sufficed for all internal purposes; the revenue, which in the preceding eight years had sometimes fallen to 20,000 rupees, rose in 1820 to 2,67,000; whilst assured tranquillity gave confidence to the cultivators of the soil.

In the following year a marriage took place between the young Rájá, Ramchunder Puar, and Unpúra Bai, niece of Daolat Ráo Sindhia. The age of the bridegroom was twelve, that of the bride eight years. The marriage was celebrated at Gwáliár with great pomp and ceremony, and gave satisfaction to the nobles of both states. The satisfaction at Dhár was, however, somewhat diminished when it was ascertained that the dower of the bride, which had been estimated at territories bringing in an annual revenue of a lakh of rupees, consisted only of the district of Dektan, a district which, I may add, Sindhia subsequently attempted to resume.

A second visit was paid to Daolat Ráo Sindhia by the Rájá of Dhár in 1826, with the hope of extracting from

PART II.

Daolat Ráo during the sickness which had then overtaken him, some material sign of his goodwill. That, naturally, was not the ostensible reason for the journey. Others more natural were not wanting. The bride of the young Rájá had remained since the wedding at Gwáliár; and it was to show no unchivalrous impatience that the Rájá himself should set forth to escort her to her new home. Besides, Daolat Ráo was sick, and it seemed but natural to go to offer him the condolence of a near relative. Again, however, were the hopes entertained doomed to be disappointed. Ramchunder Puar returned to Dhár, indeed, with his wife, but without any accession of territory.

Some rearrangement of the stipulations of the treaty with the British were made in 1828, 1831, and 1835, but as they were of a technical character, not affecting the property of the country or its good relations with the British power, it seems unnecessary particularly to allude to them. Their result may thus briefly be stated. Instead of a fixed sum for the cession of the district of Bairsía, the British agreed to pay the surplus revenues of that district after meeting all its expenses. But in 1832 an event occurred which reproduced disorder and rapine in the country. This was the insurrection occasioned by the pretensions of a youth who gave himself out to be the son of Morári Ráo and grandson of Jeswunt Ráo Puar, first Rájá of Dhár, killed at the battle of Pánipat.

The insurrection assumed grave proportions from the fact that the Bhíls, who had been greatly attached to Morári Ráo, rose as one man in its favour. Its consequences were most disastrous, for besides the plundering and burning of numerous villages, the insurgents are computed to have driven off to their fastnesses and jungles no less than 3,000 head of cattle, besides other booty. In at last invoking the aid of the British to quell these outrages, the minister of Dhár, Bapú Ragonáth, stated that all the villages were deserted and that the country would

CHAP. IV.

be lost unless something were done at once. The British first mediated, but mediation having proved fruitless, they interfered. Finally the leader of the insurrection, Úchét Ráo, and his followers, agreed to submit their claims to the arbitration of the British. The evidence adduced being greatly in favour of the claim to parentage urged by Úchét Ráo, and the grievances of the Bhíls having been substantiated, it was decided that a maintenance allowance for life of 200 rupees per mensem should be assigned to Úchét Ráo, on condition that he should desist from his pretensions and restore the cattle and other booty carried off during the insurrection. The grievances complained of by the Bhíls were at the same time redressed.

Rájá Ramchunder Ráo Puar died in October 1833, after a short illness of eleven days. He had not quite attained the age of twenty-four. He left no male issue, and but one daughter. Agreeably to the Hindú custom, therefore, his widow, Unpúra Bai, adopted the son of one of the nearest relatives of the family of Jeswunt Ráo Puar, of Múltán—a descendant of Údají Puar, before referred to. The adoption having received the sanction of the British Government, the young Rájá, by name Mulhar Ráo Puar, was installed in the month of April following. He was about eleven years old at the time. His name on his accession was changed to Jeswunt Ráo. It was less than two years after the accession of this prince that Sindhia resumed possession of the district of Dektan, which had formed the dower of the wife of the late Rájá. He did not, however, hold it long. His generals fell out amongst themselves, and the local authorities of Dhár seized that opportunity to recover it. To make assurance doubly sure for the future, the Dhár minister requested the British to hold and manage the province, paying to Dhár the surplus revenues. This request was complied with.

The able minister who had so long conducted the

PART II.

affairs of the State, Bapú Ragonath, died in 1836. He was succeeded by his third son, a man of excellent character. The following year the young Rájá was affianced to Náná Bai, daughter of the Patél of Tankwa, a village in the Púna territory. The marriage took place later, but no issue proceeded from it.

Nothing occurred to disturb the tranquillity of the country till 1857. In that year the two events happened of which the good effects of one would seem to have neutralised the evil effects of the other. The first was the death of the Rájá, to be succeeded by a minor, his half brother, Anund Ráo; the second, that the State took advantage of the mutiny to rebel against the British. The rebellion was crushed, and the State was confiscated. Various causes, however, contributed to induce the British Government to take a lenient view of the outbreak—one of these being, I believe, the minority of the Rájá at the time of its occurrence. The country was, therefore, restored as an act of grace, but retained under British management until the young Rájá should attain his majority. The only punishment inflicted was the excision of the district of Bairsía—which had for years been under British management—from Dhár, and its transfer to the Begum of Bhopál.

Anund Ráo Puar attained his majority in 1863, but the Government was deterred from making over to him the management of the country by the reports of the local political agents as to his unfitness to undertake so grave a responsibility. But in August 1864, the Viceroy, Sir John Lawrence, determined to give him a fair trial, and on October 1 the administration was made over to the young prince. Certain conditions, however, accompanied the transfer. Anund Ráo Puar agreed to maintain the then existing system of management; to respect all leases and engagements until the expiration of the term of settlement; to be guided in the choice of a prime minister by the advice of the Governor-General's agent; to maintain the revenue arrangements as regards roads;

to alienate no territory or reversion to any of the neighbouring chiefs without the concurrence of the agent, and to keep the Dhár fort in its existing condition. CHAP. IV.

Bound by a promise to fulfil these stipulations, it was necessary only to keep it to maintain peace and order, and to ensure contentment amongst the people.

The Rájá of Dhár has received a sunnud granting to him the right of adoption. He receives a salute of fifteen guns.

CHAPTER V.

DEWÁS.

AREA—256 sq. miles. POPULATION—25,000.
REVENUE—4,25,000 rupees.

IN my account of the principality of Dhár, I stated that the Sambají Patél left one son, Krishnají, that he left three sons, Bábájí, Ryají, and Kerújí, and that Bábájí had two, Sámbají and Kalújí, distinguished military leaders under the Rájá Sahú. I have also shown that the Puars of Dhár were descended from Sámbají. I have now to relate how the descendants of his brother Kalújí also founded a state which still lives. Kalújí had four sons, Krishnají, Túkají, Jíwají, and Mánají. Of these, the second and third, Túkají and Jíwají, accompanied Bájí Ráo Peshwa into Málwá in 1725–26. In the subsequent division of that province they were assigned the districts of Dewás, Sárungpúr, Alót, and others, yielding a nominal revenue of 2,42,900 rupees, but subject to a yearly payment of 26,000 rupees to several Grásia chiefs. To this was added an assignment of the tribute of certain districts to the amount of 78,922 rupees, and at a later date, the province of Hamerpúr, in Bundelkhand, and CHAP. V.

PART II.

of Kandobá, in the Duáb. These, however, they did not very long retain.

The constitution of Dewás is peculiar. Originally assigned to the two brothers, Túkají and Jíwají Puar, a disagreement between them caused a division of the territory. Their descendants, however, agreed to revert to the original union of power and authority. And so it has since continued. The two Rájás are equal in rank and pretensions, and share equally in all receipts. 'An inquiry was made,' writes Sir John Malcolm, 'into their exact relations to ascertain how they were to be treated in points of form and ceremony. It was explained by one of their officers saying with a smile, "If a lime is presented by a villager, it must be cut into two equal parts and divided between our two Rájás." It was easily found,' continues Malcolm, 'that though their chiefs were on good terms, their principal servants often came in collision, and in making arrangements for their future welfare, a primary object was to induce them to appoint one minister. To this they agreed, and the nomination of a respectable old servant of the family to this office, has tended greatly to the improvement of their territories.'

The immediate successors of Túkají and Jíwají Puar passed through troublous times. Unhappily for them, more so still for their subjects, their principality lay in the most distracted part of Central India. Unable to maintain any force they were alternately plundered and oppressed, not only by Sindhia and Holkar, but by the Pindárí chiefs, and indeed by every freebooter of the day. In this way they lost the outlying districts of Hamerpúr and Kandapá. At one time, indeed, their district of Sárungpúr was seized by Sindhia, and only restored after the conclusion of the Pindárí war (1817–19). The wonder is, that, living in such an age, and under such conditions, they were allowed to retain even the smallest portion of their dominions.

Túkají Puar left no children. He adopted his grand-nephew, Krishnají, grandson of his eldest brother of that name. Krishnají dying likewise without male offspring, adopted his nephew, Túkají, son of his brother Ránojí. Túkají died in 1824, and was in his turn succeeded by an adopted son, Rúkmanund Ráo, commonly known as Khásch Sahib. He died in 1860, and Krishnají Ráo, whom he had adopted, was recognised as his successor. He was a minor, and was not invested with full powers till March 23, 1867.

It is a curious though by no means a rare fact in connection with the native dynasties of India, that in this branch of the family, not one single instance occurs of its representatives having been succeeded by a son naturally begotten. In every instance the heir has been adopted.

The other founder of the State. Jíwají Puar, left two sons—Sudasío, whose line became extinct with the death of his son, Rukma, and Anund Ráo. This prince was succeeded by his son Hybut Ráo. Hybut, dying childless, adopted Nílkant Ráo, grandson of Mánají, the youngest son of Kálojí, founder of the family. Nílkant Ráo, on adoption, assumed the name of Anund Ráo, but dying without male issue in 1837, was succeeded by his adopted son, Hybut Ráo. This prince adopted a son in 1858, on the understanding that his claims should give way to those of a legitimate son in the event of his being blessed with offspring. This occurred in December 1860. On the death of Hybut Ráo, nearly four years later (May 12, 1864), this son, called Narain Ráo Puar, was recognised as his successor. The State was managed during the minority of the two Rájás by the Kámdar, Govind Ráo Ramchunder, subject to the general control and supervision of the agent to the Governor-General. This state of things lasted till March 23, 1867, when the representative of the elder branch, Krishnají Ráo Puar, having attained his majority, was, as I have already stated, invested with full powers.

PART II.

Like the cognate principality of Dhár, Dewás owes its present state of comparative prosperity to the interference of the British in 1818. Still bleeding from the exactions of Sindhia, Holkar, and the Pindárís, it was then taken under British protection. Sindhia was forced to restore its native district of Sárungpúr; the two Rájás were recognised as, in every respect, rulers of their possessions, consisting of the districts of Dewás, Alót, Sárungpúr, Gúrgúchah, Bingnaod, Baghaod; they were also recognised as being entitled to a share of the collections, amounting to seven per cent., of the third parts of the province of Sandarsí, and an equal share of the collection of the province of Dúngelah. Subsequently, in 1828, the outlying district of Baghaod, too distant to be properly controlled, was taken under British management, the Rájás being entitled to the surplus revenues.

Subsequently to the arrangements thus made in 1818 with the British, the peace of Dewás has been but little disturbed. It is true that some of their dependants, notably the Thákur of Ragúghur, endeavoured for some time to parade an affected independence, either by withholding the tribute due to the Rájás, or by engaging in acts of plunder and robbery. But these lawless acts came to a crisis in 1834 by the imprisonment of the Thákur, caught in an act of daring robbery. Since that time similar depredations have become rare.

Both Rájás of Dewás rendered good service in 1857. On March 11th, 1862, a sunnud was transmitted to them conveying the right of adoption.

CHAPTER VI.

JÁORÁ.

AREA—872 sq. miles. POPULATION—85,456.
REVENUE—6,55,240 rupees.

CHAP. VI.

THE State of Jáorá was founded by Gafúr Khan, brother-in-law of the famous Amír Khan, the sketch of whose life is recorded under the heading of Tonk, in the States of Rájpútáná.

Gafúr Khan would appear to have been born in Rohilkhand, of Afghán parents, in the last quarter of the eighteenth century. He joined Amír Khan when that leader took service under Holkar in 1798, distinguished himself by his capacity for affairs, and when Jeswant Ráo became insane in 1808 was nominated by Amír Khan, of whom he had become the brother-in-law, a member of the regency formed for administering the affairs of Indúr. Of this regency Túlsa Bai, the mistress of the late Rájá, was the nominal head. Of the conduct of such an administration, Grant Duff records the following judgment:—'There was no regular collection of revenue; the government had not the power of reducing its army; and the finances of the state, even under the most skilful management, were inadequate to the support of the establishments. . . . . The government, if such it may be designated, was alternately swayed by two factions, the Marhátás and the Patháns, which were constantly intriguing against each other, and nothing could exceed the state of anarchy which prevailed throughout the country. At the court, bribery, executions, and murders; in the provinces violence, rapine, and bloodshed.'

It need scarcely be stated that of the rival factions Gafúr Khan led the Patháns. Thenceforward he was

PART II.

alternately the accomplice and the opponent of the dark intrigues which characterised the career of Túlsa Bai.[1] In one of the moments of the ascendency of the Marhátá party, Gafúr Khan retreated with the troops devoted to him to Jáorá, the lands of which had been assigned to him, and there began not only to exact contributions, but to plunder neighbouring districts as well. The Marhátá party sent a force against him, but Gafúr Khan was joined by his brother-in-law, who, after a contest lasting over fifteen days, forced the enemy to retire. The Pathán party then regained the ascendency. Amír Khan returned to Rájpútáná, and Gafúr Khan assumed the position of protector of the infant sovereign, Mulhar Ráo. Still intrigue succeeded intrigue, until at last Gafúr Khan incited the movement upon the town of Gungrao, which forced Túlsa Bai to take flight, and brought matters to a crisis. He finally concluded the long contest by assuring himself, on the eve of the battle of Mehidpúr, of the person of the young Rájá, and by consigning Túlsa Bai to death.[2]

The next day Gafúr Khan and the army of Holkar were completely defeated at Mehidpúr. But by the twelfth article of the treaty which followed (January 6, 1818) Gafúr Khan was guaranteed the districts of the Sujít, Mulhargurh, Taul, Mundáol, Jáorá, and Burόde; likewise the tribute of Píplaodá, and the customs of the whole. He was further guaranteed the descent of those districts to his heirs on the condition of his maintaining in constant readiness for foreign service a body of six hundred horse; 'and further that this quota of troops shall be hereafter increased in proportion to the increasing revenue of the districts granted to him.'[3]

It is true that Amír Khan himself claimed the lands thus granted to Gafúr Khan, on the ground that the latter had acted only as his agent in the matter, and that he

[1] *Vide* Holkar.

[2] For a detailed account of these intrigues, *vide* Malcolm's *Central India*, vol. i. chap. vi., vii.

[3] Aitchison's *Treaties*.

was entitled to them by virtue of his engagements with the British Government. But it was proved upon inquiry that Gafúr Khan held them on his own account as a member of Holkar's administration, and that his real dependence on Amír Khan, though the origin of his influence at that court, had ceased before the war of 1817. Amír Khan's claim was therefore rejected.[1]

Such was the origin of the principality of Jáorá—the successful audacity of an adventurer of Afghán descent, his race being as much a foreign race in the eyes of the aboriginal inhabitants as is that of the British.

Gafúr Khan survived the treaty of Mundisúr but seven years. He was succeeded in 1825 by his son, Nawáb Ghous Mahomed Khan, then only two years old. The arrangements for the management of the state were made by the British Government, but as Jáorá was nominally a fief of the Holkar state, though really independent of it, the investiture of the young Nawáb was made in the name of Mulhar Ráo Holkar, to whom a nuzzerana of two lakhs of rupees was presented, with the approval of the British Government. The elder widow of Gafúr Khan was nominated guardian, her son-in-law, Jehángír Khan, was appointed her agent; and they were required to keep open accounts of the State revenues for the inspection of the Governor-General's agent at Indúr. Two years later, in consequence of gross mismanagement and neglect of the agent's advice, the Begum was removed from the guardianship. It was also decided that, in the event of Ghous Mahomed's death, the male relatives of Gafúr Khan should succeed, in preference to those in the female line.[2]

In the year 1825 the arrangements of the treaty of Mundisúr were modified so as to fix the quota of troops to be maintained by the Nawáb of Jáorá, at 500 horse, 500 foot, and two guns. But in 1842 the contingent furnished by Jáorá was amalgamated with that furnished

[1] Aitchison's *Treaties*.

[2] *Ibid.*

PART II.

by Holkar and Dewás, and in lieu a money payment was required. This was slightly reduced in 1859, in reward for the services of Nawáb Ghous Mahomed during the mutinies.[1]

Ghous Mahomed died on April 29, 1865, leaving a son, Mahomed Ishmaël Khan, eleven years of age. Immediately, upon the recommendation of the Governor-General's agent, a council of regency was nominated, consisting of Huzrut Núr Khan, the Kámdar, or general manager, of the late Nawáb; two members of the family, and the widow,—mother of Mahomed Ishmaël. This lady, however, died two days after her husband, and it was found that the single association of the Kámdar with the members of the family would simply serve to revive old family dissensions. It was decided then to maintain the fiction by which Jáorá was regarded as a fief of the Holkar family. Accordingly the Governor-General's agent was instructed to cause the investiture of the young chief to take place under the authority of the British Government, but in the name of the Máhárájá Holkar, to whom two lakhs of rupees were to be presented as the offering due to a suzerain on succession. But meanwhile, other complications arose. The chief wife of the late Nawáb, then absent on a visit to her half-brother, the Nawáb of Tonk, claimed the throne for herself. Her half-brother, the Nawáb of Tonk, demanded it also for himself, basing his claims on those preferred by Amír Khan in 1818, and rejected by the British Government, and on the statement that the son of the late Nawáb, Mahomed Ishmaël Khan, was illegitimate.

These claims were considered by the Government of

[1] The services of the Nawáb of Jáorá during the mutinies were by no means inconsiderable. It was mainly owing to him that the British Government was indebted for correct information in more than one important conjuncture. It was the Nawáb who made the Governor-General's agent, the late Sir Henry Durand, aware of the understanding between Holkar's troops and the insurgents; and when Sir H. Durand took the field the Nawáb of Jáorá was the only chief who boldly and promptly joined him in his camp.

India, and by it after due investigation were rejected. Accordingly the investiture took place in the manner directed, the khillut, or honorary dress, being bestowed in the name of the British Government.

The administration of Jáorá was conducted during the minority of the young chief by the Kámdar, subject to the supervision of the political officer on the spot. But this arrangement ceased on the Nawáb attaining his majority in 1872.

The Nawáb of Jáorá received a sunnud from the Governor-General in 1862, guaranteeing the succession to his State according to Mahomedan law, in the event of the failure of natural heirs. He is entitled to a salute of thirteen guns.

PART III.—BUNDELKHAND.

CHAPTER I.

REWÁ.

AREA—12,723 sq. miles. POPULATION—1,280,000.
REVENUE—About 22,50,000 rupees.

PART III. THIS principality is bounded on the north by the districts of Alláhábád and Mírzápúr; on the north-east by Mírzápúr; on the south-east by Koreá; on the south by Saugor, and on the west by a portion of the central provinces and Bundelkhand.

Rewá would appear to have formed part of the ancient kingdom of Kálinger, and to have been severed from it and nominally annexed to Alláhábád during the reign of Aurangzíb. The sovereignty over it of the Mogul empire, however, was apparently limited to the exaction of tribute. It is inhabited by a race called Bhagelás. On the disruption of the Mogul empire, the Bhagelá chief—who is said to have been a descendant of Sid Rai Jai Singh, famous in the twelfth century—gained a quasi-independence under the nominal suzerainty of the Peshwa. The events which led to the treaty of Bassein (1802–3), and that treaty itself, freed the chief even from that nominal suzerainty. Then it was that the British Government made to him overtures to extend to him its protection. Thinking probably he could stand his ground without such protection, the chief, known as Rájá Jai Singh Déo, refused it. And certainly, his dominions being removed from the highway of hostilities, he for some years plumed himself upon his prudence. But, in 1812, he went a step beyond keeping aloof. In the course of that year a body of Pindárís, bent on plunder, were aided and abetted by Rájá Jai Singh Déo, in a marauding incursion into the British district of Mírzápúr. The complicity of the Rájá in this act of hostility having been established to the satisfaction of the British Government, he was called upon to accede to a treaty, by which, whilst the British Government acknowledged his rank and title as Rájá of Rewá, and bound itself to friendship and protection towards him, he was required to refer all disputes between himself and neighbouring chiefs to the arbitration of the British Government, and to permit British troops to be marched through, or stationed within, his territories. The Rájá was bound likewise to deliver up enemies, rebels, and criminals who might be found therein.

Rájá Jai Singh Déo did sign this treaty, but he did not keep it. On the contrary, he seized the first opportunity of the passage of a body of British sepoys through his territories to attack them (1813). He attempted likewise to reduce them by starvation. In both these attempts he failed, but the act of aggression was palpable. Such conduct called for the display of military force. Troops were accordingly sent into his country. Their appearance was sufficient. The Rájá made no defence, expressed contrition, and submitted unconditionally. The result was the conclusion of a second treaty (June 1813), whereby the Rájá bound himself to engage in no correspondence of a political nature with any foreign State; to receive a news-writer or other agent; to permit the establishment of postal arrangements throughout his country, and to punish or aid in punishing certain large landowners who had evinced a contumacious or hostile spirit towards the British Government.

This treaty, too, was agreed to by the Rájá, but

PART III.

having imbibed the idea that its provisions were only binding upon himself personally, he abdicated in favour of his son, Bishnáth Singh, before any of them could be put into execution. But this *finesse* did not succeed. The British Government called upon Bishnáth Singh to execute an instrument binding himself to abide by the terms of the treaties negotiated with his father. Bishnáth was most unwilling to do this, and it was only after having exhausted evasion that he complied.

By a third treaty, made in 1814 with the Rájá, the British Government restored to him certain lands which had previously been forfeited, and renounced the right to interfere between him and his feudatories.

Nothing of moment occurred during the following twenty years. In 1834 Rájá Bishnáth Singh died, and was succeeded by his son Ragráj Singh, who, according to the native annals, is the thirty-second in order of succession. In 1847, this prince abolished satí throughout his dominions. In 1857 he rendered good and faithful services. For these he was rewarded by the grant of two districts in sovereignty.

The right of adoption has been granted to the Rájá of Rewá. In October 1864, he was invested by the Viceroy with the Order of the Star of India.

In the following year gangs of robbers from his dominions plundered the adjoining districts, but the Rájá, warned by the British Government, succeeded in repressing and capturing them.

The Rájá of Rewá is entitled to a salute of seventeen guns.

CHAPTER II.

ÚRCHAH or TEHRÍ.

AREA—2,160 sq. miles. POPULATION—200,000.
REVENUE—About 5,50,000 rupees.

CHAP. II.

THIS principality, lying south-east of Agra, and north of Saugor, ranks first among the States of Bundelkhand as being the only State in that province which was never held in subjection by the Peshwa. It is said that when the Rájá presented a nuzzer to the Governor-General in 1818, he remarked that it was the first time that the family had acknowledged the supremacy of any other power.

The chronicles of the house of Tehrí exhibit, according to its legendary annals, seventy-two generations, from the first Rájá, the celestial Ramchunder, who reigned at Ayodhia (Oudh). He was succeeded by his second son, Ankúsh, from whom Gungrakh, who founded some splendid temples at Gayá, in Behar, is sixteenth in lineal descent. The twentieth Rájá, Buldéo Rakh, founded those at Pryág, or Alláhábád, and his son, Indradmun, built the celebrated temples of Juggernâth. It is from Rant Singh, the second son of the thirty-second Rájá, that the Burgúzur Rájpúts derive their origin. The thirty-fourth Rájá, Kurmshya, conquered the province of Banáras. Kemkuru, the second son of the forty-sixth Rájá, having, says the chronicle, performed some religious austerities on the summit of Hinda-Chul, succeeded in propitiating the tutelary goddess of the mountain. He was about to sacrifice himself, but suddenly, when in the very act, the goddess appeared in all her glory, and a drop of blood having fallen from the wound which he had inflicted on himself, she conveyed to it a portion of the water of immortality, and it assumed the form of a child, afterwards the famous Bír Singh, who called his people Bundelás, from Búnd, a drop. He soon acquired a dominion, and ruled his people with justice. The sixtieth Rájá, Purtáb Rúdra, having founded the city of Úrcha, entrusted the government to his son while absent on an expedition, from which he never returned. Mudhúkur, proverbial for his justice, power, and charity, was the sixty-second Rájá; he reigned in the time of Akbar. His eldest son, Rámásá, was appointed to the government of Ayodhia, while the younger son, Nursingh Déo, was confirmed by Jehángír in Úrcha, and the district of Chanderí was given to Rámásá to reconcile him to the loss of an hereditary demesne. Nursingh Déo had twelve sons; the third, Pahar Singh, accompanied, at a later period, Aurangzíb to Aurangábád, and founded a suburb which now bears his name. With Bhagwán Das, the fourth son, originated the tribe of Kúrers. The sixty-eighth prince was Champut Rae. In consequence of his refusal to pay tribute to Shah Jehán, Bundelkhand was twice invaded by the imperial armies, and the country became a prey to licence and anarchy. But Úrcha was not taken, the Rájá did not submit, and the retiring army was harassed almost to annihilation by the Bundelás. Champut Rae afterwards joined Aurangzíb against his brother Dára; his son, Chutter Sál, then thirteen years old, being placed in the van of the army. To the knowledge possessed by these princes, father and son, of the passes through the country and across the Jamna the success of Aurangzíb has been ascribed. The emperor, however, as was his wont, forgot these services, for, after the death of Champut Rae, he sent an army into Bundelkhand and endeavoured forcibly to convert the inhabitants to the Mahomedan faith. The son, Chutter Sál, was at that time serving in the Dekhan, under the orders of Rájá Jai Singh, of Jaipúr. He had formed, then, the acquaintance of the renowned Sivají, against whom he was acting in the field. At one of their interviews, Sivají forcibly reminded Chutter Sál of his duty to his religion and his country. Then, girding a sword on his loins, and commending him to the goddess Bhawání, he urged him to return to his country and achieve its independence. He followed that advice, and after the death of Aurangzíb, expelled the invaders, and conquered a great part of Bundelkhand.

Such is the legendary history.[1] It would appear certain, however, that the territory conquered by Chutter Sál included Datiá, Samptar, Jhansí, and a part of Rewá. After his death, Datiá became a separate principality under a prince of the same family; whilst the portion of his territory which subsequently constituted the State of Jhansi, was bequeathed by him to the Peshwa Bájí Ráo in 1735. The independence of the portion called Tehrí, with Úrchah for its capital, was never threatened. But the effect of these severances was great. The revenues of Chutter Sál, after he had achieved the independence of Bundelkhand generally, were estimated at 20,000,000 rupees; in 1837 the revenues of Tehrí had dwindled down to 600,000: and they are believed since to have decreased.

The first communications between the Rájá of Tehrí and the British power occurred in 1809, when the Rájá solicited to be admitted amongst the number of protected allies of the British, on terms similar to those which had been concluded with the Bundelá Rájás who had been granted British protection by the terms of the treaty of Bassein. Apparently, however, the policy of totally abstaining from all interference in the affairs of native states introduced by Lord Cornwallis, and adhered to by his immediate successors, prevented the entertainment of his request. But events were too strong for the devotees of that policy. The incursion of the Pindárís into

[1] *The Princes of India*, by an officer of the East India Company. There are other legends differing in many essentials from this, and it is difficult to decide which contains the true story.

Mírzápúr in 1812, to which I have alluded in the preceding chapter, showed the British Government the advantage that would accrue to it by adopting a policy of conciliation and protection towards the independent Rájás of Bundelkhand. A treaty was thereupon negotiated and concluded with Bikramájít Molunder, Rájá of Úrchah, by which the Rájá was admitted among the number of the allies of the British; his territory, without payment of tribute, was guaranteed to him and his successors, and the British protection assured to them. On the other hand, the Rájá bound himself to refer disagreements, claims, and causes of dispute with foreign powers and other chiefs to the arbitration of the British; to defend the roads and passes of his country against predatory bodies attempting to enter the British territories; and to allow the British Government to send its troops through, or to station them within, his dominions.

When, four years and a half later, the Marquis of Hastings passed through Tehrí with a portion of the army that was to act against the Pindárís, Rájá Bikramájít presented his nuzzer in token of fealty. It was upon this occasion he remarked that it was the first time a Rájá of Úrchah had ever acknowledged the supremacy of another power.

Rájá Bikramájít died in the year 1834. His only son, Dhurm Pál, had died before him. The succession therefore devolved upon his brother, Tej Singh. This prince died in 1842, having previously adopted the son of his cousin, Súrjun Singh. But another claimant appeared in the widow of Dhurm Pál, who preferred her right to adopt a successor to the State. Serious disturbances ensued, and it became necessary for the British authorities to make a military demonstration. Finally, the British Government having recognised Súrjun Singh, and his claims having been considered well founded by the neighbouring chiefs, he was preferred, the Rání being appointed to act as regent until he should attain his majority. Súrjun

Singh, however, lived long enough to assume the reins of power, and no longer. On his death his widow was permitted, with the advice of the principal Bundelá chiefs, to adopt a collateral relation of the family, Hamír Singh. The representatives of this prince, who is now about twenty-four years old, rendered good service in 1857. In consideration of this the tribute previously paid by him to Jhansí for the district of Teráolí was remitted. In 1862 he received a sunnud conferring upon him the right of adoption.

The Rájá is entitled to a salute of eleven guns. Satí was prohibited in his dominions in 1847.

DATIÁ.

AREA—850 sq. miles. POPULATION—120,000.
REVENUE—10,00,000 rupees.

THE Rájás of this State belong to the same family as those of Úrchah or Tehrí. Datiá was severed from Tehrí about the year 1735; but even then it attained only a quasi-independence, the suzerainty of the Peshwa being acknowledged. When the Peshwa was forced in 1802-3 to sign the treaty of Bassein, the States in Bundelkhand which acknowledged fealty to him transferred their allegiance to the British Government. Of these Datiá was one. Consequently on March 15, 1804, a treaty was entered into with the ruler of the country, Ráo Rájá Párichét, on the usual terms on which protection was accorded.

The Ráo Rájá having evinced his attachment to the British interests by zealous co-operation during the war which terminated in 1817 in the deposition of the Peshwa, a tract of land on the east of the river Sindh was added to his dominions, and a new treaty, making over to him this tract, was signed July 31, 1818.

Rájá Párichét died without issue in 1839, and was succeeded by a foundling whom he had adopted, named

PART III.

Bejéy Bahadúr. His claims were opposed by a collateral branch of the late Rájá's family on the plea of an old agreement that in the event of the Rájá dying without issue the succession should lie in that branch. But the claim was rejected, on the ground that the British Government had recognised Bejéy Bahádúr; that he was governing the country fairly; and that his succession was agreeable to the people.

Bejéy Bahádúr died in 1857, leaving an adopted son, Bhawáni Singh, and an illegitimate son, Urjún Singh. The claims of the former were preferred as being consonant to Hindú law and custom. But Urjún Singh did not acquiesce in this view, and his claims were supported by the Rání regent. It became necessary, therefore, to remove him from Datiá. Shortly after this the Ráni regent rose in revolt and seized the fort of Seonda. It then became necessary to employ British troops. These reduced the fort, and took the garrison prisoners. The leading rebels were sentenced to life imprisonment in the fort of Chunar, and the Rání was placed under close surveillance. The claims of the collateral branch of the family were again preferred in 1861 and were again rejected.

The Rájá is entitled to a salute of eleven guns. He has been granted the right of adoption. Satí was prohibited in 1847.

SAMPTAR.

AREA—175 sq. miles. POPULATION—30,000.
REVENUE—About 4,50,000 rupees.

THE small state of Samptar formed part of the Datiá territory till about the year 1762, when it was separated from it under circumstances which have apparently evaded all research. Probably, as Datiá acknowledged the suzerainty of the Peshwa, and Samptar claims to have been always independent, it represents that portion of the united territory which took advantage of the humiliation of the Márhátás after Pánipat, to recover freedom and assert independence. Certainly it always claimed to be independent, and ever regarded the Márhátás as the enemy most to be dreaded. This was shown in 1805, when, after the defeat of both Sindhia and Holkar, the Rájá, Ranjít Singh, pressed to be taken under British protection. A draft of an engagement for that purpose was actually prepared, when the arrival of Lord Cornwallis entirely altered the policy of the British Government, and Samptar was left out in the cold. Subsequently to that period the Rájá made repeated applications to be admitted within the pale, but his entreaties were not acceded to until the middle of 1817. Samptar was then comprehended in the arrangements made with other powers similarly situated. By the treaty made with him (November 12, 1817), his possessions were guaranteed to him, and protection against enemies was promised, on condition of his furnishing a contingent of horse, and attaching himself to British interests. The body of horse which the Rájá at once furnished was attached to the centre division of the army, and rendered good service.

Rájá Ranjít Singh died in 1827, and was succeeded by his son Nindúpat.

Nindúpat was only six months old when his father died. His mother was appointed regent. But as Nindúpat grew up he discovered symptoms akin to unsoundness of mind. He married, indeed, and begat children, but his mental powers remained conspicuous by their absence. As soon as he became of age, then, the Rání, with the concurrence of the officials and Thákurs of the state, placed Nindúpat under restraint, and administered the affairs of the state ostensibly until her eldest son Chutter Singh, known as Rájá Bahádúr, and who was born about 1843, should attain his majority. But in 1864, Rájá Bahádúr, being then twenty-one, complained to the political agent that not only had his mother excluded him from the government, but that she was squandering and mismanaging the resources of the State. He brought another charge against her, which need not, however, be more particularly alluded to.

In consequence of this representation, the British Government directed that the administration should at once be conferred upon Rájá Bahádúr. In compliance with instructions received this was done, and the insane Rájá and the Rání were moved to the district of Alma, there to receive a fourth of the revenues during their natural lives. A council of six was nominated to assist the young Rájá in his administration.

The Rájá of Samptar has received the right of adoption. He is entitled to a salute of eleven guns.

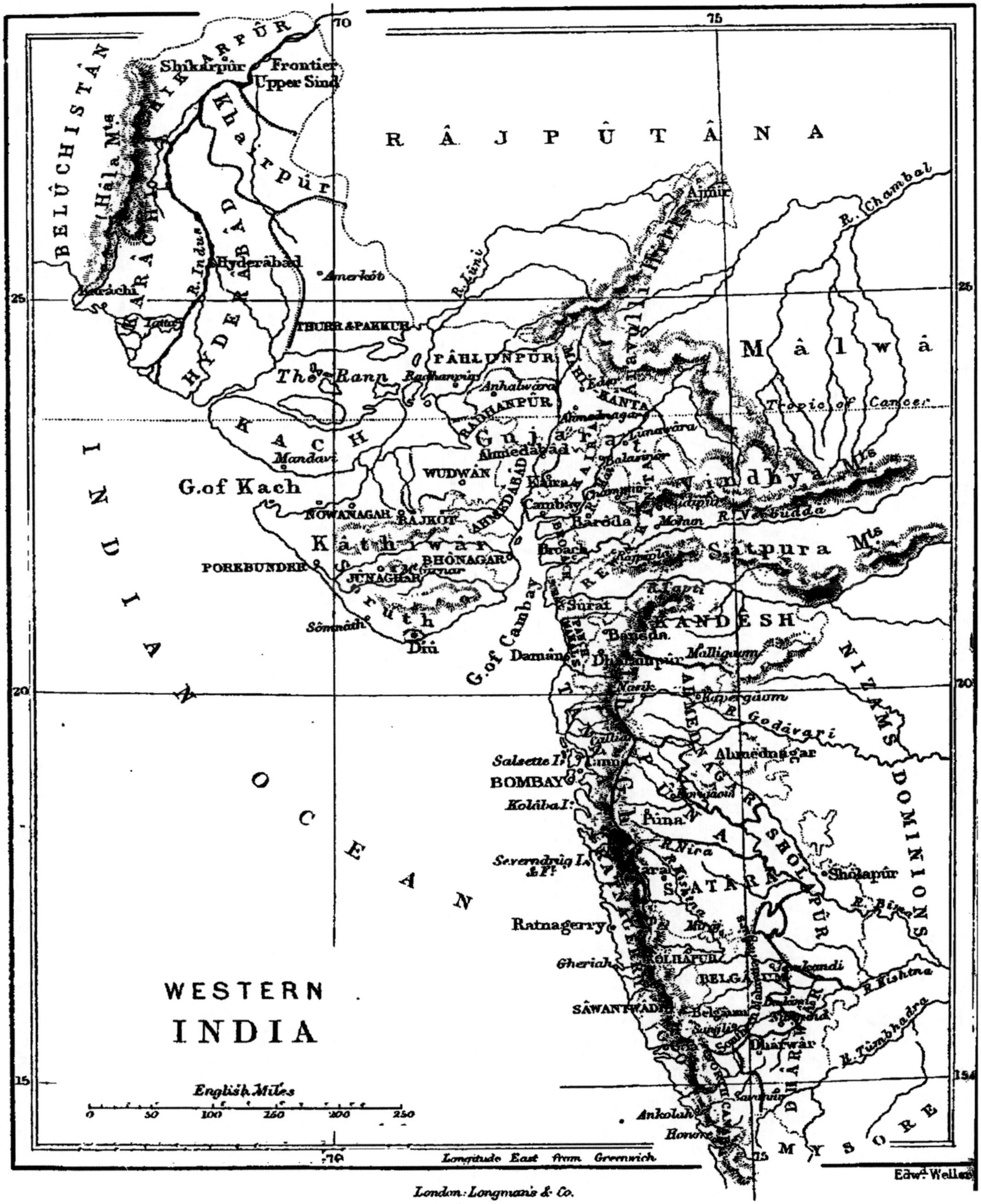

London: Longmans & Co.

PART IV.—WESTERN INDIA.

CHAPTER I.

BARODAH, OR THE DOMINIONS OF THE GÁIKWÁR.

AREA—4,399 sq. miles. POPULATION—1,710,400.
REVENUE—60,00,000 rupees.

CHAP. I.

THE first member of this family of whom any mention is made in Indian history was Dámají Gáikwár, an officer who had greatly distinguished himself in the military employ of the Márhátás, especially under the command of one of the most eminent of the leaders of that people, Khandí Rao Dhabárí. Dámají died in 1720. He was succeeded in his military office and appointments by his nephew, Pílají, a man of talent and energy. Pílají used these qualities to such advantage that in 1731 he was raised to the office of Sená Kháss Kheyl, or 'Commander of the sovereign's tribe,' under the governor of Gujrát. He did not long enjoy his new dignity, for the following year he was assassinated by the emissaries of Abhí Singh, Rájá of Jodhpúr, who had been nominated by the court of Delhi Súbadár of the province.

Pílají was succeeded in his offices by his son Dámají. A circumstance which occurred shortly afterwards led to the preferring of a claim by the Gáikwárs always to salute with the left hand. It appears that there was some delay in the recognition of Dámají Gáikwár. He thereupon raised an army to support his claims, and marched at its head into the Dekhan. He was induced

PART IV.

by the Rájá of Satára, on a solemn promise to accord him satisfaction, to disband this army. No sooner, however, had he done this than the Peshwa, by the Rájá's orders, attacked and plundered him. This induced Dámají solemnly to swear that he would never pay the compliment of a salaam with the hand which had been pledged in that of his prince with a false oath.

Dámají did not allow a long time to elapse before he avenged his father's death. In concert with his uncle, Mádhají Gáikwár, he attacked and took Barodah, which thenceforth became the seat of his administration, then occupied many of the principal districts in the east of Gujrát, and finally, extending his incursions as far as Jodhpúr, forced the Rájá of that country to resign Ahmedábád to a deputy in order to proceed to the defence of his paternal dominions. Ahmedábád was not finally taken till 1755, when it surrendered to the united efforts of Ragonáth Ráo and Dámají Gáikwár. From that time the authority of the court of Delhi over Gujrát ceased entirely, and the country was divided between the Peshwa and the Gáikwár.

I have already stated that the Gáikwárs were the confidential servants of the Dhabárí family. Dámají Gáikwár was destined to become its successor. Unrestrained debauchery had entirely unfitted the representative of the Dhabárí family, Jeswant Ráo, from carrying on the duties devolving on the head of a State, and some time before the conquest of Ahmedábád, that nobleman had retired before the increasing influence of the commander of his forces. When, then, the division of the conquered lands of Gujrát took place, the partition was made, as I have stated, between the Peshwa and the Gáikwár, to the entire exclusion of the Dhabárí interest. From the period of that partition dates the rule of the Gáikwár family.

Dámají employed the early period of his rule in consolidating the territories he had thus gained. He was not deaf, however, to the call of his suzerain, and he led his troops in 1761 to the fatal field of Pánipat. Escaping from that defeat, he returned to Barodah to nurse the resources which had been so terribly tried. But he was not destined to remain in peace. The restlessness of the ambitious Ragonáth Ráo had brought about a rebellion against the Peshwa, and in this Dámají Gáikwár was induced to take part. He sent to Ragonáth Ráo troops under the command of his son Góvind Ráo. But after a campaign, in which no decisive action had been fought, terms were agreed upon very favourable to the Peshwa. The Gáikwár was punished by the imposition of an annual payment of 5,25,000 rupees, and by an obligation to furnish 3,000 horse in times of war. He was also compelled to pay 2,54,000 rupees for certain districts which the Peshwa promised to restore to him.

The same year, 1768, Dámají Gáikwár died. He left four sons: Syají, an idiot, Góvind Ráo, Mánají, and Futteh Singh. Góvind Ráo claimed the succession, and by means of a large nuzzer to the Peshwa and by signing the unsigned treaty of 1768—the purport of which is given in the preceding paragraph—succeeded in obtaining recognition. His right was not, however, acknowledged by his brothers. The youngest, Futteh Singh, proceeded in 1771 to Púna, to advocate the rights of his idiot brother, Syají. His arguments were effectual, it being the Peshwa's object to weaken as much as possible the power of the Gáikwárs, and he received the nomination of coadjutor to his brother. The terms of the treaty of 1768 were likewise modified in his favour. By this arrangement Futteh Singh became virtual ruler. Moreover, he had divined the designs of the Peshwa, and he determined if possible to baffle them. With this object he sought an alliance in 1772, offensive and defensive, with the English. To this proposal, however, the Governor of Bombay was not authorised to accede, and the idea fell for the moment to the ground. A short contract was entered

PART IV.

into between the two governments on January 13th in the following year, conveying an agreement on the part of the British Government to pay to the Gáikwár his share of the revenues of Bharoch, which the British had captúred.

Futteh Singh administered the affairs of the country for eighteen years. Eleven of these were years of almost unceasing hostility in his neighbourhood. First came the wars of the Peshwa, the restless Ragonáth Ráo, and his contests with the party that had driven him from his office. Then followed the contests between Mádhají Sindhia and the English, ending in the convention of Wargaum, followed up by the campaigns of General Goddard. In none of these was the Gáikwár a principal, and their details scarcely belong to the history of his country. It is sufficient to state that on the whole Futteh Singh displayed tact and discrimination. For although he at first attached himself to the losing cause of Ragonáth Ráo, he had the good sense in 1780 to unite with the English and espouse their side. The result was that the Gáikwár emerged in 1782 from these long troubles, without any loss of territory or prestige.

Seven years later, December 31, 1789, Futteh Singh died from a fall from the upper story of his house. His younger brother, Mánají, who was on the spot, at once assumed charge of the person and government of the idiot brother, Syají. But the second brother, Góvind Ráo, who, elbowed out by Futteh Singh, was then residing in a village in the neighbourhood of Púna, presented a petition to the Peshwa, praying to be acknowledged as regent of the Gáikwár's possessions. His claim was just, but Mánají, by paying a nuzzer of thirty-three lakhs thirteen thousand and one rupees, and agreeing to pay up the thirty-six lakhs of arrears due by Futteh Singh, was confirmed in his usurpation. But Mádhají Sindhia espoused the cause of Góvind Ráo, and procured the reversal of this arrangement. Upon this Mánají appealed to the Government of Bombay. A compromise was then suggested. This was unpalatable to Góvind Ráo. The question, however, was suddenly settled by the death of Mánají (August 1793). Góvind Ráo thus became undisputed regent. He set out to assume this office on December 19, 1793, having first signed an engagement to pay large sums to the Peshwa. From other attempted exactions he was released by the interference of the English.

A few years after Góvind Ráo Gáikwár had thus assumed the reins of government we find him engaged in a conflict with Ábá Shelúkur, the deputy-governor of the Peshwa's share of Gujrát, who had made raids into the territories of the Gáikwár. Whilst hostilities were in progress the Nawáb of Súrat died. The Governor of Bombay proceeded at once by orders of the Governor-General to Súrat, to assume charge of the government of that city, and to arrange for the grant to the Nawáb's brother and heir of an annual pension, on condition of his renouncing all pretensions to the exercise of authority. The Governor, Mr. Duncan, took advantage then of the arrival of two envoys from Góvind Ráo Gáikwár to prefer a request that the district immediately surrounding Súrat, and known as the district of Chourasí, might be added to the grant. Góvind Ráo, hoping to secure the aid of the English in his contest with Ábá Shelúkur, readily promised the cession, provided the Governor could obtain the sanction of the Peshwa, without which it would not be valid. Notwithstanding this, the Governor evaded his request for aid. But just at this conjuncture, Góvind Ráo succeeded in taking Ahmedábád, the capital of his enemy, and with it that enemy himself. In consequence of this success, the Peshwa granted his share of the revenue of Gujrát in form to the Barodah government for five years, at five lakhs of rupees annually. But before the agreement could be executed Góvind Rao Gáikwár died (September 1800).

Góvind Rao left behind him eleven sons, four of whom

were legitimate. He was succeeded by his eldest legitimate son, Anund Ráo. But as he was a man of weak intellect and incapable of ruling, various parties began to plot to secure the direction of public affairs. That headed by Kánhojí Ráo, the eldest of the illegitimate sons, and who, for his turbulent behaviour, had been placed in confinement prior to his father's death, but had subsequently been released, seemed at first to take the lead. Kánhojí became first minister, then dictator. But the usurpation was not acquiesced in. A formidable party, headed by the late prime minister, Raojí Áppají, went into active opposition, and succeeded in wresting the seals of office from Kánhojí. Both sides then appealed to the Bombay Government to support them in their recourse to arms. Each party had formidable adherents. Raojí was supported by his brother Bábájí, who commanded the Gujrát cavalry, and by the seven thousand Arab mercenaries who formed the garrison of the town. Kánhojí, on the other hand, was aided by the courage, talent, and enterprise of his father's first cousin, Mulhar Ráo Gáikwár. This chief, believing that success depended upon taking an active initiative, attacked the town with such vigour as to spread alarm in the highest circles of Barodah.

Then came the Bombay Government's opportunity. The Governor had early pressed upon the Governor-General the propriety of interfering efficiently in favour of the old prime minister; but, receiving no reply, he had recourse to the half measure of interfering inefficiently. He sent a small auxiliary force of 1,600 men to the support of Raojí, under the command of Major Walker. This officer received instructions to settle the affair amicably if possible; if not, by acting with Bábájí. The second course was pursued. The united forces advanced against Mulhar Ráo Gáikwár. Mulhar Ráo, having lulled his enemies into security by evincing a disposition to retreat, suddenly assailed them, and was only repulsed after he had inflicted a perceptible loss. Soon after, it was discovered that Mulhar Ráo had succeeded in gaining over many of Bábáji's troops. Major Walker's position then became critical. He had an open enemy in front of him, and he had secret enemies in his very camp. Fortunately for Major Walker, Mulhar Ráo's plans were not quite ripe, and he had time to send to Bombay for reinforcements. These arrived on April 29, 1801. The next day Mulhar Ráo's camp was attacked, and after a desperate resistance and suffering severe loss, was carried. Mulhar Ráo soon afterwards surrendered. He was assigned the town of Neriad and an income of 1,25,000 rupees per annum, with a promise of increase should he behave well. Kánhojí was made prisoner and confined in Barodah. The terms imposed by the British were such as marked their policy in dealing with native States at that period. The Gáikwár was to receive a subsidiary force from the British Government, and to cede the chouth[1] of Súrat and the district of Chourásí. A private agreement was also made with the minister, Raojí Áppají, guaranteeing to him permanently the post of minister, and extending the protection of the British Government to him, his son, brother, nephews, relations, and friends. A political resident was also nominated to the court of the Gáikwár.

But order had not been entirely restored. The finances were in a state of terrible confusion. The Arab mercenaries occupied a position similar to that, in former days, of the janissaries at Constantinople. Some rebels remained still in arms.

The third difficulty was first met and solved. The first was also boldly encountered and was in process of solution, when it became absolutely necessary to meet the second. In fact, the reforms, retrenchments, and re-organisations going on around them had alarmed these mercenaries. They saw that unless they struck they would

[1] A fourth part of the revenue.

PART IV.

be swept away. They therefore confined the Gáikwár, permitted Kánhojí to escape, and entered into negotiations with Mulhar Ráo. Vainly did the British Resident try to bring them to terms. He therefore called in a regiment of Europeans to aid the subsidiary force, and sent that to assail them in Barodah. After a siege of ten days, in which great losses were inflicted on the besieging force, they surrendered. Liberal terms were made with them, and they agreed to quit the country.

Kánhojí was shortly afterwards defeated in a desperate encounter at Saurí (February 6), and again near Kaperwanj a month later. He then fled to Ujjén. Finally, in 1812, he was removed as an incorrigible disturber of public order, to Madras. Mulhar Ráo Gáikwár eventually died a prisoner at Bombay.

Amongst the terms made with the Arab mercenaries that which pressed the most heavily on the resources of the State was the liquidation of the arrears of pay due to them. To effect this liquidation it became necessary to raise a loan of 41,38,732 rupees. Of this loan the East India Company advanced about one-half, and guaranteed the remainder to the native bankers who might advance it. The debt thus incurred was to be repaid in three years, with interest at the rate of 9 per cent.; in default of which certain districts were to be assigned, and their revenues collected and applied by the Company to its extinction. No part of this advance having been repaid in April 1805, it became necessary to draw up a definitive treaty, which should consolidate the stipulations of all former engagements. By this treaty (April 21, 1805) the subsidiary force, which had been augmented to 3,000 men in June 1803, was made permanent, and certain territories together rated as yielding 11,70,000 rupees, were assigned in perpetual sovereignty to the Company to provide for its payment. Other lands were also assigned, rated at 12,95,000 rupees, for the liquidation of the debt due by the Gáikwár to the British Government.

The cession in perpetuity of the districts of Chourási, Kaira, Súrat, and Chickly was confirmed by this treaty.

But under such a steadying load of debt, increased every year by the high rate of interest charged on the loan, the affairs of the Gáikwár did not progress, and in 1809, only four years after the conclusion of the last treaty, they appeared to be almost inextricably involved. It must be admitted that—to state the matter as fairly as possible—he had not in the interval been assisted by any forbearance on the part of his main creditors. On the contrary, in 1807, the British Government, finding that the ceded districts did not yield a revenue equal to the support of the subsidiary force, forced the Gáikwár (June 18) to yield more districts, yielding an annual revenue, in addition, of 1,76,168 rupees. The Government of Bombay, unmindful of the heavy loan pressing upon his Highness, offered, in 1812, to restore him all these ceded territories on the payment of a million sterling of money. This would have been a remarkably good bargain for the British, but it was objected to by the Governor-General.

The following year a general famine added greatly to the disasters of the country, and rendered the collection of revenue difficult, the meeting the demands of creditors impossible.

I have already alluded to the appointment of a British officer as Resident at the court of the Gáikwár in the year 1802. The choice of the British Government had fallen then upon Major Walker, the same who had been sent to support Raojí Áppají against Mulhar Ráo. Major Walker would appear to have been an officer of singular capacity and prudence. After he had succeeded in introducing some sort of order in the Barodah councils, he had to report to his Government (1805) that whilst the receipts of the State amounted to only fifty-five lakhs of rupees the disbursements reached eighty-two. He received then the sanction of the Supreme Government to exercise a more marked and decided interference, with a view to bring

PART IV. about an equilibrium. This he partially effected by the disbandment of the Arab mercenaries and the obtaining of the loans already alluded to. At this period the Gáikwár himself, from his natural imbecility, took no part in State affairs. These were administered nominally by a council of State under the control of the Resident—in reality by the Resident aided by the advice of the members of the council of State.

Major Walker retired in 1811, to be succeeded by Captain, afterwards Sir James Rivett Carnac. Major Walker's talents and industry had accomplished much, but much still remained to be done.

The famine of 1813 threw matters back considerably; so much so that though in 1809 Major Walker had calculated that the debt, which in 1805 amounted to about forty-one lakhs, might be paid off in five years, it had risen in 1816 to fifty-five lakhs!

Two years prior to that, in 1814, an agreement which had existed between the Peshwa and the Gáikwár regarding the farming of Ahmedábád and Káthiwár, to the latter, for 4,50,000 rupees per annum having expired, the proposal to renew the agreement was met by counter claims preferred by the Gáikwár for the revenues of Bharoch, which the Peshwa had ceded, without his consent, to the British, and for the pay of extraordinary troops kept up for the defence of the Peshwa's possessions in Gujrát. To settle the differences which had arisen, the council of State at Barodah despatched one of their members, Gungadhur Shastry, under the guarantee of the British Government, to Púna. Here he was basely murdered by an unprincipled favourite of the Peshwa, Trimbukjí Angria. The British, who had guaranteed his safety, at once interfered. They did so with such effect that the assassin was surrendered, though most reluctantly, by the Peshwa. Unfortunately, however, he managed to elude the vigilance of his guards, and appeared in the field at the head of a considerable body of men, with the countenance and support of the Peshwa. The British Government remonstrated, but ineffectually. They then threatened recourse to arms, and even to surround and attack the city of Púna. The troops had actually surrounded it when the Peshwa gave in, and signed a treaty (June 1817) virtually dictated by the British Resident, Mr. Elphinstone.

This satisfactory termination of the dispute led to a new arrangement with the Gáikwár, bringing him important advantages. By the treaty of Púna, the Peshwa's claims upon him as the head of the Márhátá confederacy were renounced for ever; his unadjusted pecuniary claims were settled for an annual payment of four lakhs of rupees; the farm of Ahmedábád was renewed on the former terms, but the tribute of Káthíwár was transferred to the British Government as part of an additional subsidy, leaving the Peshwa no pretext for interfering in the affairs of Gujrát. On the other hand, by a treaty made by the British immediately afterwards with the Gáikwár, the subsidiary force was to be increased; all the rights the Gáikwár had acquired by the farm of the Peshwa's territories in Gujrát were ceded to the English; the territories of both governments were consolidated by the exchange of certain districts, whilst the co-operation of their troops in time of war and the mutual surrender of criminals were agreed upon.

Anund Ráo Gáikwár died October 2, 1819. His demise had been preceded by that of his brother, Futteh Singh, who during twelve years had exercised the nominal powers of regent, in which he had been succeeded by his younger brother, Syají Ráo. On the death of Anund Ráo, Syají succeeded to the sovereignty, to the exclusion of the two sons of his elder brother.

On the accession of Syají Ráo Gáikwár, the British Government did not consider it expedient to continue the same absolute direction of the internal affairs of the Barodah government, which had been authorised in consequence of the imbecility of Anund Ráo. But whilst it specified as a condition of this withdrawal that the Gáikwár should respect the guaranteed allowances of his ministers, the agreements with his tributaries, and the arrangements with his bankers, it did not withdraw from the Resident the power of control. But to place the relative conditions of the two powers to each other on as clear and satisfactory a basis as possible, the Governor of Bombay, the Hon. Mountstuart Elphinstone, paid a visit in 1820 to Barodah. Here he held several conferences with Syají Ráo, and finally both parties agreed to conditions which may thus be summarised :—

1. That all foreign affairs were to remain, as before, under the exclusive management of the British Government.

2. That the Gáikwár should have the unrestrained management of his internal affairs, provided he fulfilled the arrangements, guaranteed by the British Government, with the bankers. The Resident, moreover, was to be made acquainted with the financial plan of the year; to have access to the accounts, and to be consulted regarding any new plan of large expenditure.

3. That the Gáikwár should observe scrupulously the guarantees of the British Government to ministers and other individuals.

4. That the Gáikwár might choose his own ministers, on condition of consulting the Resident before nominating them.

5. That the British Government should retain the power of offering advice.

It would seem that, placed in these leading strings, it would have been easy for Syají Rao to run a straight course. But he did not. He failed to pay regularly the instalments due on his debts, which, even in 1820, had increased to upwards of 107 lakhs of rupees, and when, to remedy the evil thus created, the British Government caused, with the Gáikwár's consent, certain districts to be farmed for seven years to respectable bankers under regulations which would ensure the ryots against oppression, Syaji Ráo entered upon a line of conduct which placed him at direct issue with the Government of Bombay. Eager to amass a private treasure of his own, he had accumulated all the State moneys on which he could lay hand. To this end he paid no regard whatever to the guarantees the British Government had afforded to the State creditors, whilst he oppressed individuals for whose protection that Government stood pledged. In fact, he openly and directly violated the agreement made with Mr. Mountstuart Elphinstone in 1820.

Sir John Malcolm, who had succeeded Mr. Elphinstone as Governor of Bombay, exhausted every effort to persuade Syají Ráo Gáikwár to act in a manner more conformable with his engagements. Nor was it until he had found advice, remonstrance, and threats alike unavailing, that he determined to sequestrate such a portion of his territories as would enable him to provide for the gradual extinction of the guaranteed debt. This was done in 1828, and districts yielding a gross revenue of twenty-seven lakhs per annum were sequestered by the Bombay Government. Nor was this all. The Gáikwár had bound himself to maintain a body of 3,000 effective cavalry to co-operate with the subsidiary force. The treaty gave, indeed, no right to the British Government to the services of this cavalry except on occasions when the subsidiary force should be employed; but the practice had grown up of holding it available for police duty in the tributary states. But it was not at all in an efficient condition, and the British Government only exercised a right when in 1830 it called upon the Gáikwár to render two-thirds of it fit for service. He failed to do so; whereupon the British Government sequestrated lands yielding about 15,00,000 rupees to secure funds for the punctual payment of the force.

There can be no doubt that these sequestrations, how-

PART IV.

ever much he might have brought them on himself, pressed hard on the Gáikwár, and when Lord Clare visited Barodah in 1832 the subject was discussed in more than one interview. Eventually a settlement was arrived at. The British Government was released by the bankers from its guarantee on their coming to a satisfactory understanding with the Gáikwár for the adjustment of their debts. The bankers were at the same time promised protection against any persecutions which the Gáikwár might subject them to on account of the part they had taken in the discussions regarding the loan. The sequestrated districts, yielding 15,00,000 rupees, were restored to the Gáikwár on his depositing 10,00,000 rupees with the British Government to provide for the pay of the effective cavalry in case his own payments should fail.

But Syají Ráo Gáikwár was incorrigible. After the visit of Lord Clare the British Government lost no opportunity of kindly advice or friendly remonstrance to induce him to keep his promises. But he was deaf to both. Nay, more, emboldened by impunity, he had the audacity to deny the validity of the engagements made with the British, and this although one was his personal act, and the others had been those of his immediate predecessors. The third article of the arrangement made in 1820 with Mr. Elphinstone, by which he had agreed to observe scrupulously the guarantee of the British Government to ministers and other individuals, was treated as non-existent. He went so far at last as to bid defiance to all remonstrances. In consequence of this the British Government, under orders from England, was forced in 1837 to retain in deposit collections made by it in certain districts under its agency, and due to the Gáikwár, to fulfil his and its engagements ; and in the following year the district of Nausárí was taken possession of for the same purpose.

But all this had no effect on Syaji Ráo Gáikwár. He still continued the same course. Aided by his minister, Venírám, he acted as though he were anxious to testify to the British Government his absolute contempt for their advice and his indifference to their threats. It would be needless to enumerate the never-ending causes of dissatisfaction he gave to the British Government. He kept faith with no one; and it is hard to say which of the two most deserved reprobation, his internal administration or the relations he assumed and the conduct he exhibited to the paramount power. Up to the year 1839 [1]

[1] Up to the date of the sequestration of Pitlaod, the following leading demands had accumulated, and been in vain pressed against Syají:—

1. The dismissal of Venírám and the appointment of another minister, to be approved by the British Government.

2. The surrender of Narain Ráo Venkatsh, an officer of the Gáikwár's government, formerly in charge of Okamandel, charged with having instigated certain piracies on British vessels, and with having participated in the booty.

3. The punishment of Mahbúla Khan, formerly manager of Amrellí, for violating our tributary engagements in Káthíwár.

4. A retrospective confirmation of a settlement concluded by Mr. Blane of the claims of the Chullala Kattís.

5. The surrender of all persons concerned in the murder of Múrejo Manik, in Káthíwár.

6. A settlement of the claims of Bawa Komaun, a Kathí chief in Káthíwár.

7. Satisfaction for a robbery committed in a village of the Ján of Naonagár, in Káthíwár.

8. The introduction of a better system of administration in Káthíwár, and a due observance of our tributary engagements in that province.

9. Satisfaction for the past, and prevention for the future, of the complaints received from British authorities in Gujrát against the Gáikwár and his officers, of a systematic want of co-operation in matters of police.

10. The surrender of the prisoners captured at Kansípúr, a settlement of the complaints and claims of Pertáb Singh of Aghúr, and the removal of certain obnoxious authorities in charge of the district of Bíjapúr.

11. Reparation for the violation of the guarantee held by Bhasker Ráo Wittal.

12. That the British representative at Barodah be treated with the respect and attention due to his rank and station, and that free and unrestricted intercourse be allowed between him and all persons at Barodah with whom he may have occasion to communicate.

These demands were exclusive of many others of a pecuniary nature, which the British had previously adjusted by resorting to the funds collected on account of tribute.

There also were at the above date, either under investigation, or which had been so, the following claims against the Gáikwár:—

1. The surrender for trial of the persons concerned in the murder of two coolies of the Mahí Kantá, and the grant of compensation to the families of the deceased.

2. Reparation for the infraction of the guarantee of the British Government, held by the late Pílají Ráo Gáikwár, son of the late Anund Ráo Gáikwár.

3. The case of the family of the late Súbanjí, commandant of the fort of Kaira, who as the price of surrendering the fort without opposition, obtained a provision under our guarantee.

4. Satisfaction for the conduct of

PART IV.

numberless demands had been in vain pressed upon Syají; time had been given him; he had left them all unanswered and neglected.

Such a state of things could not be allowed to continue very long. It was determined in 1839 to sequestrate Syají Ráo's share of the district of Pitlaod, bringing in a revenue of 7,32,000 rupees, as alike a punishment for his misconduct and a material mark of the displeasure of the sovereign power. He was likewise threatened with deposition, and with the transfer of his dominions to another member of the family. Subsequently to this, a further reform of his contingent took place. To this Syají Ráo was also opposed, when suddenly, influenced, as has been imagined, by the conduct of the British Government in deposing the Rájá of Satára, Pertáb Singh (1839), he tendered his submission and declared his readiness to comply, with one or two exceptions, with all the demands made upon him. The district of Pitlaod was then restored to him, and the sum of 10,00,000 rupees deposited with the British Government in 1832 was refunded. Thenceforth he was more amenable to advice, though it would be difficult to affirm that his internal administration improved.

the Gáikwár officers in respect to certain persons who committed a robbery attended with murder at Rájkót, in Káthíwár.

5. Satisfaction for the culpable conduct of the Gáikwár's officers in Káthíwár, in conniving at the disturbances committed during several years in that province by a notorious outlaw, named Chamraj Walla.

6. Case of Gopal Ráo Ganpat Gáikwár of Sunkheira.

7. Satisfaction for a robbery committed by the Gáikwár's subjects on the property of certain British officers in the vicinity of Barodah.

8. Satisfaction for a robbery committed by certain Waghírs of Okamandel, at the village of Inkhau, in Kachh.

9. Measures of prevention against offenders obtaining an asylum in the Gáikwár's territory.

All the chief demands were embodied in a written statement, and the Gáikwár was allowed a fixed period within which to comply with them. Unwilling to push matters to extremities, another period was to be allowed him—at the expiration of which the revenue of the still sequestrated territory was to be declared forfeited, and applied to public works and other useful purposes. The written statement of the British demands was finally delivered to the Gáikwár on October 1, with explicit information of what would ensue, if he did not comply. This producing no effect, Pitlaod was taken possession of by a British force on November 1.

Syají Ráo Gáikwár died on December 19, 1847. He was succeeded by his eldest son, Ganpat Ráo.

The reign of this prince, extending over a short period of nine years, was not in itself in any way remarkable. It was at least undistinguished by any occurrence bringing the Gáikwár himself into direct collision with the English. Ganpat Ráo Gáikwár, like most Oriental rulers born in the purple, cared more for sensual pleasures than the welfare of the people entrusted to his care. In the year of his demise (1856), the only act by which his rule may be regarded as worthy of notice took place. In that year he ceded to the British the lands required for the construction of the Bombay and Barodah Railway, on condition that he should not suffer by the loss of transit duties. Such losses as might be proved were to be calculated every year, and compensated year by year.

Ganpat Ráo Gáikwár died on November 19, 1856, and, leaving no issue, was succeeded by his next brother, Khandé Ráo.

Very few months after Khandé Ráo Gáikwár had assumed the direction of affairs, the storm of the mutiny burst over India. The Gáikwár proved true and loyal. In the words of Lord Canning, 'he identified his own cause with that of the British Government.' It is fair to add that his power of doing mischief was small, and his interests were bound up with those of the British, for the power of the Gáikwár could never have survived the fall of British rule. For his services he was rewarded in the manner most agreeable to himself. The payment of 3,00,000 rupees annually for the Gujrát Irregular Horse was remitted, whilst the power given to him by a former treaty to reduce the contingent to 1,500 men was cancelled. The contingent was thus replaced on the footing on which it had been fixed by the treaty of 1817, with the additional provision that it should perform ordinary police duties in the tributary districts.

PART IV.

As a further mark of the satisfaction of the British Government a sunnud was addressed to the Gáikwár, dated March 11, 1862, conferring upon him the right of adoption. In this he is designated as His Highness the Máhárájá Gáikwár of Barodah.

Of the internal administration of the country but little can be advanced in praise. Khandé Ráo was, especially in his late years, a spendthrift, careless of his people, a lover of luxury and pomp, and not unamenable to the charge of cruelty. In July 1866, the Governor of Bombay, Sir Bartle Frere, had to 'call him to order' for having directed that an offending sepoy—a man condemned to death for conspiracy—should be trampled to death by an elephant. And, in the following year, the same Governor felt it incumbent upon him to disallow the right of the Gáikwár to appoint as his prime minister a man whose name had not been previously submitted to the British Government for approval.

Khandé Ráo died November 28, 1870, and was succeeded by his brother, Mulhar Ráo.

The short reign of this prince has been fraught with evil to the people of Barodah. The circumstances of his previous life had not been calculated to mould him into the form of a good ruler. Neglected during his childhood, having received but little education, he was charged in 1863 with having attempted the life of his brother, Khandé Ráo. In consequence of an investigation which followed that attempt, he was incarcerated as a State prisoner during the remainder of his brother's life. On the death of his brother in 1870, Mulhar Ráo jumped at once from a prison to a throne, having received none of the training that would enable him to perform satisfactorily the duties of his new position. As might have been expected under the circumstances, he at once plunged into a career of misrule, extravagance, and folly. To such an extent did his misgovernment extend that in 1873 the British Government was constrained to appoint a Commission to investigate the complaints brought against him. Every branch of his administration—revenue, political, and judicial—was then inquired into. CHAP. II.

Upon the report of this Commission, Mulhar Ráo was informed that, unless great improvement should be manifested by the end of the year 1875, he would 'be deposed, in the interest of his people, and for the peace and security of the empire.' This warning did not, unfortunately, produce the desired effect. But an unexpected event brought matters to an early crisis. Towards the close of the year 1874 an attempt was made at Barodah to poison the British Resident, Colonel Phayre, C.B. Subsequent inquiry led the Government of India to suspect that the Gáikwár himself had instigated the criminal attempt. Upon this the Viceroy issued a proclamation, in which he announced the suspension of the Gáikwár from power, with a view to give him an opportunity of clearing himself before a competent Court of Inquiry from the grave suspicions attaching to him; and, in consequence, the temporary assumption by the British Government of the administration of Barodah.

A subsequent notification of the Government of India published the charges on which Mulhar Ráo was to be tried. They are as follows:—

1. The offence charged against Mulhar Ráo was that he did by agents and in person hold secret communications for improper purposes with some servants employed by Colonel Phayre or attached to the British Residency.

2. That Mulha Ráo gave bribes to such servants, or caused bribes to be given them.

3. His purpose for holding such communications and giving such bribes was to use the said servants as spies on Colonel Phayre, thereby improperly to obtain information of secrets and to cause injury to Colonel Phayre, or remove him by means of poison.

PART IV.

4. That, in fact, an attempt to poison Colonel Phayre was made by persons instigated thereto by the Gáikwár.

The Commissioners appointed to conduct the inquiry, —viz., the Chief Justice of the High Court of Calcutta, the Máhárájás of Gwáliár and of Jaipúr, the Chief Commissioner of Mysore, Sir Dinkur Rao,[1] and a Commissioner in the Punjáb have been requested to meet for that purpose February 23, 1875.

The Gáikwár receives a salute of nineteen guns. In 1840 satí was prohibited within his territories; the sale of children in 1849, and slavery in 1856.

CHAPTER II.

KOLHAPÚR.

AREA—3,184 sq. miles. POPULATION—546,156.
REVENUE—10,00,000 rupees.[2]

THE principality of Kolhapúr is bounded on the north and north-west by Satára; on the east and south by Belgáon; and on the west by Sawunt-wárí and Ratnagirí. It is ruled over by the representative of the younger branch of the family which gave birth to the famous Sivají Bhonslá.

According to Márhátá tradition, Sivají claimed descent from that branch of the royal family of Údaipúr which reigned in Dongarpúr. One of the disinherited sons of the thirteenth ruler of that family left his father's house for Bíjapúr, entered the service of the king of that place, and was recompensed for his services by the grant of the district of Modhul, comprising eighty-four villages, and the title of Rájá. This

[1] *Vide* pp. 171, 172.

[2] Two-fifths of this sum are enjoyed by the independent Jaghírdárs.

man, who was called Sujunsí, had four sons, from the youngest of whom, Sugají, Sivají claims to be directly descended. Sugají had one son, Bhosají. Bhosají left ten sons, the eldest, father of Shahjí, father of Sivají; the tenth, who settled at Khanwata, is the direct progenitor of the Kolhapúr family.

This is not the place in which to enter into a history of Sivají. It will suffice to say that, by the exercise of great talents, indefatigable perseverance, matchless audacity harassed by no scruple—by the aid of great faith in his own mission, and by the spirit which he infused into his followers, Sivají founded an empire destined to replace for a time the already tottering edifice of the Moguls. He died on April 5, 1860, and was succeeded by his son, Sámbají. This degenerate son, after an inglorious reign, chiefly marked by tyranny towards his subjects and by sensual indulgence, was, in 1694, surprised by the troops of Aurangzíb, and carried captive, with his eldest son, to the camp of the monarch. He was put to death in the most barbarous manner, whilst his son, Sivají, was spared, and confided to the charge of a daughter of the emperor. By this lady his name was changed to Sáhú.

Meanwhile the younger son, Rájá Rám, had been raised to the regency (1695). He lived, however, only three years, dying in June 1698, and leaving two sons, Sivají and Sámbají, by his two wives, Tárá Bai and Rájis Bai. Sivají succeeded as regent for Sáhú, but becoming insane, he was deposed, and confined, in 1703, by his mother, Tárá Bai, who thenceforth, till 1707, governed in his name. In that year, however, Sahú was released from confinement, and returned to claim his inheritance. Tárá Bai resisted his pretensions: but in 1712 the death of Sivají, and a revolution in favour of her stepson, Sámbají, removed her from power. Thenceforth Sáhú and Sámbají were the rival claimants for the power and possessions of their great ancestor.

PART IV.

The division between the two branches of the family continued unhealed till 1730. In that year Sámbají was surprised, attacked, and completely defeated by the adherents of his cousin. This defeat brought about an accommodation (1731) by which Sámbají was forced to acknowledge the right of Sáhú to the whole of the Márhátá country, Kolhapúr and the territory dependent on it excepted. This was assigned to himself, with the title of Rájá.

Sámbají, great-grandson of the renowned Sivají, was thus the first Rájá of Kolhapúr. He died, without issue, in 1760. His widow, called upon then to adopt an heir, selected a son of the tenth branch of the family of Bhosají, great-grandfather of Sivají, called the Khanwata branch. The child, for he was a minor, was called, in memory of his great relative, Sivají.

During the minority of the young prince, the State was administered by the widow of Sámbají. She held the reins with a loose and careless hand, permitting her subjects to support themselves by plunder and piracy, the victims being the inhabitants of other States, and especially, in the matter of piracy, the subjects of the English Government of Bombay. To put a stop to this the British Government fitted out and despatched (1765) an expedition against the fort of Mulwán. This was reduced, and the Regent Rání then agreed to the conditions imposed by the British Government. She promised to pay seven lakhs and a half of rupees for the expenses of the expedition; to allow the British to build a factory on the coast in her dominions; to grant them a monopoly for the importation and sale of cloths and other commodities from Europe; to put a stop to piracy, and to act as a good friend in general. Upon this Mulwán was restored. But the Rání fulfilled none of her engagements. Piracy by sea and plunder by land continued to be the two guiding principles of her administration until her death, in 1772.

Nor with the accession of the young Rájá did they cease. He, however, found himself hard pressed by his enemies. The Peshwa attacked him, and took from him some districts which were given to the Putwurdun family. They were, it is true, subsequently restored, but the original cession had begotten covetousness on the part of the Putwurduns, and a family feud, extending over a third of a century, was the result. In the course of this feud, Kolhapúr was reduced to very great extremities, and was only saved in the end by the intervention of the Peshwa.

Then, again, Kolhapúr fought with its neighbour, Sawunt-wárí. This war lasted twenty-three years, and did not tend to the prosperity of the country. Nor, whilst these contests were raging, was there any improvement in the internal administration. In fact there was no administration. A puppet Rájá, factions struggling for plunder, and plunder supplied by piracy and robbery,—such was Kolhapúr towards the close of the last century. In the end the British Government, whose traders had suffered greatly from the depredations, was forced to interfere. A second expedition was fitted out (1792) but before it proceeded to action the Rájá signed another treaty by which he bound himself to compensate the British traders, and to allow factories to be erected at Mulwán and at Kolhapúr.

But the great Márhátá empire was approaching the close of its turbulent career. Whether by accident or by calculation, the British seemed to be guided in dealing with it by the sound principle 'Divide et impera.' In October 1812, Kolhapúr being then at war with Nipání, the British interfered, and in return for the renunciation of claims on Nipání and other districts, over which the Peshwa claimed dominion, and for the cession to the British of the harbour of Mulwán, with the lands and ports dependent upon it, the territories that remained to the Rájá were guaranteed to him. He received the

PART II.

protection, and admitted the superiority of the British power.

The same year Rájá Sivají died, and was succeeded by his eldest son Sámbají, also called Abba Sáhib. He was ruling Kolhapúr when there broke out with Bájí Ráo Peshwa the war which terminated (June 3, 1818) by his surrender and political annihilation. In that war Abba Sáhib acted as a true and faithful ally of his liege lord, the British Government. In return for the services then rendered, the districts (Chikórí and Menaoolí) which he had been forced to surrender to the Peshwa by the treaty of 1812 were restored to him. In the reign of this prince the internal administration of the country greatly improved.

In the course of his proceedings it happened that the Rájá found it necessary to resume an estate which had been granted to one of his chiefs, Saejí Bai, of the Mohíté family. The chief came to Kolhapúr for remonstrance or revenge. He gratified the latter by shooting the Rájá dead in his own palace (July 1821). Abba Sáhib left an infant son, who died the following year. The succession then devolved upon Shahjí or Báwá Sáhib, second son of Rájá Sivají. Báwá Sáhib possessed none of the talents or right feelings of his brother, but was oppressive and profligate. He was governed, too, by an ill-regulated ambition which would fain have shaken off the protecting influence of the British. It happened that in the year 1824 the town of Kittúr in Belgáon was the scene of great disturbances, attaining the pitch of actual insurrection. About the same time Southern India was pervaded by rumours that a great disaster had befallen the British arms in Burma. The event at Kittúr and the rumours regarding Burma seemed to announce to the spirit of Báwá Sáhib that the time for action had arrived. He suddenly left his capital at the head of 5,000 infantry, 1,000 horse, and seven guns, nominally on account of a dispute with his neighbour of Sawunt-wárí; and, in defiance of his engagements with the British, positively refused either to submit the cause in dispute to their arbitration or to accept their award.

Not content with this display of independence he attacked the fort and jaghír of Kungal, and captured the fort; notwithstanding that a sunnud for the possession of both had been granted by his father to Hindú Ráo, a relation of the Máhárájá of Gwáliár. Having effected this highway robbery he, without any communication with the British Government, marched to the frontiers of Satára, with intentions so palpably hostile as to induce the Rájá of that State to implore British intervention.

It would, indeed, have been impossible for the British to delay interference longer. Towards the close of 1825 a British force therefore marched into Kolhapúr and compelled the Rájá to sign a treaty, binding himself to attend to the advice of the British Government in all matters affecting the public peace; to respect the rights of Hindú Ráo and of certain jaghírdars mentioned; to reduce his force and to maintain it only at a strength not calculated to affect public tranquillity within or without his territories; and never to grant an asylum to rebels.

Shortly after the conclusion of this treaty, Rájá Báwá Sáhib proceeded to Púna with the avowed object of inducing the Government of Bombay to release him from the conditions by which he was bound. Failing in this, he returned to Kolhapúr, committing extravagancies and aggressions on his road, and behaving himself—as indeed he had at Púna—in a manner that showed him hardly to be of sane mind. On his arrival at Kolhapúr he increased, instead of diminishing, his army, and seized on the possessions of jaghírdars guaranteed to them by the British. Nor did he stop there, but began, as soon as he could, to commit aggressions on his neighbours.

Again was a British force levied, and this time it reached the capital,—the garrison, consisting of between two and three thousand Arabs and Belúchís, evacuating

PART IV.

it as the British force entered. Again was a treaty forced upon the Rájá. By this he bound himself to reduce his army to 400 horse and 800 foot, exclusive of garrisons for his forts according to a stated list. The districts granted to his brother for good service rendered in 1817 were resumed. The forts of Kolhapúr and Panálágarh were to be garrisoned by British troops at the expense of the Rájá. He had to restore villages which he had resumed, and to see the jaghírdars whom he had molested invested with perpetual, instead of life, guarantees by the British. He had to pay 1,47,948 rupees for damage done by him to his neighbours, material guarantees being taken for such payment; and to accept a minister appointed by the British Government, and irremovable by him, to administer the affairs of Kolhapúr.

Ultimately the right to garrison the port of Panálágarh was surrendered, and at a later period, the garrison was withdrawn from Kolhapúr. Later still, the Rájá having indicated some signs of amendment, the minister, who had sadly disappointed the expectations formed regarding him, was withdrawn, and the management of affairs was resumed by the Rájá, he having been informed by the Governor of Bombay, at a personal interview, that should it ever again become necessary to send a garrison to Kolhapúr, it would become there a permanent fixture.

The Rájá Báwá Sáhib died on November 29, 1838, leaving a minor son, Sivají. A council of regency was at once formed, consisting of the mother and aunt[1] of the young Rájá, and four officials. But the members of the council were apparently not formed to act harmoniously together. The strongest mind and most determined will amongst them were possessed by the aunt, Iárá Bai, and she so managed as to assume the entire control of affairs. Henceforth she is known in the history of Kolhapúr as Dewán-Sáhib.

[1] She was aunt by marriage—being the widow of Abba Sáhib.

The usurpation of this lady was recognised by the British Government. She managed or rather mismanaged the State for three years. It was a bad time for Kolhapúr, for misrule could scarcely have reached a greater pitch. At length the British Government was forced to interfere. Mild measures were at first tried with her, but as these produced no improvement, the British Government, acting upon the right secured by the treaty of 1827, removed her from the regency, and nominated a minister in whom it had confidence, Dají Krishna Pandit, to administer affairs. The efforts which this minister made in the way of reform excited the bitter hostility of the old corrupt *régime*—the partisans of the Dewán Sáhib—and culminated, in 1844, in a general rebellion, a rebellion which extended to the neighbouring State of Sawunt-wárí. The rebellion was, however, put down by force of arms, and the entire management of the Kolhapúr State assumed by the British Government.

Under the *régime* thus introduced great reforms were effected. The forts were dismantled, the system of hereditary garrisons was abolished, the military force was disbanded, and a local force entertained in its stead. The cost of suppressing the rebellion was required to be paid by Kolhapúr. In the various administrative departments order, regularity, and system were introduced.

In 1862 matters had so improved, and the system of management had become so well understood, that Rájá Sivají was entrusted with the administration. By the treaty made with him upon that occasion, he bound himself in all matters to follow the advice of the British Government. Rájá Sivají had previously displayed, in the crisis of 1857, a desire to remain faithful to his engagements, notwithstanding that his brother, Chimma Sáhib, had joined the mutineers.

Rájá Sivají lived only four years after his installation, dying on August 4, 1866. He had no male children, but before his death he adopted Nágújí Ráo Patankar, an intelligent boy of sixteen years of age, who at once assumed the name of Rájárám.

This prince, with a spirit beyond the majority of his countrymen, resolved in 1869 to visit Europe. Unhappily he died at Florence the following year.

The present Rájá, his adopted successor, who has assumed the name of Sivají, is still a minor. He is receiving a capital education under the auspices of the Political Agent, by whom, meanwhile, the country is administered.

CHAPTER III.

SAWUNT-WÁRÍ.

AREA—900 sq. miles. POPULATION—152,506.
REVENUE—2,00,000 rupees.

WÁRÍ, or Sawunt-wárí, is a small State situated between Goá and the district and harbour of Mulwán, and forms the southern part of the territory known as the Konkan. Khem Sawunt, to whom the rulers of the Wárí tribe trace their origin, was an officer serving under the Mahomedan kings of Bíjapúr, and held part of the Wárí country in jaghír during the declining period of that monarchy. When the celebrated Sivají was in the zenith of his glory, Khem Sawunt transfered his allegiance to him, and was by him confirmed as *Sar-Dessaye* over all that part of the Konkan, half of the revenue being made available for Sivají and the other moiety assigned for the maintenance of a body of three thousand infantry for foreign service, besides the requisite number for garrisons. This arrangement, however, proving unsatisfactory to both parties, Khem Sawunt took the opportunity of a reverse of fortune befalling Sivají to break it, and to return to his allegiance to Bíjapúr. In 1662, however,

Sivají, having proved his superiority to the king of that country, attacked Wárí, and speedily overran it, forcing the Sawunts to throw themselves on his clemency. He generously restored to them the country, under the same conditions as had previously existed, and he ever afterwards found them faithful vassals. In 1707 Khem Sawunt received from Sahú Rájá, grandson of Sivají, a deed confirming him in his possessions in full sovereignty, and assigning to him, conjointly with the chief of Kolába, half the revenues of the Salsí Mahal.

Khem Sawunt was succeeded (1709) by his nephew, Phónd Sawunt, the first of the family who came in contact with the British. About the beginning of the eighteenth century British commerce had suffered greatly from the piratical attacks upon it sanctioned or connived at by the rulers of Kolába. To put an end to these depredations, and to enlist on their side one at least of the rulers of the western coast, the British concluded in 1730 an offensive and defensive treaty with Phónd Sawunt. By this the contracting parties agreed to mutually assist each other against the mutual enemy of both, Kánojí Angria, ruler of Kolába. It was also agreed that on the conclusion of the war all the conquests made should be given up to Sawunt-wárí, with the exception of Ghéria and the island of Kennerí, which should be retained by the British.

Phónd Sawunt died in 1738, and was succeeded by his grandson, Rámchunder Sawunt. After a reign of seventeen years, unmarked by any incident worthy of special record, he gave way to his son, Khem Sawunt, a minor. This ruler found himself engaged at a very early period in a war with his neighbour of Kolhapúr. The quarrel between the two powers traced back its origin to a period long anterior, and was due to a jealousy entertained by the Rájás of Kolhapúr of the position of independence assumed by the Sawunts. Undoubtedly it was provoked by Kolhapúr, and was excited and fed by purely per-

PART IV.

sonal feelings But this was not the only embarrassment felt by the guardians of the Sawunt. They fell out, too, with their neighbours of Goá, the Portuguese, and with the British. Both these quarrels arose from the same cause, the practice of piracy by the subjects of the Sawunt. We have seen that to repress that atrocious trade, the ancestor of Khem Sawunt had allied himself with the British. But now the guardians of Khem Sawunt connived at its practice on the British. It was impossible for the latter to allow such a state of things to continue; accordingly, early in 1765 they despatched an expedition from Bombay, under the joint command of Major Gordon, and Captain John Watson of the Bombay Marine, with instructions to stop the piracies carried on by Kolhapúr and Sawunt-wárí. This they effectually did for the time. From Sawunt-wárí they took the fort of Yeswuntgarh or Reví, and changed its name to Fort Augustus, intending to keep it. But finding that the acquisition was unprofitable, they agreed to restore it to the Sawunt, on condition of his promising not to molest their ships or trade, to cede all the lands between the rivers Karlí and Sarsí from the sea to the foot of the hills, to pay a lakh of rupees for the expenses of the expedition, and to allow the British to build a fort in his dominions.

It is probable that had Khem Sawunt been of age, and possessed the ability to manage his affairs, he would have observed the conditions of this treaty. But his turbulent relations, greedy for plunder, broke out almost as soon it had been signed; consequently, another treaty was forced upon his government. By this the money payment was increased to two lakhs; and as this money could only be raised by a mortgage on the district of Vingorla for thirteen years, the town, port, and district of Vingorla were made over to the British Government for that period, Sawunt-wárí furnishing two hostages for the due observance of the treaty.

CHAP. III.

A very curious circumstance happened shortly after this, discreditable alike to both contracting parties. The mortgagee, who was to advance to the British the stipulated sum, was one Vittojí Kommotim. To enable him to recoup himself for his payments, the British placed him in charge of the district of Vingorla under the security of the British flag and British Sepoys. But very soon after the treaty had been signed the hostages made their escape. Then the Sawunt, levying troops, marched into Vingorla, drove away the agents of Vittojí engaged in collecting the revenue, and then returned home. Strange to record, this outrage was met by nothing stronger than remonstrance. Nor, when the thirteen years had expired, was any opposition made to the Sawunt, when he attacked Vingorla, took it (June 1780) and appropriated a large quantity of public and private property belonging to the British! It would seem that the main sufferer, though he had the British guarantee, was the mortgagee, Vittojí, who in the interval had been forcibly prevented from collecting the rents of the district. It resulted from the impunity with which the Sawunt was allowed to perpetrate these outrages that the piracy received a fresh impetus; nor was it checked during the thirty-two years that followed.

The system of public plunder was at its height when Khem Sawunt died (1803). He had reigned for forty-eight years—years of almost unceasing warfare; and when he died the war with Kolhapúr was raging with as much fury as ever.

Khem Sawunt left four widows, the eldest of whom, Lukshmi Bai, became regent, on account of the minority of Khem Sawunt's only son by Déví Bai, his third wife.[1] Shortly after the assumption of the regency by this lady, the Sawunt-wárí troops were defeated by those of Kolhapúr, and the fort of Wárí was immediately

[1] Grant Duff (Bombay edition), vol. iii. p. 244. Mr. Aitchison says he died without male issue. *Vide Treaties,* vol. vi. p. 115.

besieged. In this extremity Lukshmi Bai called upon Wiswas Ráo Ghatgay and Appa Dessaye, adherents of Sindhia and the Peshwa, to assist her. Appa Dessaye, with the secret concurrence of the Peshwa, afforded the required aid; the siege of Wárí was raised; and the war was carried into the enemy's country. But this result had hardly been obtained, when Appa Dessaye endeavoured to establish his own authority over Sawunt-wárí. At the instance of his chief confidant, and with the concurrence alike of the regent, Lukshmi Bai, and of Phónd Sawunt, the next heir to the principality, the young prince was strangled (1807). But Appa Dessaye derived no profit from this atrocious deed. Phónd Sawunt took advantage of the diminished number of his troops to assault and drive from the country Appa Dessaye, and to possess himself of the government.

Shortly after this the ex-regent, Lukshmi Bai, died. The second widow of the late Sawunt, Dúrga Bai, laid claim to the office. Phónd Sawunt, however, refused to recognise her pretensions, and insisted upon carrying on the government himself.

Under the earlier rule of this prince there was no diminution in the practice of piracy. In fact, this mode of raising a revenue seemed to have become a time-honoured principle of administration. But in 1812 the British Government had become alive to the absolute necessity of repressing it at all hazards. Action was accordingly taken, and Phónd Sawunt, Dessaye of Sawunt-wárí, was bound down (October 1812) to cede the fort of Vingorla and the battery of Gunarámo Tembe, with its port and limits, and to promise to cede the ports of Rérí and Neótí if piracies should be committed in the future. British merchants were to be allowed free ingress and egress to and from the Sawunt-wárí territory, on paying the customary duties; but all articles of consumption required for British troops stationed within the territory were to pass duty free.

CHAP. III.

Soon after the conclusion of this treaty Phónd Sawunt died (1813), and, his son being a minor, the second widow of the late Dessaye, Dúrga Bai, became regent. This lady commenced her administration by an attack upon Kolhapúr, and seized two forts which had been guaranteed to that State by the British Government. As she obstinately refused to restore them, war was declared against her by the British. Two outlying districts were at once taken possession of, and preparations made to march on the capital. But meanwhile an insurrection had broken out in Sawunt-wárí—Duda Bai, the fourth widow of the Dessaye, Khem Sawunt, having produced a child whom she endeavoured to pass off as the true heir to the principality,—the son of Khem Sawunt, who, she alleged, had escaped the murder attempted upon him by Appa Dessaye. Her cause found a large number of adherents, many of whom thought the opportunity a good one to plunder on their own account. But at length the party of Dúrga Bai gained the upper hand. This, however, unfortunately for her, happened when the Peshwa was engaged in a life-struggle with the British, and she did all in her power to aid and sustain him. It became at length necessary to put an end to this state of things. A force was marched into the country, and a treaty was dictated (February 1819) by which the British Government agreed to protect Sawunt-wárí, that State acknowledging British supremacy, ceding the line of sea-coast from the river Karlí to the boundaries of the Portuguese possessions, and to receive British troops into Sawunt-wárí. In consequence of the readiness with which these terms had been accepted, a portion of the ceded territory, yielding a net revenue of 30,000 rupees, was restored the following year.

The regent, Dúrga Bai, had died before this treaty had been signed, and had been succeeded in her office by the two widows of the preceding chief, Savitrí Bai and Naranda Bai. These ladies were very anxious to retain

PART IV.

the power which had thus devolved upon them, and attempted to debar the young chief, though he had attained his legal majority, from all participation in affairs. At length, however, in 1822 the claims of this youth, Khem Sawunt, could no longer be resisted, and he was installed as ruler. He proved himself incapable, and quite unfit for his position. Affairs under his mode of administration soon drifted into such disorder that he had to invoke, in 1830 and 1832, British aid to suppress the rebellion he himself had caused. On the second occasion he signed a treaty with the British, in the preamble to which he made this humiliating confession: 'My country has been thrown into disorder and confusion more than once through my own misconduct;' and he bound himself to appoint as his minister a man approved of by the British Government, and not to remove him without the sanction of that Government; to adopt the measures of reform advised by his minister and sanctioned by the British; to abdicate, if necessary, should he fail to keep those conditions; and to pay the cost of any troops required for the settlement of his affairs.

Yet, notwithstanding this humiliating confession, the promise, and the self-imposed punishment for breach of faith looming in the future, Khem Sawunt continued to sail very close to the wind. He never, in fact, had any intention of keeping the treaty if he could avoid keeping it. He made constant and repeated complaints against his minister, many of which, on investigation, were proved to be malicious, and all unfounded. His barons became virtually independent, and defied his authority. In 1836 and 1838, British intervention was required for the maintenance of order. On the second occasion—the fourth within eight years—the state of the country was thus officially described:—'The Sar-Dessaye (the chief) again exhibits the same imbecility and unfitness for the control of his territory. The same insecurity for life and property exists. Phónd Sawunt's band is still out, increasing in numbers; other bands of plunderers have broken out, setting defiance to the Sar-Dessaye, plundering the peaceful inhabitants of his villages, and threatening, if not actually causing, disturbances and depredations in our adjoining districts. The leaders of this band have refused the amnesty offered to them by the chief. The Sar-Dessaye exhibits the same obstinacy, surrounded by and under the influence of favourites of an evil and designing character, and refuses support and concurrence in the measures taken by the minister appointed by the British Government, to whose advice he is bound by agreement to attend.'

The consequence of such a mode of government showed itself in the rapid abandonment of the country by the best class of the inhabitants, and the prevalence of anarchy amongst those who remained.

Under these circumstances, forced, in 1838, to intervene, the British Government found it would be impossible to give its support to a system so ruinous and so subversive. It decided, therefore, to remove Khem Sawunt from power, making for him an ample provision, and to assume the direct management of the country.

This was accordingly done. Under the firm rule of the British, order was restored, confidence returned, and rebellion was crushed. It was no easy task. In 1839 and 1844 the turbulent chiefs who had successfully resisted their liege lord broke into revolt. Even the chief's son, Phónd Sawunt, known as Anna Sáhib, tried to shake off the firm control of the British. But these rebellions were successfully put down. Gradually a better feeling was introduced into the country, and when the mutiny broke out in 1857, the old chief and Anna Sáhib, deprived as they were of power, showed themselves firmly attached to British interests.

Khem Sawunt died in 1867. Anna Sáhib was acknowledged as his successor by the British Government, but in consequence of his having addicted himself largely to

PART IV.

the practice of opium-eating, certain restrictions were placed upon his exercise of power, with a view to prevent the administration from falling into disorder. These restrictions will be open to revision in the event of his being succeeded by a more competent ruler.

The chief of Sawunt-wárí has been granted the right of adoption.

CHAPTER IV.

KACHH.

AREA—6,500 sq. miles.[1] POPULATION—409,522.
REVENUE—15,00,000 rupees.

THE State of Kachh is bounded on the north and north-west by the province of Sindh; on the east by the dominions of the Gáikwár; on the south by the peninsula of Káthíwár and the Gulf of Kachh, and on the south-west by the Indian Ocean.

'In ancient times,' says Hamilton, 'the province of Kachh appears to have been occupied by pastoral tribes, for the Kúmbís or cultivators do not appear at any time to have formed an essential part of the community; and the Chaoras, though formerly the governing class, are now extinct. The Jhárejas are a branch of the Samma tribe, which emigrated from Sindh about the fifteenth century, under the leadership of Jám Lakha, son of Jhára.' To distinguish the family of this celebrated chief, Jhára, whose faith, whether it were Hindú or Mahomedan, is still a matter of controversy in Kachh, the surname of Jháreja was applied to it, whilst its representative took the title of Jám. The possessions in Kachh were divided by the three grandsons of Jám Lakha. About the year 1540, the three branches of the family were represented by Jám Dádur, Jám Humír, and Jám Ráwul. Dádur ruled over Wagur, or

[1] Exclusive of the Ran of Kachh, which covers 9,000 square miles.

the eastern district of the province; Ráwul, after murdering his kinsman Humír, usurped his possessions and united the western districts, or Kachh proper, under his own government. But Khengah, the son of the murdered Humír, with the help of the king of Ahmedábád, from whom he received the district Morví and the title of Ráo —a title held ever since by the rulers of Kachh— succeeded not only in recovering his father's possessions, but in expelling Jám Ráwul from Kachh and reducing Dádur to subjection.

Kachh is mentioned by Abul Fázal in 1582 as an independent State, but its power appears to have reached its zenith about the middle of the eighteenth century, when Ráo Dásal is said to have held garrisons in Sindh, Parkar, and Káthíwár. The hold on these provinces was however lost by Ráo Lakha, who succeeded in 1751. After a short reign this chief was followed by Ráo Ghór, an incapable ruler, under whom anarchy and disorder prevailed. Ráo Ghór died in 1778, and was succeeded by Ráo Roydhun, the eleventh in succession from Ráo Khengar. Ráo Roydhun was a man of passionate and uncontrollable temper, indulged in to such an extent as to render him insane, and to cause him to be placed by his chiefs in confinement (1786). There ensued then a struggle for power which was ultimately decided (1792) in favour of a soldier of fortune, Jemadár Futteh Mahomed, who had commenced life as a private horseman. A revolution, headed by Bháijí Báwá, brother to the Ráo, expelled Futteh Mahomed in 1802; but he speedily recovered a portion of the country, which he governed from Anjar, leaving the remainder in the real power of Hunsráj, the Dewán of the party opposed to him, and having his head-quarters at Mandaví; the capital, Bhúj, being occupied by the deranged Ráo.

Kachh was thus in the possession of two rival parties, each ruling independently of the other. No long time elapsed before Futteh Mahomed recovered Bhúj, whence

PART IV.

he made inroads into Gujrát and Káthíwár, at the same time that he lent his countenance to piracy on a large scale. These depredations provoked the interference of the British, who, in October 1809, entered into an engagement with Futteh Mahomed and Hunsráj, whereby they bound themselves not to interfere in the countries to the east of the Gulf of Kachh and the Ran; to suppress piracy; and to exclude Americans and Europeans from their possessions. Hunsráj was also guaranteed the separate possession of Mandaví until such time as the Ráo should re-assume the government.

Shortly after this Hunsráj died. This event, and the accession of his son, Sheo Ráj, caused a renewal of the civil war, and the British troops were forced to interfere. Ultimately both parties were left in the position they had occupied before the death of Hunsráj.

The British Government was forced again to interfere (1813) in consequence of the non-observance of the treaty of 1809. Whilst the negotiations on this subject were pending, Vizír Futteh Mahomed died (October 1813). The insane Ráo, Roydhun, survived him only a month. He was succeeded, thanks to the support of the two sons of Futteh Mahomed, by his illegitimate son, Ráo Bharmul, then eighteen years of age, to the exclusion of the rightful heir, his legitimate nephew.

Ráo Bharmul suffered under the same infirmity as his father, and he commenced his reign by acts of cruelty and aggression on his neighbours. He soon lost the support of the sons of Futteh Mahomed—the one being assassinated in public durbar, the other resigning from conscious incapacity. Uncontrolled, the Ráo became then wholly unmanageable, his natural malady being increased by constant intoxication. The outrages perpetrated increased so much in atrocity, that it became necessary that the British should forcibly introduce some sort of order in the country. A force was accordingly marched in, and in January 1816 a treaty was concluded, by which the

Ráo agreed to pay an indemnity for the losses caused by the inroads of his subjects, to suppress piracy, to give no shelter to outlaws; and to yield in perpetuity the fort of Anjar, the port of Túrea and adjacent villages, and to pay in perpetuity also an annual sum equal to 70,000 rupees. In return for this cession and payment the British Government agreed to reduce his country to obedience and to restore order within it. This last stipulation was carried out within a month. A few months later, in consideration of the great impoverishment of the country, caused by twenty years of turmoil and misrule, the British Government voluntarily remitted the whole of the military expenses it had incurred, and the annual sum which the Ráo had agreed to pay.

Yet scarcely had these terms been concluded when the Ráo returned to his evil ways. He murdered his cousin, the legitimate son of his uncle, the rightful heir, before himself, to the throne. He then began to levy troops for the purpose of assaulting Anjar; he attacked, too, one of the Wágur chiefs whose possessions were under the guarantee of the British, in order 'to show others,' as he openly avowed, 'the punishment which awaited those who depended for protection on the British Government.' His tyranny became at last so insupportable that the principal Jháreja chiefs earnestly requested the British Government to interfere.

There was no other course to pursue. The provisions of the treaty of 1816 were therefore declared to be suspended, and a force, under Sir William Grant Keir, marched into the country. A new arrangement was then made. The Ráo, whose intellect was greatly deranged, was deposed, and his son Daisul was appointed ruler in his place. As Ráo Daisul was a minor, a regency was formed of six members, one of whom, in compliance with the earnest request of the chiefs, was the British Resident. A British force was left in the country for its protection, to be reduced or withdrawn at the option of the British

Government. By the terms of the treaty then concluded, October 1819, it was arranged that the government of Kachh should pay for maintaining that force. The provisions of the former treaty, with some trifling additions, were renewed. Amongst these latter was one which guaranteed their estates to the Jháreja chiefs, and generally to all the Rájpút chiefs in Kachh and Wágur the full enjoyment of their possessions. One of the first acts of the regency was to restore their estates to certain Wágur chiefs on their engaging to preserve the peace.

In 1822 the town, fort, and district of Anjar were restored to Kachh, in consideration of an annual payment of 88,000 rupees. The annual contribution demanded by the British Government for the maintenance of its subsidiary force in that country had been fixed at two lakhs of rupees. But the inability of the Durbar to pay this sum had led to constant remissions. At length, in 1832 the Court of Directors came to the conclusion that the demands on Kachh on account of the cession of Anjar were excessive, and that they should be permanently relinquished. This was done, all arrears were remitted, and the total payment limited to two lakhs. And regarding this sum the British Government arranged that it should diminish in proportion as the British should diminish the number of troops in Kachh; that should the cost fall below 88,000 rupees annually, or should the troops be withdrawn altogether, then only should the amount of the Anjar compensation be demandable. This measure of justice and policy proved a great relief to the resources of Kachh.

The following year, 1833, the conduct of the ex-Ráo, Bharmul, came under consideration. It had been ascertained that by evil counsels and in other ways he was endeavouring to unsettle the right principles which it had been endeavoured to instil into his son; and that his conduct had caused great uneasiness to those whose special care it was to watch over his proceedings. In consequence of this, it was determined to remove him to another palace, under such restrictions as would put a stop to the evil complained of. At the same time that this was done, the young Ráo was admitted to the council of regency, and encouraged to take part in public affairs. In these he displayed so much aptitude that in the month of June 1834, he being then nearly nineteen, he was placed in sole charge of the administration.

Ráo Daisul showed by the course he pursued that he well deserved the confidence reposed in him. In December 1835 he entered warmly into the views entertained by the British Government regarding the suppression of the traffic in slave children, and issued a proclamation prohibiting, on pain of confiscation, the importation of slaves into his country after six months from the date it bore.

In 1838, when the British Government plunged into the Kábul war, the Ráo exerted himself to the utmost to afford assistance to the British forces, procuring camels and supplies. In carrying out this policy he incurred considerable expense, for which he refused to accept reimbursement. As an acknowledgment of this liberality, when, the following year, a succession of unfavourable harvests forced him to solicit the postponement of the British demands for one year's subsidy, and the distribution of the payment over the four succeeding years, the British Government agreed without hesitation to his request.

It may be added that in 1840 he signed an agreement exempting from duty vessels forced into Mandaví by stress of weather, and in 1852, with the assent of the Jháreja chiefs, he abolished satí.

Ráo Daisul died in 1860, and was succeeded by his eldest son, Ráo Pragmul. Since the accession of this prince the affairs of Kachh have called for little comment. The country is prosperous, and it is to be hoped will remain so.

PART IV.

The Ráo of Kachh has been granted the right of adoption. It may be added that, owing to the measures taken by the British Government, the crime of infanticide has greatly diminished in this state. In 1842 the proportion of males to females of the Jháreja tribe was eight to one. In 1852 it was as three to one.[1]

[1] Aitchison's *Treaties*.

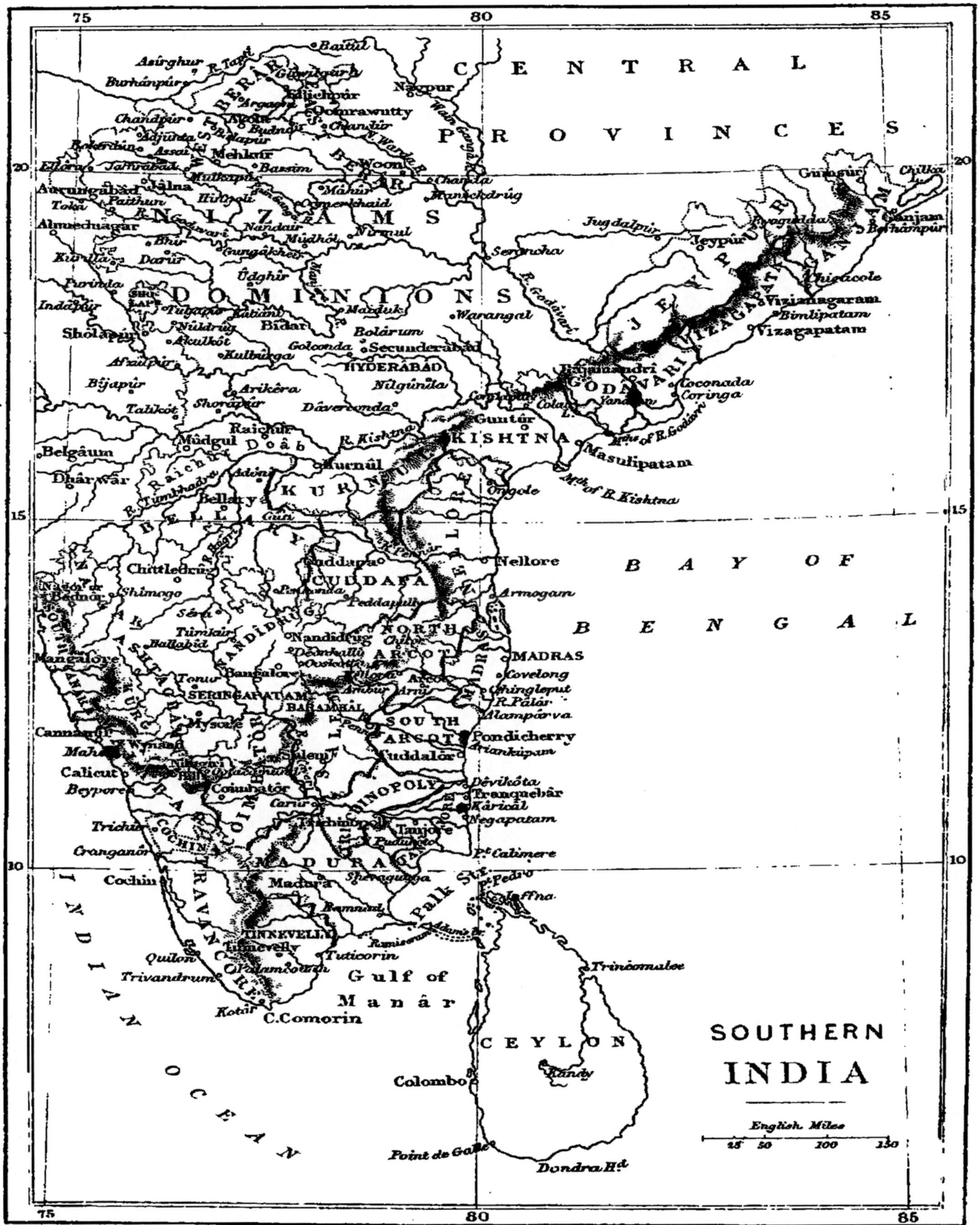

London. Longman's & Co. Edwd. Weller

PART V.—SOUTHERN INDIA.

CHAPTER I.

HAIDERÁBÁD, OR THE DOMINIONS OF THE NIZÁM.

AREA—95,337 sq. miles. POPULATION—10,666,080.
REVENUE—About 2,00,00,000 rupees.

CHAP. I.

THE country known generally under the name of the Dekhan formed a portion of that ruled by Mahomedan kings of Afghán descent, distinguished as the Bráhmaní[1] kings, from the year 1347 to 1526. In that year the dynasty finally disappeared from the Haiderábád country to make way for the Túrkomán family of Kúli Kútb. The country was invaded by Akbar in 1599, again by Jehángír in 1612, again by Shah Jehán in 1620 and 1621, and again by Aurangzíb in 1650. On the last occasion the Mogul emperor, with the words of peace in his mouth, suddenly and treacherously attacked the city of Haiderábád, capital of the kingdom of Golkonda. The city was taken and sacked, then restored under very hard conditions to its sovereign. But the final intentions of Aurangzíb were only veiled. By another equally treacherous attack, made in 1687, he overthrew the ancient dynasty and annexed the country (1688). The viceroyalty of the new conquest was first placed by Aurangzíb in the hands of his favourite

[1] Elphinstone states that the name is derived from the word 'Bráhman,' the founder of the race having leased a field from a Bráhman. In that field he found a treasure, which he made over to his landlord, who thenceforth devoted himself to pushing his fortunes.

PART V.

son, Prince Kámbuksh. On the succession of Bahádúr Shah, however, Kámbuksh revolted (1708), was defeated, and died of his wounds. The victorious monarch then bestowed the viceroyalty upon his ablest general, Zúlfikár Khan; but his services being required at court, he left as his lieutenant, to administer the state, Dáúd Khan Pání, a Pathán officer, who had distinguished himself in the wars of Aurangzib. In 1713 Dáúd Khan was removed, and three years later was defeated and slain by Húsén Ali, commander-in-chief of the Emperor Farokhsír. The successor of Dáúd Khan was Chin Kilich Khan, afterwards well known under the titles of Nizám-úl-Múlk and Azof Jáh, the founder of the reigning family.

Azof Jáh, as he will be called, was of a respectable Túrk family, the son of Ghází-ú-dín, a favourite officer of Aurangzíb. He was a man of ability and craft, and utterly without scruple. He continued to exercise the office of viceroy under the Emperor of Delhi until the year 1724, with only a short interlude, during which he officiated as prime minister to the emperor. In 1724, the emperor, who feared him, incited Mobáriz Khan, the local governor of Haiderábád, to rise against and supersede him. He attempted to do so, but was defeated and slain in October 1724. Azof Jáh wrote to congratulate the emperor on the victory he had obtained over his master's nominee, and forwarded with the letter the nominee's head! From that date Azof Jáh conducted himself as an independent prince.

To record his intrigues and his wars would be foreign to my present purpose. It will suffice to state that he founded a dynasty, and when he died in 1748, his sway extended from the Narbadá to Trichinápalí and from Masulípatam to Bíjapúr.

Azof Jáh left behind him six sons and six daughters, legitimate and illegitimate. It is necessary to refer to the marriage of one of his daughters, because from it sprang an issue which affected greatly the contest for supremacy between the French and English. Whilst, then, the elder legitimate daughter married the Subadar of Lahore, the younger espoused a nobleman of Haiderábád. She bore to him a son, Mozuffer Jung, towards whom Azof Jáh showed so great an affection, that he was universally regarded as his destined heir. In fact Azof Jáh had taken care to obtain a firman from the court of Delhi nominating Mozuffer Jung as his successor.

It was not to be supposed that this arrangement would be quietly acquiesced in. Of the six sons, indeed, the eldest, Ghází-ú-dín Khan, was high in the imperial service, and preferred pushing his fortunes at the court of Delhi to risking all for a doubtful succession. The second Názir Jung, had been engaged in constant rebellion against his father, but he was with him when he died. Of the other four, the fifth, Nizám Ali, proved eventually to be a man of some mark, but he was yet young, and they had all been kept in comparative seclusion.

When Azof Jáh died, Mozuffer Jung, his intended successor, was at his government at Bíjapúr, whilst the second son, Názir Jung, was on the spot. This prince acted in accordance with the traditions and customs of his age and country. He seized his father's treasures, bought over the leading men of the army, and proclaimed himself Subadár of the Dekhan.

Mozuffer Jung not lightly renouncing an inheritance he had been brought up to consider as his own, invoked the aid of the Márhatás, and having obtained the promise of that, succeeded then in securing the important support of the great ruler of Pondichéry, M. Dupleix. This last adherence was not at first decisive. At Ambúr, indeed, his ally, Chunda Sáhib, defeated and slew the Nawáb of the Karnátik. But the first events that followed were unpropitious, ending in the surrender by Mozuffer Jung of his own person to Názir Jung, by whom he was at once put in irons.

But the French alliance saved him. On April 12 1750, Názir Jung's camp was surprised by a party under M. de la Touche. On September 1 his lieutenant, Mahomed Ali, was completely beaten by M. d'Auteuil. On the 11th of the same month Bussy captured Jinjí; and on December 16 de la Touche again surprised Názir Jung's camp, and that leader lost his life. Mozuffer Jung was released, and was at once proclaimed Subadár.

But he did not long enjoy the dignity. On his way to take possession of Haiderábád, he was treacherously murdered by the Nawábs of Kadapah, Karnúl, and Savanúr (February 1751). He was at once succeeded in his government by Salábat Jung, the third son of Azof Jáh. Salábat Jung's reign lasted ten years. It was full of incidents all intimately connected with the rise and fall of the French power in India.

This part of the history of Haiderábád is so completely, indeed, the history of the French in India that it would be foreign to the purpose of this book to enter at any length into the subject, more especially as I have dealt with it completely in another work.[1] It will suffice to state that on the overthrow of M. Conflans by Colonel Forde, January 1759, Salábat Jung, who had been marching with a large force to the aid of the former, was terrified into signing a treaty with the English—a treaty whereby he renounced the French alliance, agreed never to allow a French contingent in the Dekhan, and ceded to the English a territory yielding an annual revenue of four lakhs. Salábat Jung did not long survive the disruption of the French alliance. His brother, Nizám Ali, conspired successfully against him in 1761, imprisoned him, and had him murdered two years later.

Nizám Ali, though unscrupulous and fond of power, was a man of small capacity. In 1761 he repulsed an invasion of the Márhátás. Four years later, watching

[1] *History of the French in India.* Longmans.

his opportunity, he made an irruption into the Karnátik, then under the protection of the English, and plundered it. This act was naturally resented, but the English, not being prepared at the moment for active hostilities, deputed Major Calliaud to negotiate with the Nizám—as he began then to be styled—and to endeavour to place matters on a pacific and satisfactory footing. Calliaud's mission resulted in the treaty of Haiderábád, by virtue of which the East India Company consented to hold the northern Sirkárs[1] from the Nizám at an annual rent of nine lakhs of rupees, from which was to be deducted the cost of a subsidiary force, which the Company undertook to furnish whenever that force might be required. The Nizám also engaged to assist the English with his troops.

True to this engagement, the English despatched two battalions to aid Nizám Ali in the siege of Bangalúr, then held by Haider Ali. But, with his usual management, Haider succeeded in persuading Nizám Ali to desert the English alliance for his own. The two princes then joined forces and invaded the Karnátik (August 1767). Encouraged by the little opposition they met, they attacked the English detachment, which, under the command of Lieut.-Col. Smith, had been sent to co-operate with Nizám Ali. Smith was forced to retreat to Trinkamalí. But, sallying subsequently from this place, he inflicted so much loss on the enemy, that the latter expressed a desire to negotiate. The only terms the Nizám would accept being, however, inadmissible, Smith, who had received reinforcements, again attacked him and his ally near Ambúr, and drove them to Kávárípatam. This action forced Nizám Ali to reason; he accepted the terms offered, and signed a new treaty on February 26, 1768. By this he revoked all sunnuds granted to Haider Ali by the Subadárs of the Dekhan; agreed to cede to the English the administration of the Karnátik above the ghâts, which had been seized by Haider Ali, on

[1] Comprising the districts of Ganjam, Vízagapatam, Godávéri, and Khrisna.

condition of their paying him seven lakhs of rupees a year; not to interfere with the possessions of the Nawáb of the Karnátik; and to accept a reduced payment for the northern Sirkárs. Lastly, the English agreed to furnish the Nizám, on requisition, with two battalions of sepoys and guns, on condition of his paying their expenses, and on the understanding that the force was not to be employed against any ally of the English. The provisions of this treaty, so far as they concerned Haider Ali, were not carried out, peace having been concluded with that chief the following year.

In 1779 another complication arose, which threatened to embroil the Nizám again with the English, and, it must be admitted, with right and justice on his side. His brother, older than himself, Basálat Jung, held in jaghír from Nizám Ali the district of Guntúr, which appertained to the northern Sirkárs; but the Company having acquired, by a sunnud from the emperor, a right to the Sirkár, it had been settled that on the demise of Basálat Jung, it should devolve on the English. This had been confirmed, with certain provisos, by the second article of the treaty of 1768. Now, about 1774, Basálat Jung was induced to take into his pay a body of French troops, and it became necessary to Nizám Ali, as his liege lord, to order him to remove them, as being contrary to his engagements with the English. Basálat Jung did not remove them; but five years later, threatened by Haider Ali, he implored the aid of the British, agreed to dismiss his French levies, and to replace them by a British detachment; and, what was more, he was induced to allow the British to take possession of the district of Guntúr on lease. Nizám Ali was naturally incensed at this transaction. He had been no party to it—he had not even been consulted; and it violated the second article of the treaty of 1768. That he was right was shown by the subsequent conduct of the Home Government, who, for this and other offences, showed their displeasure by dismissing the Governor of Madras, Sir Thomas Rumbold, and by removing some of the members of his council.

But for the moment he obtained no redress. He therefore again united with Haider Ali, and threatened to attack Basálat Jung unless he should cancel his engagements with the English. At the same time, encouraged by the success which had attended Mádhají Sindhia in the operations which led to the convention of Wargaum, he concerted with Haider and the Marhátás a system of hostilities on a large scale which should rid the native powers of their common foe.

But Nizám Ali was incapable of the large views of Mádhají. He possessed besides little stability of character. The decision of the Madras Government regarding Guntúr having been overruled in Bengal, that district was restored to him.[1] At the same time, attempts were made to soothe and bring him to reason. These efforts were so far successful that, with the power to yield important, perhaps decisive, aid, he held aloof from the Haider in the last war that leader waged against the British.

Basálat Jung died in 1782. Guntúr lapsed then by right to the British. But Nizám Ali held it, nor did he surrender it for six years (September 1788). The rent, 72,000*l.*, continued to be paid to him until 1823, when it was redeemed by a payment of 1,16,66,666 rupees, or 1,201,201*l.* sterling, the value of the annuity, to relieve the Nizám from a debt due by him to the firm of Messrs. Palmer and Co., at Haiderábád, incurred to pay off an accumulation of arrears due to an augmented military establishment, arising principally out of the war of 1817–18.

The following year, 1789, war ensued between Tippú Sultan and the English. Nizám Ali was forced to take a side. He distrusted Tippú because he felt that, should

[1] The Nizám took the French corps into his own service.

PART V.

he succeed against the English, he himself would fall a certain victim to the ambition of his ally. Every motive of policy, then, induced him to side with the English; and to stimulate this there was at hand also the urgent solicitation of Lord Cornwallis, who promised him full participation in the advantages which might result from the war. Nizám Ali was anxious indeed that his own territories should be guaranteed to him, fearing lest, whilst his armies should be engaged with Tippú, the Márhátás should sweep upon his defenceless cities. This guarantee, however, Lord Cornwallis refused to give him, and the treaty was signed without it.

By this treaty, to which the Peshwa acceded, it was stipulated that the contracting parties should prosecute the war with vigour, that peace should not be made without the consent of all, and that an equal partition of the conquests should be made.

The war did not last very long. In February 1792, Tippú was compelled by the treaty of peace, dictated under the walls of Seringapatam, to yield half his dominions. The share of the territory apportioned to the Nizám yielded an annual revenue of about 52,64,000 rupees, besides a third of the amount in cash, amounting to three millions sterling, levied upon Tippú.

I have already stated that the Nizám had pressed on the attention of Lord Cornwallis the desirability of granting him a guarantee for the retention of his territories prior to his entering into the alliance against Tippú, and that his desire for a guarantee had been inspired by a fear of double-dealing on the part of the Márhátás. A very short interval of time showed that he had had reason for that fear. An unsettled account between the two powers had been allowed to accumulate. The balance was against the Nizám, and as he professed his inability to pay it, the Márhátás signified their intention, in 1794, to enforce their claims. In vain did the Governor-General, Lord Teignmouth, proffer his mediation. The

Peshwa refused it, and in February 1795, hostilities commenced. The war was conducted by Nizám Ali with blundering imbecility, and with a caution bordering on pusillanimity. He did indeed fight a drawn battle with the enemy, and had he only encamped where he fought, as urged to do by the leader of his French levies, Raymond, he would probably have seen them flee before him. But he himself retreated in the night, and took refuge in the small fort of Kurdla. Followed up with vigour by the Márhátás, he was soon hemmed in. His supplies were cut off, and he was forced to sue for peace. The terms granted him were humiliating in the extreme. He was compelled to cede to the Márhátás territories yielding an annual income of thirty-five lakhs; to pay three millions sterling; and to yield up his prime minister as a hostage for the fulfilment of these conditions. It may here be added that three-fourths of the territory ceded on this occasion were afterwards recovered during the dissensions which followed the demise of Madho Ráo Peshwa.[1]

Prior to the commencement of hostilities, the Nizám had implored the Governor-General for the aid of two battalions of British sepoys. Lord Teignmouth, unwilling to break with the Peshwa, with whom he had no quarrel, had refused. But though he refused his active aid, the Governor-General, with a consideration which the Peshwa might have construed as exceeding the bounds of permissible courtesy, had allowed the British sepoys to maintain the internal peace of the Nizám's dominions, whilst he should concentrate all his forces against the enemy. But notwithstanding this extreme display of goodwill, the refusal of active aid rankled in Nizám Ali's mind. To be entirely independent of British support for the future, he determined to dismiss the subsidiary force furnished him by the British, and to augment the corps

[1] Aitchison's *Treaties*.

in his service commanded by French officers, some of whom he had previously taken over from his brother, Basálat Jung. The British battalions, however, had not only received their orders to leave, they had actually started, when an event occurred which induced Nizám Ali to send pressing messengers to recall them. This event was the rebellion of his eldest son, Ali Jáh. In rebelling against his father Ali Jáh had only followed the traditions of the family. By rebellion against his brother his own father had obtained the post he occupied, and Ali Jáh considered the road shorter and more secure than the uncertain process of time and a father's caprice. So he rebelled. He might have succeeded had he possessed more than a small modicum of brain. As he did not possess even that modicum, he failed. The French battalions sent after him captured him. Escorted to Haiderábád on an elephant, the minister directed that the howdah in which he sat should be veiled. Ashamed of the indignity thus offered, the greatest a Mahomedan can receive, that of being treated as a woman, Ali Jáh took poison and died. Meanwhile the British contingent had returned, and Nizám Ali, feeling still insecure, determined to retain it.

But the augmentation of the battalions officered by Frenchmen still continued to be an offence to the British Government. In 1798, the Nizám had in his pay a body of fourteen thousand men, armed and disciplined in the European fashion, and officered by one hundred and twenty-four Frenchmen, giving, in addition to staff officers, about eight officers to a regiment a thousand strong. This formidable body was commanded by M. Raymond.

This remarkable man is referred to by many English writers simply as 'an adventurer named Raymond.' That he was an adventurer is true, but he was one in the best sense of the term. Chivalrous, daring, trustworthy, and a splendid organiser, he was one of those 'adventurers' who, like the Garibaldi of our own days, leave their mark on the history of the country in which their deeds have been achieved. His story, briefly summarised, is this. Born in 1755, at Sérignac, in the province of Gascony, he engaged at the age of twenty as sub-lieutenant in a French corps, commanded by the Chevalier de Lassé in the service of Haider Ali. His distinguished conduct on several occasions brought him to the notice of the French authorities. He obtained the grade of captain in the French army, and when Bussy came out in 1783 to co-operate with Haider Ali against the English, he made Raymond his aide-de-camp. After the death of Bussy, Raymond was recommended, in 1786, by the then Governor of Pondichéry, to the Nizám, as an officer upon whom he could entirely rely. Nizám Ali commissioned him to raise a regiment of infantry, granting him at the same time a monthly salary of five thousand rupees. The regiment so raised was in every respect so superior to any the Nizám had seen before that Raymond was encouraged gradually to increase the number to fourteen. It may be truly said that no Indian prince, not even Mádhají Sindhia, nor his successor, Daolat Ráo, ever had a finer or more efficient body in his service. In the campaign against the Márhátás in 1796, it was Raymond and his troops who repulsed the charges of the Márhátá cavalry, and would have beaten them back altogether, had not the Nizám and his irregular troops abandoned the field. His reputation, great at the time, still survives him, and it may be said with truth that the name of no European connected with India has survived seventy-six years after the demise of the body, to live with such eternal greenness in the hearts of the people of the country with which he was connected, as does the name of Raymond in the memories and traditions of the great families of Haiderábád!

The French force under Raymond was in its highest state of discipline and perfection when the Marquess Wellesley, who had succeeded Lord Teignmouth, saw looming

PART V.

in a very proximate future that contest with Tippú Sultan which ended in the overthrow of the Mussulman dynasty in Mysore. To enter upon such a contest with doubtful allies in a high state of discipline on his flank, was totally opposed to those sound maxims of policy by which the Marquess Wellesley was ever guided. He urged therefore upon the Nizám the absolute necessity under which he lay to disband them. Nizám Ali did not at all relish the idea. He looked upon his French officers and their troops as Napoleon regarded his guard. But just at the crisis of his hesitation two circumstances came to sway him. Raymond died—it has been said, with what truth I know not, by poison. The second concurring influence was the release of the minister left as a hostage with the Peshwa, a minister not only favourable to British interests, but who brought with him a remission of three-fourths of the cessions, territorial and pecuniary, settled by the convention of Kurdlah in 1796.

Then the Nizám yielded. He gave his consent to the dismissal of the French corps and the increase of the British subsidiary force. A treaty was concluded, September 1, 1798, which regulated the duties on which the subsidiary force was to be employed, secured the Nizám in the sovereignty of his dominions, prohibited his entering into political negotiations with other States, and made the British Government the arbiter of his disputes with other powers.

No sooner had the treaty been concluded than four battalions of British sepoys with their guns marched to Haiderábád and joined the two battalions formerly stationed there. Some hesitation was even then displayed by the Nizám to break up the French corps, then commanded by Perron; but a movement of the British contingent forced him to issue a proclamation informing his disciplined sepoys that he dismissed his French officers from his service. The episode that ensued can scarcely be wondered at. These men had learned to look up to their European officers with pride; they felt that they owed the prestige they had acquired to them alone; they would have followed them to the end of the earth; they knew that their dismissal was owing, not to the wish of the Nizám, but to the insistance of the English. They were not slow to resent this indignity. They broke into open mutiny; but, unfortunately for them, this probable issue had been foreseen and provided for by the English commander. He surrounded their cantonments. From every commanding point cannon were pointed on them. Resistance they saw to be hopeless, and they allowed themselves to be disarmed. Their officers were not treated as prisoners of war, but were sent, *viâ* England, to France.

In the war with Tippú Sultan, which followed, the troops of the Nizám took a part. After the death of that sovereign and the partial dismemberment of his territories, the Nizám received districts yielding about 24,00,000 rupees. To these were subsequently added two-thirds of the territory offered to, but rejected by, the Peshwa. But all the territories thus acquired, as well as those acquired by the treaty of 1792, and yielding an annual income of about 100,00,000 rupees, were in 1800 ceded to the English in perpetuity, to defray the expenses of the subsidiary force, then augmented to 8,000 infantry, 1,000 cavalry, and a proportion of artillery. It was stipulated in the treaty that, in the event of war, of this force 6,000 infantry with the cavalry and artillery, joined by 6,000 foot and 9,000 horse of the Nizám's own troops, should march to oppose the enemy. Subsequently an article was added to the treaty, requiring the contracting parties to admit the troops of either party into their forts when called upon to do so.

Nizám Ali died in 1803. He had eight sons by different wives. The fate of the eldest, Ali Jáh, has been already recorded. The second, Sekunder Jáh, who succeeded him, had commanded the contingent which ope-

PART V.

rated in alliance with the English against Tippú Sultan in 1792. The others lived obscure lives, and died unnoticed.

Sekunder Jáh.

This prince had many of the defects common to oriental princes born in the purple. Only thirty-four years of age, he was fond of ease and luxury and careless of his people's welfare. His want of intellect bordered upon folly. He disliked the English. To this dislike he gave utterance, first, by requesting the Emperor of Delhi to confirm his authority—an act which, in the then condition of the Mogul empire, conveyed with it no security—and secondly, by evincing something more than apathy in the war which the British Government were prosecuting with Sindhia and Holkar. The British Government, far from resenting these displays of dislike, renewed with him the treaties made with his father, and, on the successful close of the Márhátá war, treated him as though he had materially aided to bring about that issue by allowing him to partake of the spoil. His northern frontier was thus extended to the Indyadrí hills and the Wardá river.

Nothing of any moment disturbed the surface of affairs till 1808. In that year the prime minister, Mír Alim, died. His death threatened to disturb the relations between Haiderábád and Calcutta, for it was due mainly to the influence of the deceased minister that the innate aversion of Sekunder Jáh to the British had been partially veiled, and it was feared lest he might appoint as a successor a man who might be incompetent or hostile, or both. There were good reasons for that fear. Then ensued a curious struggle between the strength of will of the predominant, and the obstinacy of the protected, power. The result was quite in accordance with the teachings of all experience. The Nizám contented himself with the shells, and allowed the British Government to take the oyster. He nominated his own favourite as prime minister, on condition that the prime minister was never to interfere actively in the affairs of the State. The real power was bestowed upon a dependent of the British, a Hindú, who was, it was imagined, ready to pull the strings as he might be directed. CHAP. I.

This man, Chundú Sál by name, possessed great acuteness, but his method of administration was extremely primitive in theory, and in action oppressive. Its sole merit, if merit it can be called, was simplicity. He farmed the revenue of the several districts to middlemen. The State was thus made secure of a certain revenue without the trouble of collection, whilst the taxpayers and people were absolutely without protection. This misgovernment resulted in universal disorganisation and unchecked tyranny. The people, ground down to the earth, were forced in their turn to become robbers. To repress these again the military were called in; and as the regular army was officered by British officers, the unseemly spectacle was presented of British officers hunting down the poor wretches who had only risen under the most dire oppression.

To put an end to this scandal the British Government sent Sir Charles Metcalfe as Resident in 1820. Under the firm and vigorous guidance of this able administrator sweeping reforms were inaugurated. British officers were sent to the several districts with instructions to define the amount of revenue which the government, the district and village officers, were respectively entitled to levy from the people. The several amounts having been settled, the officers were directed to watch, for a series of years, that no more than this amount should be levied. From the inquiries made by these officers, from past averages, from the amount of land in cultivation or fit for cultivation, it became possible generally to form an assessment for a period of five years. On these terms leases were then granted, and a written acceptance of the conditions, and a promise to abide by them, were taken from the people.

PART V.

These just and simple measures had a wonderfully restorative effect. The country became tranquillised as if by magic. It no longer became necessary to employ troops for the collection of revenue. The government, from having been hated, became popular; cultivation increased; and after a few years there was a natural augmentation of revenue.

Prior to the inauguration of these reforms, and partly during the early period of their introduction, the Nizám, or rather his minister acting for him, had taken part with the British in the wars against the Pindárís and the Peshwa, 1817-22. In acknowledgment of the good service rendered by the Haiderábád troops on these occasions, the Nizám received, December 12, 1822, an increase of territory, bringing in an additional annual revenue of 6,26,375 rupees. He bound himself, however, to protect the rights of the landholders in the districts made over to him—a promise which subsequently led to 'constant and unpleasant discussions' [1] with the British Government.

It was a little before this period that the minister, Chundú Sál, effected a reform in the regular army. Its number was fixed at 10,244 men, divided into six regiments of infantry and four of cavalry. The regiments were clothed like the native regiments in the British service, and were officered by English gentlemen and adventurers.

Sekunder Jáh lingered on till the middle of 1829. He led a life of seclusion, taking for many years no part in public affairs. He died on May 24, and was succeeded by his eldest son, Násir-úd-Daola.

Almost the first act of this prince after his accession to the Nizámat was to claim the right of administering the affairs of his country in his own way. He requested the British Government, therefore, to withdraw the

[1] Aitchison's *Treaties*.

officers introduced by Sir C. Metcalfe, and whose earnest endeavours had re-introduced order and prosperity. His request was complied with; but he was required to maintain inviolate the settlements made by the British officers until the period for which they had been made should expire. Yet, scarcely had the British officers left than these conditions were violated, and renewed misrule produced renewed disorder. 'Every department of the State became disorganised, and the credit of the State was so bad that bankers refused to grant loans.'[1] The disorder was increased by the state of arrears into which the payment of the army was allowed to fall.

To remedy this state of things the British Government was forced once more to interfere. After many negotiations, characterised by generosity and candour and sound counsel on the one side, and the making of promises only to break them on the other, a settlement on the basis of a material guarantee was arrived at in 1853. A treaty was signed that year by which the Nizám ceded, in trust to the British, certain districts yielding a gross annual revenue of fifty lakhs of rupees. For this sum the British engaged to maintain for his Highness's service an auxiliary force of not less than 5,000 infantry, 2,000 cavalry, and four field batteries of artillery, to be officered and commanded by British officers. 'By this treaty the Nizám, while retaining the full use of the subsidiary force and contingent, was released from the obligation of furnishing a large force in time of war; the contingent ceased to be the Nizám's army, and became an auxiliary force kept up by the British Government for the Nizám's use.'[2] It must be added that it was provided that the accounts of the ceded districts should be rendered annually to the Nizám, and that he should receive all the surplus that might accrue after the cost of the contingent had been met.

[1] Aitchison's *Treaties*. [2] *Ibid.*

PART V.

It deserves to be recorded that so greatly did the evenues of the ceded districts rise under British administration that at the end of two years they were found so much to exceed the requirements, that the Governor-General, Lord Dalhousie, restored to the Nizám territory yielding three lakhs of rupees. His successor, Lord Canning, subsequently, in 1860, restored all the districts that had been ceded, with the exeption of Barár, the revenues of which were found then to cover the entire cost of the contingent.

Násir-úd-Daola died in 1857. He had laboured all his life under the unhappy misfortune of estimating his own abilities more highly than he was warranted by their intrinsic value to estimate them. Thus, he began his reign by determining to be his own minister. He soon found himself helplessly drifting into mismanagement and disorder. Finding he could not manage without ministers, he laboured to undermine them. But here again he was foiled. Fond of pomp and show, he strove to keep up an expensive force, whilst every year plunged him more deeply into debt. So heavily was he involved at one time that even the bankers refused him credit. Like his father, and his father's father, he owed his extrication from the difficulties which more than once threatened to overwhelm him to the forbearance, the kindly aid, and the generosity of the Government of India.

Násir-úd-Daola was succeeded by his son, Afzal-úd-Daola. The year had dawned unpropitiously for British interest. In the centenary of Plassey the descendants of the sepoys who had helped to gain that battle for the English had revolted to undo, and more than undo, all that Plassey had enabled their masters to accomplish. For a few brief moments it seemed as though the felon stroke might be fatal. It seemed so, that is to say, to a few princes, to very many soldiers, to all the fanatics, and to a large proportion of the ignorant. It seemed so, certainly, to a not inconsiderable number of the population of Haiderábád. Nor were those who formed that number content with the idea. They determined that, if possible, it should become a fact. Assembling then, on July 17, these conspirators attacked the palace of the British Resident. But the Resident repulsed them. More than that, they were attacked likewise by one who did not belong to any one of the classes I have enumerated—by one who was neither a prince, nor a soldier, nor a fanatic, nor ignorant. They were attacked by the prime minister, Sir Salar Jung, one of the ablest of living Indian statesmen, and were dispersed. Guided by the counsels of that enlightened man, the Nizám steered a straight course during the cyclone of the mutiny.

It was partly in reward for his loyalty on this trying occasion, partly to remove difficulties connected with the commercial treaty of 1802, that a new treaty was concluded in December 1860, by which the debt of fifty lakhs due by him to the British was cancelled, and through cessions and exchanges of districts, the territories to be held by the British in trust were reduced to an area yielding 32,00,000 rupees, instead of one yielding 50,00,000 rupees, as had been specified in the treaty of 1853.

Afzal-úd-Daola, like all his ancestors, did not love the British. He and his family had been under too many obligations to do that. But at his court British influence was preponderant. This was entirely due to the influence of Sir Salar Jung. When then, in 1861, the Nizám took the resolution to remove that minister from office, the weight of British influence was thrown so forcibly into the opposite scale that the resolution was rescinded. Sir Salar Jung remained, and still remains, notwithstanding an attempt made in 1868 to assassinate him—the prime minister of the State,[1] and the hope of the country.

[1] The attempt to assassinate Sir Salar Jung was made by a Mussulman named Reshna Ali, who had long borne a grudge against the ad-

PART. V.

His master, Afzal-úd-Daola, died February 27, 1869. He had been nominated a Knight of the Star of India, and he had received from the Government of India a guarantee that any succession to his State, made in accordance with Mahomedan law and the customs of the country, would be recognised.

Mír Mábúb Ali Khán.

Afzal-úd-Daola was succeeded by his infant son, Mír Mábúb Ali Khán, who was placed on the musnud on March 1, 1869.

Being of a very tender age, only four years old, a council of regency was appointed to conduct, with the aid of the British Resident, the affairs of the country. Of this council the Nawáb Shums-úl-Amra and Sir Salar Jung are members.

Little has occurred from that date to the present time to call for remark. The young Nizám has been kept in seclusion in the palace of his grandmother. From this he emerged for the first time on July 24, 1874. Mounted on a richly caparisoned elephant, and followed by about 20,000 armed men, he paraded the city, *en route* to the tomb of a pious Mahomedan who had died half a century before. He paid his first visit to the Resident on August 1 following.

ministration on account of a divorce case which had been decided against him by a district Kází in strict accordance with law and justice. The escape of Sir Salar Jung was hailed with joy by the nobles and people of Haiderábád. The assassin was executed March 21 following the attempt.

CHAPTER II.[1]

MYSORE. (MAISÚR).

AREA—27,004 sq. miles. POPULATION—5,055,412.
ANNUAL REVENUE—1,08,20,000 rupees.
SUBSIDY PAID TO BRITISH GOVERNMENT—2,450,000 rupees.

CHAP. II.

THE early history of the territory known as Mysore is involved in obscurity. According to the Hindú legend, a small territory to the west of the Karnátik, consisting of two fortified places and a few villages, was raised to an independent condition by two young men of the Yadu[2] tribe, who, coming as strangers to a marriage festival at Hadana, near Mysore, slew, with the connivance of the bride and her relatives, the destined bridegroom, a chief of Karúgalí. One of them, the elder, married the bride, and became the acknowledged lord of the united territories. This fact, we are informed by Colonel Wilks, is recorded in many manuscripts, but its date is uncertain. There are, however, authentic records to show that in 1507, the country was under the rule of Chám Ráj, called the Sixfingered, from his being marked by that peculiarity.

At this time, however, the territories under his rule comprehended only a few villages, two or three of which were fortified, and Chám Ráj was more of a zamindar than a king. But small as were his possessions, they were subdivided by his successor, Betad Chám Ráj, in 1524, amongst his three sons. To the youngest of these, Chám Ráj, surnamed the Bald, was assigned the fort of Púragarh with some adjacent villages. This fort was, however, repaired or re-erected in the same year, and its name was changed to Mahesh Asúr, 'the buffalo-headed monster.' Thence is derived the more modern appellation of Maisúr or Mysore.

[1] The contents of this chapter were contributed by the author to the *Calcutta Review* some years ago.

[2] *Yadu*, a name of Krishna.

PART V.

Chám Ráj, the Bald, may thus be styled the first ruler of Mysore, for though not the founder of his family—though indeed by the failure of issue in his family, his territories devolved afterwards on the descendants of his brothers—he was the first ruler of the territory known as Mysore. Not many years after the subdivision I have recorded, the Mahomedan power began to make itself felt south of the Dekhan. In 1564, the Hindú kingdom of Bijianagar succumbed to the four Mussulman sovereigns of Daolutábád, Bijapúr, Golkonda, and Bíder. This event proved in the main eminently advantageous to the possessor of Mysore. That little fort, for it was then no more, was situated too much to the south to tempt, at that period, the attacks of the Mahomedans; whilst the fall of the great Hindú house of the Dekhan released its occupier from the state of vassalage in which he had hitherto been held. For several years, then, the descendants of Chám Ráj struggled to obtain an independent position, and at the same time to aggrandise their territories.

The representative of the dynasty of Bijianagar had fled after his expulsion from that place to Seringapatam, where he kept up a sort of regal state. In reality, however, he was weak and powerless, and none knew this better than Híra Chám Ráj, the successor of Chám Ráj the Bald. He accordingly evaded the payment of tribute, erected a line of fortifications, expelled the royal collectors, and bade defiance to the Rájá himself. I may pause to note a circumstance which is strongly characteristic of the proceedings of the various houses which have reigned in Hindostan. There has never existed any real loyalty towards the great representative reigning house of the country. When such a house has been struck down, the minor princes, though of the same religion and having the same real interests, have almost invariably hastened to endeavour to profit by its fall, instead of to work towards its recovery. The history of the subversion of the Hindú dynasty of Bijianagar forms no exception to this rule. In all its struggles to recover from the blow dealt by the Mahomedans and to re-assert its sovereignty, it was thwarted by its ancient vassals, likewise of the Hindú persuasion, and suffered at least as much from their attempts at independence as from the attacks of its foreign invaders.

In 1576 Mysore received an accession of territory. In that year Híra Chám Ráj died childless. The succession fell consequently to Betád Wadiar, the grandson of the Rájá who had originally partitioned the territory. The second third, represented by the fort of Hemunkali and the surrounding villages, was therefore reunited to Mysore.

A few years later, Betád Wadiar gave way to his brother Ráj Wadiar, who conquered from his cousin the remaining third and the original territory represented by the fort of Kembala. Under the rule of this Ráj Wadiar, who appears to have been a man of considerable ability, the limits of Mysore were greatly extended, and its power was considerably increased. Perhaps the most important of his acquisitions was the famous city of Seringapatam, originally called Siri Runga Pattan, or the city of the holy Runga, and which had long been the seat of the expelled sovereign of Bijianagar. There are several versions current as to the manner in which this city came into the hands of Ráj Wadiar, but Colonel Wilks is of opinion that on the death of the Bijianagar sovereign it devolved upon him as the ablest of the Hindú princes in the vicinity. Thenceforth Seringapatam became the seat of government of the Ráj of Mysore. It is curious to note that the occupation of this city was followed by a change of religion on the part of the Rájá. Before that time the family had professed the religion of the Jangam; thenceforth

PART V.

they adopted the forms prescribed for the followers of Vishnú. Several other conquests followed the acquisition of Seringapatam.

Ráj Wadiar died in 1617, leaving behind him a very great reputation. Not only had he re-united the three portions of the territories divided by his ancestor, and considerably added thereto, but by the possession of Seringapatam on the demise of the ruler of Bijianagar, he had come to be regarded as the chief of the Hindú sovereigns south of the Krishna. He left his policy behind him. During a reign of twenty years, his grandson, Chám Ráj, added to his dominions, and continued his policy of treating the conquered with leniency. On his death in 1637, he was succeeded by his uncle Ímadí Ráj, born after the death of his father. This prince, however, who inherited the martial qualities of Ráj Wadiar, was poisoned, after a reign of eighteen months, by his minister. As he left no offspring, the throne reverted to the son of the elder brother of Ráj Wadiar, by name Kantiréva Narsa Ráj.

This prince had hitherto lived in obscurity, but he was endowed with a chivalrous spirit, and with unusual strength and courage. Colonel Wilks relates an instance of his having gone in disguise to the court of Trichinápalí to meet in single combat a celebrated champion whose fame was in everyone's mouth. He encountered and slew him; then, with a modesty equal to his courage, notwithstanding the solicitations of the king, returned to his humble abode. It is probable that the minister, who, to retain the actual power in his own hands, had murdered his predecessor, little knew the real character of Kantiréva, when he invited him to assume the reins of government at Seringapatam; nor was the prince aware, when he accepted the offer, of the circumstances which had attended the death of his cousin. The insolence of the minister soon after the prince's arrival brought matters to a crisis; Kantiréva was informed of the fate which had

CHAP. II.

befallen his predecessor, and which probably awaited himself; he determined therefore to strike the first blow. The minister was accordingly waylaid, and, after a severe struggle, despatched.

The throne had been gained just in time, for the following year Kantiréva had to sustain the first invasion of the Mahomedans. The general of the king of Bíjapúr attacked his dominions, and even besieged Seringapatam. A breach was effected in the walls, and a general assault was delivered. Kantiréva, however, not only beat back the assailants, but pursued them with great slaughter beyond the border. He then proceeded to consolidate the conquests previously made, to settle the lands, and to introduce an organised system of administration. Amongst other matters he enlarged the fortifications of Seringapatam, and established a mint. Nor was he less inclined to military enterprises than the most warlike of his predecessors. He extended his dominions, by a succession of conquests in the direction of Bijianagar and Madura, and concluded his warlike achievements by gaining a great victory over the Rájá of Mágrí, whose territories he annexed.

On the death of Kantiréva childless, in 1659, the sovereignty of Mysore devolved upon a distant relative, a descendant of one of his ancestors. The name of this prince was Dúd[1] Déo Ráj. He repulsed a serious invasion by the Rájá of Bednúr, defeated the Naik of Madura, and by conquests from both, as well as by the absorption of some petty states, added greatly to his dominions; he died in 1672, just about the time when the French were struggling with their early difficulties in a corner of the Karnátik.

At this time Mysore may be said to have emerged from the *status* of a Zamíndárí, and to have assumed a position of importance in Southern India. Until this

[1] Dúd, in the language of Mysore, signifies 'great;' Chick 'little;' or senior and junior.—Wilks.

period the rulers of the little territory, struggling to enlarge it, had had but little leisure and little opportunity for indulgence in luxury. The desire to extend the limits of the State had been handed down as an hereditary maxim from each sovereign to its successor. We have seen how, up to this point, they had endeavoured to carry with them the feelings of the people, by rating the ryots of the conquered lands at no heavier assessment than their own vassals. The real difficulties of governing were now to begin. The State was, from its size, beginning to attract attention. The Mahomedan power in Southern India, too, was at its zenith. It ruled not only the district known as the Dekhan, but possessed the Karnátik on the eastern, and Bijapúr on the western, coast; it was also known to be actuated by designs on Trichinápalí. On the western coast, besides, there was rising a power destined to become the enemy of all authorities, Hindú or Mahomedan—the great power of the Márhátás. Mysore would have, indeed, to contend with difficulties in its further progress to greatness.

Dúd Déo Ráj was succeeded in 1672 by Chick Déo Ráj. In the reign of this monarch the Márhátá power had become really formidable. The important posts of Jinjí and Vellúr fell into the hands of Sívají, the kingdoms of Bíjapúr and Golkonda were pushed hard, Tanjúr was overrun and conquered. Yet, though thus approached by such a powerful enemy, Mysore was too far south of the direct line of his movements to fear an attack, unless indeed she should provoke it. But this her sovereign was especially careful not to do. Whilst maintaining a constant look-out on the frontier, and even taking every opportunity of extending it imperceptibly, he devoted his main energies to placing the internal affairs of the kingdom on a permanent basis. He established a post office, openly for the transmission of letters, really for obtaining for himself a knowledge of their contents. The knowledge he thus acquired he used to make himself the centre of all the power of the State. He compelled the abolition by all his feudatories and dependants of the title of Rájá, forcing them to fix their residence at Seringapatam, and converting them from rebellious princes into obsequious courtiers. His policy in this respect bears a striking analogy to that of Richelieu in France, during the reign of Louis XIII., and was influenced by the same motives—the desire to repress feudal and quasi-independent rights, and to establish an almost absolute monarchy on their ruins. His other measures were not dictated by the same wisdom. To increase the amount receivable from the land assessments, he had recourse to a variety of vexatious taxes upon the husbandmen, with the view to induce them to compound for the removal of the most objectionable by agreeing to pay a larger amount in the shape of revenue. From this, as a matter of policy, were exempted only lands granted for military service. The vexatious nature of these taxes, which will be referred to hereafter, and which, if applied to Bengal, would startle the ryots of that province, produced a passive resistance amongst the agricultural population of Mysore. The mode in which the resistance was crushed, by one of the most enlightened monarchs who ever reigned in Mysore, affords a striking contrast to the mild measures adopted in cases of passive resistance to authority by the western rulers of India. It should be recollected that on this occasion there was no revolt, no actual outbreak. It was simply this:—that the children of the soil, crushed by the multifarious taxes which interfered with their sowing, their reaping, their gathering into store, and the selling of the produce of their fields, suspended their inverted ploughs at the gates of their villages, and generally announced their intention to emigrate from a land which denied them the fruits of their labour, rather than cultivate on the terms proposed. A few, and only a few, talked of revenge; the rest were prepared peaceably to depart. But Chick Déo Ráj was

PART V.

too sensible of the value to himself and his kingdom of these cultivators to allow them to leave. And this is the mode he adopted to prevent them. I tell the story as related by Colonel Wilks:—'An invitation was sent to all the priests of the Jangam,'—to which religion the people belonged,—'to meet the Rájá at the great temple of Nanjangód, about 14 miles south of Mysore, ostensibly to converse with him on the subject of the refractory conduct of their followers. Treachery was apprehended, and the number which assembled was estimated at about four hundred only. A large pit had been previously prepared in a walled enclosure, connected by a series of squares composed of tent-walls with the canopy of audience, at which they were successively received one at a time, and, after making their obeisance, they were desired to retire to a place where, according to custom, they expected to find refreshments prepared at the expense of the Rájá. Expert executioners were in waiting at the square, and every individual in question was so skilfully beheaded, and tumbled into the pit, as to give no alarm to those who followed; and the business of the public audience went on without interruption or suspicion.' Having thus quietly rid himself of four hundred priests, the Rájá proceeded to put in operation the plans he had concerted for the extermination or dispersion of their followers. 'Wherever a mob had assembled, a detachment of troops, chiefly cavalry, was collected in the neighbourhood, and prepared to act on one and the same day. The orders were distinct and simple: to charge without parley into the midst of the mob; to cut down in the first selection every man wearing an orange-coloured robe (the peculiar garb of the Jangam priests); and not to cease acting until the crowds had everywhere dispersed.' Having thus paralysed the people by terror, the Rájá, it is said, with very little difficulty 'exacted from every village a written renunciation, ostensibly voluntary, of private property in the land, and an

CHAP. II.

acknowledgment that it was the right of the State.' This occurrence affords one of the few instances on record of the successful warfare by a sovereign against his own people on a question with reference to which the people are of all others the most sensitive—the question of their right to the proprietorship of the soil.

Meanwhile Sivají had died. Aurangzíb, then at the height of his power, had returned to the Dekhan, conquered the independent Mahomedan sovereignties of Bíjapúr and Golkonda, and was engaged in exerting all his energies to crush the Márhátás. Then it was that the chief of Mysore first came into contact with the rivals contending for the possession of Southern India. The Márhátá ruler of Tanjúr, who then held possession of the district of Bangalúr, finding that in the coming conflict his hold upon that territory would be precarious, and might lead him into difficulties, sold it to the Rájá of Mysore for three lakhs of rupees.[1] And though the troops of Aurangzíb anticipated the action of the purchaser and seized the country, they were too glad to yield it to Mysore, on the transfer to themselves, instead of to Tanjúr, of the promised purchase money. Allying himself then with the great Mahomedan sovereign, the Mysore ruler made conquests at the expense of the Márhátás and the Rájá of Bednúr; and although his own capital was on one occasion suddenly besieged by an army of the former warriors, the invaders were, by the combined skill and stratagem employed by his son, driven ignominiously from the kingdom. It was soon after this that the ruler of Mysore, till then known at the imperial court only as the zamíndár of that country, obtained from Aurangzíb the title of Rájá, with the privilege of sitting on an ivory throne. The throne made for this purpose was, we are

[1] Colonel Wilks very justly remarks (vol. i. p. 91), that the sale of the important district of Bangalúr for so small a sum as three lakhs of rupees is a striking instance of the insecurity of the tenure of property in those days of native rule.

informed by Colonel Wilks, always used by the successors of the Rájá; 'it is the same which, in the year 1799, was found in a lumber room of Tippú Sultan's palace; was employed in the installation of the present Rájá; and is always used by him on occasions of public ceremony.'

Chick Déo Ráj died in 1704, after having added thirteen important districts to his territories, and obtained from Aurangzíb the recognition of himself as a sovereign prince independent of all but the Mogul.

The dynasty, which had for nearly two hundred years reigned over Mysore, and raised it from a small zamíndárí to the dignity of a kingdom, was now, however, about to suffer a fate inseparable from all despotic dynasties, viz., the fate either of being sterile or of failing to produce a competent representative. The successor of Chick Déo Ráj, by name Kantiréva Ráj, had the misfortune to be born deaf and dumb. He did not possess the commanding intellect requisite to balance so great a misfortune, and although the energy infused by his predecessor into all branches of the administration continued to exercise a perceptible influence during his life-time, yet his own inability to control actively the governing machine contributed to foster a state of things such as eventually led to the overthrow of the dynasty. In despotic States the sovereign, if he wishes to govern, must be everything; if he cannot take upon his own shoulders the responsibilities of his position, some one else must and will. And the experience of such states has fully shown —it shows every day—that the man who has once enjoyed the substance of authority, will use all the means in his power to make its possession hereditary in his family. So it was in Mysore. Kantiréva died after a reign of ten years, leaving the crown to his son, Dúd Kishen Ráj. This sovereign, let it be recollected, was but the third in succession from the prince who had raised Mysore to the dignity of a kingdom. Prior to that date its rulers had been struggling for a position. That position had been obtained. But from the moment of its obtainment how rapid is the downfall! Kantiréva a nonenity, Dúd Kishen an imbecile, leaving to his successors but an empty title and a pageant throne! CHAP. II.

It would answer no purpose were we to follow Dúd Kishen in his inglorious reign. The process of his fall is thus described by Colonel Wilks: 'Whatever portion of vigour or wisdom,' writes this historian, 'appeared in the conduct of this reign, belonged exclusively to the ministers, who secured their own authority by appearing with affected humility to study in all things the inclinations and wishes of the Rájá. Weak and capricious in his temper, he committed the most cruel excesses on the persons and property of those who approached him, and as quickly restored them to his favour. While no opposition was made to the establishment of almost incredible absurdity, amounting to a lakh of rupees annually for the maintenance of an alms-house to feed beasts of prey, reptiles, and insects, he believed himself to be an unlimited despot; and while amply supplied with the means of sensual pleasure, to which he devoted the largest portion of his time, he thought himself the greatest and happiest of monarchs, without understanding or caring to understand, during a reign of nineteen years, the troublesome details through which he was supplied with all that is necessary for animal gratification.' It is easy to understand that under such a sovereign, the ministers who affected humility, in order, by gratifying his inclinations, to secure their power, were not unfaithful to the traditions of their class. Prominent amongst them were two, Déva Ráj, and his cousin Nanjá Ráj. So long as the Rájá lived they allowed him to enjoy the empty pageantry of power, contenting themselves with its practical exercise; but upon his death in 1701, they treated his distant relative and successor, Chám Ráj, with undisguised contempt. They were at first, indeed, a little too outspoken in their proceedings, for Chám Ráj, though a man of contemptible intellect, possessed that special quality of the weak-minded, that he knew how to conspire. Suddenly he removed his ministers, and filled their places with creatures of his own. But he did not possess the force of mind necessary to strengthen his position, and to improve his victory. Déva Ráj plotted in his turn, and taking advantage of the absence of the Rájá from the city, with a slender escort, he seized the palace, gained over the troops, and, seizing the Rájá, sentenced him to life-imprisonment on the hill of Kabal Drúg—the climate of which was sufficient to ensure death. As if that were not enough, the Rájá was supplied during his captivity with unwholesome food—a procedure which immediately put an end to his sufferings.

From the deposition of Chám Ráj, Colonel Wilks dates the extinction of the dynasty which had reigned for two hundred years in Mysore; thenceforward, though a member of the old family held the nominal office of Rájá, all the authority in the state was in the hands of Hindú or Mahomedan usurpers. In tracing the further history of the country, the names of the ministers or actual rulers will principally engage my attention, as the Rájás were seldom permitted to emerge from the precincts of the palace.

The first of these minister rulers, under the nominal sovereign, Chick Kishen Ráj, were the two cousins, Déva Ráj and Nánjá Ráj. Shortly after they had secured to their adherents all the important posts in the kingdom, Nanjá Ráj died. A few months later, Mysore was invaded by the Nawáb of the Karnátik, Dóst Ali. He was foiled, however, by the superior address of Déva Ráj, and his army was defeated with great slaughter. Shortly afterwards Déva Ráj acknowledged the supremacy of the Emperor of Delhi by paying tribute to Nizám-úl-Múlk, Subadar of Dekhan, who demanded it at the head of an army. Then, too old himself to take the field with his troops, he continued his attention to the internal administration of the kingdom, making over the command of the army to a younger brother, also named Nanjá Ráj, and whose exploits against, and in alliance with, the French and English for the possession of Trichinápalí, are recorded at great length in the pages of Orme. To secure his position Nanjá Ráj married his daughter to the titular king, Chick Kishen.[1]

But Déva Ráj was destined to find that neither he nor his brother, able as they were, were secure against the same means which he himself had employed against his master. The successful seizure of power always acts as an incentive to men who feel within themselves the consciousness of the possession of great capacities to follow the example thus set them. It happened that amongst the soldiers employed by Nanjá Ráj, was one Haider Sahib, or Haider Ali, the grandson of Mahomed Bhelól, a religious person, who, coming from the Punjâb, founded a small mosque near Haiderábád, and the son of Futteh Mahomed, who was killed when fighting for Abdúl Rasúl Khan against Sádut-Ulla for the possession of Séra. This Haider was nearly thirty years old when he entered the service of Mysore, but his talents soon brought him to the notice of Nanjá Ráj, and at the close of the first campaign he was appointed to the charge of an independent corps.

From that time the name of Haider Ali becomes inseparably connected with Mysore. It would be, however, foreign to my purpose to enter into a history of his exploits, or of the exploits of the army which, under the command of Nanjá Ráj, assisted first the English, and afterwards the French, in their contest for empire. For a long time the two brothers held their power with a firm hand, never allowing a single opportunity to escape them of adding to their wealth. Under their rule the interests

[1] The descendants of this marriage by the female line were alive in 1811; I believe that some of them still survive.

PART V.

of the peasantry were but little regarded. The traditions, however, of the persecutions of Chick Déo Ráj, and their own experience of the imbecility of Dúd Kishen, were sufficient to prevent the ryots from indulging in any wish in favour of the confined Rájá of the ancient dynasty. Other causes contributed at this time to the weakness of the kingdom. Its resources had been considerably impaired by foreign war; they received a further blow when, in 1755, Déva Ráj, to save Seringapatam from the hands of Salábat Jung, aided by a French force under Bussy, was forced to promise payment of a contribution-tribute of fifty-six lakhs of rupees, a portion of which was supplied by the spoils of the Hindú temples and the plunder of the private property of the Rájá.

The year following, a quarrel ensued between the two usurping brothers on the subject of the treatment of the young Rájá, who was beginning to chafe very mildly under his captive state. Déva Ráj would have preferred mild measures, but Nanjá Ráj, deeming severity to be the best lesson, opened an artillery fire upon the palace—the gates of which had been closed by the Rájá—stormed it, and placing the Rájá upon his throne, caused the noses and ears of his principal adherents to be cut off in his presence. This occurred less than a year before the victory of Plassey gave England her first firm footing in Bengal.

A few months later the Márhátás appeared before Seringapatam, and compelled Nanjá Ráj to resign a large portion of the territory of Mysore. Meanwhile Déva Ráj, not approving of the conduct of his associate, had left Seringapatam, laden with the plunder he had amassed by his oppression of the people, and the supreme power remained in the possession of Nanjá Ráj. But the division between the brothers had been Haider's opportunity. Hitherto, though feared, Haider had been caressed and petted by Nanjá Ráj, and had been assigned territories which added greatly to his power and influence; he had been saluted by the Rájá and by Nanjá Ráj himself as Futteh Haider Bahádúr, and Nanjá Ráj had invariably plumed himself upon the sagacity he had evinced in bringing forward a man who had shown talents so remarkable. He was now to see that Haider had two sides to his character. This chieftain had determined to attain supreme power. To that end Nanjá Ráj was the first obstacle. To remove him he concerted a plan with the Queen Dowager, by which he so worked upon the nerves of the usurper, that Nanjá Ráj resigned, and, after some show of opposition, agreed to take up his residence at Kúnúr, twenty-five miles from Mysore. The revenues of more than one-half the kingdom were then assigned to Haider Ali. He continued, however, on one pretence or another, to ask for more, until in 1760, he had obtained complete possession of the whole, and this,—notwithstanding a desperate and nearly successful attempt to oust him in that very year,—he retained to the day of his death.

The reign of Haider, his contests with the English, his devastation of the country up to the gates of Madras, are familiar to all the readers of Anglo-Indian history. It will not be necessary then to refer, in this place, to the warlike exploits of this adventurer and his son. It devolves upon us rather to inquire what, during the period of their usurpation, had become of that Hindú dynasty. On the death of the titular Rájá Chick Kishen, in 1766, Haider had invested his eldest son with all the dignities of a sovereign prince; but learning soon after that the young prince, Nanjá Ráj Wadiar, had evinced some of the yearnings for liberty natural to man, he resumed the amount that had been allotted for the maintenance of the sovereign, plundered the palace of all its cash and valuables, with the exception of the ornaments on the persons of the women, reduced the household, and replaced those who were expelled by his own

PART V.

spies. Five years later, during a crisis in Haider's fortunes, this Rájá attempted to open negotiations with the Márhátás. Detected in this, he was strangled by the order of Haider, and his brother, Chám Ráj, invested in his place. Chám Ráj died in 1775. He was the last male representative of the family, and, for any practical service to the country, the Hindú dynasty might then and there have been pronounced to be extinguished. But it suited the whim of Haider to have a pageant Rájá. He rejected, however, the nearest in order of relationship, the grandson in the female line—and adopted a mode of his own to provide a successor. The details of this method we transcribe at length from Colonel Wilks :—

'About this period,' he writes, 'the pageant Rájá Chám Ráj died; Haider had hitherto professed to hold Mysore in behalf of the Hindú house; and amused his subjects on every annual feast of the Dasahrá by exhibiting the pageant, seated on his ivory throne, in the balcony of state; himself occupying the place of minister and commander-in-chief. This ceremonial, in most countries, would have excited feelings dangerous to the usurper; but the unhappy Hindús saw their country everywhere sustaining the scourge of Mahomedan rule; the singular exception of the Márhátá state, a wide-spreading example of still more ruthless oppression, restrained their natural preference for rulers of their own persuasion; and they were soothed with the occasional condescension which treated them and their institutions with a resemblance of respect. Haider saw and indulged the working of these reflections, and determined to have another pageant. The lineal male succession was extinct, and he ordered all the children to be collected from the different branches of the house, who, according to ancient precedent, were entitled to furnish a successor to the throne. The ceremonial observed on this occasion, however childish, was in perfect accordance with the feelings which he intended to delude, and sufficiently adapted to the superstition of the fatalist. The hall of audience was strewed round with fruits, sweetmeats, and flowers, playthings of various descriptions, arms, books, male and female ornaments, bags of money, and every varied object of puerile or manly pursuit; the children were introduced together, and were all invited to help themselves to whatever they liked best; the greater number were quickly engaged in a scramble for the fruits, sweetmeats, and toys; but one child was attracted by a brilliant little dagger, which he took up in his right hand, and soon afterwards a lime in his left. "That is the Rájá," exclaimed Haider, "his first care is military protection; his second to realise the produce of his dominions: bring him hither, and let me embrace him." The assembly was in an universal murmur of applause; and he ordered the child to be conducted to the Hindú palace, and prepared for installation. He was of the same name as his predecessor, viz., *Chám Ráj*, and was the father of the present (late) Rájá, who was placed by the English at the head of the Hindú house of Mysore on the subversion of the Mahomedan dynasty in 1799.'

This Chám Ráj survived the death of Haider Ali in 1782, but continued till his own demise, in 1795, to be kept a prisoner in the palace. On the occurrence of that event, Tippú Sultan determined to continue the farce of a pageant ruler no longer. The son of the late Rájá was but two years old; yet the palace was ransacked, and he, his mother, and all his relations, were despoiled of their personal ornaments. They were then removed to a wretched hovel in the neighbourhood. In this hovel they were found when Seringapatam was captured on May 4, 1799.

Then ensued a new phase in the history of the country. Dividing between himself and the Nizám a considerable portion of the conquered country, Lord Wellesley placed as ruler over the remainder—a territory

PART V.

yielding then an annual revenue of 49 lakhs of rupees—the boy whom he had found in the hovel, and whose father had owed his elevation to the regal dignity not to birth, not to merit, but to the chance of having on one occasion in his childhood preferred a toy dagger to the other playthings by which he was surrounded. At this time, the family, deprived for many years of power, had entirely lost their influence in the country. Lord Wellesley, however, was apparently influenced in the course he adopted by the fact that he saw in it the means of escape from a choice of difficulties. He could not restore even a dismembered portion of Mysore to the representatives of the warlike house of Haider Ali, without, he thought, laying in store for the English Government the chances of future contests as desperate as those which had gone before; nor could he, on the other hand, appropriate to the British the entire country without exciting the jealousy, and, with it, the probable hostility of the Nizám and the Márhátás. The assignment to the last recognised descendant of the Hindú house of Mysore of a considerable portion of the dismembered territory, in a state of vassalage to the British, seemed to present to the English statesman the means of escape from his dilemma. These were his reasons for placing upon the throne of Mysore a child, six years old, the accident of one of the fancies of Haider Ali, and who had been nurtured in indigence and misery.

The arrangements made during the minority of the child, who assumed the name of Krishna Ráj Wadiar, seemed to be dictated by the soundest considerations. Sir Barry Close, one of the ablest political officers of the day, was appointed Resident, the troops were commanded by Colonel Arthur Wellesley, whilst the administration of the country was entrusted to the ablest of the ministers of Tippú, the Brahman Púrnia. I cannot do better than extract the story of this experiment from the Report of the Administration of Mysore for 1872.[1] In a concise style, and with the most absolute accuracy, the writer summarises the history of Krishna Ráj Wadiar. Yet it should be always borne in mind by those who, perusing it, might be inclined to regard as hopeless all future attempts to inaugurate native rule, that neither had Krishna Ráj, nor had any of his predecessors, the advantage now bestowed upon the present Rájá, the advantage of a sound education. The education of Krishna Ráj reminds the historical student of the account of the education of Louis XV. as told by Michelet.

'During the infancy of the Rájá,' states the Report, 'viz. from 1799 to 1810, Púrnia virtually governed the country. His rule was despotic, and it may be questioned whether he did not enrich the treasury at the expense of the State by narrowing the resources of the people, for by 1811 he had accumulated a surplus of seventy-five lakhs of pagodas. He was a minister of the old school, and viewed with chagrin any attempts which the Rájá, as he came to years of discretion, made to assert his prerogative. This provoked the resentment of the young Rájá, surrounded as he was by parasites who constantly urged him to take the government in his own hands. In 1811 the Rájá expressed to the Resident a wish to govern for himself. The Resident endeavoured to secure a share in the administration for Púrnia, but the latter declined office in the position of a subordinate, and retired to Seringapatam, where he soon after died.

'The Rájá assumed the government under the best of auspices, with the goodwill of the British Government, and with a well-filled treasury. His youth was his misfortune, and unhappily he never found a good minister. He was, besides, fond of pleasure; and although he was shrewd and observant, his aspirations to govern absolutely were in excess of his capacity. He was generous to a

[1] This report, though official, is not private, copies being sent to the press.

fault, and lavish in benefactions to temples. Under such conditions it is not surprising that the administration broke down. In less than two years after the Rájá's accession to power, the Resident was obliged to report to the Supreme Government that the Rájá had dissipated all the treasure accumulated by Púrnia. All remonstrances failed to check the Rájá's downward course. High offices of state were sold to the highest bidder, while the people were oppressed by the system of "Sharti," which had its origin under Púrnia's regency. "Sharti" was a contract made by the Amildar that he would realise for the government a certain amount of revenue; that if his collections should fall short of that amount he would make good the deficiency, and that if they exceeded it, the surplus should be paid to the government. The amount which the Amildar thus engaged to realise was generally an increase on what had been obtained the year preceding. In the mutchbolika or agreement the Amildar usually bound himself not to oppress the ryots, nor impose any new taxes, nor compel the ryots to purchase the government share of garden; but this proviso was merely formal, for any violation of the contract in any of these points when represented to the government was taken no notice of. The consequence was that the ryots became impoverished, the revenues most embarrassed; and the Amildars themselves frequently suffered losses. The distress arising from this state of things, and from the neglect of duties incumbent upon government, fell heavily upon the ryots, who groaned under the oppression of every tyrannical Sharti, Fouzdar, and Amildar.

'In 1830 the ryots in portions of the Nagar division (which, it should be observed, formed no part of the dominion of Mysore before Haider's time, and in which, therefore, the hereditary influence of the Rájá was weaker than elsewhere,) broke into open revolt; several of the Páligars assumed independence, and a pretender was set up as the representative of the Rájá who, as we have seen, was dispossessed by Haider. Although the Rájá's troops were generally successful in their skirmishes with the rebels, they failed in subduing the revolt, and the Rájá found it necessary to ask for the aid of British troops, who completely quelled the insurrection.

'The state of Mysore had been for some time attracting the notice of the Government of India, and as it was considered that the insurrection was of so serious a character as to call for special inquiry, the Governor-General ordered the formation of a committee to 'investigate the origin, progress, and suppression of the recent disturbances in Mysore.' Their report showed that the misgovernment of the Rájá had produced grave and widely-spread discontent, that the revenues were rapidly failing, that maladministration was rampant in all departments of the state. The Governor-General therefore determined upon acting on the fourth and fifth articles of the subsidiary treaty. In a letter addressed to the Rájá, after recounting at some length and in forcible terms the circumstances under which the Rájá had been placed on the throne, the objects of the subsidiary treaty, and the mismanagement, tyranny, and oppression of the Rájá's government, Lord W. Bentinck went on to say—"I have in consequence felt it to be indispensable, as well with reference to the stipulations of the treaty above quoted, as from a regard to the obligations of the protective character which the British Government holds towards the State of Mysore, to interfere for its preservation, and to secure the various interests at stake from further ruin. It has seemed to me that in order to do this effectually, it will be necessary to transfer the entire administration of the country into the hands of British officers, and I have accordingly determined to nominate the Commissioners for the purpose, who will proceed immediately to Mysore.

'"I now, therefore, give to your Highness the formal

PART V.

and final notice, and I request your Highness to consider this letter in that light—that is, as the notice required by the treaty to be given to your Highness of the measure determined upon for the assumption and management of the Mysore territory in the case stipulated. I beg of your Highness, therefore, to issue the requisite orders and proclamations to the officers and authorities of Mysore, within ten days from the date when this letter may be delivered to your Highness, for giving effect to the transfer of the territory, and investing the British Commissioners with full authority in all departments, so as to enable them to proceed to take charge and carry on affairs as they have been ordered, or may be hereafter instructed." To the Rájá, in accordance with the treaty, one lakh of star pagodas per annum was allotted for his private expenses.

'The Rájá peacefully surrendered the reins of government, and continued to reside in his palace at Mysore. The Governor-General vested the government in the hands of two Commissioners, the senior of whom was appointed by himself, and the junior by the Madras Government. The senior Commissioner, who possessed what was termed a 'casting vote,' and was therefore enabled to overrule his colleague on every point, fell into very much the position of the Rájá, and was aided in financial matters by the Déwan, which latter post was not abolished until 1834. Up to June 1832 the Commissioners were under the Government of Madras; but in that month they were made immediately subordinate to the Government of India. It was soon found that a Board of two Commissioners, who, naturally, constantly differed in opinion, was an agency ill adapted for the organisation of a proper system of government. Accordingly, on April 28, 1834, one Commissioner (Colonel Morison) was appointed for the whole province.

'The necessity of a still more sweeping change in the

administration soon afterwards became apparent. The instructions of the Governor-General to the Madras Government on the first assumption of the province had been to the effect that "the agency under the Commissioners should be exclusively native; indeed, that the existing native institutions should be carefully maintained." These views were subsequently confirmed by the Court of Directors in their letter, dated September 25, 1835, in which they stated that they were "desirous of adhering, as far as can be done, to the native usage, and not to introduce a system which cannot be worked hereafter by native agency." The above instructions were as far as possible adhered to in the early days of the Commission. But in process of time it became known that the machinery of government was rotten to the core. As an instance of maladministration which prevailed, it may be mentioned that the courts of justice had no power to pass sentence, their prerogative being limited to the mere finding of "Guilty," or "Not guilty." The Rájá, who had retained the power of passing sentence, was too indolent to attend to business, and the result was that the jails had remained for years crowded with prisoners, who, if guilty at all, were only guilty of light offences. The powers of the various descriptions of courts were ill-defined, and involved endless appeals. The evils involved by this state of things lay too deep to be remedied by one Commissioner, aided by the existing native agency, and it was therefore determined to substitute four European superintendents for the native Fouzdars. The "Huzur Adalat," composed of native judges, was allowed to remain the highest judicial authority in the province, but its sentences were made subject to the confirmation of the Commissioner, and not long afterwards a Judicial Commissioner was substituted for it. The post of Resident was abolished in 1843.

'Such was the form of administration under General (afterwards Sir Mark) Cubbon, who succeeded Colonel

Morison as Commissioner in June 1834, and occupied that post until February 1861. The history of the province under his rule affords a brilliant illustration to those who maintain the superiority of British over native rule; for it is the history of a people made happy by release from serfdom, and of a ruined state restored to financial prosperity. The gradual rise of the revenue will be shown in the financial chapter of this Report. At the same time no less than seven hundred and sixty-nine petty items of taxation were swept away. Among these were such whimsical taxes as taxes on marriage, on incontinency, on a child being born, on its being given a name, and on its head being shaved. In one village the inhabitants had had to pay a tax because their ancestors had failed to find the stray horse of a Pálígar, and any one passing a particular spot in Nagar without keeping his hands close to his side had to pay a tax. All of these taxes were formerly entered in the government records as part of the resources of the State, and all were swept away under Sir Mark Cubbon. In addition, the abuses in the working of the land revenue which had crept in since the time of Púrnia were removed; the payment of assessment was made as easy as possible to the ryot by dividing it into five instalments payable with reference to the periods of harvest; the system of "batayi," or payment of assessment in kind, which exposed the ryot to numberless exactions, was in great measure abolished, and the land assessment in many cases was lowered.

'In order to close the historical summary it is only necessary to recur briefly to political affairs. The Rájá, until his death in 1868, continued to reside at Mysore. He had no political power, but the assignment to him of a fifth of the revenue of the province for his personal expenditure enabled him to give reins to the princely liberality which formed one of the main elements of his character. In June 1865, he adopted a scion of one of he leading families of his house, who, on his adoption, received the name of Chámrájendra. Whether the British Government would recognise the adoption was for some time doubtful. In April 1867, the Home Government decided that it should be recognised. Accordingly, on September 23, 1867, six months after the death of Rájá Krishna Ráj, his successor, Chámrájendra Wadiar, at that time between six and seven years of age, was duly installed at Mysore. The following proclamation issued after the death of Krishna Ráj Wadiar by the Governor-General may not unaptly close this historical summary:—

'"His Excellency the Right Honourable the Viceroy and Governor-General in Council announces to the chiefs and people of Mysore, the death of His Highness the Máhárájá Krishna Ráj Wadiar Bahádúr, Knight, Grand Commander of the Most Exalted Order of the Star of India. This event is regarded with sorrow by the Government of India, with which the late Máhárájá had preserved relations of friendship for more than half a century.

'"His Highness Chámrájendra Wadiar Bahádúr, at present a minor, the adopted son of the late Máhárájá, is acknowledged by the Government of India as his successor and as Máhárájá of the Mysore territories.

'"During the minority of his Highness, the said territories will be administered in his Highness's name by the British Government, and will be governed on the same principles and under the same regulations as heretofore.

'"When his Highness shall attain the period of majority, that is, the age of eighteen years, and if his Highness shall then be found qualified for the discharge of the duties of his exalted position, the government of the country will be entrusted to him, subject to such conditions as may be determined at that time."'

To carry out the scheme thus announced it was decided to place the young Rájá under the immediate

PART V.

charge of a British officer, who should exercise the functions and duties of his guardian, training him for his high position, and guarding him from the temptations and evils which had beset the path of his predecessor.

The task of the guardian appointed by the British Government began virtually in August 1869. Then, for the first time, was the Rájá allowed to leave the walls of the fort in which he had resided. A school was formed in one of the palaces in the healthiest localities of Mysore. To it were invited the sons of the nobles and officers of state, and there, in September 1869, did the Rájá, then six years and a half old, begin his education.

From that time to the present his progress has been steady and satisfactory. He is being taught all, with the exception of Latin and Greek, which would be taught in an English school. He has learned to ride, even to hunt with the hounds, to play cricket, to drive. He has manifested a cheerful, steady, and painstaking disposition. He is punctual and methodical in his habits, and evinces an amiability of character which promises well for the future. It requires only the care and interest hitherto bestowed upon him to be continued to make him eminently qualified to fulfil the duties which will devolve upon him.

To give an idea of the nature of the resources of the country over which he will be called to rule, I append the statistical return from the latest published annual reports :—

Revenue Collections for 1872–3.	Rupees	*Expenditure for* 1872–3.	Rupees
Land Revenue	73,50,285	Interest and Refunds	41,440
Sayer (Customs)	8,85,824	Land Revenue proper	7,51,500
Forests	3,76,185	Revenue Survey	2,47,043
Abkari (Excise)	10,80,826	Inam Commission	84,787
Assessed Taxes	3,88,008	Sayer (Customs)	39,210
Salt	13,437	Miscellaneous Revenue Charges	18,983
Stamps	1,88,243	Forests	1,86,081
Post Office	44,876		

CHAP. II.

Revenue Collections for 1872-3—cont.

	Rupees
Law and Justice . .	4,13,130
Education . . .	1,41,604
Other items . . .	1,14,274
Total . .	1,09,96,692
Local and Municipal Funds . . .	9,83,223

Expenditure for 1872-3—cont.

	Rupees
Abkari (Excise) . .	19,695
Stamps	12,971
Mint	25,625
Post Office . . .	1,51,346
Administration . .	2,91,589
Palace charges . .	8,53,829
Minor departments .	17,716
Law and Justice (Judicial Courts)	8,59,856
Jails	1,09,561
Registration . . .	17,576
Police	4,44,794
Education	2,45,732
Religious and Charitable Institutions . .	2,82,510
Medical	1,30,265
Stationery and Printing	33,374
Assignments under Treaties and Engagements	25,66,666
Miscellaneous . .	84,096
Superannuation and Compassionate Grants .	1,14,583
Local Force . . .	10,86,529
Public Works Department Establishments	5,13,594
Works	9,10,188
Total . .	1,01,31,148
Local and Municipal Expenditure . . .	17,88,666

CHAPTER III.

TRAVANKÚR.

AREA—6,653 sq. miles. POPULATION—1,262,647.
REVENUE—42,85,000 rupees.

TRAVANKÚR is bounded on the north by Kochin and the British district of Koimbatúr, on the east by Madura and Tinnivéli, and on the south and west by the Indian Ocean.

This State presents the example of a territory which, from the earliest tradition, has always been under Hindú rule, and governed by Hindú laws. Its early history is obscure. The code of laws which prevailed till 1811 dated from 1496. According to one of those fundamental laws the succession to the throne invariably descends in the female line. Thus, if the sovereign have two sons and a daughter, he is succeeded by the male offspring of his daughter. According to tradition the princesses exercised the authority themselves up to the year 1740, when the reigning princess was persuaded to make over the sovereignty to the Rájá, both for herself and all succeeding princesses. This probably was caused by the fact that, prior to 1740, the country was divided into a number of petty chiefships, all of which claimed independence, and the arm of a strong man was felt necessary to reduce them to submission to one master.

Such a man appeared, in 1740, in Mastanda Wurmah, in whose favour the reigning princess resigned her pretensions. Between that date and the year 1758 Rájá Mastanda subdued many of the petty chiefs, mainly by the aid of a body of troops disciplined in the European fashion by a Flemish officer, named De Lanoy. Rájá Mastanda died in 1758. His successor, Wanjí Baula Perumal, continuing De Lanoy in his service, completed the task so well begun by Rájá Mastanda, subduing all the remaining chiefs.

It was the fortune of this prince, however, to come into contact with Tippú Sultan. He had given offence to Tippú and his father, Haider Ali, in 1778, by granting a free march through his territory to the British troops sent to attack Mahé; and again in 1783, when, alone of all the native princes in Southern India, he resisted the offers of the usurper of Mysore, and boldly avowed himself the friend of the British. His troops contributed to the victory gained by Colonel M'Leod at Paniáni (November 1783), at that time important in its consequences. His zealous co-operation having entitled him to be ranked as an ally, the British Government included him as such in the treaty with Tippú in 1784.

When, subsequently, Malabár and Kanará had been completely subdued by Tippú, the independent principality of Travankúr bècame isolated by the territories he had acquired. The only obstacle to its immediate absorption was the treaty of 1784. Tippú, however, sought every opportunity to disturb the neutrality observed by the Rájá of Travankúr, and did succeed by the movement of troops on his frontiers in completely frightening him. In his first moments of terror the Rájá applied to the Madras Government (June 1788) for four officers and twelve sergeants to discipline six battalions of infantry. In reply he was informed (August 1788) that it was contrary to the system of the Madras Government 'to lend officers to command any troops except such as are actually in their own pay;' but if the Rájá would 'suggest any plan by which one, two, or even three battalions of the Company's army might be employed in securing the Travankúr territory against any sudden attack of its enemies, it would be taken into consideration.' In consequence of this communication the Rájá agreed to entertain a subsidiary force of two battalions, the monthly subsidy for each of which, during peace, was fixed at 1,755 pagodas,[1] to be paid in cash or pepper.

This force had hardly reached its station, on the island of Vipen, before Tippú found a ground of offence against the Rájá, for having purchased from the Dutch the town of Kranganúr, to which he laid claim as being situated on the territory of his tributary, the Rájá of Kochin. Regardless, then, of the defensive alliance subsisting between the Rájá and the British Government, he attacked the Travankúr lines early on the morning of December 29, 1789. He was, however, well received

[1] About 7,000 rupees.

PART V. and repulsed with great loss, escaping almost alone. His palanquin, seals, rings, and all his ornaments fell into the enemy's hands. But he was resolved on revenge. Endeavouring to blind the British as to his real intentions, he made earnest preparations for a renewed attack. This attack took place on May 7 following, and was completely successful. The victorious troops spread desolation over the country, and probably would have endeavoured to occupy it permanently, but that Tippú was called to his own country to defend himself against the British, who had declared war against him for attacking their ally.

In the war which followed, Tippú lost half his dominions, and the territories which had been wrested from Travankúr were restored to that country.

The following year (January 1793) the Rájá concluded a commercial treaty with the British Government by which he bound himself to supply a considerable quantity of pepper to the Bombay Government, in exchange for broadcloth, arms, and other articles. The same year, too, he proposed to subsidize three battalions of sepoys, a company of European artillery, and some Lascars, to be stationed in his country, or on the frontier near it, or in any other part of the British territory, as the Rájá might desire. A treaty carrying out these proposals was agreed to in November 1795.

Rájá Wanjí Baula Perumal died in 1799, and was succeeded by Rájá Rámá Warmá Perumal. This prince had hardly ascended the throne when a circumstance happened which tended to cool very much his feeling of attachment to the British Government. Travankúr had been united with the British in that crusade against Tippú Sultan, which terminated in May 1799, by the death of that ruler at Seringapatam. But the demise of their common enemy proved fatal likewise to the independence of Travankúr. At no remote period subsequent to that event, January 1805, the Rájá was called upon to pay annually an additional sum (to that previously agreed upon) in order to provide for one more regiment, in return for being relieved of the obligation to furnish troops. He was required to concede to the British the power, under certain circumstances, of regulating the administration of all branches of public affairs, and of bringing them under the direct management of the officers of the British Government. Under such circumstances a guarantee would be given to the Rájá that his income should not be less than two lakhs of rupees, plus one-fifth of the revenue annually. The Rájá was also to bind himself to attend to the advice of the British Government, to hold no communication with any foreign State, and to admit no European foreigner into his service or within his territories without the permission of the British Government.

This treaty, in fact, reduced Travankúr to the position of a dependent and protected state.

This was a position not at all palatable to a large party in Travankúr. Discontent spread widely, and rapidly became general. The leader of the malcontents was the Dewán or prime minister, a man who was not disposed to look on calmly whilst his authority was thus virtually taken from him, even though his hopes of success might not be very cheering. The insurgents assembled, to the number of 30,000, and surrounded the subsidiary force. With vigour they might have gained the day, but that necessary aid to success was wanting. Several actions were fought, but in the end the insurrection was suppressed. Then the Rájá, feeling himself unfit to rule and having no one in whom he could confide, was inclined to make over the management of the affairs of the country to the British Resident. At this crisis he died, and was succeeded by Lutchmí Ráni, until a male heir should be born to her. On her assumption of office the British Resident took charge of the administration. For the country it must be admitted the change was beneficial.

PART V.

The ancient and obsolete code of laws which punished severely where a light penalty would have sufficed, and lightly where a severe example was required, and which dated back to the year 1496, was abolished; and a new code, more in accordance with sound principles, was introduced. Effectual reforms were also carried out in the departments of revenue and finance.

Lutchmí Ráni was delivered of a son on April 18, 1813. She continued to act as regent for him, but the following year she bore a second son and died. The regency was then assumed by her sister, and to her, at the close of the year 1814, the Resident made over the duties of the administration. Aided by his counsels, this lady performed her task with great ability and success. In 1829 the young Rájá, having attained the age of sixteen, was formally invested with the sovereignty. Three years later, the new order of government being regarded as firmly established, the subsidiary force was withdrawn.

The Rájá died in 1846, and was succeeded by his brother, Mastanda Rájá. His reign of fourteen years presents no marked incidents for review. On his death, in 1860, the government devolved upon his nephew, Rámá Warma, the present ruler.

A curious incident in connection with the succession occurred in 1857. I have before referred to the custom of the country which provides that the succession must descend in the female line, that is, to the male children of daughters. But it sometimes happens that a failure in the direct female descent occurs. Such a failure requires the selection and adoption of two or more females from the immediate relatives of the family who reside at certain places in Travankúr. Such an adoption occurred in 1788, when two sisters were selected and adopted. The younger sister died after giving birth to a female child, which also died. From the elder sister the present family of Travankúr is descended, the late Rájá being her daughter's son, and the present her daughter's daughter's son. In 1857 the line of Travankúr was again threatened with eventual exhaustion. The sister of the late Rájá—daughter's daughter of the eldest of the two sisters adopted in 1788—left five children, four sons, the second of whom is the present Rájá, and one daughter. This daughter died suddenly, leaving only two sons. The race whence future Rájás were to be supplied thus became extinct, and, on the death of all the male members, the line, unless recruited by adoption, would expire with them. Under these circumstances, the Rájá, with the concurrence of the British Government, adopted, to continue the line, two of the most eligible from amongst his female relatives.[1]

The right of adoption has been granted to the Rájá of Travankúr.

CHAPTER IV.

KOCHIN.

AREA—1,131 sq. miles. POPULATION—399,060.
REVENUE—10,57,497 rupees.

THIS small principality is bounded on the north by the province of Malabár, on the south by Travankúr, on the east by Dindigal, and on the south-west by the Arabian Sea. Its rulers claim to hold the territory in right of direct descent from the potentates who are said to have wielded in the ninth century supreme authority over the whole extent of territory stretching from Gokuru in North Kanará to Cape Kumárí. It is difficult to trace their history back to a period so remote. There are, however, authentic records to show that the Rájás succumbed at an early period to the Portuguese, who built a fort at

[1] Aitchison's *Treaties*.

Kochin. In 1662 the fort and town yielded to an attack made upon them by the Dutch, under whose management the town of Kochin attained a high degree of prosperity. The Dutch made no attempt to conquer the remainder of the country, but left the Rájá there to reign supreme. Here, in 1759, the Rájá was attacked by the Zamorin of Malabár; but he in his turn was expelled by the Rájá of Travankúr, to whom, as a reward for his assistance, the Rájá of Kochin transferred a portion of his territories.

Kochin preserved her independence till the year 1776, when the country was conquered by Haider Ali. Haider contented himself with exacting a tribute from the Rájá, who continued in a state of dependence to him and his son Tippú till the breaking out of the war of 1790.

In the following year, the Rájá, known as Rájá Verulam Tamburan, succeeded, with the aid of the British, in shaking off the Mysore yoke. He simply, however, transferred his allegiance to a new master, the British, he agreeing to pay them an annual subsidy of 100,000 rupees, the same amount he had till then paid to Haider Ali and Tippú.

Meanwhile the town of Kochin continued to be occupied by the Dutch. But on the breaking out of the war with Holland, the British took possession of it, continuing, however, the practice of Dutch law in all the places where it had theretofore prevailed. The British protection was deemed essential by the Rájá to the preservation of his authority so long as the dynasty of Haider Ali ruled at Mysore, and he clung to it with all his energy. But on the downfall of Tippú, in 1799, his mind was relieved from his fears, and he was gradually led to regard the British connection as pressing upon him with undue might. In 1809 these ideas took practical form. His minister, in correspondence with the minister of Travankúr, suddenly raised troops and attacked the British, having previously failed in an attempt to assassinate the

Resident. The insurrection was put down with little trouble, and a new treaty made with the Rájá, by which he was obliged to receive a subsidiary force of a battalion of native infantry. To pay for this force his tribute was raised from one lakh of rupees to 276,037 rupees, payable yearly in six equal instalments. He was forbidden also to admit Europeans or foreigners into his service without the sanction of the British Government. That Government also reserved to itself the right, under certain circumstances, to take over the management of the country, making a suitable provision for the Rájá.

The increase in the amount of the subsidy, making it exceed a moiety of the revenues—which at that time amounted only to 480,000 rupees—caused great embarrassment at Kochin. This reached at last such a height that the British Resident was forced to act himself as Dewán, or minister. But even he was unequal to the task of bringing about an equilibrium. Almost his first act, then, was to reduce the subsidy to 240,000 rupees, or an exact moiety of the estimated revenue. It was subsequently still further reduced to 200,000, at which amount it now stands. The Resident likewise introduced reforms in the revenue, agricultural, and trading departments, which have borne good fruit. The revenue in the present day exceeds ten lakhs of rupees.

In 1814 the Dutch finally ceded their rights in the town of Kochin to the British. A large number of the inhabitants of the town are descendants of that people, who held it in possession for about a century and a half.

In 1839 the misconduct of the reigning Rájá rendered it necessary that the Resident should once again assume the administration of affairs. The result was highly satisfactory. Under the present Rájá, Rávi Vurma, who succeeded to power in 1853, the prosperity of the country has been progressive. Notwithstanding the great improvements that have been made, by the construction of bridges, canals, roads, and other works of public utility,

PART V.

the revenue shows a surplus. Great facilities have been afforded to commerce by the removal of all unnecessary imposts and by placing the port of Kochin on the same footing, with certain specified exceptions, as the British ports in India.

The Rájá of Kochin has received the right of adoption. The succession descends, as in Travankúr, through the female branch of the family.

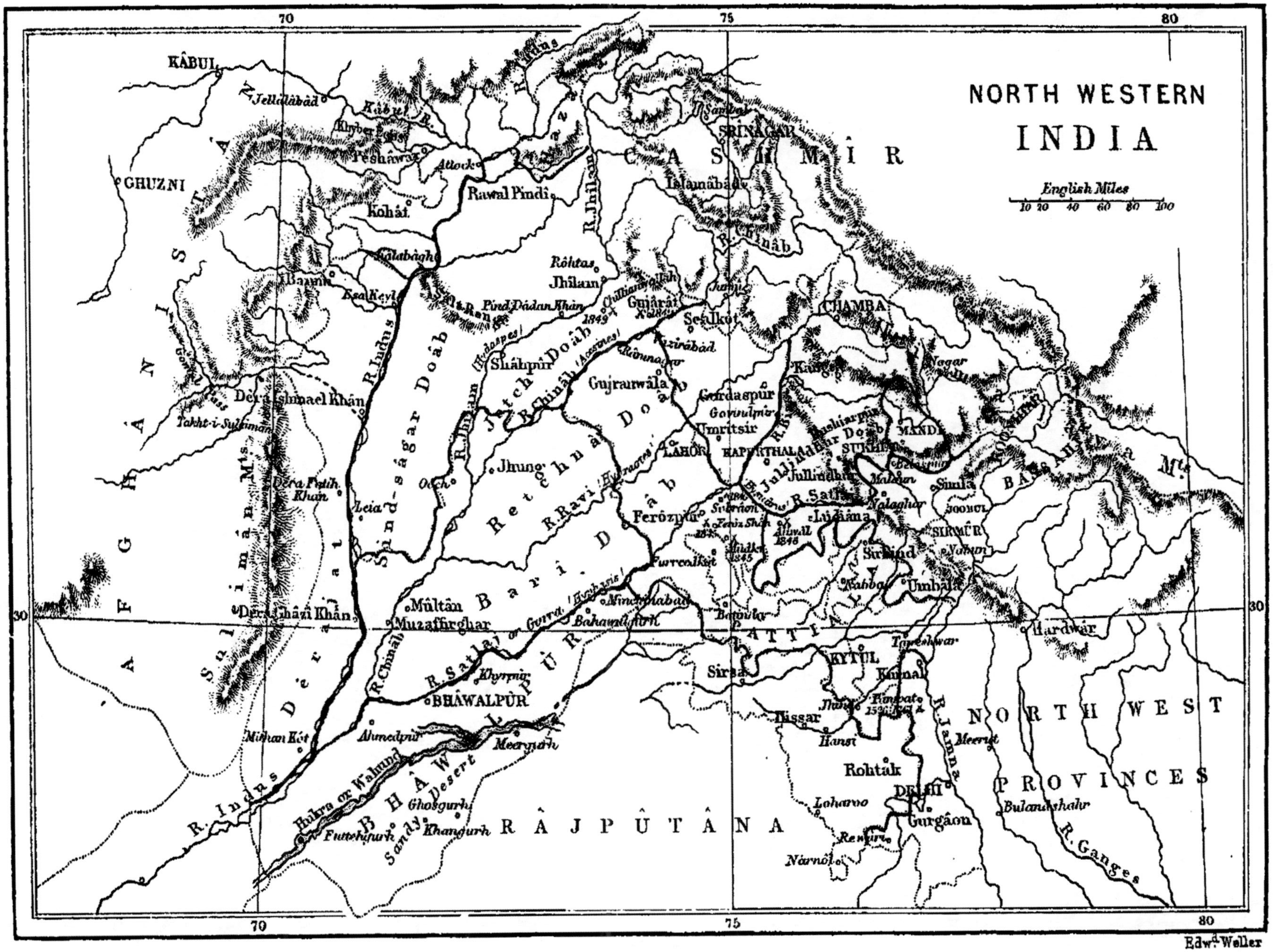
NORTH WESTERN
INDIA
English Miles
10 20 40 60 80 100
KÂBUL
GHUZNI
Jellalâbâd
Peshâwar
Attock
Rawal Pindi
Kohât
Kâlabâgh
Rôhtas
Jhilam
Pind Dâdan Khân
Gujarât
Sealkot
Shâhpûr
Gujranwâla
Gurdaspûr
Umritsir
LAHOR
Jhung
Leia
Dera Ismael Khân
Dera Fatih Khan
Dera Ghâzi Khân
Mûltân
Muzaffirghar
BHÂWALPÛR
Ahmedpûr
Mithan Kôt
Ferôzpûr
Jullindhar
Lûdiâna
Simla
CHAMBA
MANDI
SIRMÛR
Umbala
Hardwâr
Sirsa
KYTUL
Karnal
Hissar
Hansi
Rohtak
DELHI
Gurgâon
Meerut
Bulandshahr
A F G H Â N I S T Â N
C A S H M Î R
S u l e i m â n Mts.
D é r a j a t
Sind-sâgar Doâb
Retchnâ Doâb
Bari Doâb
R Â J P Û T Â N A
N O R T H W E S T
P R O V I N C E S
R. Indus
R. Jhilam
R. Chinâb
R. Ravi
R. Satlaj
R. Jamna
R. Ganges
Sandy Desert
London: Longman's & Co.
Edwd. Weller

PART VI. NORTHERN INDIA.

CHAPTER I.

THE CIS-SATLAJ STATES.

I. *Patiálá.*

AREA—5,412 sq. miles. POPULATION—1,586,000.
REVENUE—30,00,000 rupees.

CHAP. I.

THE Máhárájá of Patiálá is the recognised chief of the Phulkean tribe, so called from the ancestor, Choudri Phúl, a peasant, who founded a village in the Nabhá territory. The second son of Phúl, by name Rámá, laid the foundations of the sovereign state now known as Patiálá. Though belonging to the Jât tribe, the Máhárájá is a Sikh.

I have been unable to gather any important materials throwing light on the infancy of this State. In the year 1806, it was ruled by one of the descendants of Ráma, and stood in a proud position between Ranjít Singh and the British, owing allegiance to neither. But its possession was coveted by Ranjít Singh. In that year, accordingly, deeming that his action would be unnoticed, or at all events would be unobstructed by the British, then in the peaceful mood which followed the departure of Marquess Wellesley, Ranjít determined to strike a blow at the independence of the Cis-Satlaj states. Fortune, at the time, seemed to favour him. A violent quarrel had taken place between the Rájás of Patiálá and Nabhá, and the latter, the weaker of the two, invoked the assistance of

PART VI.

Ranjít Singh. Nothing could have been more opportune. In October of that year (1806) Ranjít crossed the Satlaj with his army and dictated terms of reconciliation to the rival sovereigns. He then recrossed into his own territories. He had accomplished all that he desired. He wished, before positively committing himself, to see in what light his interference would be regarded by the British Government. He had cleared up that point. The British Government had made no objection to his proceeding, and he thought that the game was in his hands.

The following year, 1807, he again crossed into the dominions of Patiálá. This time he had been appealed to by the wife of the Rájá of that country, who was at variance with her husband. But his action alarmed all the Cis-Satlaj princes, and they made an appeal to Calcutta, protesting themselves the servants of the British Government, and imploring its protection. Before a reply could arrive, the Rájá and Rání had settled their differences, and Ranjít had no excuse for remaining. He had received the thanks of both Rájá and Rání, and the present of a diamond necklace and a brass gun. But baulked in his plans, he was foolish enough to show his anger by seizing the forts and confiscating the lands of some petty Rájás. Learning, too, that preparations were being made at Delhi in a sense hostile to his views, he wrote to the Governor-General, claiming all the country west of the Jamna as his own, except the stations occupied by the English.

This claim was not at the moment openly resisted, but an envoy was sent to Ranjít Singh to remonstrate on its extravagance. This mild procedure only inflamed the passion of Ranjít, and he deliberately recrossed the Satlaj, and seized upon Ambála. Nor was it until the British, convinced of the necessity of strong measures, assembled an army, that he finally withdrew his pretensions, and consented to treat.

By the treaty then concluded (April 1809) Ranjít

Singh engaged neither to commit nor to suffer any encroachments on the possessions or rights of the chiefs on the left bank of the Satlaj. The following May the British Government issued a proclamation, extending its protection to the chiefs of Sirhind and Málwá, without demand of tribute, requiring service in time of war, and defining generally the relation of the protected states to the paramount power.

The general scope of the proclamation of 1809 was to establish the chiefs in the states they held before they were received under British protection. At that time there were ten of these chiefs. These were, Sáhib Singh, Rájá of Patiálá; Bhailal Singh, of Kaital; Jeswunt Singh, of Nabhá; Bhag Singh, of Jhínd; Gurú-Dayal Singh, of Ladüa; Jodh Singh, of Kalsia; Daya Kunwar, Rání of Ambála; Bhanga Singh, Rájá of Thánesur; Soda Singh, of Mahawut; and Jawahir Singh, of Bharup. By the action of the British Government these chiefs were relieved from all dread of their powerful neighbour on the other side of the Satlaj. But there ensued from this relief a consequence which had not been foreseen. They began to quarrel among themselves—the stronger to oppress the weaker, thus practically to demonstrate the need for the intervention of a strong power. This necessity soon forced itself on the recognition of the British, and in 1811 a second proclamation was issued, directing the restoration of estates that had been usurped, and prohibiting the encroachment of one State upon another.

Three years later the British engaged in war with Nipál, and in accordance with the terms of the proclamation of 1809, called upon the Rájá of Patiálá to aid them with troops. The aid was cheerfully rendered, and was, in its way, effective. As a mark of the appreciation of the British Government portions of the Keonthal and Baghat states, yielding a revenue of 35,000 rupees, were conferred upon him by sunnud, the Rájá paying for them in exchange the sum of 280,000 rupees.

PART VI.

In 1830, the hill territory of Simla was ceded to the British by the Rájá in exchange for three villages in the district of Beraoli.

Nothing further occurred till the first war with the State of Lahore broke out at the close of 1845. In that memorable contest the Máhárájá of Patiálá cast in his lot with the British, whilst the Rájá of Nabhá showed great sympathy with the invaders. As a reward for his loyal service the Máhárájá was granted a portion of the territory confiscated from the Rájá of Nabhá for his misconduct. At the same time the Máhárájá was confirmed by sunnud for ever, for himself and his heirs, in possession of his ancient estates and those added by the British Government, with all the rights appertaining thereto. In consideration of his renouncing the right to impose custom and transit dues, he was awarded an additional grant of territory confiscated from the Lahore Durbar, with a rental of 10,000 rupees.

The service rendered by the Máhárájá to the British Government during the mutiny of 1857 can scarcely be exaggerated. The prompt action of himself and the Rájás of Jhínd and Nabhá had a marked influence alike on the state of affairs in the Punjáb and on the march of the British troops to Delhi. It is not too much to say that hostility or lukewarmness on the part of the Cis-Satlaj Rájás at the early stage of the mutiny would have greatly imperilled the position of the British. The gain of their hearty co-operation can then scarcely be over-estimated.

But the Máhárájá of Patiálá did something more than aid the British by his troops. Whilst these were usefully employed in keeping open the communications and aiding in the field, he lent his money freely, a favour in those troublous times most highly to be appreciated.

For his fidelity the Máhárájá was amply rewarded by the gift of estates that had been forfeited, bringing with them a considerable accession of income. A sunnud likewise was given him (1860) granting him and his successors the exercise of sovereign powers over their ancestral and acquired possessions, and binding all dependants and feudatories of every degree to render them obedience. The British Government engaged never to demand any tribute on account of revenue, service, or on any other plea. Other conditions very favourable to the Máhárájá were contained in this sunnud. Subsequently, another sunnud was granted, making over to the Máhárájá certain lands in liquidation of the debt due to him by the British.

Máhárájá Narender Singh was granted the right of adoption. He was invested on November 1, 1861, with the insignia of the Most Exalted Order of the Star of India.

This Máhárájá, who, in the language of Earl Canning, 'had surpassed the former achievements of his race by the constancy and courage he evinced during the mutiny of 1857–8,' whose loyalty had been 'unswerving and conspicuous,' died suddenly on November 14, 1862. He was succeeded by his son, then thirteen years old.

This prince was associated in 1864 in an investigation which took place at Nabhá in October of that year regarding the causes of the death of the Rájá of that state. This is more specially referred to under the head of Nabhá.

The Máhárájá of Patiálá is entitled to a salute of seventeen guns.

II. *Jhínd.*

AREA—1,236 sq. miles. POPULATION—311,000.
REVENUE—4,00,000 rupees.

THE Rájá of Jhínd is of the same family as the Máhárájá of Patiálá, being like him, descended from Choudri Phúl. The rise of the two states was contemporaneous. The Raja of Jhínd, however, had relations with the British earlier than the other. In the pursuit of

PART VI.

Holkar by Lord Lake (1805) Bhag Singh, then Rájá of Jhínd, who was maternal uncle of Ranjít Singh, showed the greatest interest in the success of the British, and after the conclusion of the campaign he offered to transfer to them his allegiance. Lord Lake gave him many marks of his esteem and appreciation.

In the attempts of Ranjít Singh to annex the Cis-Satlaj states, the Rájá of Jhínd sided with his relative of Patiálá, and the history of both the states in this crisis and in the Sikh war of 1845–6 is identical. He received also, in money and lands, a proportionate reward for his services.

In 1857 the Rájá of Jhínd had the merit of being the first person who marched against the mutineers at Delhi. His troops acted as the vanguard of the British army. He remained in the camp before Delhi until the re-occupation of the city, and his troops also took part in the assault. For these services he received territory yielding 1,16,813 rupees per annum, on condition of fidelity and political and military service in time of difficulty and danger. He also received in 1860 a sunnud similar to that given to the Máhárájá of Patiálá.

The present Rájá of Jhínd, Sangat Singh, succeeded his predecessor as the nearest of kin, being, however, only a remote kinsman. He did not therefore inherit the acquisitions which had been made by the successors of his and their common ancestor. These, amounting to one-half of the principality, were declared an escheat, and Sangat Singh succeeded only to the ancient family possessions, added to the later grants of the British Government.

In October 1864, the Rájá was engaged in an investigation at Nabhá, which will be more especially referred to when dealing with that principality.

The Rájá of Jhínd has been granted the right of adoption. He is entitled to a salute of eleven guns.

III. *Nabhá.*

AREA—863 sq. miles. POPULATION—276,000.
REVENUE—4,00,000 rupees.

CHAP. I.

THE Rájá of this principality is of the same family and stock as the two Rájás previously noticed. Up to the year 1845, the history of his dynasty does not vary from that of Patiálá. But in that year the Rájá who represented it, Devindar Singh, showed sympathy with the Sikh invaders. He was, in consequence, on the conclusion of the war, deposed, and assigned a pension of 50,000 rupees per annum. One-fourth of his territory also was confiscated, and divided between the Rájás of Patiálá and Farídkot. The remainder of the principality was made over to his eldest son, Bhurpúr Singh.

When the mutiny broke out, this chief made ample amends for his father's lapse. Like the rulers of Patiálá and Jhínd he rendered splendid service to the British. For this, he was rewarded by a grant of lands out of the Jhujhar territory, yielding 1,06,000 rupees per annum. He likewise (1860) received a sunnud similar to that granted to the Rájá of Patiálá, and like him obtained a fresh acquisition of territory in liquidation of the debt due to him by the British Government.

On November 9, 1863, this Rájá, Bhurpúr Singh, died without male issue, and was succeeded by his brother, Bhugwán Singh. But, shortly after the accession of the latter, a rumour was spread that the late Rájá had died from the effects of poison administered by members of his own court, and that a lady of rank had also been murdered at the instigation of some people about the court. These rumours obtained so great a currency that an investigation was ordered, presided over by a British officer, with whom were associated the Máhárájá of Patiálá and the Rájá of Jhínd.

The investigation made it clear that the late Rájá had

PART VI.

died a natural death; and the actual murderer of the lady was subsequently shown to be a person not at the time suspected; but it was made evident, likewise, that a native official of high rank, Gurbúksh Singh, had abetted the murder. He was tried for that offence, and though acquitted on account of the unreliable nature of the evidence produced, yet he and two other dangerous characters were prohibited from residing henceforth in the territory of Nabhá.

The Rájá of Nabhá has been allowed the right of adoption. He is entitled to a salute of eleven guns.

IV. *Kálsiá.*

AREA—155 sq. miles. POPULATION—62,000.
REVENUE—1,30,000 rupees.

THERE is nothing worthy of record in the history of this state. The family came originally from Kálsiá, a village in the Manjha. Its chief, after some hesitation, accepted British protection in 1809, and since that time he has been faithful to his engagements. He receives from the British Government, in perpetuity, an annual money payment of 2,851 rupees, to compensate him for custom duties which have been abolished. The Sirdar of Kálsiá has received the right of adoption.

V. *Maler Kotlá.*

AREA—165 sq. miles. POPULATION—462,000.
REVENUE—1,00,000 rupees.

THIS little state is represented by a Pathán family which originally came from Kábul and occupied places of trust in Sirhind under the Mogul emperors. The connection of the family with the British dates from 1805, when its chief joined Lord Lake, and was granted in 1809 the British protection. The present chief is Nawáb Sekunder Ali Khan. He has received a sunnud assuring him that any succession in his state, in conformity with the Mahomedan law, will be respected. The near relatives of the chief enjoy a share in the family estates, and exercise sovereign powers therein, in general subordination to the Nawáb.

The Nawáb of Maler Kotlá is entitled to a salute of nine guns.

VI. *Farídkot.*

AREA—643 sq. miles. POPULATION—51,000.
REVENUE—75,000 rupees.

THE family ruling Farídkot traces itself back to the reign of Akbar, when its representative, named Bhullun, a member of the Burar Jât tribe, rendered signal service and acquired considerable influence. His nephew built the fort of Kôt-Kapúra and made himself an independent ruler. Early in the present century the Kôt-Kapúra district was seized by the prime minister at Lahore, Mokam Chand. It remained in the possession of his family till the conclusion of the Sikh war in 1845–6, when it was confiscated by the British Government and restored to the chief of Farídkot. That chief, as an additional reward for his services rendered during the campaign, was likewise raised to the rank of Rájá.

In 1857 the Rájá of Farídkot rendered good service to the British cause. He is entitled to a salute of eleven guns. The right of adoption has been conferred upon him.[1]

[1] For this, and for the history of the other Cis-Satlaj Rájás, I have indented largely on Mr. Aitchison's collection of Treaties. Nowhere else have I been able to obtain so complete an account of them. All of them being of comparatively modern origin, the short sketch of them given in the text will probably be deemed sufficient.

CHAPTER II.

CASHMERE (KASHMÍR).

AREA—25,000 sq. miles. POPULATION—1,500,000.
REVENUE—6,50,000 rupees.

PART VI.

ACCORDING to tradition, the valley of Kashmír was colonised by the Hindús about 2,666 years before the commencement of the Christian era, and ruled by a regular succession of kings of that race. It appears certain, however, that, even at an early period, these princes were subjected to desultory invasions, and even to the temporary occupation of their country by Tartar and other chiefs. Thus it seems clearly ascertained that Ogyges, probably a name of Oghuz Khan, the Scythian, attempted an entrance into the country some time antecedent to the Christian era, and though at first repulsed by the ruler of the country, by name Jagma, he eventually, after a year's struggle, succeeded in forcing his way into the valley. Others of the stream of invaders who followed him must have made similar attempts, for it is recorded that from 150 to 100 B.C., the country was governed by three Tartar princes. From that period until the predatory attacks of Mahmud of Ghizní, the record is uncertain and the details are scanty. But it would appear that, though often temporarily occupied by invaders, Kashmír continued, in the main, under the rule of its Hindú princes.

Mahmud of Ghizní is said to have overrun the valley in 1011 and 1012. On the second occasion, however, his army, in retiring, was led into the wrong pass, and suffered very considerably. He passed the passes in 1017, but did not enter them again.

Kashmír would seem to have enjoyed comparative peace from that time till the beginning of the fourteenth century, when it was definitively conquered by a Tartar prince of the family of Chug. It was ruled with one or two trifling breaks by the descendants of this prince till the year 1587, when it was conquered by Akbar, and its king enrolled among the nobles of Delhi, and assigned a large jaghír in Behar. Akbar himself only paid three visits to Kashmír after his conquest of it, but it became the favourite summer retreat of his successors.

Kashmír continued under the dominion of the Moguls till some time after the year 1739, when the conquest of Delhi placed it in the hands of Nadir Shah, by whom it was annexed to the kingdom of Kábul. It remained attached to that kingdom till 1809, when the governor of the province, Mahomed Azim Khan, disavowed his allegiance, claimed independence, and set the sovereign of Kábul at defiance. Seven years later an army was sent from Kábul to reconquer the country, but there was a traitor in the camp, and the army was forced to retreat with heavy loss. In 1819 Ranjít Singh conquered the city of Kashmír, and some portions of the country in its vicinity. The chief of the country, Mahomed Azim Khan, did not, however, readily surrender the remainder, for in 1820 two persons arrived at Delhi, charged by him with overtures for a treaty of alliance, and with an earnest request that Kashmír should be taken under British protection. The request was refused, and thenceforth the whole country, gradually but surely, fell under the domination of Ranjít Singh.

During the whole of this prince's life, and subsequently till 1846, Kashmír was governed by a nobleman appointed by him. On the defeat of the Sikh army in 1845–46, a treaty was negotiated at Lahore (March 1846), by one of the clauses of which Kashmír was transferred to British rule. But the Governor-General of the day, deeming his resources insufficient to guard all

PART VI.

the acquisitions obtained by the treaty, whilst he was obliged to keep a watchful eye on the Sikh nation, humiliated though not vanquished, determined to make a friend of the astute chief of Jammú, Goláb Singh, by conferring upon him for a pecuniary consideration the territory of Kashmír, with the rank and title of an independent sovereign, and to make with him a separate treaty.

The chieftain so elevated bore the character of being alike cautious and cunning, a watcher of the atmosphere, always holding back from committing himself, but ever ready to seize the ball when it lay at his feet. He had begun life as a horseman in a troop of cavalry commanded by the favourite chamberlain of Ranjít Singh. He soon raised himself to an independent command, and in this he distinguished himself by taking prisoner Ágar Khan, chief of Rajaorí. For this service Ranjít Singh conferred upon his family the principality of Jammú. Here Goláb Singh took up his residence, and from it managed soon to extend his authority over his Rájpút neighbours, and eventually into Ladákh. In the revolutions which preceded the outbreak of the war he was elected minister of the Khalsa, and he took an important part in the negotiations which followed the battle of Sobraon, casting the weight of his influence in favour of the restoration of friendly relations with the British.

In the second Sikh war, Goláb Singh was true to the character I have recorded of him. From his eyrie in Jammú he watched the course of events. He had an instinctive notion that the victory would be with the British, and though he might have been shaken by the doubtful battle of Chillianwala, yet the fall of Multán and the 'crowning mercy' of Gujrát soon came to reassure him.

Goláb Singh died in 1857, and was succeeded by his son Ranbír Singh. This chief performed excellent services in the year of the mutiny, sending his troops to Delhi, where they behaved well and loyally. Subsequently

Máhárájá Ranbír Singh was invested with the insignia of the Most Exalted Order of the Star of India. In 1867 he reduced all transit duties through his territories to a payment of five per cent. *ad valorem*. In this and in other respects the Máhárájá has shown a laudable desire to meet the wishes of the British Government. CHAP. II.

The Máhárájá of Kashmír has been granted the right of adoption.

CHAPTER III.

MINOR TRANS-SATLAJ STATES.

I. *Kapúrthalá.*

AREA—598 sq. miles. POPULATION—212,721.
REVENUE—5,77,000 rupees.

THE founder of the Kapúrthalá family was one Jussa Singh, who at the period of turmoil towards the close of the last century, acquired possessions, by conquest and by gift, from Ranjít Singh, on both banks of the Satlaj. Those on the left bank were, by the treaty made with Ranjít Singh in 1809, brought under the suzerainty of the British. By that treaty the Sirdar of Kapúrthalá became bound to furnish with supplies British troops moving through or cantoned in Cis-Satlaj territory, and, by the British proclamation to those states issued in the month of May following, to join the British during war.

In 1826 Ranjít Singh made an aggression on the Sirdar of Kapúrthalá, who appealed to the British Government for protection. This was accorded, and Ranjít ceased to molest him. Nevertheless in the first Sikh war (1845-6), the Sirdar sided with the Sikhs against the British.

PART VI.

For this act of hostility his possessions on the left bank of the Satlaj were confiscated. Those on the right bank, containing the city of Kapúrthalá, were, however, left to him and his heirs on condition of his paying to the British Government a commutation in cash of the service engagements by which he had previously been bound to the government of Lahore. He was likewise required to be loyal to his suzerain, to govern well, to levy neither customs nor duties, and to keep the high roads in repair. His military service was commuted for an annual payment of 1,38,000 rupees, subsequently reduced to 1,31,000, at which sum it now stands assessed.

After the annexation of the Panjáb by the British, 1849, the Sirdar of Kapúrthalá, Nihál Singh, was created a Rájá. He died in 1852, and was succeeded by his son, Randhir Singh. This prince rendered good service in the stormy years of 1857-58, alike in the Panjáb and in Oudh. As a reward for this he received an hereditary jaghír in the Barí Daáb, which his father had held in life tenure, but which had been resumed on his death by the British Government; and, in addition, two estates in Oudh in perpetuity, with remission of half the revenue.

Rájá Randhir Singh set out for England towards the end of 1869. But, taken ill at Aden, he died before he could reach Bombay on his return (1870). He was succeeded by his son, Khurruk Singh.

II. *Mandí.*

AREA—1,080 sq. miles. POPULATION—139,259.
REVENUE—3,00,000 rupees.

THIS is an ancient Rajpút principality, regarding the earlier history of which I have been unable to glean any specific information. It was under the suzerainty of Ranjít Singh in 1810, and continued so till after the first Sikh war, when it was transferred to the British, full sovereignty being conceded to the Rájá, to his heirs, and those of his brothers, according to seniority. The present Rájá was born in 1847. He has received the right of adoption. He pays a tribute of 1,00,000 rupees to the British.

III. *Chambá.*

AREA—3,216 sq. miles. POPULATION—120,000.
REVENUE—1,20,000 rupees.

THIS principality fell into British possession under circumstances precisely similar to the preceding, and under conditions nearly similar. Part of the country was, however, made over in 1846 to Goláb Singh, but in the following year the whole was brought under the British suzerainty. The Rájá pays a tribute of 10,000 rupees. The British Government has conferred upon him the right of adoption.

IV. *Sakít.*

AREA—420 sq. miles. POPULATION—44,552.
REVENUE—80,000 rupees.

This state also came under British suzerainty in 1846, and was treated in the same manner as the others. It has no special history. The Rájá pays a tribute to the British Government of 11,000 rupees. He has the right of adoption.

CHAPTER IV.

BHÁWALPÚR.

AREA—14,483 sq. miles. POPULATION—365,000.
REVENUE—3,00,000 rupees.

THE territory of Bháwalpúr is a long narrow tract of country, bounded on the north-west by Sindh and the Panjáb, and on the east, south-east, and part of the south by the Rajpút states of Bikanír and Jaisalmír, and by Bhattiána.

The Nawáb of Bháwalpúr is the head of a clan known as the Daúdpútri, or sons of David. The clan was originally collected by Dáud Khan, or David Khan, a man of some consequence at Shikarpúr in Sindh. Driven thence by his sovereign, the ruler of Kandahar, he and his followers found refuge in the country where they now reside, then peopled for the most part by Hindús of the Jât tribe. Since that period the immigration of pure Hindús, of Belúchís, and of Afghans, has greatly changed the character of the population, in which, now, the Mahomedan element predominates.

Dáud Khan, taking refuge from his liege lord in a country so barren that it was not considered worth while to pursue him, gradually extended his authority to the fertile strips on the eastern bank of the river line, and assumed the sovereignty of the territory occupied by his followers. He was succeeded by Mobárik Khan. Mobárik improved on the acquisitions of his father, and annexed the district of Khádál, which he conquered from the Bhátí tribe, and made its chief town, Derráwul, his capital. Bháwal Khan, who succeeded him, added further to the territories left him by his uncle. On the site of an old Bhátí city, on the south bank of the river Ghára, he built a new capital which, after himself, he named Bháwalpúr. But whilst this was yet building, Bháwal Khan was attacked (about 1780) by an army from Kandahar; Derráwul was invested and taken, and he was forced to acknowledge the suzerainty of the liege lord of his family, and to give his son Mobárik in hostage as a pledge of his fidelity. Mobárik remained three years in Kábul, at the end of which time, returning, he appeared in Bháwalpúr as the declared rival of his father. He was imprisoned, but shortly before his father's death was released, only, however, to be assassinated by the chiefs who had taken part against him during the lifetime of Bháwal Khan. His death paved the way for the succession of his brother, Sádik Mahomed. But this prince had to fight for the throne with his nephews and brothers, and it was not until he had disposed of these that he felt secure in his seat.

The rule of Sádik Mahomed was mainly noticeable for his disputes with his kinsmen and the too powerful chiefs of the country. But as he, by degrees, felt his power, he shook off the suzerainty of Kandahar and asserted his independence. His son and successor, Bháwal Khan, had, however, to fear the encroachment of a new power that had risen. During the first two decades of the present century the overshadowing power of Ranjít Singh filled him with dismay, and he made several applications to the British, tendering his allegiance and asking their protection. The applications were, however, declined, but the treaty made in 1809 with Ranjít Singh, referred to in the first chapter of this part, really did give him the protection he sought, as it confined Ranjít Singh to the right bank of the Satlaj.

The British subsequently (1830) entered into a commercial treaty with Bháwal Khan, by which his independence within his own territories was acknowledged. The terms of this treaty, which related mainly to the tolls to be levied on the traffic passing through his territories, were modified in 1835, 1838, 1840, 1843, 1847, and 1855. But it is a treaty of another sort, negotiated in 1838 to which it is necessary more particularly to refer. The Nawábs of Bháwalpúr had always been *de jure* vassals of the lords of Kandahar and Kábul, and although the predecessor of Bháwal Khan had broken the yoke from off his neck, yet the prospect of restoring, in the person of Shah Súja, the Duráni family, naturally filled him with concern. To maintain his independence the Nawáb then negotiated a treaty with the British Government (October 1838), by the terms of which he placed himself under its supremacy, and bound himself to act in

PART VI.

subordinate co-operation with it, receiving its protection and being recognised as the absolute ruler of the country. In the war which followed, the Nawáb acted in perfect good faith, and rendered no unimportant assistance in the way of supplies and in facilitating the passage of the British troops. For the services thus rendered he was rewarded by receiving as an addition to his dominions a portion of the northern part of Sindh, including Subzulkót and the fertile district of Bhúng Bárá.

In the first contest of the British with the Sikhs the Nawáb of Bháwalpúr was not concerned, but on the breaking out of the second war, 1848, he volunteered to aid the British with the whole of his disposable force. The offer was accepted. In May of that year, therefore, his army, amounting to about 9,000 men, crossed the Satlaj, and effecting a junction with Captain Herbert Edwardes and General Cortlandt, sustained an attack at the village of Kinéri from the army of Múlráj, amounting to 8,000 men and four guns, and repulsed them at all points, forcing them to retire into Multán. For this service the Nawáb was rewarded with a life pension of a lakh of rupees per annum, besides being reimbursed the expenses of the campaign.

Nawáb Bháwal Khan died in 1852. He was succeeded by his third son, Sádik Khan—the eldest, Futteh Khan, having been disinherited by his father. Futteh Khan did not, however, acquiesce in this arrangement, but, escaping from the place in which he had been confined, began to levy troops. A large number of the chiefs rallied to his standard, and Sádik Khan was driven out. An appeal was then made to the British Government, but it refused to interfere in the internal affairs of the country. Finally it was arranged that Sádik Khan should reside in British territory, receiving from his brother an allowance of 1,600 rupees per mensem, he relinquishing for ever, on the part of himself and his heirs, all claim to the principality. Subsequently, however, it became necessary to place him in confinement.

CHAP. IV.

Futteh Khan died in October 1858, and was succeeded by his eldest son, Rahím Yar Mahomed, seventeen years old, who took the name of his grandfather, Bháwal Khan.

The short reign of this prince, lasting only eight years, was wild and stormy. For the first moiety of this period he ruled wisely and well, attending to the counsels of the vizír of his father. But he then fell into bad courses, put the vizír, who remonstrated, to death, and provoked a rebellion on the part of the leading nobles of his clan. In the course of the contest which followed he caused, it is believed, his three uncles to be murdered, and was only induced by the threats of the British Government to send to the safe custody of British authorities the widow of his grandfather and the two children of one of the murdered uncles. Even then he sent them in an impoverished condition and without decent clothing.

The following year, 1865, another outbreak took place, which though contemptible as to strength, yet, by showing the Nawáb to be pusillanimous and nerveless, encouraged a more effective demonstration. This took place in 1866, and was yet undecided when the Nawáb died. An interregnum followed. Factions were rampant. Adventurers had clambered into high places, and the safety of the State seemed involved in the maintenance of the legitimate heir, the son of the late Nawáb, supported by a power sufficient to put down disorder. After a short interval, during which many changes of fortune occurred, and scenes, sensational if not tragical, were enacted, this policy was followed. The young Nawáb, then a mere child, was nominated successor to his father, whilst, during his minority and until he should attain the age of eighteen, the administration was entrusted to a British officer appointed by the British Government.

PART VII.—MEDIATIZED AND MINOR CHIEFS.[1]

PART VII.

ALTHOUGH (writes Mr. Aitchison) there is very great diversity in the tenures of the guaranteed chiefs, they may all be divided into two great classes : those chiefs in the administration of whose affairs the interference of the feudal superior is excluded by the express terms of the guarantee, and those chiefs whose sunnuds contain no such stipulation ; and the policy of the British Government towards them is governed by the following general rules :—

I. The guarantee given by the British Government descends in all cases to direct heirs.

II. When there are no direct heirs, the previous recognition by the British Government of an adopted heir is, as a rule, essential to the continuance of the guarantee; with this previous sanction the guarantee descends to an adopted heir.

III. When this previous sanction has not been obtained, the guarantee does not descend to adopted heirs unless the adoption subsequently obtains the formal sanction of the British Government.

IV. When there are no heirs, direct or adopted, the escheat of the guaranteed estate or tankah is to the suzerain chief and not to the British Government.

V. When the interference of the feudal superior in the affairs of the subordinate chief is expressly barred by

[1] The details contained in this Part have mostly been condensed from Mr. Aitchison's valuable work, 'Treaties, Engagements, and Sunnuds relating to India.'

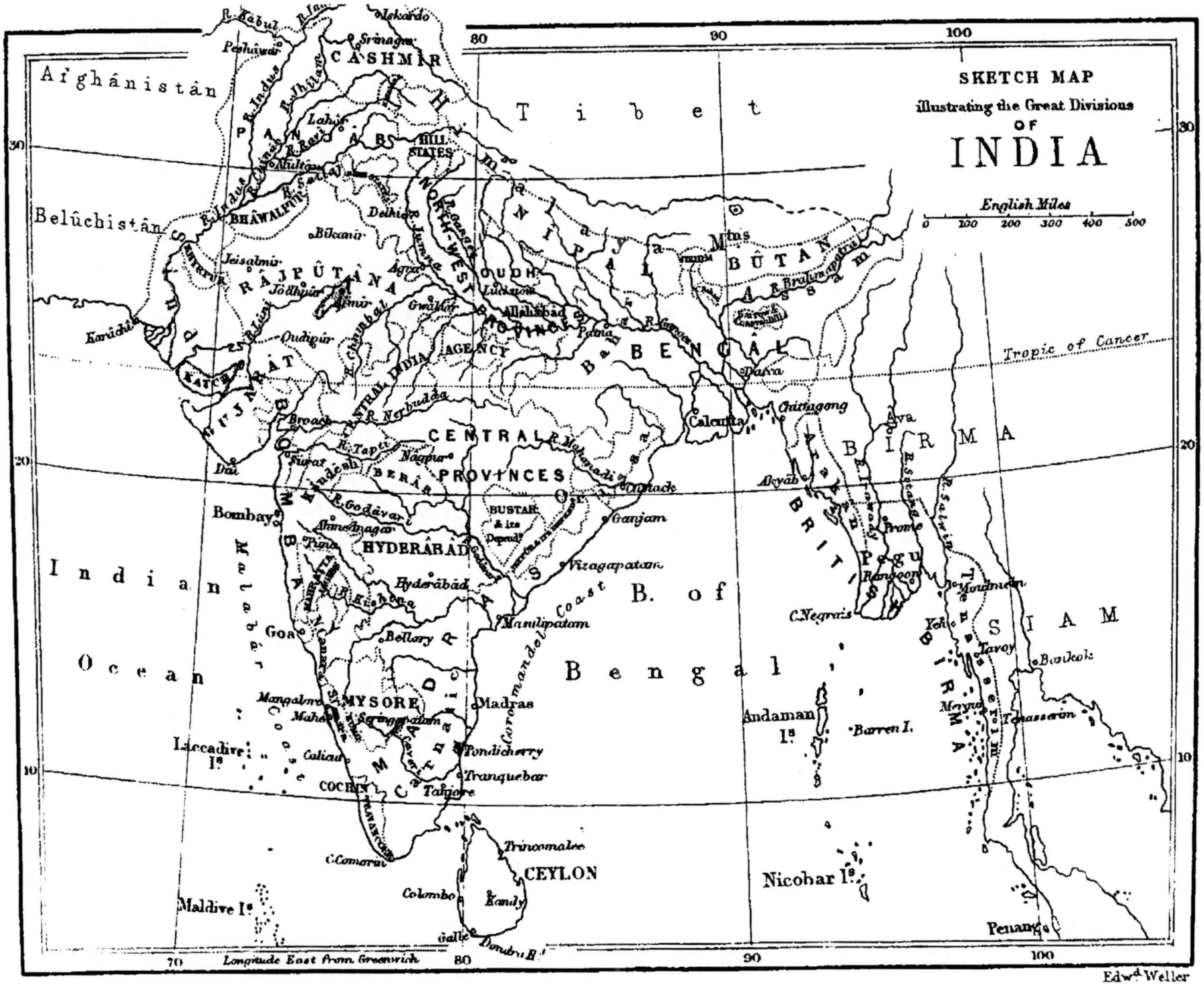
SKETCH MAP
illustrating the Great Divisions
OF
INDIA
English Miles
0 100 200 300 400 500
Afghânistân
Belûchistân
Tibet
CASHMIR
PANJÂB
HILL STATES
BHÂWALPUR
RÂJPÛTÂNA
NORTH-WEST PROVINCES
OUDH
NIPÂL
BÛTÂN
ASSAM
BENGÂL
AGENCY
CENTRAL INDIA
CENTRAL PROVINCES
BERÂR
BOMBAY
HYDERÂBÂD
BUSTAR & its Depend.
MADRAS
MYSORE
COCHIN
TRAVANCORE
CEYLON
BRITISH BIRMA
Pegu
SIAM
Tropic of Cancer
Indian Ocean
B. of Bengal
Malabâr Coast
Coromandel Coast
Laccadive Is
Maldive Is
Andaman Is
Barren I.
Nicobar Is
Peshâwar
Srinagar
Iskardo
Lahôr
Multân
Delhi
Bîkanîr
Jeisalmîr
Jôdhpur
Ajmîr
Agra
Gwâlîor
Lucknow
Allahâbâd
Patna
Dacca
Calcutta
Chittagong
Akyab
Ava
Prome
Rangoon
Moulmein
Tavoy
Mergui
Tenasserim
Bankok
Penang
Karâchi
Oudipûr
Broach
Surat
Daman
Bombay
Nâgpur
Ahmednagar
Poona
Hyderâbâd
Cuttack
Ganjam
Vizagapatam
Masulipatam
Bellary
Goa
Madras
Mangalore
Mahe
Seringapatam
Calicut
Pondicherry
Tranquebar
Tanjore
C. Comorin
Trincomalee
Colombo
Kandy
Galle
Dondra Hd.
C. Negrais
R. Kabul
R. Indus
R. Jhîlam
R. Râvî
R. Chinâb
R. Satlaj
R. Jumna
R. Ganges
R. Brahmaputra
R. Chambal
R. Nerbudda
R. Tapti
R. Godâvari
R. Kishna
R. Cavery
R. Mahanadi
R. Irawady
R. Sitang
R. Salwin
Longitude East from Greenwich
70
80
90
100
10
20
30
Edwd. Weller
London: Longmans & Co.

the terms of the guarantee, the decision of all questions relating to succession, direct or by adoption, rests solely with the British Government.

VI. When there are direct heirs to an estate or tankah, the sunnud for which does not expressly bar the interference of the suzerain chief, the decision regarding the succession and the continuance of the guarantee rests solely with the British Government; but the superior chief has a right to be heard if he has any reasonable objections to bring either (*a*) to the legitimacy, or (*b*) the direction of the descent.

VII. When there are no direct heirs to such an estate or tankah, and the British Government sanction the succession of an adopted heir, the feudal superior is entitled to a patient hearing of his claim to the escheat; but he has no concurrent authority with the British Government in deciding the question of succession, nor, where a British guarantee is involved, can he take any steps in recognition of an adopted heir prior to and independently of, the preliminary action of the British Government.

VIII. Tankahdars have no power over the tankahs beyond their own lines, and no right to burden them with sums payable after their death.

IX. When the terms of the guarantee exclude the interference of the superior chief, the subordinate chief is not subject to the payment of nuzzerana. In other cases, a nuzzerana equal to one-fourth of the net revenue of the guaranteed estate or tankah may be levied by the superior chief on the occurrence of a succession by adoption to the guaranteed estate or tankah. On such occasions the superior chief gives to the subordinate a dress of honour equal to one-fourth of the nuzzerana.

X. None of the mediatized chiefs have power of life and death. They must submit all trials for heinous crimes and all sentences of death or transportation or imprisonment for life to the local officer of the British Government.

PART VII.

1. Central India and Málwá.

Mediatized and Guaranteed Chiefs.

Rutlam, Rájá of; descended from Ratna, seventh son of Udai Singh, Rájá of Jodhpúr, to whom Rutlam was granted by the Emperor Shah Jehán. Area, 500 square miles; population, 94,839; revenue, 3,64,064 rupees; tribute, 84,000 Salim Shahí rupees, equal to 66,150 of British currency.

Sillana, Rájá of; originally a part of Rutlam, from the chiefs of which the Rájá is descended (1709). Area, 103 square miles; population, 88,978; revenue, 2,49,000; tribute, 42,000 rupees.

Sítamau, Rájá of; also originally a part of Rutlam, from the chiefs of which this Rájá is descended (1660). Area, 95 square miles; population, 20,000; revenue, 1,50,000 rupees; pays a tribute of 55,000 Salim Shahí rupees to Sindhia.

Punth Píploda, Chief of; receives the tribute of ten villages in the district of Mundavul and Soubah of Mundisúr.

Píploda, Thákur[1] of; a feudal vassal of the Nawáb of Jáorá.

Jamasca, Thákur of; holds several villages in quit-rent tenure, and receives tankah[2] from Sindhia, Holkar, and Dewás; possesses also lands under Sindhia and Holkar, for which he has no sunnuds.

Naolana, Thákur of; receives tankahs from Sindhia and Holkar, and holds certain villages in jaghire, for which he has no sunnuds.

Sheogurh, Thákur of; receives tankahs from Sindhia and Holkar.

Dabrí, Thákur of; receives tankahs from Sindhia.

Bichród, Thákur of; receives tankahs from Sindhia, Holkar, and Dewás; holds a small amount of land in jaghire under Sindhia, for which he has no sunnud.

Kalúkhêra, Ráo of; receives tankahs from Sindhia and Holkar; holds also certain villages under Sindhia.

Narwar, Thákur of; receives tankahs from Sindhia, Holkar, and Dewás, and three villages from Sindhia in quit-rent tenure.

[1] Thákur, a lord, heriditary landowner.

[2] Tankah, originally forced tribute; now, an allowance for superintendence of the villages for which it is paid.

Salgurh, Thákur of; receives tankahs from Sindhia, Holkar, and Dewás; holds also villages in jaghire and in quit-rent tenure.

Piplia, Thákur of; receives tankahs from Sindhia and Holkar.

Naogong, Thákur of; receives a tankah from Sindhia, and holds small lands from him in jaghire.

Dutana, Thákur of; is in a position similar to the preceding.

Ajraoda, Thákur of; receives tankahs from Sindhia and Holkar.

Dhúlatia, Thákur of; receives tankahs from Sindhia and Holkar, and holds lands in jaghire in the Mehidpúr district.

Bichród, Thákur of; receives tankah from Sindhia, and holds in quit-rent tenure half the village of Bichród, paying Sindhia an annual rent for the same.

Biloda, Thákur of; receives tankahs from Sindhia and Holkar, and holds the village of Biloda in quit-rent tenure under Holkar.

Burdia, Ráo of; receives tankahs from Sindhia, Holkar, and Dewás; also holds villages in jaghire and quit-rent tenure, and one from Sindhia in perpetual tenure at a fixed rent.

Alirájpúr, Rájá of; pays a tribute of 10,000 rupees per annum to Dhár, through the British Government. The Rájá is a Rájpút.

Jhabúa, Rájá of; descended from the royal family of Jodhpúr; did good service during the mutinies. Area, 1,500 square miles; population, 55,000, chiefly Bhíls; revenue, 1,23,000 rupees, of which 35,000 rupees accrue to Holkar from districts held by him.

Nunkhera or *Tirla*, Bhúmia[1] of; holds the village of Tirla in hereditary succession, paying tankah to Dhár.

Khota Burkhera or *Sorepur*, Bhúmia of; holds villages on three different tenures, paying tankah to Dhár.

Mota Burkhera, Bhúmia of; holds villages under various tenures, paying tankah to Dhár and Sindhia.

Kali Baurí, Bhúmia of; holds several villages, paying tankah to Dhár; receives an annual sum for protecting the district of Dhurrumpurí from robberies, and receives tankah from Sindhia for the village of Bíkanír.

[1] For Bhúmia, *vide* Appendix F.

PART VII.

Múltan, Thákur of; a vassal of the Dhár state, to which he pays a tribute of 18,044 Halí rupees, and makes reports.

Kachi Baroda, Thákur of; is in a similar position; his tribute is 9,459 rupees.

Bukhtgurh, Rájá of; is in a similar position; the amount of his tribute is 16,502 rupees.

Baisola or *Dotra*, Thákur of; is in a similar position; his tribute amounts to 2,501 rupees.

Narwar, Rájá of; possesses under Sindhia the district of Parone and six villages. He joined the rebels in 1857, but surrendered on condition of a free pardon and suitable maintenance being granted him. His former possessions were restored.

Khaltoun, Thákurs of; own three villages under Sindhia, yielding 4,000 rupees annually, on condition of serving the Government faithfully and protecting the high road.

Sirsi, Chief of; receives three-fourths of the district of Sirsi, on certain fixed conditions.

Ragúgarh, Rájás, now Thákurs of; representatives of the third of the twenty-four branches of the Chohan race, called Kychí, one of the oldest families in India. After many reverses of fortune, the Kychíwára lands were divided (1843) amongst the three brothers, representatives of the family, one receiving fifty-two villages, bringing in a rental of 15,000 rupees; the second, thirty-two villages with 8,000; the third, one hundred and twenty villages, supposed to yield a revenue of 31,555 rupees. Certain formal conditions were attached by Sindhia, their liege lord, to the first two allotments, but no sunnud would appear to have been granted for the third.

Baroda or *Sheopur*, Rájá of; a Rájpút and a vassal of Sindhia. He holds twelve villages.

Burra, Thákur of; receives tankahs from Sindhia and Holkar, amounting to 5,400 rupees.

Barudpúra, Bhúmia of; receives 500 rupees annually for protecting from robberies that part of the district of Dhurmpúri which lies between the Mán and Karan rivers; holds three villages from Dhár, and one in Mandú, paying 367 rupees annually.

Jamnia or *Dabir*, Bhúmia of; receives 2,505 rupees tankah from Holkar for several districts, and pays him 751 rupees for a village; pays 652 rupees to Sindhia for five villages, for which, however, no engagement is forthcoming; he received the villages of Dhár on a quit-rent of 150 rupees, and receives 65 rupees from that state on condition of being responsible for robberies in a portion of the Dhurmpúri districts.

Rajgurh, Bhúmia of; pays Dhár 101 rupees for a village in Dhurmpúri, and receives 500 rupees from that district to be answerable for all robberies therein; receives also 50 rupees from Holkar for Hashpúr on similar conditions.

Ghurri, or *Bhysa Kheri*, Bhúmia of; holds certain villages in Dhúrmpúri; pays a small annual sum for the same on condition of being responsible for robberies effected in them and within others specified.

Sillani and Bukhtgurh, Thákurs of; receive tankahs of 4,038 rupees from Sindhia, and of 778 from Holkar; also a monthly assignment of 400 rupees from the British Government in continuation of an agreement made in 1820. They also receive annually 1,350 rupees as zamindárí dues; 250 rupees from rent-free lands, and 1,100 rupees from other sources.

Khangurh, Rájá of: holds a jaghír from Sindhia of seventeen villages, bringing in an annual income of 800 rupees.

Jumti, Turvís of; hold from Sindhia a village which, with cash allowance granted by him, brings in 1,900 rupees a year.

Chota Kusrawul, Chiefs of; holds in life tenure from the British Government the village of Chota Kusrawul, subject to a payment of 1,699 rupees per annum; receives dues from other sources in Nimar aggregating 8,500 rupees per annum; and ináms and dues elsewhere amounting annually to 28,000 rupees.

Pithari. Thákur of; receives a tankah of 4,835 rupees from Dewás, under which he holds twelve villages; also one of 2,687 rupees from Sindhia, and one of 1,145 rupees from Holkar.

Bagli, Thákur of, a dependant of Sindhia; holds fourteen villages on a quit-rent of 6,471 rupees per annum; and nine other villages at a fixed rent. The time has expired, and it is possible these may have been resumed.

Karodia, Thákurs of; enjoy from Sindhia, Holkar, and Bhopál tankahs amounting to 3,427 rupees per annum; they

PART VII.

received, in 1838, from Sindhia the village of Khairi Rájpúra as blood money. They also hold other villages on quit-rent; but the amount paid is small, and is not guaranteed.

Tonk, Thákur of; receives tankahs from Sindhia, Holkar, and Dewás, aggregating 9,140 rupees per annum; holds a village and some lands from Sindhia and Holkar, not guaranteed.

Patharea, Thákur of; holds one village on a quit-rent of 701 rupees.

Dhungong, Chief of; holds thirty-six villages from Sindhia, on payment of 1,001 rupees per annum; receives tankahs from Sindhia and Holkar aggregating 1,540 rupees.

Singhana, Thákur of; pays to the British Government 240 rupees and to Holkar 56 rupees as tankah; received a life grant of three villages.

Baí, Thákur of; for maintaining the security of the Simrol Pass receives annually a cash payment of 750 rupees, and pays to Holkar 52 rupees 10 annas as collection dues.

Mayne, Chief of; seven of the adherents of this chief receive from Holkar two villages on rent, subject after the seventh year to a payment of two rupees per bígah[1] on condition that the chief made no further collection on passengers and goods between Man and Jám, and was responsible for all robberies, &c. For this purpose they receive 50 rupees per mensem.

Dhawra Kanjara, Chief of; receives 80 rupees per mensem for the protection of the roads between Simrol Ghât and Sigwar.

Ragúgarh, Thákur of; receives a family allowance of 1,500 rupees from the chiefs of Dewás; holds a village from Sindhia on a quit-rent of 250 rupees per annum. Neither grant is guaranteed.

Kaytha, Thákur of; receives 1,427 rupees per annum from the chiefs of Dewás.

Khursi Jhalaria, Thákurs of; receive annually 225 rupees from Dewás, and 1,750 rupees from Sindhia.

Phúngat, Thákur of; holds Phúngat and twelve villages from the British Government, subject to an annual payment of 401 rupees; received a tankah of 112 rupees from Sindhia, and subsequently another of 32 rupees.

Bhoja Kheri, Chief of; pays to Kotá annually 100 rupees for the village of Sidra.

[1] Varies from one third to two thirds of an acre.

Petty chiefs immediately dependent on the British Government.

Kúrwai, Nawáb of; rules over a territory having an area of 162 square miles; a population numbering 22,349, and returning a revenue of 75,000 rupees; pays neither tankah nor tribute.

Mahomedgurh, Nawáb of; pays neither tankah nor tribute; of the same family as the preceding; area of country, 80 square miles; population, 4,000; revenue, 7,000 rupees.

Basonda, Chief of; the state is an offshoot from Mahomedgurh; area, 68 square miles; population, 5,000: revenue, 7,000 rupees.

Mediatized and Guaranteed Chiefs.

Rájgarh, Ráwut of; belongs to the inferior class of Rájpúts. The state, which for the misconduct of the family had been taken under the management of the British Government, was restored free of debt in 1856. The revenues amount to about two lakhs of rupees, of which 85,000 Chunderí rupees are paid to Sindhia for certain villages, and 1,050 rupees of the Kotá currency to Jháláwur for another. On the other hand he receives annually from Sindhia a tankah of 3,187 rupees.

Nursingarh, Chief of; draws a revenue of about 3,25,000 rupees, and expends about 2,25,000 per annum; pays a tribute of 85,000 Bhopál rupees to Holkar, and receives from Sindhia and Dewás tankahs aggregating 6,301 rupees per annum.

Khilchipur, Déwán of; pays a tribute of 13,138 Halí rupees to Sindhia. Area of the territory, 204 square miles; population, 35,500; revenue, 83,317 rupees.

Pathari, Nawáb of; administers a small territory of 22 square miles, with a population of six, and a revenue of three, thousand.

Agra Burkhera, Thákur of; holds a grant of twelve villages from Sindhia, for which he pays 1,001 rupees annually as quit-rent; receives a tankah of 300 rupees from Kúrwar.

Dubla Dhir, Thákur of; receives tankahs from Holkar, Sindhia, Dewás, and Bhopál, aggregating 4,250 rupees annually; holds also three villages in Shujawulpúr, for which he pays annually a quit-rent of 1,401 rupees.

Duria Kheri, Thákur of; receives from Sindhia, Dewás, and Bhopál, tankahs aggregating 4,480 rupees; holds also two villages in Shujawulpúr on a quit-rent of 925 rupees per annum.

PART VII.

Kumalpúr, Thákur of; receives 4,600 rupees as tankah from Sindhia; holds one village in Shujawulpúr on a quit-rent of 700 rupees annually.

Dubla Ghosi, Thákur of; receives from Sindhia, Dewás, and Bhopál, tankahs aggregating 5,000 rupees; holds a village in Shujawulpúr on a quit-rent of 1,054 rupees.

Khursia, Thákur of; receives from Sindhia a tankah of 1,750 Halí rupees per annum.

Jhalera, Thákur of; receives from Sindhia a tankah of 1,200 Halí rupees per annum.

Hírapúr, Ráo of; receives from Holkar, Sindhia, and Bhopál, tankahs aggregating 6,449 rupees per annum. He holds also two villages on a perpetual rent of 600 rupees.

Rámgarh, Thákuráni of; receives from Holkar, Sindhia, Dewás, and Bhopal, tankahs aggregating 8,615 rupees.

Kakurkheri, Thákur of; receives a tankah of 800 rupees; holds a village in Shujawulpúr on a quit-rent of 171 rupees 8 annas.

Sutatea, Jaghírdar of; holds in Rajgurh a lease of twelve villages, for which he pays a tankah of 3,400 rupees to the chief of that state.

Jabria Bhil, Chiefs of; the descendants of the brother of the notorious Pindárí Kheetú. On the death of the brother the estate was divided amongst his five sons, with whom and their children it remains.

2.—Bundelkhand.

Chiefs who hold their states under sunnuds are bound by Ikrarnamas, or deeds of allegiance, and are vassals and dependants of the British Government.

Pannah, Rájá of, is descended from a long line of ancestors, who played a conspicuous part in the history of Bundelkhand. The most famous amongst them was Chutter Sál, whose eldest son, Hirdi Sah, inherited from him, with Pannah, territories estimated at an annual value of 38,46,123 rupees.

By wars, internal and external, the importance of Pannah has much diminished since that period. The revenues are reduced to four lakhs of rupees; the area of the country is 688 square miles, and the population 67,500.

The present Rájá, Nírpát Singh, is fifth son in descent from the son of Chutter Sál. He has received the right of adoption, and is entitled to a salute of eleven guns. After much trouble, he was induced about fourteen years ago to abolish the rite of satí throughout his territories.

Logassi, Ráo of. The ancestor of this chief was grandson of Hirdi Sah, above mentioned. He was in possession of seven villages when the British Government assumed supremacy in Bundelkhand, and he was confirmed in these after executing the usual deed of allegiance. The grandfather of the present held, as his predecessors, the title only of Déwán; but for his services in 1857 he received that of Ráo Bahadúr, a jaghír of 2,000 rupees per annum, a dress of honour worth 10,000 rupees, and the privilege of adoption. The name of the present Ráo is Híra Singh. The area of Logassi is about 30 square miles, the population about 3,500, and the revenue 17,000 rupees.

Chirkari, Rájá of. This was a portion of the country over which, by the treaty of Bassein, 1803, the Peshwa ceded to the British his sovereign claims. The ruler of it was then Rájá Bikramajít, a direct descendant from Chutter Sál, who, not however without some repugnance, subscribed to terms of allegiance to the British in 1804.

Rájá Ratañ Singh, grandson of Bikramajít, rendered good service in 1857. For this he was rewarded by receiving an accession of territory of 20,000 rupees per annum, a dress of honour, the privilege of adoption, and the right to a salute of eleven guns.

The name of the present Rájá is Jaí Singh Déo. He rules over a territory, the area of which is 880 square miles, the population 81,000, and the revenue about 5,00,000 rupees.

Bijáwur, Rájá of. The founder of the little state of Bijáwur was Bursing Déo, an illegitimate son of Juggut Ráj, who was the second son of the famous Chutter Sál. The present ruler, Bhao Pertáb Singh, is fourth in descent from Bursing Déo. He rendered good service in the mutinies, for which he received a dress of honour, and the hereditary right to a salute of eleven guns. He has been allowed the right of adoption.

The area of Bijáwur is 920 square miles, the population 90,000, and the revenue 3,50,000 rupees.

Ajaigarh, Rájá of, originally styled Rájá of Banda. This state was comprised originally in the kingdom of Jaitpúr, left

PART VII.

to Juggut Ráj by his father, Chutter Sál. But the dominions of Juggut Ráj were dissevered by internal wars, and his descendant, Bukht Singh, was reduced to such indigence that in the latter part of the reign of Ali Bahadúr, he was constrained to accept from that sovereign a pittance of two rupees per diem. His condition improved on the occupation of Bundelkhand by the British, and in 1807 he received a sunnud restoring to him a portion of his ancestral possessions. The present chief, Ranjúr Singh, is the fourth in descent from Bukht Singh. The area of his territory is 340 square miles, the population 50,000, and the revenue 1,75,000 rupees. He has received the right of adoption.

Surila, Rájá of; also a lineal descendant of Chutter Sál; rules over 35 square miles of territory, with a population of 4,500, and a revenue of about 24,000 rupees. The Rájá, whose name is Hindúput, has received the right of adoption.

Jigni, Ráo of; likewise a descendant of Chutter Sál. His territory has an area of 27 square miles, with a population of 2,800, and a revenue of 12,500 rupees. The chief has been granted the privilege of adoption.

The present Ráo, Bhopál Singh, is of unsound mind, and the state has been, since 1855, under the direct control of the British Government; but its affairs are administered by a native superintendent.

Jussú, Rájá of; an adopted descendant of Chutter Sál, the line having died out in 1860. The present Rájá, Satterjít Singh, who belonged to a branch of the same family, was recognised by the British Government in 1862. The area of his territory is 180 square miles, the population 24,000, and the revenue about 30,000 rupees. He has received the right of adoption.

Behri, Chief of; also a descendant of Chutter Sál; administers 30 square miles of territory, with a population of 2,500, and a revenue of 25,000 rupees. The present chief, Bijéy Singh, was the cousin and nearest relative of his predecessor. He has received the right of adoption.

Chaterpúr, Rájá of. This state may be said to have been founded by Súní Sah, a servant of Hindúput, great grandson of Chutter Sál.

Hindúput was the second son of his father, but murdering his elder brother and confining the younger, he succeeded to the inheritance left by Chutter Sál to his eldest son Hirdi Sah. After his death, however, civil war ensued, the inheritance was dissipated, and Súní Sah saw his way to appropriating a portion to himself. After some vicissitudes, he was recognised by the British Government in 1808 as chief of Chaterpúr.

In 1827, the son of Súní Sah, Pertáb Singh, was made a Rájá by the British Government.

The Rájá having died without issue in 1854, the Court of Directors ruled that the state of Chaterpúr was clearly an escheat; but in consideration of the fidelity of the family and the good government of the late Rájá, they decided, as an act of grace and favour, to grant the state to a nephew of the late Rájá, Juggut Ráj, the succession being limited to him and his male descendants.

Juggut Ráj attained his majority in 1867, but died in 1868, leaving an infant son. His succession was recognised by the British Government, by whom the state is administered through a native superintendent. The Rájá has received permission to adopt. The area of Chaterpúr is 1,240 square miles, the population 120,000, and the revenue 300,000 rupees.

Beronda, Rájá of; belongs to a very ancient family of Rájpúts totally unconnected with Bundelkhand. The state has neither increased nor diminished in extent since it came under British rule. It contains an area of 275 square miles, a population of 24,000, and a revenue of 45,000 rupees. The Rájá, Surubjít Singh, has received the right of adoption.

The Chohey family. The Chohey jaghírs are jaghírs administered by members of the Chohey family, whose ancestors possessed themselves of Kalinjer and other districts during the distractions which followed the invasions of Ali Bahádúr. They had been retainers of the family of Chutter Sál and had no right to the dominions they had usurped, but the British on assuming sovereignty in Bundelkhand left them in possession, on condition of allegiance.

Subsequently political necessity required that the fort of Kalinjer should be surrendered, but other lands were given in exchange.

It is a rule of succession in this family that when heirs fail to any sharer in the family estates, the share shall be divided amongst the surviving branches of the family.

There now remain six sharers.

The area of the Chohey jághírs is estimated at 90 square

miles, the population at 14,000, the revenue at 35,500 rupees.

Behut, Ráo of; is descended from the earlier members of the Tehrí family; administers a state of 15 square miles, with a population of 2,500, and a revenue of 15,000 rupees. Has received the power to adopt.

Alipúra, Ráo of; a lineal descendant in the direct male line of Chutter Sál; rules over a state having 85 square miles, a population of 9,000, and producing a revenue of 50,000 rupees. Has received the right of adoption.

Kotí, Jaghírdar of; belongs to an old family of the Bhagelás, which have held the jaghír from time immemorial. The area of the state is 100 square miles, the population 30,000, and the revenue 50,000 rupees. The Jaghírdar has received permission to adopt.

Úchera and *Nagód*, Rájá of; belongs likewise to a very old family. The present Rájá, Rugovind Singh, did good service in 1857, for which he was rewarded by the grant of an additional jaghír. His estates had been for some time under British management to free them from debt; but they were restored to him in May 1865. The area of the state is 450 suqare miles; the population 70,000; and the revenue 72,400 rupees.

Sohâwal, Chief of; descended from Jaghírdars who were feudatories of the Rájás of Pannah; his independence was recognised by the British in 1809. In consequence of the improvidence of the present Jaghírdar, the state has been for some time under British management. It has an area of 300 square miles; a population of 50,000; and a revenue of 30,000 rupees. The chief has been guaranteed the right of adoption.

Gorihar, Ráo of; descended from ancestors in the service of the Rájás of Ajaigarh, who first rebelled against their masters, and then started as the leaders of a band of professed plunderers. At the time of the early British occupation, the British Government sanctioned an offer of 30,000 rupees for the capture of the leader, Rám Singh. He finally surrendered on the promise of receiving a territorial possession on terms similar to those granted to the Bundelkhand chiefs. This was done in November 1807.

The son of this adventurer rendered good service in 1857. For this he was nominated Ráo Bahádúr, received a dress of honour worth 10,000 rupees, and the privilege of adoption.

This state comprises an area of 76 square miles, with a population of 7,500, and a revenue of 65,000 rupees.

Geraoli, Jaghírdar of; also the descendant of an adventurer, the most active and daring of all who opposed the occupation of Bundelkhand by the British. The father submitted, however, on condition of receiving a full pardon and a provision of land. This was granted in 1812.

The present chief, Randbir Singh, whose conduct in 1857 was not satisfactory, administers a state with an area of 50 square miles, a population of 5,000, and a revenue of 15,000 rupees. He has received the right of adoption.

Niagaon Rebai, Jaghírdar of; also a descendant of one of the banditti leaders of Bundelkhand. The property consists only of five villages, which are to lapse absolutely at the death of the present Jaghírdar, Juggut Singh.

Myhere, Thákur of; descended from a dependant of the Rájás of Rewá. The state has an area of 400 square miles, with a population of 70,000, and a revenue of 74,200 rupees. In consequence of its having been deeply involved in debt by its native ruler, it was for many years under British management. It was made over to the Thákur in 1865.

Baoni, Nawáb of; is a lineal descendant of Azof Jáh; otherwise known as Chin Kilich Khan, the founder of the family which now rules at Hyderabad. This state is the only state in Bundelkhand ruled by a Mahomedan. It covers an area of 127 square miles, has a population of 19,000, and yields a revenue of 100,000 rupees.

The Husht Bhya Jaghírs, Jaghírdars of; are descended from Dewan Rai Singh, himself descended from one of the Rájás of Tehrí. Déwán Rai Singh left an estate called Baragún, which on his death he willed to be divided into eight shares among his eight sons, whence the name of the Husht Bhya Jaghírs. Of these eight shares two were at an early date merged into the remainder; one reverted to Tehrí, and a fourth was, in 1841, confiscated for the rebellion of its owner.

There now remain four Jaghírdars, and four jaghírs covering 85 square miles. The population of all is estimated at 18,000, and the revenue at 81,000 rupees.

Kanýadhána, Jaghírdar of; administers a small jaghír formerly part of the state of Tehrí. It first came formally under British sovereignty in 1862. It has a revenue of 30,000 rupees. The population numbers about 6,000.

PART VII.

3.—Western India.

Satára Jaghírdars whose possessions have been guaranteed by the British Government.

N.B.—These Jaghírdars do not possess the power of life and death.

Akulkót, Jaghírdar of, administers an area of 986 square miles, with a population of 77,339, and a revenue of 150,000. The tenure of the jaghír in the present family dates from about 1730.

Pant Sachéo Jaghír; Chief of, is descended from one of the eight hereditary ministers of the old Márhátá empire. The area of the jaghír is 500 square miles; the population 110,193; the revenue 120,000 rupees. The Pant Sachéo pays a tribute of 5,275 rupees to the British Government.

Pant Prithi Nidhi Jaghír, Chief of; is descended by adoption from a family high in esteem under Sivají, and upon whose representative Rájá Rám conferred the title of 'Prithi Nidhi,' a title higher than that of the Peshwa.

The area of the jaghír is 350 square miles; the population 67,967; and the revenue amounts to 75,000 rupees.

Jaghír of the Duflay, Chief of; is called the Duflay from Duflapúr, a village in the district of Jut. The area of the jaghír is 7,000 square miles; the population 58,794, and the revenue 65,000 rupees, of which nearly 5,000 are paid to the British Government.

Jaghír of the Nimbalkur, or *Phultun*, Chief of; is descended by adoption from a family which long held the jaghír under the Mahomedan kings of Bíjapúr, and distinguished itself by its bold opposition to Sivají. The area of the jaghír is 400 square miles, the population 47,100, and the revenue 75,000 rupees.

Pasurni, Jaghírdar of; belongs to the Mahomedan family of Waekur, the representative of which received the jaghír from Rájá Sahú for his fidelity. The income of his lands is about 6,647 rupees, all of which, except a small subsistence allowance, is assigned to his creditors.

Southern Márhátá Jaghírdars.

N.B.—Of these the first-mentioned, the Putwardhur, has alone power to try for capital offences any person but British subjects. The others have power to try for capital offences their own subjects only.

The Putwardhur; a family founded by Húri Bhut, a

Brahman, who became family priest of an influential family in the vicinity of Kólhapúr, and whose three sons rose to high military command under the first Peshwa, receiving grants of land on condition of military service. His grandson, Purusrám Bhao, was well known to the English as the leader of the Márhátá division which co-operated in the reduction of Mysore in 1792. He was killed in battle in 1800, fighting against Kólhapúr. The family estates are now divided into five separate parts, held by separate members of the family. They produce in the aggregate a revenue of 980,000 rupees, of which they pay 49,429 rupees to the British Government, in lieu of maintaining a contingent force. To each of the chiefs the right of adoption has been granted.

Ramdrúg, Chief of; descended from a family to which the Márhátás confided, in the early part of the eighteenth century, the defence of the two strongest forts in the Konkan, Nurgúnd and Ramdrúg. The two forts became regarded in course of time as separate appanages for members of the same family, and as such they were regarded, when, on the fall of the Peshwa, 1818, they came into British possession.

The ruler of Nurgúnd rebelled and murdered the British political agent in 1857. For this he was hanged, and his estate was confiscated.

The Chief of Ramdrúg, on the other hand, remained faithful, and was granted the right of adoption. His revenue amounts to about 50,000 rupees.

Múdhól, Chief of; is descended from a family which rose to eminence under the Mahomedan Kings of Bijapúr, from whom its members received their estates. The revenues amount to about 1,00,000 rupees, of which 2,618 are paid to the British Government in lieu of military service.

Abyssinian Chiefs.

Jinjíra, Sídí of, is descended from the Abyssinian admirals of the Mahomedan fleet which served the Kings of Bijapúr. In course of time, hard pressed in the fort of Jinjíra by the Márhátás, the captains of the fleet formed themselves into a kind of republic, and offered their services to Aurangzíb. Their services were accepted; their chief was appointed admiral of the imperial fleet, for the support of which an as-

PART VII.

signment was granted on the revenues of Súrat, the trade of which port, together with the ships which annually conveyed the pilgrims to Mecca, the admiral was specially bound to protect. The admiral in 1733, Sídi Kásim Yakút Khan, entered in that year into an offensive and defensive alliance with the British Government, to which he and his successors were ever faithful.

In 1834 Jinjíra was declared to be subject to the British power.

It pays no tribute. The area of the territory is 324 square miles, its population 71,000, and its revenues 1,70,000 rupees. The chief has power to try his own subjects only for capital offences.

Sachín, Nawáb of; descended from a Sídí of Jinjíra, to whom the Peshwa made over lands in lieu of Jinjíra, of which, however, he never obtained possession. The estate consists of seventeen villages, the revenues from which amount to 85,000 rupees. The population is about 13,000. The Nawáb has power to try his own subjects only for capital offences.

Other States.

Bansda, Rájá of; administers a small state, forty-five miles south-east of Súrat, the early history of which is unknown. Its population is 19,000, and the revenues amount to 61,000 rupees, of which 7,351 rupees are paid as tribute. The Rájá has power to try his own subjects only for capital offences.

Dhurmpúr, Rájá of; administers a small state, south of Bansda, the population of which amounts to 15,000, and the revenue to 90,000 rupees, of which about 6,500 are paid as tribute. The Rájá has only power to try his own subjects for capital offences.

Jowar, Rájá of; descended from a freebooter, who, till checked by the Márhátás in 1760, raised a large revenue by robberies and exactions. At present the state thus acquired covers an area of 300 square miles, has a population of 8,000, and yields a revenue of 25,900 rupees.

The powers of the Rájá are similar to those of the Rájá of Dhurmpúr.

Kambay, Nawáb of; is descendedfrom the last but one of the Mahomedan governors of Gujrát. He rules over a small but compact country with an area of 350 square miles, a population of 175,000, and a revenue of 3,50,000 rupees.

The Nawáb has received a sunnud guaranteeing any succession that may be legitimate according to Mahomedan law. He has power to try for capital offences any persons except British subjects.

Káthíwar.

PRELIMINARY.—Of the chiefs in the Gujrát Peninsula, or Káthíwar, one hundred and thirty-seven were, in former days, tributary to the Peshwa, and one hundred and eleven to the Gáikwár. The tributes, as settled with each chief individually, amounted, in 1809, on account of the former, to 8,54,700 rupees; on account of the latter to 9,79,882. The Peshwa's share of the tribute was ceded to the British Government in June 1817, and in 1820 the Gáikwár agreed to allow his share to be collected by the British, and to send no troops into Káthíwar. From that date the supreme authority in the whole of the peninsula has rested with the British Government.

Under the authority thus recognised the British Government established in 1831 a criminal court of justice in Káthíwar, to be presided over by the political agent, aided by three or four chiefs as assessors, for the trial of capital crimes on the estates of chiefs who might be too weak to punish such offences, and of crimes committed by petty chiefs against one another, or otherwise than in the legitimate exercise of authority over their own dependants. Sentences exceeding imprisonment for seven years require to be submitted to the Bombay Government for approval. Of the chiefs, the first five in the order laid down below have power to try for capital offences any persons except British subjects; the remainder have power to try their own subjects only.

The area of Káthíwár is 21,000 square miles; the population is estimated at 14,75,685; the gross income of the chief may be set down as at least 100,00,000 rupees; the gross tribute and collections realised in 1862 amounted to 11,81,140 rupees, of which 7,23,370 were for the British Government; 3,10,000 for the Gáikwár; 64,000 for the Nawáb of Júnágarh, and 83,270 for local funds.

Subjoined is a list of the chiefs who exercise legal jurisdiction.

PART VII.

Júnágarh, Nawáb of; is the representative of a family founded by Shír Khan Bábi, a soldier of fortune, who, during the confusion occasioned by the struggles between the Márhátás and Mogul for supremacy in the province, established himself in the district of Soreth, of which Júnágarh is the capital. The present Nawáb is seventh in descent from the founder.

The revenues of the state are about 6,00,000 rupees; the Nawáb pays to the British Government 28,394, and to the Gáikwár 36,413. He has received the assurance that any succession to his state, legitimate according to the Mahomedan rule, will be upheld.

Nawánagar, Jám of; is the head of the Jahrejah Rájpúts. The family, of which he is the representative, emigrated from Kachh to Káthíwar, and founded Nawánagar about the year 1542, driving before them the Jetwa family, who formerly possessed the country, but who are now confined to the small state of Púrbandur.

A predecessor of the present Jám made a futile attempt to shake off the British suzerainty in 1811-12, but he failed to evoke even sympathy with his projects.

The Jám of Nawánagar has received power to adopt. His revenues amount to about 6,00,000 rupees. He pays to the British 50,312, to the Gáikwár 64,183, and to the Nawáb of Júnágarh 4,843 rupees.

Bháonagar, Thákur of; is descended from a Rájpút family, which settled in the peninsula about the year 1200 A.D. He is the richest chief, and his territories are in the most flourishing condition of any, in the peninsula. His revenues are estimated at over 8,00,000 rupees. He pays in tribute 1,30,000 rupees to the British Government. He has been guaranteed the right of adoption.

Púrbandur, Ráná of, is a Rájpút belonging to the Jetwa tribe, expelled in 1542 from Nawánagar by the family now ruling there. In the year 1808, in return for the aid of the British in the suppression of a rebellion, the ruling Ráná ceded to them half the port dues of the port of his chief town. These are rated at about 15,000 rupees per annum. The total revenues of his state amount to 2,50,000 rupees. Besides the 15,000 for a moiety of the port dues, he pays the British a tribute of 25,202 rupees. To the Gáikwár he pays 7,196, and to Júnágarh 5,106. He is considered to be specially entitled to the assistance of the British Government.

Durangdra, Chief of; is head of the Jhalla Rájpúts. His country has become much impoverished from various causes. His revenue is rated at about 1,60,000 rupees, and his tribute to the British Government at 40,000.

Wánkanir, Thákur of; has a small district in Muchhú-Kantá. His revenue is not more than 26,000 rupees; the tribute taken is, or was, 12,000 rupees.

Morewí, Chief of; is the principal chief in Muchhú-Kantá; is stated to be descended from the Ráos of Kachh. His estate comprises ninety-seven villages; his revenue is rated at 1,68,641 rupees, and his tribute is 40,001.

Rájkot, Thákur of; belongs to a Márhátá family. His revenues are about 75,000 rupees; he pays a tribute to the British of 17,421 rupees, and receives, on the other hand, 2,803 rupees as compensation for land granted by him for a civil station. He pays annually 2,330 rupees to the Nawáb of Júnágarh.

Gúndul, Chief of; administers a large district in the division of Hálar. His revenue was rated at 4,00,000 rupees, derived from one hundred and seventy-nine villages, and two flourishing towns. He pays a tribute to the British of 53,000 rupees, and to the Gáikwár of 1,15,000 rupees. He is a Rájpút.

Limri, Chief of; is a Rájpút. His revenues are estimated at 1,60,000 rupees. His annual tribute to the British amounts to 51,931 rupees annually.

Wudwan, Rájá of; is one of the principal chiefs in the Jhaláwar division of Káthíwar. His revenues amount to 2,50,000 rupees; his tribute to the British to about 32,500, and to the Nawáb of Júnágarh to 62,812.

Palitána, Rájá of; is a relation of the Rájá of Bháonagar, being descended from the same stock. His capital is the chief place of pilgrimage in Gujrát.

Dhérol, Chief of; belongs to the Jhareja Rájpúts.

Jaffarábád, Sídí of; is subject to the Sídí of Jingúra (*vide* 'Abyssinian Chiefs,' *ante*). His revenues amount to 30,000 rupees. He pays no tribute, either to the British, or to the Gáikwár.

Sindh.

Khairpúr, Amír of; rules over the remnant left to the Talpúr family after the conquest of Sindh by Sir Charles

PART VII.

Napier in 1843. Previous to that conquest, Ali Murád had been recognised as chief of Khairpúr. After it, to obtain a larger share of the territory for himself, he did not hesitate to forge an alteration of the treaty which had made him ruler of the country guaranteed to him before it. The fraud was detected, and on investigation clearly established. Ali Murád was then degraded from the rank of Ráis of Khairpúr, and deprived of all his territories except those which he held under his father's will. The country still ruled by the Amír is estimated at an area of 5,000 square miles; it has a population of 105,000, and a revenue estimated at 3,50,000 rupees.

The Amír has power to try for capital offences all persons but British subjects.

Páhlanpúr Agency.

PRELIMINARY.—There are eleven states under this agency, of which four are Mahomedan and seven Hindú. The total area of the states is 6,041 square miles, the population 321,645, and the gross revenues 6,40,000 rupees per annum. The chiefs of Páhlanpúr and Rádhanpúr alone have power to try for capital offences any persons except British subjects.

Páhlanpúr, Déwán of; claims his descent from the leader of a tribe of Afgháns who occupied Bahár in the reign of Humáyun. The head of the family derived his title of Déwán from the Emperor Akbar.

The present chief rendered good service in 1857, and has been assured that the British Government will uphold any succession in the state which may be legitimate according to Mahomedan law. The area of the territory is 2,384 square miles; the population 178,051; and the revenues 3,00,000 rupees. The chief pays a tribute of 45,512 rupees to the Gáikwár.

Páhlanpúr, Nawáb of; derives his descent from a family which came from Ispahan about two centuries and a half ago. An ancestor, Shír Khan Bábi, was Thanadar of the district of Chowál in 1659; and in 1713, his grandson, Jawan Murd Khan, was appointed Foujdar of Rádhanpúr. He had several sons, the elder of whom, bearing the same name, is conspicuous in the Gujrát annals of the period. This chief usurped the Súbadhári of Gujrát. Subsequently the family lost several of their possessions to the Gáikwár, but received a sunnud for the remainder. The family came under the suzerainty of the British in 1820.

The area of Rádhanpúr is 833 square miles; the population 45,293, and the revenue 2,50,000 rupees. The state pays black mail to the neighbouring tribes of Kúli plunderers, but no tribute.

The Nawáb has received the right of appointing a successor according to Mahomedan law.

Warái, Nawáb of; administers a state the area of which is 204 square miles; the population 12,000, and the revenue 18,000 rupees. He is a Mahomedan of the Jhut tribe.

Terwara, Nawáb of; possesses an area of 100 square miles; with a population of 4,488, and a revenue of 2,000 rupees.

Thurad and Morwara, Chief of; possesses an area of 113 square miles, a population of 27,000, and a revenue of 21,000 rupees; pays no tribute.

Wao, Chief of; is a Chohan Rájpút; pays no tribute; has a revenue of 8,600 rupees. The area of his territory is 360 square miles, and the population 13,000.

Súegaum, Chief of; also a Chohan Rájpút. The area of his territory is 161 square miles, the population 5,813, and the revenue 5,500 rupees.

Déodur, Chief of; is a Rájpút. The area of his territory is 240 square miles, the population 9,000, and the revenue 5,000 rupees.

Chorwai and Charchut, Chief of; is a Rájpút of the Jhareja tribe. The area of his territory is 440 square miles; the population 12,000, and the revenue 13,000 rupees.

Bhabur, Chief of; rules over an area of 72 square miles, with a population of 2,000, and a revenue of 800 rupees.

Kankraj, Chief of; rules over an area of 507 square miles, with a population of 12,945, and a revenue of 18,000 rupees. The chief pays 5,593 rupees as tribute to the Gáikwár.

Mahíkantá States.

Preliminary.—The area of Mahíkantá is 4,000 square miles; the population is 311,046; and the entire revenues amount to 5,14,000 rupees, of which the Gáikwár receives 1,29,483 as tribute. Besides that of Ídar and Ahmadnagar, which will be separately noticed, there are the following

PART VII.

families notorious chiefly as freebooters, and to whom it seems unnecessary to make further reference. The chief of Amhara; the Kúlís of Sohar; the Thákur of Ahima; the Thákur of Titóví; the chief of Gajan; the chief of Anovia; the heads of villages in the Megráj district. The engagements made with the chiefs may be generally summed up as being engagements on their part not to rob or steal. I proceed now to the only important state in Mahíkanta, that of Ídar and Ahmadnagar.

Ídar and Ahmadnagar, Rájá of; is a descendant of the brother of Abhi Singh, Rájá of Jodhpúr. In the second quarter of the eighteenth century his brother, Anand Singh, with another, Rai Singh, left in Gujrát, where their father had been Viceroy, conquered the districts of Ídar, Ahmadnagar, and ten others. In the wars which followed they and their descendants were stripped of a considerable portion of the territories he thus acquired. Then followed family dissensions, which ended in the dismemberment of the territory, and its division into two distinct principalities of Ídar and Ahmadnagar.

This separation lasted until on the failure of heirs to Maun Singh, Rájá of Jodhpúr in 1843, the chief of Ahmadnagar was elected, as one of the nearest collaterals, to succeed him in that ancient kingdom. As a consequence it was decided in 1848, after some objection on the part of her late ruler, that Ahmadnagar should revert to Ídar.

The Rájá of Ídar has received the right of adoption. He possesses the power to try for capital offences any persons except British subjects.

Rewá Kantá States.

Preliminary.—Of the chiefs in these states the first in order of place in this record alone has power to try for criminal offences any person except British subjects; the remaining five have power only to try their own subjects for such offences. But besides these there are fifty-six small proprietors, mostly Bhíls and Mewasses, plunderers by instinct, and with whom the engagements made relate principally to the prohibition and punishment of plundering, and to the harbouring of plunderers. It would be tedious to give even the designation of the petty holdings. It will suffice to state that the revenues of the chiefs ascend to 33,000 rupees, and descend to 50 rupees per annum. With the exception of three, they are all tributaries of the Gáikwár. I now proceed to notice the six principal chiefs.

Rájpíplá, Chiefs of; are Rájpúts whose ancestors maintained their independence till the time of Akbar. On the decline of the Mahomedan power they fell under the domination of the Gáikwár. In consequence of a quarrel between that prince and the nominal ruler for the nine years antecedent, the British Government interfered in 1819. Two years later the Gáikwár relinquished his control over the territory to the British Government, engaging to receive his tribute through the hands and by the sole intervention of that power.

The British Government then assumed, the Rájá being a minor, the management of the country, which was almost bankrupt. Since that time the finances have been in a measure restored; the disputes with the Gáikwár satisfactorily settled by the transfer to him of certain villages, and the government restored to its native ruler.

The area of Rájpíplá is 4,500 square miles, and the revenue 3,75,000 rupees, of which 20,000 rupees are paid annually to the British Government towards the maintenance of the Gujrát Bhíl corps.

Déogarh Baria, Rájá of; is descended from the Páwaichas of Páwagurh, one of the branches of the Chohan race. Driven from Páwagurh by the Mahomedans, they took refuge in the country of the Bhíls, and founded there a new principality. The state was brought under the protection of the British Government after the defeat of Sindhia in the war of 1802-3.

Subsequently, however, the country underwent great tribulation from Márhátá invasions and internal strife. In 1819 it was taken under direct British management, and its finances, which were half ruined, were in a measure restored. The present Rájá, Maun Singh, is nineteen years old. The area of the state is 1,600 square miles, and its revenues 75,000 rupees. It pays a tribute of 12,000 rupees to the British Government.

Chota Udaipúr, Rájá of; is descended from the same family as the preceding. The state became subject to the British Government in 1822. Its area is about 3,000 square miles, and its revenue about 1,00,000 rupees. It pays an annual tribute of 8,770 rupees to the Gáikwár.

Lúnáwárá, Rájá of; ruler of a territory which came under

British protection at the time and under the circumstances related regarding Déogarh Bária. The area of the state is 1,736 square miles, and the revenue 42,000 rupees. It pays 10,653 rupees tribute to the British, and 2,300 rupees to the Bábí of Bálásínúr.

Súnth, Rájá of; rules a territory the area of which is 900 square miles, and the revenue 22,000 rupees. He pays a tribute to the British Government of 6,108 rupees. He claims descent from the ancient Rájás of Málwá.

Bálásinúr, Bábí of; is descended from the same family as the Nawábs of Júnagárh in Káthíwár, and is the representative of the younger branch. It came under the political jurisdiction of the British after the downfall of the Peshwa in 1818.

The area of the territory is 400 square miles; and its revenue about 40,000 rupees. It pays a tribute of 11,079 rupees to the British Government.

4. Southern India.

Pudukottá, Rájá of; is known as the Tondiman Rájá. His connection with respect to the British Government is peculiar. He has no treaty with it, pays no tribute, and his courts of justice are under no exterior supervision. Yet he is under the suzerainty of the British. His small state, possessing an area of 1,037 square miles, is surrounded by British districts; he keeps up only 126 regular infantry and 21 troopers, besides militia and watchmen; and the British Government receives complaints from his servants, and sends them to be dealt with by the political agent, who is also entitled to advise and remonstrate with the Rájá on all subjects, but more especially as regards expenditure. His subjects, too, are amenable to British courts for crimes committed within the British territory.

The Tondiman Rájás are the oldest and truest allies of the British in Southern India. They most materially aided them in their contest for supremacy with the French, especially in the stirring events in the neighbourhood of Trichinápalí, and subsequently in the wars against the Mahomedan dynasty of Mysore.

The British Government of former days was not backward in recognising and substantially rewarding those services.

The Rájá has received the right of adoption. The population of his territory is 268,780 square miles, and the revenue 3,24,136 rupees. The present Rájá, as a punishment for his reckless expenditure, has been deprived of some of his titles.

Sandúr, Rájá of; is descended from the family of the famous Morári Ráo, of whose principality Sandúr formed a part. It was conquered by the British in 1817, restored in 1818, and a sunnud granting it to the present family for ever issued in 1826. The present Rájá was an adopted son. He has received power to adopt.

The area of the territory is 145 square miles; its population 13,446; and its revenue 37,821 rupees.

Bángapáli, Jaghírdar of; administers a territory having an area of 500 square miles, a population of 35,200, and a revenue of 1,66,175 rupees. He administers civil and criminal justice except in cases involving capital punishment. Certain conditions are imposed on him to ensure as far as may be security against oppression for his subjects. He has received the power to adopt.

Kananúr, Rájá of; is a Mápillah. He holds, in addition to his estate on the mainland, the southern Laccadive islands. The descent, as in the royal families of Travankúr and Kochin, lies with the male descendants of sisters.

N.B.—Besides Kananúr, there are on the Malabar coasts several other states subordinate to British authority, with whom engagements on revenue matters have been made by the British Government. None of these states have any political status, and it is unnecessary to enumerate any of them in a work of this kind. The mention even of Kananúr is superfluous.

5. Eastern India.

Hill Tiparah, Rájá of; has no treaty with the British Government, though he receives his investiture from it. His country was never subjected by the Mogul or his lieutenants and representatives. The area of his territory is 2,879 square miles; the population 69,000.

Kasaá Hill States. These are twenty-five in number; over five of these, called the semi-independent states, their chief exercise civil and criminal jurisdiction over their own people only.

The twenty minor states, which it is unnecessary to enumerate, are virtually dependent on the British Government.

Chutiá Nagpúr, tributary Mahals of; consist of several petty states which it is unnecessary to enumerate, as they are all under the undefined authority of the British commissioner.

Orísá, tributary Mahals of; sixteen in number, held by petty Rájás, who administer criminal and civil justice, controlled only by the undefined authority of the British superintendent.

Manípúr, Rájá of; is in subordinate alliance with the British. The relations with him are conducted through a political agent. The area of his territory is 7,584 square miles; the population 75,840, and the revenue 14,250 rupees. He pays no tribute.

Koch Bihár, Rájá of; descended from a family which began its connection with the British in 1772 by its chief, then a minor and a prisoner in the hands of the Bhútías, offering to pay to them half his revenue if they would assist him to expel the Bhútías from his country.

They were expelled. Since that period Koch Bihár has remained annexed to Bengal, and half its revenues are paid to the British Government. The management of the country is left, however, in the sole care of the Rájá and his officers.

The area of the country is 1,300 square miles, the population 100,000, the revenue 7,00,000 rupees.

6. North-Western India.

Rámpúr, Nawáb of; is the lineal descendant of Ali Mahomed Khan, the adopted son of Daúd Khan, himself the son of an Afghán who settled in Rohilkhand. Ali Mahomed Khan was the first to establish absolute supremacy in Rohilkhand, and to take the title of Nawáb.

The commotions prevalent in North-Western India upon the break-up of the Mogul empire, affected the position of the heir of Ali Mahomed, and in the end he was glad to compound for the possession of the estate of Rampúr, on condition of military service to the Vizír of Oudh, a condition commuted in 1783, under the guarantee of the British Government, to a cash payment of 15,00,000 rupees. A portion of the estate was subsequently cut off and annexed to Rohilkhand, but when that province came into British possession in 1801, the position then held by the Nawáb was continued to him.

The Nawáb of Rampúr, Mahomed Yússúf Ali Khan, rendered good service in 1857. For this he received a grant of land yielding 1,04,000 rupees. He was subsequently nominated a Knight of the Most Exalted Order of the Star of India, and received a sunnud assuring him regarding the succession.

The area of Rampúr is 1,140 square miles, the population 3,90,232, and the revenue about 10,00,000 rupees.

Banáras, Rájá of; is descended from the nephew of Cheít Singh, the chief who made himself famous in the time of Warren Hastings. Had he displayed in that crisis a presence of mind and directness of aim corresponding to the circumstances in which he had been placed, the history of India might have been changed. As it was, he was dethroned, and his territory given, with greatly restricted powers, and a considerable increase of tribute (from twenty-two and a half to forty lakhs), to his nephew.

The family derives its origin from a Zamíndár named Mansa Rám, who originally possessed no more than half the village of Gungapúr, but who, through the favour of the Subadar of the province, and by the modes then usual in Hindostan, acquired in nineteen years districts yielding a gross revenue of 24,50,000 rupees. These, his son, Balwant Singh, increased to a yield of 35,00,000 rupees. Cheít Singh was the son of Balwant Singh.

From the time of the expulsion of Cheít Singh, the administration has been entirely in the hands of the British, the Rájá retaining his authority only over certain patrimonial lands of inconsiderable extent, a certain share of the surplus revenue or excess above the fixed tribute being assigned for his personal expenses. He has received the right of adoption, and is allowed a salute of thirteen guns.

Garhwál, Rájá of; administers a country possessing an area of 4,500 square miles, with a population of 200,000 and a revenue of 80,000 rupees. This comprises only a portion of the territory formerly held by his house. But prior to the Nipál war of 1834-5, the Gúrkhas had deprived him of the whole, and the British who, on the conclusion of the war, found him living in great poverty at Déhra, restored him the portion which lay to the west of the Alikamanda river.

The Rájá rendered valuable service to the British in 1857. A sunnud has been granted to the present ruler guaranteeing to him the right of adoption.

PART VII.

Shahpúra, Rájá of; is descended from an ancientRáná of Údaipúr, from whom he is tenth in lineal descent.

The founder of the family acquired the district of Kheirar in Méwar from his father, whilst his son received the possessions in Ajmír as a reward for his gallant services to Shah Jehán. The present Rájá thus holds under two suzerains, the Ráná of Údaipúr and the British Government. His revenue is estimated at 3,00,000 rupees. He pays a tribute to the British Government of 10,000 rupees, an amount liable to decrease under certain circumstances. He has been guaranteed the right of adoption.

Minor Cis-Satlaj Chiefs.

These are eighty in number, receiving revenues varying from 250 rupees to 68,303 rupees per annum, and paying tribute from 36 rupees to 5,645 rupees. With the exception of two of them, the Nawáb of Kúnipúra and the Mír of Kolatiar, they possess no higher status than that of ordinary Jaghírdars. Certain privileges, which it is not necessary to enumerate, have been extended to a limited number amongst them for their lives.

Succession to these estates is governed by the following rules:—

1. That no widow shall succeed.
2. That no descendants in the female line shall inherit.
3. That on failure of a direct heir, a collateral male heir may succeed, if the common ancestors of the deceased and of the collateral claimant should have been in possession of the share at or since 1808-9.

The Delhi Territory.

Dojana, Nawáb of; holds his estates on condition of fidelity to the British Government and military service when required. The sunnud conferring the tenure in perpetuity dates from 1806, but accessions of territory have since been made.

Lohárú, Chiefs of; trace their descent from a Vakíl of the Rájá of Alwar, from whom, at the beginning of the present century, the head of the family received Lohárú in perpetuity. The conduct of the two chiefs in 1857 was suspicious, and they were placed under surveillance after the capture of Delhi, but they were subsequently released and reinstated.

The family at one time possessed the district of Ferozpúr,

but it was confiscated on account of the murder, by one of its members, of Mr. Fraser, the Governor-General's agent at Delhi, in 1835. The gross revenue of the district is about 60,000 rupees.

Patáodí, Nawáb of, grandson of the original grantee, who received the estate in 1806 in perpetual jaghír as a reward for co-operating with Lord Lake against Holkar. The revenue is about 45,000 rupees.

These three Nawábs have received sunnuds guaranteeing the succession according to Mahomedan law.

Hill States.

Sirmúr, or *Náhan*, Chief of; is a Rájpút. Came under the suzerainty of the British in 1815. The population of his country is 75,000, and the revenue is about 1,00,000 rupees. He pays no tribute, but is bound to render feudal service. The Rájá rendered good service in the mutinies, and received in reward a salute of seven guns, and a khillut of 5,000 rupees.

Kahlúr (*Bilaspúr*), Rájá of; also a Rajpút. Came under British suzerainty in 1815. The population of his country is 66,848, and the revenue 70,000 rupees. In other respects the remarks made regarding the Rájá of Sirmúr apply to him.

Hindúr (*Nálágarh*), chief of; also a Rájpút. The population is 49,678, the revenue 60,000 rupees; pays a tribute of 5,000 rupees.

Búsáhir, Rájá of; is a Rájpút. The population of Búsahír is 55,025; the revenue 70,000 rupees. The Rájá pays a tribute of 3,945 rupees.

Keonthal, Rájá of; is a Rájpút. Receives tribute from four chiefs, aggregating 1,500 rupees, as their liege lord. The population is 18,083, the revenues are 30,000 rupees. The father of the present chief was created a Rájá for his services in 1857, and received also a dress of honour worth 1,000 rupees.

Júbul, Ráná of, first became independent after 1815, having previously been tributary to Sirmúr. The population is 17,262; the revenue 18,000 rupees. The Ráná pays 2,520 rupees tribute, and is bound to render feudal service.

Bhují, Ráná of; rules over 9,000 people, and draws a revenue of 15,000 rupees. He pays 1,440 rupees annually to the British Government; is bound in case of war to join the British in person, with all his retainers; is bound likewise to 'construct roads four yards broad in his territory.'

Kumhársin, Ráná of; is a Rájpút. The family first became independent in 1815. The population amounts to 7,829; the revenue to 9,000 rupees. The Ráná pays a tribute of 2,000 rupees to the British.

Kothar, Ráná of; a Rájpút. The sunnud of his state dates 1815. The population amounts to 3,990, the revenue to 5,000 rupees; pays a tribute of 1,080 rupees.

Dhami, Ráná of; first became independent in 1815. The population amounts to 2,853; the revenue to 4,000 rupees; the tribute to 360 rupees.

Baghát, Ráná of; a Rájpút. This state has been twice treated as a lapse, and has twice been restored. Its size is but one-fourth of what it was before the Gúrkha war, during which the conduct of the chief was unfriendly. The present Rájá was restored in 1862.

Bulsun, Ráná of; dates his separate existence from 1815. The present chief was created a Ráná in 1858 for his services in the mutiny. The population is 4,892; the revenue amounts to 6,000 rupees; the tribute to 1,080 rupees.

Meilog, Thákur of; possesses a territory containing a population of 7,358, and producing a revenue of 8,000 rupees. He pays a tribute of 1,450 rupees.

Bijah, Thákur of; rules over a population of 981, with a revenue of 2,000 rupees; pays a tribute of 180 rupees, but receives 100 rupees as compensation for land used by the British.

Turoch, Thákur of; is lord of a population of 3,082, and receives a revenue of 2,500 rupees; pays a tribute of 280 rupees.

Kúnhiar, Thákur of; rules over a population of 1,906, and receives a revenue of 3,000 rupees: pays 180 rupees as tribute.

Mungul, Ráná of; is chief amongst a population of 917, and receives a revenue of 1,000 rupees; pays 92 rupees tribute.

Durkotí, Ráná of, pays no tribute; has an income of 500 rupees. The population numbers 612.

All these chiefs are, with respect to each other, as nearly as possible in the same position as they had been before they were brought under British suzerainty in 1815. The right of adoption has been guaranteed to all of them. In 1847 transit duties were abolished throughout their states. A yearly sum of 13,935 rupees is paid to them in compensation by the Government of India.

APPENDIX A.

I APPEND the letter from Ráná Ráj Singh to the Emperor Aurangzíb, erroneously attributed by Orme and the writers who followed him to Jeswunt Singh. Colonel Tod states that his Múnshi obtained a copy of the original letter at Údaipúr, where it is properly assigned to the Ráná Ráj Singh. The following is the text of it:— APPX. A.

Letter from Ráná Ráj Singh to Aurangzíb.

'All due praise be rendered to the glory of the Almighty, and the munificence of your Majesty, which is conspicuous as the sun and moon. Although I, your well-wisher, have separated myself from your sublime presence, I am nevertheless zealous in the performance of every bounden act of obedience and loyalty. My ardent wishes and strenuous services are employed to promote the prosperity of the Kings, Nobles, Mírzás, Rájás, and Rájs of the provinces of Hindostan, and the chiefs of Irán, Turán, Rúm, and Shán, the inhabitants of the seven climates, and all persons travelling by land and by water. This, my inclination, is notorious, nor can your royal wisdom entertain a doubt thereof. Reflecting, therefore, on my former services, and your Majesty's condescension, I presume to solicit the royal attention to some circumstances in which the public as well as private welfare is greatly interested.

'I have been informed that enormous sums have been dissipated in the prosecution of the designs formed against me, your well-wisher, and that you have ordered a tribute to be levied to satisfy the exigencies of your exhausted treasury.

'May it please your Majesty, your royal ancestor, Mahomed Julál-ú-dín Akbar, whose throne is now in heaven, conducted the affairs of this empire in equity and firm security for the space of fifty-two years, preserving every tribe of men in ease and happiness, whether they were followers of Jesus, or of Moses, of David, or Mahomed; were they Brahmans, were they of the sect of Dharians which denies the eternity of matter, or of that which ascribes the existence of the world to chance, they all equally enjoyed his countenance and favour, insomuch that his people, in gratitude for the indiscriminate protection he afforded them, distinguished him by the appellation of Juggut Gúrú (Guardian of Mankind).

'His Majesty Mahomed Núr-úl-dín Jehángír, likewise, whose dwelling is now in paradise, extended for a period of twenty-two years the shadow of his protection over the heads of his people. Successful by a constant fidelity to his allies and a vigorous exertion of his arm in business.

'Nor less did the illustrious Shah Jehán, by a propitious reign of thirty-two years, acquire to himself immortal reputation, the glorious reward of clemency and virtue.

'Such were the benevolent inclinations of your ancestors. Whilst they pursued these great and generous principles, wheresoever they directed their steps, conquest and prosperity went before them; and then they reduced many countries and fortresses to their obedience. During your Majesty's reign many have been alienated from the empire, and further loss of territory must necessarily follow, since devastation and rapine now universally prevail without restraint. Your subjects are trampled under foot, and every province of your empire is impoverished; depopulation spreads, and difficulties accumulate. When indigence has reached the habitation of the sovereign and his princes, what can be the condition of the nobles? As to the soldiery, they are in murmurs; the merchants complaining, the Mahomedans discontented, the Hindús destitute, and multitudes of people wretched, even to the want of their nightly meal, are beating their heads throughout the day in rage and desperation.

'How can the dignity of the sovereign be preserved who employs his power in exacting heavy tributes from a people thus miserably reduced? At this juncture it is told from east to west that the Emperor of Hindostan, jealous of the poor Hindú devotee, will exact a tribute from Brahmans, Sanoras, Jógís, Berágís, Sanyásís; that, regardless of the illustrious honour of his Timúrean race, he condescends to exercise his

APPX. A.

power over the solitary inoffensive anchoret. If your Majesty places any faith in those books, by distinction called Divine, you will there be instructed that God is the God of all mankind, not the God of Mahomedans alone. The Pagan and the Mussulman are equal in his presence. Distinctions of colour are of his ordination. It is he who gives existence. In your temples to his name the voice is raised in prayer; in a house of images, where the bell is shaken, still he is the object of adoration. To vilify the religion or customs of other men is to set at naught the pleasure of the Almighty. When we deface a picture, we naturally incur the resentment of the painter; and justly has the poet said, 'presume not to arraign or scrutinise the various works of power divine.'

'In fine, the tribute you demand from the Hindús is repugnant to justice; it is equally foreign from good policy, as it must impoverish the country. Moreover, it is an innovation and an infringement of the laws of Hindostan. But if zeal for your own religion hath induced you to determine upon this measure, the demand ought, by the rules of equity, to have been made first upon Rám Singh, who is esteemed the principal amongst the Hindús. Then let your well-wisher be called upon, with whom you will have less difficulty to encounter, but to torment ants and flies is unworthy of an heroic or generous mind. It is wonderful that the ministers of your government should have neglected to instruct your Majesty in the rules of rectitude and honour.'

TOD'S 'Rajásthán.'

APPENDIX B.

APPX. B.

THE subsequent adventures of Prince Amra, as given by Colonel Tod, are so extraordinary, that I transcribe them from the 'Annals of Rajásthán'—'In the month of Bysak, S. 1690 (A.D. 1634), five years before the death of Rájá Guj, in a convocation of all the feudality of Marú,[1] sentence of exclusion from the succession was pronounced upon Amra, accompanied by the solemn and seldom practised rite of Dés-vatoh or exile. This ceremony, which is marked as a day of mourning in the calendar, was attended with all the circumstances of funeral pomp. As soon

[1] Marú-Márwár.

APPX. B.

as the sentence was pronounced that his birth-right was forfeited and assigned to his junior brother, and that he ceased to be a subject of Marú, the khelat of banishment was brought forth, consisting of sable vestments, in which he was clad; a sable shield was hung upon his back, and a sword of the same hue girded round him; a black horse was then led out, being mounted on which, he was commanded, though not in anger, to depart whither he listed beyond the limits of Marú.

'Amra went not alone; numbers of each clan, who had always regarded him as their future lord, voluntarily partook of his exile. He repaired to the imperial court; and although the emperor approved and sanctioned his banishment, he employed him. His gallantry soon won him the title of Ráo and the munsub of a leader of three thousand, with the grant of Nagore as an independent domain, to be held directly from the crown. But the same arrogant and uncontrollable spirit which lost him his birth-right brought his days to a tragical conclusion. He absented himself for a fortnight from court, hunting the boar or the tiger, his only recreation. The emperor (Shah Jehán) reprimanded him for neglecting his duties, and threatened him with a fine. Amra proudly replied that he had only gone to hunt, and as for a fine, he observed, putting his hand upon his sword, that was his sole wealth.

'The little contrition which this reply evinced, determined the king to enforce the fine, and the paymaster-general, Salábat Khan, was sent to Amra's quarters to demand its payment. It was refused, and the observations made by the Synd not suiting the temper of Amra, he unceremoniously desired him to depart. The emperor, thus insulted in the person of his officer, issued a mandate for Amra's instant appearance. He obeyed; and having reached the aum-khás, or grand divan, beheld the king, "whose eyes were red with anger," with Salábat in the act of addressing him. Inflamed with passion at the recollection of the injurious language he had just received, perhaps at the king's confirmation of his exclusion from Márwár, he unceremoniously passed the Omrahs of five and seven thousand, as if to address the king; when, with a dagger concealed in his sleeve, he stabbed Salábat to the heart. Drawing his sword, he made a blow at the king, which descending on the pillar, shivered the weapon in pieces. The king abandoned his throne and fled to the interior apartments. All was uproar and confusion. Amra continued the work of death, indifferent upon whom his blows fell, and five Mogul chiefs of eminence had fallen, when his brother-in-law, Urjún Gór, under pretence of cajoling him, inflicted a mortal wound, though he continued to ply his dagger until he expired. To avenge his death, his retainers, headed by Bullú Khampawut and Bhao Khúmpawut, put on their saffron garments, and a fresh carnage ensued within the loll kelah. To use the words of their native bard, "The pillars of Agra bear testimony to their deeds, nor shall they ever be obliterated from the record of time: they made the obeisance to Amra in the mansions of the sun." The faithful band was cut to pieces; and his wife, the princess of Búndi, came in person and carried away the dead body of Amra, with which she committed herself to the flames. The Bokhára gate, by which they gained admission, was built up, and henceforward known only as "Amra Singh's Gate;" and in proof of the strong impression made by this event, it remained closed through centuries, until opened in 1809 by Captain George Steel, of the Bengal Engineers.' APPX. B.

APPENDIX C.

APPX. C.

THE Princess Kishna Komari, daughter of Rána Bhím Singh, of Údaipúr, had the reputation of possessing extraordinary beauty. Her birth contributed to make an alliance with her the highest aspiration of a Rájpút prince. Bhím Singh, Rájá of Jodhpúr, was the fortunate aspirant to her hand. To him she had been betrothed; but Rájá Bhím Singh died in 1804. On his death Maun Singh succeeded to the throne, and with it to the hopes of his predecessor. But one Sevaí Singh, who had been formerly minister to Bhím Singh, and whose object it was to sow dissension between Jaipúr and Jodhpúr, so worked upon the sensual mind of Juggut Singh, Rájá of Jaipúr, that he determined to demand the princess in marriage for himself. He sent an embassy for the purpose, but it was contemptuously dismissed.

Thenfollowed a desolating war between the rival aspirants. The marauder Amír Khan, summoned first by one party, then selling himself to the other, ruined Rájpútáná by his exactions.

APPX. C.

There was scarcely an infamy of which he and his followers were not guilty. Treachery succeeded murder, and plunder accompanied both. But meanwhile neither of the rival princes would relinquish his claim; the country continued to be inundated with blood. So long as the cause remained, the flame would continue. It was decided then, at the instance, it is said, of Amír Khan, that the cause should disappear, that the 'Flower of Rájásthán' should die. I quote a description of her and the ruin that ensued, from the glowing pen of Colonel Tod:—

'Kishna Komari Bai, the "Virgin Princess Kishna," was in her sixteenth year. Her mother was of the Chawura race, the ancient kings of Anhulwárá. Sprung from the noblest blood of Hind, she added beauty of face and person to an engaging demeanour, and was justly proclaimed the "Flower of Rájásthán." When the Roman father pierced the bosom of the dishonoured Virginia, appeased virtue applauded the deed. When Iphigenia was led to the sacrificial altar, the salvation of her country yielded a noble consolation. The votive victim of Jephtha's success had the triumph of a father's fame to sustain her resignation, and in the meekness of her sufferings we have the best parallel to the sacrifice of the lovely Kishna. Though years have passed since the barbarous immolation, it is never related but with a faltering tongue and moistened eyes, "albeit unused to the melting mood."

'The rapacious and blood-thirsty Pathán, covered with infamy, repaired to Údaipúr, where he was joined by the pliant and subtle Ajít. Meek in his demeanour, unostentatious in his habits, despising honours, yet covetous of power; religion, which he followed with the zeal of an Asiatic, if it did not serve as a cloak, was at least no hindrance to an immeasurable ambition, in the attainment of which he would have sacrificed all but himself. When the Pathán revealed his design that either the princess should wed Rájá Maun, or by her death seal the peace of Rájwarra, whatever arguments were used to point the alternative, the Ráná was made to see no choice between consigning his beloved child to the Ráhtor prince, or witnessing the effects of a more extended dishonour from the vengeance of the Pathán, and the storm of his palace by his licentious adherents. The fiat passed that Kishna Komari should die.

'But the deed was left for women to accomplish—the hand of man refused it. The harem of an eastern prince is a world of itself; it is the labyrinth containing the strings that move the puppets which alarm mankind. Here intrigue sits enthroned, and hence its influence radiates to the world, always at a loss to trace effects to their causes. Máhárájá Daolut Singh, descended four generations ago from one common ancestor with the Ráná, was first sounded "to save the honour of Údaipúr," but horror-struck he exclaimed, "accursed the tongue that commands it! Dust on my allegiance, if thus to be preserved." The Máhárájá Jowandás, a natural brother, was then called upon; the dire necessity was explained, and it was urged that no common hand could be armed for the purpose. He accepted the poniard, but when in youthful loveliness Kishna appeared before him, the dagger fell from his hand, and he returned more wretched than the victim. The fatal purpose thus revealed, the shrieks of the frantic mother reverberated through the palace, as she implored mercy or execrated the murderers of her child, who alone was resigned to her fate. But death was arrested, not averted. To use the phrase of the narrator, "she was excused the steel—the cup was prepared," and prepared by female hands! As the messenger presented it in the name of her father, she bowed and drank it, sending up a prayer for his life and prosperity. The raving mother poured imprecations on his head, while the lovely victim, who shed not a tear, thus endeavoured to console her: "Why afflict yourself, my mother, at this shortening of the sorrows of life? I fear not to die! Am I not your daughter; why should I fear death? We are marked out for sacrifice from our birth, we scarcely enter the world but to be sent out again; let me thank my father that I have lived so long!" Thus she conversed till the nauseating draught refused to assimilate with her blood. Again the bitter potion was prepared. She drained it off, and again it was rejected; but, as if to try the extreme of human fortitude, a third was administered, and, for the third time, nature refused to aid the horrid purpose. It seemed as if the fabled charm, which guarded the life of the founder of her race, was inherited by the virgin Kishna. But the bloodhounds, the Pathán and Ajít, were impatient till their victim was at rest, and cruelty, as if gathering strength from defeat, made another and fatal attempt. A powerful opiate was pre-

APPX. C.

sented—the kasúmba draught. She received it with a smile, wished the scene over, and drank it. The desires of barbarity were accomplished. "She slept!" a sleep from which she never awoke.

'The wretched mother did not long survive her child; nature was exhausted in the ravings of despair. She refused food, and her remains in a few days followed those of her daughter to the funeral pyre.

'Even the ferocious Khan, when the instrument of his infamy, Ajít, reported the issue, received him with contempt and spurned him from his presence, tauntingly asking "if this were the boasted Rájpút valour?" But the wily traitor had to encounter language far more bitter from his political adversary, whom he detested. Sangrám Suktáwut reached the capital only four days after the catastrophe: a man in every respect the reverse of Ajít. Audaciously brave, he neither feared the frown of his sovereign nor the sword of his enemy. Without introduction he rushed into the presence, where he found seated the traitor Ajít. "Oh, dastard! who hast thrown dust on the Sísodia race, whose blood, which has flowed in purity through a hundred ages, has now been defiled; this sin will check its course for ever—a blot so foul in our annals that no Sísodia will ever again hold up his head—a sin to which no punishment were equal. But the end of our race is approaching. The line of Bappú Ráwul is at an end; Heaven has ordained this as a signal for our destruction." The Ráná hid his face with his hands, when, turning to Ajít he exclaimed, "Thou stain on the Sísodia race, thou impure of Rájpút blood, dust be on thy head as thou hast covered us all with shame. May thou die childless, and your name die with you! Why this indecent haste? Had the Pathán stormed the city? Had he attempted to violate the sanctity of the harem? And though he had, could you not die as Rájpúts like your ancestors. Was it thus they gained a name? Was it thus our race became renowned—thus they opposed the might of kings? Have you forgotten the Sakas of Chítor? But whom do I address? Not Rájpúts? Had the honour of your females been endangered, had you sacrificed them all and rushed sword in hand on the enemy, your name would have lived, and the Almighty would have secured the seed of Bappú Ráwul. But to owe preservation to this unhallowed deed; you did not even await the threatened danger. Fear seems to have deprived you of every faculty, or you might have spared the blood of your family, and if you did not scorn to owe your safety to deception, might have substituted some less noble victim. But the end of our race approaches." APPX. C.

'The traitor to manhood, his sovereign, and humanity, durst not reply. The brave Sangrám is now dead, but the prophetic anathema has been fulfilled. Of ninety-five children, sons and daughters, but one son (the brother of Kishna) is left to the Ráná; and though his two remaining daughters have been recently married to the princes of Jaisalmír and Bikanír, the Salic law, which is in full force in these states, precludes all honour through female descent. His hopes rest solely on the prince, Jowan Singh, and though in the flower of youth and health, the marriage bed (albeit boasting no less than four young princesses) has been blessed with no progeny.[1]

'The elder brother of Jowan died two years ago; had he lived he would have been Amra the Third. With regard to Ajít, the curse has been fully accomplished. Scarcely a month after his wife and two sons were numbered with the dead, and the hoary traitor has since been wandering from shrine to shrine, performing penance and alms in expiation of his sins, yet unable to fling from him ambition; and with his beads in one hand, "Ráma! Ráma!" ever on his tongue, and subdued passion in his looks, his heart is as deceitful as ever. Enough of him. Let us exclaim, with Sangrám, "Dust on his head," which all the waters of the Ganges could not purify from the blood of the virgin Kishna, but

'Rather would the multitudinous sea incarnadine.'

APPENDIX D.

The following is an extract from the order of the Government of India, issued on the occasion of the death of the late Begum of Bhopál. After stating the profound regret with which the Government had received intelligence of the demise of that illustrious lady, the document went on to add: 'Her Highness had conducted the administration of this principality since the year 1847, when she was first appointed regent, with ability and APPX. D.

[1] Jowan Singh did succeed his father, but he died without natural issue.

APPX. D.

success, until the day of her decease. In the early years of her rule she improved the system by which the revenue of the state is collected, abolished monopolies, regulated the mint, reorganised the police, and gradually increased the revenue, while she effectually diminished the public debt. In later times, by her support of the cause of male and female education, by her superintendence of works intended to supply her capital with pure and wholesome water, by the construction of serais and roads, and by other improvements, she gave convincing indications of real and abiding interest in the progress of her people and in the prosperity of her country.

'But it was by her firm conduct during the great mutiny that she established a more direct title to the acknowledgments of the head of the administration.

'Her unswerving fidelity, her skill in the management of affairs at an important crisis, the bold front which she presented to the enemies of the British power, and the vigilance with which she watched over the preservation of Englishmen, were acknowledged by Lord Canning, in open durbar, in terms of well-deserved praise and commendation, and the gratitude of the British Government was further evinced by a grant of territory which its owner had justly forfeited for open rebellion, by a recognition of the right of succession according to the custom of the principality and the Mahomedan law, and by the bestowal of one of those titles which the Sovereign of Great Britain, as the fountain of honour, has instituted to reward good services performed in India either by the natives of the country, or by the British servants of the Crown.'

APPENDIX E.

APPX. E.

I THINK that the following statement, showing the war material and fighting men at the disposal of the native chiefs of India, may not be uninteresting. It has been arranged in the order of States followed in the body of the book.

It will be seen that the native chiefs command collectively 5,252 guns, 9,390 trained artillerymen, 64,172 cavalry, and 241,063 foot soldiers. They are distributed as follows :—

APPX. E.

Names of Divisions	Guns	Infantry	Cavalry
Rájpútáná	2,003	69,028	24,287
Central India	893	55,664	15,321
Central Provinces	—	2,115	140
Western India	1,083	32,770	9,331
Southern India	734	38,401	8,262
Eastern India	109	5,264	404
Northern and North-Western India	428	37,799	6,407

The appended list will show how these forces are distributed among the more important States:—

I.

States.	Guns.	Infantry.	Cavalry.
I. Údaipúr	538	15,100	6,240
II. Jaipúr	312	10,500	3,530
III. Jodhpúr	220	4,000	5,600
IV. Búndí	68	2,000	200
V. Kotá	119	4,600	700
VI. Jháláwar	90	3,500	400
VII. Tonk	53	2,288	430
VIII. Karaúli	40	3,200	400
IX. Kishngarh	35	2,000	150
X. Dholpúr	32	3,650	610
XI. Bharatpúr	38	8,500	1,460
XII. Alwar	351	5,633	2,280
XIII. Bikanír	53	940	670
XIV. Jaisalmír	12	400	500
XV. Sirohí	—	350	375
XVI. Dongarpúr	4	632	57
XVI. Bánswárá	3	500	60
XVI. Partábgarh	12	950	275
II.			
I. Gwáliár	210	16,050	6,068
II. Indúr	102	5,500	3,000
III. Bhopál	39	4,766	1,194
IV. Dhár	4	790	370
V. Dewás	—	—	—
III.			
Rewá	35	2,000	905
Other States in Bundelkhand	421	22,163	2,677
IV.			
I. Barodah	30	11,000	3,098
II. Kolhapúr	258	1,502	154
III. Kachh	38	600	300
IV. Kathíwár	508	15,306	3,033

APPX. E.

States	Guns	Infantry	Cavalry
V.			
I. Haiderábád	725	36,890	8,202
II. Mysore	6	1,000	35
III. Travankúr	6	1,211	60
IV. Kochin	3	300	—
VI.			
I. Cis-Satlaj States	141	7,185	3,191
II. Kashmír	96	18,436	1,393
III. Trans-Satlaj States	27	3,275	300
IV. Bháwalpúr	80	2,484	360
VII.			
Petty States	302	18,000	4,000

APPENDIX F.

APPX. F.

The following graphic description of the Bhúmia class is taken from the Rájpútáuá correspondence of the 'Pioneer' newspaper, dated Allahábád, November 24, 1874:—

Some months ago I touched upon the subject of Bhúmia Thákurs and Bhúm holdings. Since then I have had access to a singularly clear report on the Bhúmia Thákurs of the Ajmír district, and I have more than once meditated giving you a *précis* of its contents. There seems to have been a considerable confusion of ideas upon the *status* and duties of this class, and no one seemed able to say what privileges they were entitled to enjoy, and what services they were pledged to render in return for their holdings. After the new order of things had been established, the Commissioner appointed a committee to sift the whole matter of their rights and duties. A very careful and interesting report was submitted by the committee, the report to which I alluded above, and on it the Commissioner framed his suggestions for the future regulation of our demands from the Bhúmia holders. The orders of the Supreme Government on his recommendations have lately been received. The proposals of the committee have been favourably entertained, and it now only remains to have them put into execution.

Let me give you some idea of who the Bhúmia Thákurs in Ajmír are, and what their history has been. In certain parts of India there is an impression abroad that the holders of Bhúm lands are little more than village watchmen. However much support there may be for this belief as regards the Bhúmias of other provinces, there is no ground for its application to Rájpútáná. So far from being a tenure of low repute, it is much sought after even by the wealthy and well-born. So far from the Bhúmias being poor, ill-born, and despised, they are very often the most influential men in the village, riding their own cattle, owning their own herds and flocks, and playing second fiddle to no man. If this apparent prosperity be not sufficient to establish his gentle blood, there is another decisive test which admits of no doubt. Watch a district official receiving the magnates of the village, and you will see that while the *patail* puts forward the mean rupee in his extended palm, the Bhúmia Thákur presents his ancestral sword. No surer sign of gentle blood in this once warlike province. This, then, is the first fact to commit to memory, namely, that whatever the circumstances of their private affairs, our friends the Bhúmias are sprung from good stock, and are circled about by a certain dignity which is not to be extinguished even by the curse of poverty. Their tenure, moreover, is the only one which is not legally resumable by the Crown, except for disloyalty and rebellion. But in order to attain this perfect security of possession it is necessary that every grant should have obtained the sanction of the power ruling at the time of the grant. There are instances, notably in Mewár, after the general pacification in 1818, when the sovereign resumed lands granted in Bhúm, on the grounds that their grant had not met with his sanction. In point of fact, therefore, until the sanction of the ruling power has been accorded, no grant professing to be Bhúm is really Bhúm.

There are four kinds of Bhúm grants:— 1. Bhúm granted for 'Mundkáti.' 2. That granted to quell a feud. 3. A gift bestowed for services in the field; and, 4, a grant from the Ráj to protect a border, or from a village to perform the duties of watch and ward. Lands surrendered on this tenure are held rent-free. Of the four kinds above-mentioned there are no examples of the first or second in the Ajmír district, and of the third there are only two authenticated instances. The

APPX. F.

fourth description may, therefore, be said to be the only one existing in the Ajmír district.

We have next to examine the duties and responsibilities of this class. They are:—

1. The protection of the property of travellers within their circle.

2. The protection of their villages from *dacoits*.

3. The pecuniary indemnification of sufferers from crime within the limits of their charge.

The committee then proceed to define Bhúm as it exists in the Ajmír district, as follows:—

1. It is a hereditary property, inalienable, rent-free, and requiring the sanction of the ruling power.

2. It is resumable for offences against the State, and other misdemeanours for which confiscation of immovable property is the penalty prescribed.

3. When resumed proprietary and revenue free rights both vanish, these being inseparable.

4. Neglect or remissness creates liability to fine or attachment till the fine is realised.

5. If alienated without sanction of the State, it is liable to forfeiture, and may be settled upon anyone.

Though the Bhúmias are described as not liable for rent or assessment, it is easy to imagine that, in the troubled times which ushered in and cradled the present century they did not get off scot-free. Accordingly, we find an exaction called the *Bhúm Báb* in full force during the Mahratta rule. One must do them the credit to admit that the idea was not of their origination. It was first levied by Máhárájá Tukht Singh in 1752, but he only exacted it once, and there is no record of the amount he took, and the number subjected to it were few. When Sívají Náná fastened on the district it seems to have struck him as an excellent idea; so he immediately reinaugurated it on true Márhátá principles, that is, he fixed no rate, but squeezed as much as he could out of them. In nine years he levied the tax three times, and his successor improved on this and introduced the custom of taking it every second year. Altogether it was collected ten times before we came into possession. It seems, however, that some escaped the infliction—a sad stain upon the Márhátá reputation for catholic rapacity. Tukht Singh was new to the work, so that it is not strange that he taxed only 16 out of some 108 holdings, and to these the investigations of the Márhâtás add 87 more, making a total of 103: but as the tax was irregularly collected, it appears that only 76 holdings had paid since 1818. Those who managed to secure exemption entirely seem to have done so through the support of influential nobles. Some years after we entered into possession we abolished some of the perquisites the Bhúmias had been in the habit of obtaining, so that they had very little to be grateful for to us, as we kept up the collection of *Bhúm Báb* up to the year 1842, when it was abolished by order of Government. The Bhúmias seem, however, to have managed to retain a number of perquisites, such as presents on the Holi and Dusserah, on the marriage of their eldest sons, and on the occasion of every marriage in their village. They received a goat or a buffalo yearly, a skin for drawing water from the well from the leather trade, seventy heads of Indian corn, or a handful of wheat from each field. Their forts were also repaired by free labour. Alas! all these delightful things followed the odious *Bhúm Báb*—all bound for the limbo of the superannuated. Meanwhile, these unfortunate men had been cruelly maligned by our district officials, who insisted on considering them no better than *chowkeedars*, thought these lofty lineaged ones *atavis editas regibus*, the counterpart of the cudgel-armed knave who coughs a guttural warning to all approaching his neighbourhood, or snores in forgetful slumbers in the verandahs. However, those days of slighted reputation are past. The patient and discriminating committee, *rem acu tetigerunt*, and in future no man shall revile the Bhúmia with the name of *chowkeedar*. His fate I must leave to another letter, for I have discoursed too much already.